PELICAN BOOKS

THE ORIGINS AND GROWTH OF
PHYSICAL SCIENCE · 2

# THE ORIGINS AND GROWTH OF PHYSICAL SCIENCE

## 2

EDITED BY
D. L. HURD AND J. J. KIPLING

BASED ON
'MOMENTS OF DISCOVERY'
EDITED BY GEORGE SCHWARTZ
AND PHILIP W. BISHOP

PENGUIN BOOKS

Penguin Books Ltd, Harmondsworth, Middlesex, England
Penguin Books Inc., 7110 Ambassador Road, Baltimore, Maryland 21207, U.S.A.
Penguin Books Australia Ltd, Ringwood, Victoria, Australia

—

First published in the U.S.A. under the title *Moments of Discovery* 1958
First published under the present title with additional material, in Pelican Books 1964
Reprinted 1970

—

Copyright © Basic Books, Inc., 1958, and Penguin Books Ltd, 1964

—

Made and printed in Great Britain
by C. Nicholls & Company Ltd
Set in Monotype Baskerville

# CONTENTS

## III

## THE ELECTROMAGNETIC SYNTHESIS

# ACKNOWLEDGEMENTS

Acknowledgements are due to the following for the use of materials from the publications stated: Harper & Bros., *Röntgen Rays: Memoirs by Röntgen, Stokes and J. J. Thomson* (Vol. III of *Harper's Scientific Memoirs*, trans. and ed. G. F. Barker, 1899); Harvard University Press, H. M. Leicester and H. S. Klickstein, *A Source Book in Chemistry*, 1952, H. F. Magie, *A Sourcebook in Physics*, 1935 (first published by the McGraw-Hill Book Co.); Philosophical Library, Max Planck, *Scientific Autobiography*, 1949; *The Philosophical Magazine*, Ernest Rutherford and Frederick Soddy, 1902, J. J. Thomson, 1897; *The Philosophical Transactions of the Royal Society*, Humphrey Davy, 1811, Michael Faraday, 1839, James Clerk Maxwell, 1865, Isaac Newton, 1672; the Royal Society of Edinburgh, Alembic Club Reprints Nos. 2, 4, 9, 19 (John Dalton, Amedeo Avogadro and Joseph Gay-Lussac, Humphrey Davy, Svant August Arrhenius); S. P. Thompson (Christian Huygens), *Treatise on Light*, 1912; University of Chicago Press, Dmitri Ivanovich Mendeleev, from *Selected Readings in Natural Science*, 1947.

Acknowledgements are also due to the Burndy Library for permission to use illustrative material.

# INTRODUCTION

## THE DEVELOPMENT OF MODERN SCIENCE

THE division of *The Origins and Growth of Physical Science* into two volumes is dictated quite simply by limitations of space. The history of science has been a continuous process, and the trends and movements to which the historian points are seldom sharply defined. They merge, one with another, into a complex and organic whole.

At the same time, there is an important sense in which the two volumes represent distinct phases in the development of the physical sciences. In the extracts in Volume 1 we have witnessed the slow and laboured emergence of a scientific outlook which gave a confidence and a new unity of purpose to the inquiries and speculations which developed in many new fields. This change we refer to as the Scientific Revolution.

The extracts in the present volume roughly cover the nineteenth century, during which time the pace of scientific investigation underwent a continuous acceleration. The scope of research both broadened and deepened, until, with the closing years of the nineteenth century, new horizons were revealed which forced a reassessment of the foundations of both physics and chemistry. It is at this point that this volume closes, for these developments brought a chapter in the history of science to an end.

The nature of this work makes it impossible to attempt to present a complete picture of the development of the physical sciences over the century or so covered by this volume. In the realm of physics alone the variety of topics is too extensive to allow of more than a small fraction to be illustrated by extracts. Accordingly, a single theme has been chosen – the rise of the theory of electromagnetism – which is not only of great importance in itself, but which must also stand as representative of that complex series of investigations that grew out of the Scientific Revolution.

In the first volume we had occasion to refer to the fact that one feature of the rapid growth of science during the eighteenth century was the gradual separation of physics and chemistry into independent fields of inquiry. The extracts of this second volume clearly show the establishment of chemistry as a subject with its own preoccupations and methods, and, with the passing of time, an increasing specialization into the three branches of inorganic, organic, and physical chemistry. It is an interesting fact that a recognizably modern chemistry emerged more than a century later than physics; for this reason the writings of the chemists form a large part of this second volume.

Despite the fact that one must recognize the growing separation between physics and chemistry, it is as well to remember that the division arose as a matter of expediency rather than from the existence of any conflict. The common origin of the two subjects is to be explicitly revealed in the extracts in the section entitled 'The Breakdown of Classical Physics', where the questioning of traditional concepts of the nature of matter is of like concern for scientists from both fields.

The history of science is more than the long sequence of theory and experiment, which the extracts of this work seek to illustrate; the activity of the scientist can never be completely divorced from the general social background of his times. During the period covered by this Volume the dedicated amateur was giving way to the professional scientist, the private laboratory to the research institute. Science today is a highly organized activity. It has become an important factor in the economy of any modern nation, and many research programmes require the investment of not thousands but millions of pounds. As Joseph Priestley so truly observed in 1775 – 'Natural Philosophy is a science which more especially requires the aid of wealth.'

Increasingly in this volume it is necessary to refer to applications which have been made of scientific findings.

# INTRODUCTION

The growth of pure scientific research has been paralleled by the growth of technology. Our modern society is founded on industries which, directly or indirectly, trace their origins to the achievements, and to the attitudes of mind, of the physicist and the chemist. In a very real sense the Scientific Revolution was the parent of the Industrial Revolution.

# I

# THE FOUNDATIONS OF MODERN
CHEMISTRY

In Volume 1 the gradual emergence of chemistry as a separate discipline within physical science was illustrated; it was predominantly an eighteenth-century change. In the nineteenth century, three major themes in chemistry can be discerned.

The first theme was the discovery of new elements. This could be regarded as a process which defined the scope of chemistry, inasmuch as all matter is formed from the chemical elements and their compounds. Boyle had defined what he meant by elements: ' . . . certain primitive and simple, or perfectly unmingled bodies; which not being made of any other bodies, or of one another, are the ingredients of which all those called perfectly mixed bodies are immediately compounded, and into which they are ultimately resolved.' If Boyle had carried out more chemical experiments to elucidate this idea, the modern concept of a chemical element would have gained acceptance much earlier. As it was, the scholastic idea of 'principles' (cf. Volume 1) had to give way gradually to the idea of separate isolable substances. One of the final stages of this process was the overthrow of the phlogiston theory. The start of the modern period in chemistry was signified by the introduction of a simplified nomenclature for which Lavoisier was responsible.

Lavoisier's text-book of 1789 listed 23 elements, but by 1849 Gmelin's *Handbook of Chemistry* was based on 61 elements, of which 49 were metals and 12 were non-metals. The list increased as new elements were discovered and also as well-known substances such as chlorine were demonstrated to be elements. The extract from Davy's work shows the kind of argument which was put forward for this second process. Similarly some substances, formerly thought to be elements, were shown to be compounds and had to be omitted.

The isolation of new elements sometimes depended on the use of techniques new to chemistry. One of these was the use of electricity. By electrolysis, Davy isolated sodium and potassium; his accounts of the isolation of these elements make fascinating reading. Aluminium, although it was isolated in 1825 by other methods, only became commercially important after 1888 when it could be produced electrolytically.

As more elements were discovered, likeness between groups of elements became apparent, and various ways of classifying them were put forward. These culminated in Mendeleev's Periodic Table which proved to be a great work of systematizing. He set the known elements in a framework, leaving gaps where no element was known which fitted into the pattern. From the gaps he was able to predict, most successfully, the properties of elements (such as germanium) which were later discovered, some during his lifetime. The Periodic Table, has, in the present century, provided the basis for interpreting chemical behaviour in terms of sub-atomic structure. It also formed a valuable guide in predicting the chemical properties of the group of new elements which have recently been prepared, but which do not occur naturally. The total number of elements now stands at over a hundred.

The second theme is that of chemical composition. The late eighteenth and early nineteenth centuries saw the enunciation of a set of laws concerning the quantitative proportions in which elements would combine together to form compounds. These laws could be understood in terms of a physical picture which Dalton put forward. Throughout history men appear to have speculated about the composition of matter, and at least since the time of Democritus to have had before them the possibility that matter consisted of discrete particles. Dalton's Atomic Theory was valuable and successful largely because it made sense of quantitative results. Elements reacted in definite proportions to form compounds because their atoms combined in definite proportions to form 'compound atoms' (molecules in present nomenclature). All atoms of a given element had the same weight, and Dalton set about establishing their relative weights, which he published in 1808. This needed revision, because it had not yet become apparent that the natural condition of some elements was to exist, not as single atoms, but as molecules. This was realized by Avogadro to be a consequence of Gay-Lussac's Law of the Combination of Gases. Avogadro's hypothesis was universally rejected in his own time, but was revived nearly fifty years later by Cannizzaro.

The great Swedish chemist, Berzelius, extended the table of atomic weights by making his own determinations. He did not use Avogadro's hypothesis, but by closely following Gay-Lussac's Law, obtained a series of values (a final table being published in 1826) which in many cases (e.g. for copper, chlorine, lead, nitrogen, and sulphur) are very close to those which we use today, when corrected from his basis of 100 for the atomic weight of oxygen. His values for potassium and silver, however, were double those used now. It is intriguing to read the arguments which he used to arrive at his values. He was also responsible for the introduction of our present use of letters as symbols for the elements, and it is surprising to find Dalton protesting that he found them horrifying, and far more difficult to use than his own pictorial symbols.

As the Atomic Theory, with amplification and modifications, gained acceptance it became a rational basis for expressing methods of analysing and synthesizing compounds. With the concept of molecules firmly established, chemists could consider the way in which the individual atoms were linked together to form the molecule. Here was the basis of structural chemistry, which developed a further stage when the shape of the molecule in three-dimensional space was envisaged. Structural chemistry has become vastly important and today new techniques continue to be invented for the elucidation of the structures of ever more complex molecules.

The third major theme is the nature of chemical reaction. The laws relating to chemical composition described the situation at the completion of chemical reactions. The progress of a chemical reaction, however, was found to vary with the conditions in which it took place. The rate at which a reaction took place varied with the proportions in which the reactants were present, with temperature, sometimes with pressure, and sometimes with the addition of extra substances. As the laws governing the progress of chemical reactions were evolved, so attempts were made to relate them to the changes taking place among the molecules themselves. This, of course, was (and still is) only possible because the Atomic Theory had led chemists to think in molecular terms. Indeed, these three themes are not separate. Chemistry is the stronger because they have interacted with one another and continue to do so in our own times.

# JOHN DALTON
## 1766–1844

## THE FOUNDATIONS OF THE ATOMIC
## THEORY

DALTON was born in the village of Eaglesfield, near Cockermouth, the son of a weaver. He began his professional life as a teacher in the village while still only a boy, teaching first in a barn and later at the Friends' meeting house. As there were five other children in the family, he was required to augment the family income, but still managed to study further and to interest himself in meteorology, a hobby which fascinated him for the rest of his life.

When fifteen, he moved to Kendal, and in 1793 to the New College at Manchester as a teacher of mathematics and natural philosophy. At the end of the century he became a private tutor. In 1800 he became secretary to the Manchester Literary and Philosophical Society, a body similar in its origins to the Lunar Society in Birmingham to which Priestley belonged, and later was elected its President.

Dalton seems to have come to his atomic theory through his interest in meteorology. He believed that the atmosphere was a mixture of gases, but wondered why the heavier components did not separate out from the lighter ones. He came to think of the ultimate particles of which they were composed, and regarded atoms, not as being infinite in variety as had been supposed by earlier philosophers, but of one kind for each element. He also supposed that, whereas atoms of a given element repelled one another, atoms of different elements attracted each other; this was one of his ideas which later had to be changed as far as chemical combination of atoms was concerned, though it led him to his law of partial pressures.

The further virtue of Dalton's theory was that he gave it a quantitative significance. He made use of the laws recently formulated by Richter and Proust, that chemical compounds always had the same composition by weight, and that the weights of the elements A and B, which would separately combine with the same weight of C, were the weights of A and B which would combine with each other. Dalton could explain this by postulating that all atoms of a given element had the same weight. Using the symbols reproduced in the diagram (p. 33) he illustrated his ideas of the combination of atoms. Moreover, he realized that the *relative* weights of the atoms could be deduced from experiments on the combination of the elements, and so came to draw up a table of atomic weights. This was based on hydrogen, the lightest element he knew. His table had subsequently to be modified in principle, because he had not recognized that elements might normally be found as 'compound atoms' instead of single atoms. His experiments led him to compare other atoms with the hydrogen molecule, which consists of two atoms, and his table had therefore to be modified when this was realized so as to relate other atomic weights to the weight of the hydrogen atom.

Dalton did, however, realize that atoms of different elements might combine in ratios other than 1 : 1. The ratios would always be simple, as is indicated in his diagram. Two given elements might combine in more than one ratio, and in this case there would be a simple relationship between the proportions present in the two (or more) compounds formed. Here Dalton added another law to those dealing with the quantitative aspects of the composition of matter.

Dalton was a crude experimenter, but using data reported by others was able to effect a synthesis which is fundamental to modern chemistry. Representative arguments are set forth in the following extracts from his *A New System of Chemical Philosophy* published in 1808. For the first and third sections, see also Alembic Club Reprints No. 2.

## ¶ On the Constitution of Bodies

There are three distinctions in the kinds of bodies, or three states, which have more especially claimed the attention of philosophical chemists; namely, those which are marked by terms *elastic fluids*, *liquids*, and *solids*. A very familiar instance is exhibited to us in water, of a body, which, in certain circumstances, is capable of assuming all the three states. In steam we recognize a perfectly elastic fluid, in water, a perfect liquid, and in ice a complete solid. These observations have tacitly led to the conclusion which seems universally adopted, that all bodies of sensible magnitude, whether liquid or solid, are constituted of a vast number of extremely small particles, or atoms of matter bound together by a force of attraction, which is more or less powerful according to circumstances, and which as it endeavours to prevent their separation, is very properly called in that view, *attraction of cohesion*; but as it collects them from a dispersed state (as from steam into water) it is called, *attraction of aggregation*, or more simply, *affinity*. Whatever names it may go by, they still signify one and the same power. It is not my design to call in question this conclusion, which appears completely satisfactory; but to shew that we have hitherto made no use of it, and that the consequence of the neglect, has been a very obscure view of chemical agency, which is daily growing more so in proportion to the new lights attempted to be thrown upon it.

The opinions I more particularly allude to, are those of Berthollet on the Laws of chemical affinity; such as that chemical agency is proportional to the mass, and that in all chemical unions, there exist insensible gradations in the proportions of the constituent principles. The inconsistence of these opinions, both with reason and observation, cannot, I think, fail to strike everyone who takes a proper view of the phenomena.

Whether the ultimate particles of a body, such as water, are all alike, that is, of the same figure, weight, etc. is a question of some importance. From what is known, we have no reason to apprehend a diversity in these particulars: if it does exist in water, it must equally exist in the elements constituting water, namely, hydrogen and oxygen. Now it is scarcely possible to conceive how the aggregates of dissimilar particles should be so uniformly the same. If some of the particles of water were heavier than others, if a parcel of the liquid on any occasion were constituted principally of these heavier particles, it must be supposed to affect the specific gravity of the mass, a circumstance not known. Similar observations may be made on other substances. Therefore we may conclude that *the ultimate particles of all homogeneous bodies are perfectly alike in weight, figure, etc.* In other words, every particle of water is like every other particle of water; every particle of hydrogen is like every other particle of hydrogen, etc.

Besides the force of attraction, which, in one character or another, belongs universally to ponderable bodies, we find another force that is likewise universal, or acts upon all matter which comes under our cognisance, namely, a force of repulsion. This is now generally, and I think properly, ascribed to the agency of heat. An atmosphere of this subtile fluid constantly surrounds the atoms of all bodies, and prevents them from being drawn into actual contact. This appears to be satisfactorily proved by the observation, that the bulk of a body may be diminished by abstracting some of its heat: But from what has been stated in the last section, it should seem that enlargement and diminution of bulk depend perhaps more on the arrangement, than on the size of the ultimate particles. Be this as it may, we cannot avoid inferring from the preceding doctrine on heat, and particularly from the section on the natural zero of temperature, that solid bodies, such as ice, contain a large portion, perhaps $\frac{4}{5}$ of the heat which the same are found to contain in an elastic state, as steam.

We are now to consider how these two great antagonist powers of attraction and repulsion are adjusted, so as to allow of the three different states of *elastic fluids, liquids, and solids*. We shall divide the subject into four Sections; namely, first, *on the constitution of pure elastic fluids*; second, *on the constitution of mixed elastic fluids*; third, *on the constitution of liquids*, and fourth, *on the constitution of solids*.

# JOHN DALTON

## ¶ On the Constitution of Mixed Elastic Fluids

When two or more elastic fluids, whose particles do not unite chemically upon mixture, are brought together, one measure of each, they occupy the space of two measures, but become uniformly diffused through each other, and remain so, whatever may be their specific gravities. The fact admits of no doubt; but explanations have been given in various ways, and none of them completely satisfactory. As the subject is one of primary importance in forming a system of chemical principles, we must enter somewhat more fully into the discussion.

Dr Priestley was one of the earliest to notice the fact: it naturally struck him with surprise, that two elastic fluids, having apparently no affinity for each other, should not arrange themselves according to their specific gravities, as liquids do in like circumstances. Though he found this was not the case after the elastic fluids had once been thoroughly mixed, yet he suggests it as probable, that if two of such fluids could be exposed to each other without agitation, the one specifically heavier would retain its lower situation. He does not so much as hint at such gases being retained in a mixed state by affinity. With regard to his suggestion of two gases being carefully exposed to each other without agitation, I made a series of experiments expressly to determine the question, the results of which are given in the Manch. Memoirs, Vol. I. *new series*. From these it seems to be decided that gases always intermingle and gradually diffuse themselves amongst each other, if exposed ever so carefully; but it requires a considerable time to produce a complete intermixture, when the surface of communication is small. This time may vary from a minute, to a day or more, according to the quantity of the gases and the freedom of communication.

When or by whom the notion of mixed gases being held together by chemical affinity was first propagated, I do not know; but it seems probable that the notion of water being dissolved in air, led to that of air being dissolved in air. –

Philosophers found that water gradually disappeared or evaporated in air, and increased its elasticity; but steam at a low temperature was known to be unable to overcome the resistance of the air, therefore the agency of affinity was necessary to account for the effect. In the permanently elastic fluids indeed, this agency did not seem to be so much wanted, as they are all able to support themselves; but the diffusion through each other was a circumstance which did not admit of an easy solution any other way. In regard to the solution of water in air, it was natural to suppose, nay, one might almost have been satisfied without the aid of experiment, that the different gases would have had different affinities for water, and that the quantities of water dissolved in like circumstances, would have varied according to the nature of the gas. Saussure found, however, that there was no difference in this respect in the solvent powers of carbonic acid, hydrogen gas, and common air. – It might be expected that at least the *density* of the gas would have some influence upon its solvent powers, that air of half density would take half the water, or the quantity of water would diminish in some proportion to the density; but even here again we are disappointed; whatever be the rarefaction, if water be present, the vapour produces the same elasticity, and the hygrometer finally settles at extreme moisture, as in air of common density in like circumstances. These facts are sufficient to create extreme difficulty in the conception how any principle of affinity or *cohesion* between air and water can be the agent. It is truly astonishing that the same quantity of vapour should cohere to *one* particle of air in a given space, as to *one thousand* in the same space. But the wonder does not cease here; a torricellian vacuum dissolves water; and in this instance we have vapour existing independently of air at all temperatures; what makes it still more remarkable is, the vapour in such vacuum is precisely the same in quantity and force as in the like volume of any kind of air of extreme moisture.

These and other considerations which occurred to me some years ago, were sufficient to make me altogether abandon the hypothesis of air dissolving water, and to explain the phenomena some other way, or to acknowledge they were inexplicable. In the autumn of 1801, I hit upon an idea which seemed to be exactly calculated to explain the phenomena of vapour; it gave rise to a great variety of experiments upon which a series of essays were founded, which were read before the Literary and Philosophical Society of Manchester, and published in the 5th Vol. of their memoirs, 1802.

The distinguishing feature of the new theory was, that the particles of one gas are not elastic or repulsive in regard to the particles of another gas, but only to the particles of their own kind. Consequently when a vessel contains a mixture of two such elastic fluids, each acts independently upon the vessel, with its proper elasticity, just as if the other were absent, whilst no mutual action between the fluids themselves is observed. This position most effectually provided for the existence of vapour of any temperature in the atmosphere, because it could have nothing but its own weight to support; and it was perfectly obvious why neither more nor less vapour could exist in air of extreme moisture, than in a vacuum of the same temperature. So far then the great object of the theory was attained. The law of the condensation of vapour in the atmosphere by cold, was evidently the same on this scheme, as that of the condensation of pure steam, and experience was found to confirm the conclusion at all temperatures. The only thing now wanting to completely establish the independent existence of aqueous vapour in the atmosphere, was the conformity of other liquids to water, in regard to the diffusion and condensation of their vapour. This was found to take place in several liquids, and particularly in sulphuric ether, one which was most likely to shew any anomaly to advantage if it existed, on account of the great change of expansibility in its vapour at ordinary temperatures. The existence of vapour in the atmosphere and its occasional condensation were thus accounted for; but another question remained, how does it rise from a surface of water subject to the pressure of the atmosphere? The consideration of this made no part of the essays above mentioned, it being apprehended, that if the other two points could be obtained by any theory, this third too, would, in the sequel, be accomplished.

From the novelty, both in the theory and the experiments, and their importance, provided they were correct, the essays were soon circulated, both at home and abroad. The new facts and experiments were highly valued, some of the latter were repeated, and found correct, and none of the results, as far as I know, have been controverted; but the theory was almost universally misunderstood, and consequently reprobated. This must have arisen partly at least from my being too concise, and not sufficiently clear in its exposition.

¶ *On Chemical Synthesis*

When any body exists in the elastic state, its ultimate particles are separated from each other to a much greater distance than in any other state; each particle occupies the centre of a comparatively large sphere, and supports its dignity by keeping all the rest, which by their gravity, or otherwise are disposed to encroach upon it, at a respectful distance. When we attempt to conceive the *number* of particles in an atmosphere, it is somewhat like attempting to conceive the number of stars in the universe; we are confounded with the thought. But if we limit the subject, by taking a given volume of any gas, we seem persuaded that, let the divisions be ever so minute, the number of particles must be finite; just as in a given space of the universe, the number of stars and planets cannot be infinite.

Chemical analysis and synthesis go no farther than to the separation of particles one from another, and to their reunion. No new creation or destruction of matter is within the reach of chemical agency. We might as well attempt to introduce a new planet into the solar system, or to annihilate one already in existence, as to create or destroy a particle of hydrogen. All the changes we can produce, consist in separating particles that are in a state of cohesion or combination, and joining those that were previously at a distance.

In all chemical investigations, it has justly been considered an important object to ascertain the relative *weights* of the simples which constitute a compound. But unfortunately the inquiry has terminated here; whereas from the relative weights in the mass, the relative weights of the ultimate particles or atoms of the bodies might have been inferred, from which their number and weight in various other compounds would appear, in order to assist and to guide future investigations, and to correct their results. Now it is one great object of this work, to shew the importance and advantage of ascertaining the *relative weights of the ultimate particles, both of simple and compound bodies, the number of simple elementary particles which constitute one compound particle, and the number of less compound particles which enter into the formation of one more compound particle.*

If there are two bodies, A and B, which are disposed to combine, the following is the order in which the combinations may take place, beginning with the most simple: namely,

1 atom of A + 1 atom of B = 1 atom of C, binary.
1 atom of A + 2 atoms of B = 1 atom of D, ternary.
2 atoms of A + 1 atom of B = 1 atom of E, ternary.
1 atom of A + 3 atoms of B = 1 atom of F, quaternary.
3 atoms of A + 1 atom of B = 1 atom of G, quaternary.

etc. etc.

The following general rules may be adopted as guides in all our investigations respecting chemical synthesis.

1st. When only one combination of two bodies can be obtained, it must be presumed to be a *binary* one, unless some cause appear to the contrary.

2nd. When two combinations are observed, they must be presumed to be a *binary* and a *ternary*.

3rd. When three combinations are obtained, we may expect one to be a *binary*, and the other two *ternary*.

4th. When four combinations are observed, we should expect one *binary*, two *ternary*, and one *quaternary*, etc.

5th. A *binary* compound should always be specifically heavier than the mere mixture of its two ingredients.

6th. A *ternary* compound should be specifically heavier than the mixture of a binary and a simple, which would, if combined, constitute it; etc.

7th. The above rules and observations equally apply, when two bodies, such as C and D, D and E, etc. are combined.

From the application of these rules, to the chemical facts already well ascertained, we deduce the following conclusions: 1st. That water is a binary compound of hydrogen and oxygen, and the relative weights of the two elementary atoms are as 1 : 7, nearly; 2nd. That ammonia is a binary compound of hydrogen and azote, and the relative weights of the two atoms are as 1 : 5, nearly; 3rd. That nitrous gas is a binary compound of azote and oxygen, the atoms of which weigh 5 and 7 respectively; that nitric acid is a binary or ternary compound according as it is derived, and consists of one atom of azote and two of oxygen, together weighing 19; that nitrous oxide is a compound similar to nitric acid, and consists of one atom of oxygen and two of azote, weighing 17; that nitrous acid is a binary compound of nitric acid and nitrous gas, weighing 31; that oxynitric acid is a binary compound of nitric acid and oxygen, weighing 26; 4th. That carbonic oxide is a binary compound, consisting of one atom of charcoal, and one of oxygen, together weighing nearly 12; that carbonic acid is a ternary compound, (but sometimes binary) consisting of one atom of charcoal, and two of oxygen, weighing 19; etc. etc. In all these cases the weights are expressed in atoms of hydrogen, each of which is denoted by unity.

In the sequel, the facts and experiments from which these conclusions are derived, will be detailed; as well as a great variety of others from which are inferred the constitution and weight of the ultimate particles of the principal acids, the alkalis, the earths, the metals, the metallic oxides and

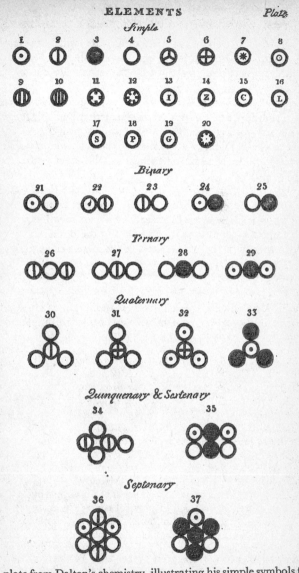

A plate from Dalton's chemistry, illustrating his simple symbols for the atoms of elements and their combination in simple and complex molecules. From John Dalton's *A New System of Chemical Philosophy*, Manchester, 1808.

sulphurets, the long train of neutral salts, and in short, all the chemical compounds which have hitherto obtained a tolerably good analysis. Several of the conclusions will be supported by original experiments.

From the novelty as well as importance of the ideas suggested in this chapter, it is deemed expedient to give plates, exhibiting the mode of combination in some of the more simple cases. A specimen of these accompanies this first part. The elements or atoms of such bodies as are conceived at present to be simple, are denoted by a small circle, with some distinctive mark; and the combinations consist in the juxtaposition of two or more of these; when three or more particles of elastic fluids are combined together in one, it is to be supposed that the particles of the same kind repel each other, and therefore take their stations accordingly.

## EXPLANATION OF PLATE

This plate contains the arbitrary marks or signs chosen to represent the several chemical elements or ultimate particles.

| | | |
|---|---|---|
| 1. Hydrog. its rel. weight | 1 | 11. Strontites | 46 |
| 2. Azote | 5 | 12. Barytes | 68 |
| 3. Carbone or charcoal | 5 | 13. Iron | 38 |
| 4. Oxygen | 7 | 14. Zinc | 56 |
| 5. Phosphorus | 9 | 15. Copper | 56 |
| 6. Sulphur | 13 | 16. Lead | 95 |
| 7. Magnesia | 20 | 17. Silver | 100 |
| 8. Lime | 23 | 18. Platina | 100 |
| 9. Soda | 28 | 19. Gold | 140 |
| 10. Potash | 42 | 20. Mercury | 167 |

21. An atom of water or steam, composed of 1 of oxygen and 1 of hydrogen, retained in physical contact by a strong affinity, and supposed to be surrounded by a common atmosphere of heat; its relative weight = 8

22. An atom of ammonia, composed of 1 of azote and 1 of hydrogen 6

23. An atom of nitrous gas, composed of 1 of azote and 1 of oxygen 12

24. An atom of olefiant gas, composed of 1 of carbone and 1 of hydrogen     6

25. An atom of carbonic oxide, composed of 1 of carbone and 1 of oxygen     12

26. An atom of nitrous oxide, 2 azote + 1 oxygen     17

27. An atom of nitric acid, 1 azote + 2 oxygen     19

28. An atom of carbonic acid, 1 carbone + 2 oxygen     19

29. An atom of carburetted hydrogen, 1 carbone + 2 hydrogen     7

30. An atom of oxynitric acid, 1 azote + 3 oxygen     26

31. An atom of sulphuric acid, 1 sulphur + 3 oxygen     34

32. An atom of sulphuretted hydrogen, 1 sulphur + 3 hydrogen     16

33. An atom of alcohol, 3 carbone + 1 hydrogen     16

34. An atom of nitrous acid, 1 nitric acid + 1 nitrous gas     31

35. An atom of acetous acid, 2 carbone + 2 water     26

36. An atom of nitrate of ammonia, 1 nitric acid + 1 ammonia + 1 water     33

37. An atom of sugar, 1 alcohol + 1 carbonic acid     35

Enough has been given to shew the method; it will be quite unnecessary to devise characters and combinations of them to exhibit to view in this way all the subjects that come under investigation; nor is it necessary to insist upon the accuracy of all these compounds, both in number and weight; the principle will be entered into more particularly hereafter, as far as respects the individual results. It is not to be understood that all those articles marked as simple substances, are necessarily such by the theory; they are only necessarily of such weights. Soda and potash, such as they are found in combination with acids, are 28 and 42 respectively in weight; but according to Mr Davy's very important discoveries, they are metallic oxides; the former then must be considered as composed of an atom of metal, 21, and one of oxygen, 7; and the latter, of an atom of metal, 35, and one of oxygen, 7. Or, soda contains 75 per cent metal and 25 oxygen; potash, 83.3 metal and 16.7 oxygen. It is particularly remarkable, that according to the above-mentioned gentleman's essay on the Decomposition and Composition of fixed alkalis, in the *Philosophical Transactions* (a copy of which essay he has just favoured me with) it appears that 'the largest quantity of oxygen indicated by these experiments was for potash 17, and for soda, 26 parts in 100, and the smallest 13 and 19.'

———

# HUMPHRY DAVY
## 1778–1829

### CHLORINE IS RECOGNIZED AS AN ELEMENT

BY contrast with Dalton, Humphry Davy was one of the most brilliant of experimental chemists. He was born in Penzance, was, like Scheele, apprenticed to an apothecary, and came to work in the Medical Pneumatic Institution in Bristol. Here, in the course of examining the properties of various recently discovered gases, he discovered the anaesthetic properties of nitrous oxide (laughing-gas).

In 1800 Count Rumford, who had come to England after the American War of Independence, secured support for the founding of a kind of mechanics' institute, which was both to educate young working-men in the new scientific knowledge of the time and to promote 'new' and 'useful' inventions. In 1801 Davy was appointed lecturer in chemistry to this organization, the Royal Institution. The Institution became an important centre of research, but, as it was dependent on private contributions, gave popular lectures to wealthy patrons rather than educational lectures to the artisan. Davy, again unlike Dalton, was an able lecturer; he introduced the Christmas lectures for children, which are still popular today. A notable commission, from the Society for the Study and Prevention of Mine Explosion, led Davy to invent the miner's safety lamp, which he refused to patent and so made free for universal use. Again, as a result of an official request, he undertook research into and lectured on agricultural chemistry at a time when imports of foodstuffs had been reduced as a consequence of the French Revolution.

Some of Davy's most valuable chemical work involved the use of a large voltaic electric battery which he found available at the Royal Institution and which became his principal interest. With this he carried out the fascinating electrolytic experiments which produced the elements sodium and potassium. Reflecting on other experiments, he came to the view, shared by Berzelius, that certain elements pair off electrically in a consistent relationship; e.g. copper is always positive relative to sulphur, and that this type of chemical affinity could form the basis of understanding chemical combination.

The selection below includes descriptions of an extensive range of experiments not in the field of electrochemistry. Lavoisier had postulated that oxygen was a component of all acids. Muriatic acid (hydrochloric acid) must therefore contain oxygen; chlorine, prepared from it by reaction with substances rich in oxygen, must contain even more, and was referred to as oxymuriatic gas. Davy's experiments were designed to find evidence that oxymuriatic gas contained oxygen, but as so many had failed to do this, he concluded that the gas was an element. Scheele had called it 'dephlogisticated marine acid air' ('marine acid air' was the vapour obtained from marine or hydrochloric acid), which accords with our present view, if hydrogen is equated with phlogiston. Davy, following Lavoisier's reform of chemical nomenclature, proposed the simpler name 'chlorine' which Gay-Lussac also used. His account is taken from two of his papers in the *Philosophical Transactions* (of the Royal Society) for 1811, and can also be found in the Alembic Club Reprint No. 9.

Davy was knighted in 1812, became a baronet in 1818, and was later elected President of the Royal Society. One of his most significant actions was his appointment of Michael Faraday to be one of his assistants.

―――――

¶ *On a Combination of Oxymuriatic Gas and Oxygene Gas*

I shall beg permission to lay before the Society the account of some experiments on a compound of oxymuriatic gas and oxygene gas, which, I trust, will be found to illustrate an interesting branch of chemical inquiry, and which offer some extraordinary and novel results.

I was led to make these experiments in consequence of the difference between the properties of oxymuriatic gas prepared in different modes: it would occupy a great length of time to state the whole progress of this investigation. It will, I conceive, be more interesting that I should immediately refer to the facts; most of which have been witnessed by Members of this Body, belonging to the Committee of Chemistry of the Royal Institution.

The oxymuriatic gas prepared from manganese, either by mixing it with a muriate and acting upon it by sulphuric acid, or by mixing it with muriatic acid, is, when the oxide of manganese is pure, and, whether collected over water or mercury, uniform in its properties; its colour is a pale yellowish green; water takes up about twice its volume; and scarcely gains any colour; the metals burn in it readily; it combines with hydrogene without any deposition of moisture: it does not act on nitrous gas or muriatic acid, or carbonic oxide, or sulphureous gases, when they have been carefully dried. It is the substance which I employed in all the experiments on the combinations of oxymuriatic gas described in my last two papers.

The gas produced by the action of muriatic acid on the salts which have been called hyperoxymuriates, on the contrary, differs very much in its properties, according as the manner in which it is prepared and collected is different.

When much acid is employed to a small quantity of salt, and the gas is collected over water, the water becomes tinged of a lemon colour; but the gas collected is the same as that procured from manganese.

When the gas is collected over mercury, and is procured from a weak acid, and from a great excess of salt by a low heat, its colour is a dense tint of brilliant yellow green, and it possesses properties entirely different from the gas collected over water.

It sometimes explodes during the time of its transfer from one vessel to another, producing heat and light, with an expansion of volume; and it may be always made to explode by a very gentle heat, often by that of the hand.*

It is a compound of oxymuriatic gas and oxygene, mixed with some oxymuriatic gas. This is proved by the results of its spontaneous explosion. It gives off, in this process, from $\frac{1}{6}$ to $\frac{2}{5}$ its volume of oxygen, loses its vivid colour, and becomes common oxymuriatic gas.

I attempted to obtain the explosive gas in a pure form, by applying heat to a solution of it in water; but in this case, there was a partial decomposition; and some oxygene was disengaged, and some oxymuriatic gas formed. Finding that in the cases when it was most pure, it scarcely acted upon mercury, I attempted to separate the oxymuriatic gas with which it is mixed, by agitation in a tube with this metal; corrosive sublimate formed, and an elastic fluid was obtained, which was almost entirely absorbed by $\frac{1}{4}$ of its volume of water.

This gas in its pure form is so easily decomposable that it is dangerous to operate upon considerable quantities.

In one set of experiments upon it, a jar of strong glass, containing 40 cubical inches, exploded in my hands with a loud report, producing light; the vessel was broken, and fragments of it were thrown to a considerable distance.

I analysed a portion of this gas, by causing it to explode over mercury in a curved glass tube, by the heat of a spirit lamp.

The oxymuriatic gas formed, was absorbed by water; the oxygene was found to be pure, by the test of nitrous gas.

* My brother, Mr J. DAVY, from whom I receive constant and able assistance in all my chemical inquiries, had several times observed explosions, in transferring the gas from hyperoxymuriate of potash, over mercury, and he was inclined to attribute the phaenomenon to the combustion of a thin film of mercury, in contact with a globule of gas. I several times endeavoured to produce the effect, but without success, till an acid was employed for the preparation of the gas, so diluted as not to afford it without the assistance of heat. The change of colour and expansion of volume, when the effect took place, immediately convinced me, that it was owing to a decomposition of the gas.

50 parts of the detonating gas, by decomposition, expanded so as to become 60 parts. The oxygene, remaining after the absorption of the oxymuriatic gas, was about 20 parts. Several other experiments were made, with similar results. So that it may be inferred, that it consists of 2 in volume of oxymuriatic gas, and 1 in volume of oxygene; and the oxygene in the gas is condensed to half its volume. Circumstances conformable to the laws of combination of gaseous fluids, so ably illustrated by M. GAY LUSSAC, and to the theory of definite proportions.

I have stated on a former occasion, that approximations to the numbers representing the proportions in which oxygene and oxymuriatic gas combine, are found in 7·5 and 32·9. And this compound gas contains nearly these quantities.*

The smell of the pure explosive gas somewhat resembles that of burnt sugar, mixed with the peculiar smell of oxymuriatic gas. Water appeared to take up eight or ten times its volume; but the experiment was made over mercury, which might occasion an error, though it did not seem to act on the fluid. The water became of a tint approaching to orange.

When the explosive gas was detonated with hydrogene, equal to twice its volume, there was a great absorption, to more than ⅓, and solution of muriatic acid was formed; when the explosive gas was in excess, oxygene was always expelled, a fact demonstrating the stronger attraction of hydrogene for oxymuriatic gas than for oxygene.

I have said that mercury has no action upon this gas in

* In page 245 of the *Phil. Trans.* for 1810 [p. 35], I have mentioned that the specific gravity of oxymuriatic gas, is between 74 and 75 grains per 100 cubical inches. The gas that I weighed, was collected over water and procured from hyperoxymuriate of potash, and at that time I conceived, that this elastic fluid did not differ from the oxymuriatic gas from manganese, except in being purer. It probably contained some of the new gas; for I find that the specific gravity of pure oxymuriatic gas from manganese, and muriatic acid is to that of common air, as 244 to 100. Taking this estimation, the specific gravity of the new gas will be about 238, and the number representing the proportion in which oxymuriatic gas combines, from this estimation, will be rather higher than is stated above.

its purest form at common temperatures. Copper and anti-mony, which so readily burn in oxymuriatic gas, did not act upon the explosive gas in the cold: and when they were introduced into it, being heated, it was instantly decom-posed, and its oxygene set free; and the metals burnt in the oxymuriatic gas.

When sulphur was introduced into it, there was at first no action, but an explosion soon took place: and the peculiar smell of oxymuriate of sulphur was perceived.

Phosphorus produced a brilliant explosion, by contact with it in the cold, and there was produced phosphoric acid and solid oxymuriate of phosphorus.

Arsenic introduced into it did not inflame; the gas was made to explode, when the metal burnt with great brilliancy in the oxymuriatic gas.

Iron wire introduced into it did not burn, till it was heated so as to produce an explosion, when it burnt with a most brilliant light in the decomposed gas.

Charcoal introduced in it ignited, produced a brilliant flash of light, and burnt with a dull red light, doubtless owing to its action upon the oxygene mixed with the oxy-muriatic gas.

It produced dense red fumes when mixed with nitrous gas, and there was an absorption of volume.

When it was mixed with muriatic acid gas, there was a gradual diminution of volume. By the application of heat the absorption was rapid, oxymuriatic gas was formed, and a dew appeared on the sides of the vessel.

These experiments enable us to explain the contradictory accounts that have been given by different authors of the properties of oxymuriatic gas.

That the explosive compound has not been collected before, is owing to the circumstance of water having been used for receiving the products from hyperoxymuriate of potash, and unless the water is highly saturated with the explosive gas, nothing but oxymuriatic gas is obtained; or to the circumstance of too dense an acid having been employed.

This substance produces the phaenomena which Mr

CHENEVIX, in his able paper on oxymuriatic acid, referred to the hyperoxygenized muriatic acid; and they prove the truth of his ideas respecting the possible existence of a compound of oxymuriatic gas, and oxygene in a separate state.

The explosions produced in attempts to procure the products of hyperoxymuriate of potash by acids are evidently owing to the decomposition of this new and extraordinary substance.

All the conclusions I have ventured to make respecting the undecompounded nature of oxymuriatic gas, are, I conceive, entirely confirmed by these new facts.

If oxymuriatic gas contained oxygene, it is not easy to conceive, why oxygene should be afforded by this new compound to muriatic gas, which must already contain oxygene in intimate union. Though on the idea of muriatic acid being a compound of hydrogene and oxymuriatic gas, the phaenomena are such as might be expected.

If the power of bodies to burn in oxymuriatic gas depended upon the presence of oxygene, they all ought to burn with much more energy in the new compound; but copper and antimony, and mercury, and arsenic, and iron, and sulphur have no action upon it, till it is decomposed; and they act then according to their relative attractions on the oxygene, or on the oxymuriatic gas.

There is a simple experiment which illustrates this idea: Let a glass vessel containing brass foil be exhausted, and the new gas admitted, no action will take place; throw in a little nitrous gas, a rapid decomposition occurs, and the metal burns with great brilliancy.

Supposing oxygene and oxymuriatic gas to belong to the same class of bodies, the attraction between them might be conceived very weak, as it is found to be, and they are easily separated from each other, and made repulsive by a very low degree of heat.

The most vivid effects of combustion known, are those produced by the condensation of oxygene or oxymuriatic gas; but in this instance, a violent explosion with heat and light are produced by their separation, and expansion, a perfectly novel circumstance in chemical philosophy.

This compound destroys dry vegetable colours, but first gives them a tint of red. This and its considerable absorbability by water would incline one to adopt Mr CHENEVIX's idea that it approaches to an acid in its nature. It is probably combined with the peroxide of potassium in the hyperoxymuriate.

That oxymuriate gas and oxygene combine and separate from each other with such peculiar phaenomena, appears strongly in favour of the idea of their being distinct, though analogous species of matter. It is certainly possible to defend the hypothesis that oxymuriatic gas consists of oxygene united to an unknown basis; but it would be possible likewise to defend the speculation that it contains hydrogene.

Like oxygene it has not yet been decomposed; and I sometime ago made an experiment, which like most of the others I have brought forward, is very adverse to the idea of its containing oxygene.

I passed the solid oxymuriate of phosphorus in vapour, and oxygene gas together through a green glass tube heated to redness.

A decomposition took place, and phosphoric acid was formed, and oxymuriatic gas was expelled.

Now, if oxygene existed in the oxymuriate of phosphorus, there is no reason why this change should take place. On the idea of oxymuriatic gas being undecompounded, it is easily explained. Oxygene is known to have a stronger attraction for phosphorus than oxymuriatic gas has, and consequently ought to expel it from this combination.

¶ *Some Reflections on the Nomenclature of the Oxymuriatic Compounds*

To call a body which is not known to contain oxygene, and which cannot contain muriatic acid, oxymuriatic acid, is contrary to the principles of that nomenclature in which it is adopted; and an alteration of it seems necessary to assist the progress of discussion, and to diffuse just ideas on the subject. If the great discoverer of this substance had signified it by any simple name, it would have been proper to have referred to it; but, 'dephlogisticated marine acid' is a term which can hardly be adopted in the present advanced aera of the science.

After consulting some of the most eminent chemical philosophers in this country, it has been judged most proper to suggest a name founded upon one of its obvious and characteristic properties – its colour, and to call it *Chlorine*, or *Chloric* gas.*

Should it hereafter be discovered to be compound, and even to contain oxygene, this name can imply no error, and cannot necessarily require a change.

* From κλωρος

# JOSEPH GAY-LUSSAC
## 1778–1850

### THE LAW OF COMBINATION OF GASES

WE may use hindsight to describe the foundations of the atomic theory as a triangle with Dalton, Gay-Lussac, and Avogadro at its vertices. As we shall see in the next selection, Avogadro's hypothesis was available, in fact, while Dalton and Gay-Lussac were engaged in their studies; but the triangle had to wait for half a century before it could be completed. Both Gay-Lussac's and Dalton's work would have been greatly advanced had they accepted Avogadro's theory and gone on from there.

Gay-Lussac belongs to the circle distinguished by Lavoisier and his collaborator, Claude Louis Berthollet (1748–1822). His basic training took place in Paris, where he served as Berthollet's assistant at the famous École des Ponts et Chaussées (school of bridges and highways). In due course he became a professor of chemistry himself, first at the École Polytechnique, then at the Sorbonne and the Jardin des Plantes. Like Berthollet, Gay-Lussac was much called upon as a consultant by the French chemical industry, his principal contributions being in connexion with the manufacture of sulphuric and oxalic acids on a commercial scale.

Given Berthollet's interest in the field of chemical combination, it was natural that Gay-Lussac should take an interest in the same problem. He also examined magnetic phenomena – literally at all levels, for he undertook balloon ascents, rising to a height of more than 20,000 feet in 1804, just a hundred years before the Wright brothers flew in their heavier-than-air machine. These experiments, reported to the French Academy, showed that the composition of the air and terrestrial magnetic effects did not change at this great height above the earth.

Gay-Lussac's first paper, published in 1802, confirmed

what is known as Charles's law or Gay-Lussac's law – that the volume of a given mass of any gas, at constant pressure, decreases by 1/273 of its volume at 0°C for every degree drop in temperature. Although the law is not followed precisely by all gases, Gay-Lussac's work cleared up a number of deficiencies in Charles's and Dalton's experiments.

Using electrochemical methods, Gay-Lussac made many useful discoveries about the nature of gaseous combinations and did considerable work with potassium, chlorine, and iodine. He thought, in opposition to Humphry Davy, that chlorine was a compound but was later convinced that Davy was right in stating that it contained no oxygen. With von Humboldt he performed experiments which showed how oxygen and hydrogen combine. Finding that, whatever the relative quantities of the gases actually present, the combination by volume was always in the proportion of 1:2, and that other gases exhibited the same tendencies, he agreed that the *weights* of equal *volumes* of gases would, in combination, be directly related to the combining weights and so to the atomic weights. This implied that the 'space' occupied by an atom was the same for all gases – in contrast with Dalton's view that the 'particles' of gases were not of the same size. Avogadro had the explanation available in 1811, but his article was overlooked. The development of the atomic and molecular theory was, as a result, held up for fifty years.

As is shown in the reading below, Gay-Lussac observed that whenever two gases combine chemically, their volumes and the volume of the resulting gas (if a gas is formed) can be expressed in a simple numerical relationship. Thus he showed that hydrogen and chlorine combine in equal volumes, and that one volume of nitrogen and three volumes of hydrogen produce two volumes of ammonia.

Gay-Lussac's work is described in a selection taken from the Alembic Club Reprint No. 4.

¶ *Memoir on the Combination of Gaseous Substances with each other*

Substances, whether in the solid, liquid, or gaseous state, possess properties which are independent of the force of cohesion; but they also possess others which appear to be modified by this force (so variable in its intensity), and which no longer follow any regular law. The same pressure applied to all solid or liquid substances would produce a diminution of volume differing in each case, while it would be equal for all elastic fluids. Similarly, heat expands all substances; but the dilatations of liquids and solids have hitherto presented no regularity, and it is only those of elastic fluids which are equal and independent of the nature of each gas. The attraction of the molecules in solids and liquids is, therefore, the cause which modifies their special properties; and it appears that it is only when the attraction is entirely destroyed, as in gases, that bodies under similar conditions obey simple and regular laws. At least, it is my intention to make known some new properties in gases, the effects of which are regular, by showing that these substances combine amongst themselves in very simple proportions, and that the contraction of volume which they experience on combination also follows a regular law. I hope by this means to give a proof of an idea advanced by several very distinguished chemists – that we are perhaps not far removed from the time when we shall be able to submit the bulk of chemical phenomena to calculation.

It is a very important question in itself, and one much discussed amongst chemists, to ascertain if compounds are formed in all sorts of proportions. M. Proust, who appears first to have fixed his attention on this subject, is of opinion that the metals are susceptible of only two degrees of oxidation; *a minimum* and *a maximum*; but led away by this seductive theory, he has seen himself forced to entertain principles contrary to physics in order to reduce to two oxides all those which the same metal sometimes presents.

M. Berthollet thinks, on the other hand – reasoning from general considerations and his own experiments – that compounds are always formed in very variable proportions, unless they are determined by special causes, such as crystallization, insolubility, or elasticity. Lastly, Dalton has advanced the idea that compounds of two bodies are formed in such a way that one atom of the one unites with one, two, three, or more atoms of the other.* It would follow from this mode of looking at compounds that they are formed in constant proportions, the existence of intermediate bodies being excluded, and in this respect Dalton's theory would resemble that of M. Proust; but M. Berthollet has already strongly opposed it in the Introduction he has written to Thomson's *Chemistry*, and we shall see that in reality it is not entirely exact. Such is the state of the question now under discussion; it is still very far from receiving its solution, but I hope that the facts which I now proceed to set forth, facts which had entirely escaped the notice of chemists, will contribute to its elucidation.

Suspecting, from the exact ratio of 100 of oxygen to 200 of hydrogen, which M. Humboldt and I had determined for the proportions of water, that other gases might also combine in simple ratios, I have made the following experiments. I prepared fluoboric,† muriatic, and carbonic gases, and made them combine successively with ammonia gas, and the salt which is formed from them is perfectly neutral, whether one or other of the gases is in excess. Fluoboric gas, on the contrary, unites in two proportions with ammonia gas. When the acid‡ gas is put first into the graduated tube, and the other gas is then passed in, it is found that equal volumes

* Dalton has been led to this idea by systematic considerations; and one may see from his work, *A New System of Chemical Philosophy*, p. 213, and from that of Thomson, Vol. 6, that his researches have no connexion with mine.

† M. Thenard and I have given the name of fluoboric gas to that particular gas which we obtained by distilling pure fluoride of lime with vitreous boracic acid.

‡ ['Alkaline' in the original.]

of the two condense, and that the salt formed is neutral. But if we begin by first putting the ammonia gas into the tube, and then admitting the fluoboric gas in single bubbles, the first gas will then be in excess with regard to the second, and there will result a salt with excess of base, composed of 100 of fluoboric gas and 200 of ammonia gas. If carbonic gas is brought into contact with ammonia gas, by passing it sometimes first, sometimes second into the tube, there is always formed a sub-carbonate composed of 100 parts of carbonic gas and 200 of ammonia gas. It may, however, be proved that neutral carbonate of ammonia would be composed of equal volumes of each of these components. M. Berthollet, who has analysed this salt, obtained by passing carbonic gas into the sub-carbonate, found that it was composed of 73·34 parts by weight of carbonic gas and 26·66 of ammonia gas. Now, if we suppose it to be composed of equal volumes of its components, we find from their known specific gravity, that it contains by weight

$$
\begin{array}{l}
71\cdot 81 \text{ of carbonic acid,} \\
\underline{28\cdot 19 \text{ of ammonia,}} \\
100\cdot 0
\end{array}
$$

a proportion differing only slightly from the preceding.

If the neutral carbonate of ammonia could be formed by the mixture of carbonic gas and ammonia gas, as much of one gas as of the other would be absorbed; and since we can only obtain it through the intervention of water, we must conclude that it is the affinity of this liquid which competes with that of the ammonia to overcome the elasticity of the carbonic acid, and that the neutral carbonate of ammonia can only exist through the medium of water.

Thus we may conclude that muriatic, fluoboric, and carbonic acids take exactly their own volume of ammonia gas to form neutral salts, and that the last two take twice as much to form sub-salts. It is very remarkable to see acids so different from one another neutralize a volume of ammonia gas equal to their own; and from this we may suspect that if all acids and all alkalis could be obtained in the gaseous state, neutrality would result from the combination of equal volumes of acid and alkali.

It is not less remarkable that, whether we obtain a neutral salt or a sub-salt, their elements combine in simple ratios which may be considered as limits to their proportions. Accordingly, if we accept the specific gravity of muriatic acid determined by M. Biot* and myself, and those of carbonic gas and ammonia given by MM. Biot and Arago, we find that dry muriate of ammonia is composed of

$$\begin{array}{lll} \text{Ammonia,} & 100 \cdot 0 & 38 \cdot 35 \\ \text{Muriatic acid,} & 160 \cdot 7 & 61 \cdot 65 \\ & & \overline{100 \cdot 00} \end{array}$$

a proportion very far from that of M. Berthollet –

$$\begin{array}{l} 100 \text{ of ammonia,} \\ 213 \text{ of acid.} \end{array}$$

In the same way, we find that sub-carbonate of ammonia contains

$$\begin{array}{lll} \text{Ammonia,} & 100 \cdot 0 & 43 \cdot 98 \\ \text{Carbonic acid,} & 127 \cdot 3 & 56 \cdot 02 \\ & & \overline{100 \cdot 00} \end{array}$$

and the neutral carbonate

$$\begin{array}{lll} \text{Ammonia,} & 100.0 & 28 \cdot 19 \\ \text{Carbonic acid,} & 254.6 & 71 \cdot 81 \\ & & \overline{100 \cdot 00} \end{array}$$

It is easy from the preceding results to ascertain the ratios of the capacity of fluoboric, muriatic, and carbonic acids; for since these three gases saturate the same volume of ammonia gas, their relative capacities will be inversely as their densities, allowance having been made for the water contained in muriatic acid.

We might even now conclude that gases combine with each other in very simple ratios; but I shall still give some fresh proofs.

* As muriatic gas contains one fourth of its weight of water, we must take only three fourths of the density for that of real muriatic acid.

According to the experiments of M. Amédée Berthollet, ammonia is composed of

> 100 of nitrogen,
> 300 of hydrogen,

by volume.

I have found (Vol. 1 of the Société d'Arcueil) that sulphuric acid is composed of

> 100 of sulphurous gas,
> 50 of oxygen gas.

When a mixture of 50 parts of oxygen and 100 of carbonic oxide (formed by the distillation of oxide of zinc with strongly calcined charcoal) is inflamed, these two gases are destroyed and their place taken by 100 parts of carbonic acid gas. Consequently carbonic acid may be considered as being composed of

> 100 of carbonic oxide gas,
> 50 of oxygen gas.

Davy, from the analysis of various compounds of nitrogen with oxygen, has found the following proportions by weight:

|  | NITROGEN | OXYGEN |
| --- | --- | --- |
| Nitrous oxide | 63·30 | 36·70 |
| Nitrous gas | 44·05 | 55·95 |
| Nitric acid | 29·50 | 70·50 |

Reducing these proportions to volumes we find –

|  | NITROGEN | OXYGEN |
| --- | --- | --- |
| Nitrous oxide | 100 | 49·5 |
| Nitrous gas | 100 | 108·9 |
| Nitric acid | 100 | 204·7 |

The first and the last of these proportions differ only slightly from 100 to 50, and 100 to 200; it is only the second which diverges somewhat from 100 to 100. The difference, however, is not very great, and is such as we might expect in experiments of this sort; and I have assured myself that it is actually nil. On burning the new combustible substance from potash in 100 parts by volume of nitrous gas, there remained over exactly 50 parts of nitrogen, the weight of which, deducted from that of the nitrous gas (determined with great care by M. Bérard at Arcueil), yields as result that this gas is composed of equal parts by volume of nitrogen and oxygen.

We may then admit the following numbers for the proportions by volume of the compounds of nitrogen with oxygen:

|               | NITROGEN | OXYGEN |
|---------------|----------|--------|
| Nitrous oxide | 100      | 50     |
| Nitrous gas   | 100      | 100    |
| Nitric acid   | 100      | 200    |

From my experiments, which differ very little from those of M. Chenevix, oxygenated muriatic acid is composed by weight of

Oxygen        22·92
Muriatic acid 77·08

Converting these quantities into volumes, we find that oxygenated muriatic acid is formed of

Muriatic gas 300·0
Oxygen gas   103·2

a proportion very nearly

Muriatic gas 300
Oxygen gas   100*

* In the proportion by weight of oxygenated muriatic acid, the muriatic acid is supposed to be free from water, whilst in the proportion by volume it is supposed to be combined with a fourth of its weight of water, which, since the reading of this paper, M. Thenard and I have proved to be absolutely necessary for its existence in the gaseous state. But since the simple ratio of 300 of acid to 100 of oxygen cannot be due to chance, we must conclude that water by combining with dry muriatic acid to form ordinary muriatic acid does not sensibly change its specific gravity. We should be led to the same conclusion from the consideration that the specific gravity of oxygenated muriatic acid, which from our experiments contains no water, is exactly the same as that obtained by adding the density of oxygen gas to three times that of muriatic gas, and taking half of this sum. M. Thenard and I have also found that oxygenated muriatic gas contains precisely half its volume of oxygen, and that it can destroy in consequence its own volume of hydrogen.

Thus it appears evident to me that gases always combine in the simplest proportions when they act on one another; and we have seen in reality in all the preceding examples that the ratio of combination is 1 to 1, 1 to 2, 1 to 3. It is very important to observe that in considering weights there is no simple and finite relation between the elements of any one compound; it is only when there is a second compound between the same elements that the new proportion of the element that has been added is a multiple of the first quantity. Gases, on the contrary, in whatever proportions they may combine, always give rise to compounds whose elements by volume are multiples of each other.

Not only, however, do gases combine in very simple proportions, as we have just seen, but the apparent contraction of volume which they experience on combination has also a simple relation to the volume of the gases, or at least to that of one of them.

I have said, following M. Berthollet, that 100 parts of carbonic oxide gas, prepared by distilling oxide of zinc and strongly calcined charcoal, produce 100 parts of carbonic gas on combining with 50 of oxygen. It follows from this that the apparent contraction of the two gases is precisely equal to the volume of oxygen gas added. The density of carbonic gas is thus equal to that of carbonic oxide gas plus half the density of oxygen gas; or, conversely, the density of carbonic oxide gas is equal to that of carbonic gas, minus half that of oxygen gas. Accordingly, taking the density of air as unity, we find the density of carbonic oxide gas to be 0·9678, instead of 0·9569 experimentally determined by Cruickshank. We know, besides, that a given volume of oxygen produces an equal volume of carbonic acid; consequently oxygen gas doubles its volume on forming carbonic oxide gas with carbon, and so does carbonic gas on being passed over red-hot charcoal. Since oxygen produces an equal volume of carbonic gas, and the density of the latter is well known, it is easy to calculate the proportion of its elements. In this way we find that carbonic gas is composed of

27·38 of carbon,
72·62 of oxygen,

and carbonic oxide of

42·99 of carbon,
57·01 of oxygen.

Pursuing a similar course, we find that if sulphur takes 100 parts of oxygen to produce sulphurous acid, it takes 150 parts to produce sulphuric acid. As a matter of fact, we find that sulphuric acid, according to the experiments of MM. Klaproth, Bucholz, and Richter, is composed of 100 parts by weight of sulphur and 138 of oxygen.

On the other hand sulphuric acid is composed of 2 parts by volume of sulphurous gas, and 1 of oxygen gas. Consequently the weight of a certain quantity of sulphuric acid should be the same as that of 2 parts of sulphurous acid and 1 of oxygen gas, i.e., 2 × 2·265, plus 1·10359 = 5·63359; seeing that, according to Kirwan, sulphurous gas weighs 2·265, the density of air being taken as unity. But from the proportion of 100 of sulphur to 138 of oxygen, this quantity contains 3·26653 of oxygen, and if we subtract from it 1·10359 there will remain 2·16294 for the weight of oxygen in 2 parts of sulphurous acid, or 1·08147 for the weight of oxygen contained in 1 part.

Now as this last quantity only differs by 2 per cent from 1·10359, which represents the weight of 1 part of oxygen gas, it must be concluded that oxygen gas, in combining with sulphur to form sulphurous gas, only experiences a diminution of a fiftieth of its volume, and this would probably be nil if the data I have employed were more exact. On this last supposition, using Kirwan's value for the specific gravity of sulphurous gas, we should find that this acid is composed of

100·00 of sulphur,
95·02 of oxygen.

But, if, adopting the preceding proportions for sulphuric acid, we allow, as appears probable, that 100 of sulphurous gas contains 100 of oxygen gas, and that 50 have still to be added to convert it into sulphuric acid, we shall obtain for the proportions in sulphurous acid

100·00 of sulphur,
92·0 of oxygen.

Its specific gravity calculated on the same suppositions, and referred to that of air, would be 2·30314, instead of 2·2650 as Kirwan found directly.*

Phosphorus is very closely connected with sulphur, seeing that both have nearly the same specific gravity. Consequently phosphorus should take up twice as much oxygen to become phosphorous acid, as to pass from this state into phosphoric acid. Since the latter is composed, according to Rose, of

100·0 of phosphorus,
114·0 of oxygen,

it follows that phosphorous acid should contain 100.0 of phosphorus, 76·0 of oxygen.

We have seen that 100 parts of nitrogen gas take 50 parts of oxygen gas to form nitrous oxide, and 100 of oxygen gas to form nitrous gas. In the first case, the contraction is a little greater than the volume of oxygen added; for the specific gravity of nitrous oxide, calculated on this hypothesis, is 1·52092, while that given by Davy is 1·61414. But it is easy to show, from some of Davy's experiments, that the apparent contraction is precisely equal to the volume of oxygen gas added. On passing the electric spark through a mixture of 100 parts of hydrogen and 97·5 of nitrous oxide the hydrogen is destroyed, and 102 parts of nitrogen remain, including that quantity which is almost always mixed with the hydrogen, and a little of the latter gas which has escaped combustion. The residue, after making all corrections, would be very

* In order to remove these differences it would be necessary to make new experiments on the density of sulphurous gas, on the direct union of oxygen gas with sulphur to see if there is contraction, and on the union of sulphurous gas with ammonia gas. I have found, it is true, on heating cinnabar in oxygen gas, that 100 parts of this gas only produce 93 of sulphurous gas. It also appeared as if less sulphurous gas than

nearly equal in volume to the nitrous oxide employed. Similarly, on passing the electric spark through a mixture of 100 parts of phosphoretted hydrogen and 250 of nitrous oxide, water, and phosphoric acid are formed, and exactly 250 parts of nitrogen remain – another evident proof that the apparent contraction of the elements of nitrous oxide is equal to the whole volume of oxygen added. From this circumstance, its specific gravity referred to that of air should be 1·52092.

The apparent contraction of the elements of nitrous gas appears, on the other hand, to be nil. If we admit, as I have shown, that it is composed of equal parts of oxygen and nitrogen, we find that its density, calculated on the assumption that there is no contraction, is 1·036, while that determined directly is 1·038.

Saussure found that the density of water vapour is to that of air as 10 is to 14. Assuming that the contraction of volume of the two gases is only equal to the whole volume of oxygen added, we find instead of this a ratio of 10 to 16. This difference, and the authority of a physicist so distinguished as Saussure, would seem to be enough to make us reject the assumption I have just made; but I shall mention several circumstances that render it very probable. Firstly, it has a very strong analogy in its favour; secondly, M. Tralès found by direct experiment that the ratio of the density of water-vapour to air is 10 to 14·5, instead of 10 to 14; thirdly, although we do not know very exactly the volume occupied by water on passing into the elastic state, we do know, from the experiments of Watt, that a cubic inch of water produces nearly a cubic foot of steam i.e., a volume 1728 times as great. Now, adopting Saussure's ratio, we find only

---

ammonia gas was necessary to form a neutral salt. But as these experiments were not made under suitable conditions – especially the last, which could only be made in presence of water, the sulphurous gas decomposing and precipitating sulphur immediately on being mixed with the ammonia gas – I intend to repeat them and determine exactly all the conditions before drawing any conclusion from them. This is all the more necessary, as sulphurous gas can be used to analyse sulphuretted hydrogen gas, if its proportions are well known.

1488 for the volume occupied by water when it is converted into steam; but adopting the ratio of 10 to 16, we should have 1700·6. Finally, the refraction of water-vapour, calculated on the assumption of the ratio 10 to 14, is a little greater than the observed refraction; but that calculated from the ratio 10 to 16 is much more in harmony with the results of experiment. These, then, are the considerations which go to make the ratio 10 to 16 very probable.

Ammonia gas is composed of three parts by volume of hydrogen and one of nitrogen, and its density compared to air is 0·596. But if we suppose the apparent contraction to be half of the whole volume, we find 0·594 for the density. Thus it is proved, by this almost perfect concordance, that the apparent contraction of its elements is precisely half the total volume, or rather double the volume of the nitrogen.

I have already proved that oxygenated muriatic gas is composed of 300 parts of muriatic gas and 100 of oxygen gas. Admitting that the apparent contraction of the two gases is half the whole volume, we find 2·468 for its density, and by experiment 2·470. I have also assured myself by several experiments that the proportions of its elements are such that it forms neutral salts with the metals. For example, if we pass oxygenated muriatic gas over copper, there is formed a slightly acid green muriate, and a little oxide of copper is precipitated, because the salt cannot be obtained perfectly neutral. It follows from this that in all the muriates, as in oxygenated muriatic acid, the acid reduced to volume is thrice the oxygen. It would be the same for carbonates and fluorides, the acids of which have for equal volumes the same saturation capacity as muriatic acid.

We see, then, from these various examples, that the contraction experienced by two gases on combination is in almost exact relation with their volume, or rather with the volume of one of them. Only very slight differences exist between the densities of compounds obtained by calculation and those given by experiment, and it is probable that, on undertaking new researches, we shall see them vanish entirely.

Recalling the great law of chemical affinity, that every combination involves an approximation of the elementary molecules, it is difficult to conceive why carbonic oxide gas should be lighter than oxygen. Indeed, that is the principal reason which has led M. Berthollet to assume the existence of hydrogen in this gas, and thus explain its low density. But it seems to me that the difficulty arises from supposing that the approximation of the elementary molecules is represented in gases by the diminution of volume which they suffer on combination. This supposition is not always true, and we might cite several gaseous combinations, the constituent molecules of which would be brought very close together, although there is not only no diminution of volume, but even a dilatation. Such, for example, is nitrous gas, whether we consider it as being formed directly from nitrogen and oxygen, or from nitrous oxide and oxygen. In the first case, there is no diminution of volume; and in the second, there would be dilatation, for 100 parts of nitrous oxide and 50 of oxygen would produce 200 of nitrous gas. We know too that carbonic gas represents an exactly equal volume of oxygen, and that the affinity which unites its elements is very powerful. Nevertheless, if we admitted an immediate relation between the condensation of the elements and the condensation of volume, we should conclude, contrary to experiment, that there is no condensation. Otherwise it would be necessary to suppose that if carbon were in the gaseous state it would combine in equal volumes (or in any other proportion) with oxygen, and that the apparent condensation would then be equal to the whole volume of the gaseous carbon. But if we make this supposition for carbonic acid, we may also make it for carbonic oxide, by assuming, for instance, that 100 parts of gaseous carbon would produce 100 parts of the gas on combining with 50 parts of oxygen. However it may stand with these suppositions, which only serve to make it conceivable that oxygen can produce a compound lighter than itself by combining with a solid substance, we must admit, as a truth founded on a great number of observations, that the condensation of the molecules of two combining substances, in particular of two gases, has no immediate relation to the condensation of volume, since we often see that whilst one is very great the other is very small or even nil.

The observation that the gaseous combustibles combine with oxygen in the simple ratios of 1 to 1, 1 to 2, 1 to $\frac{1}{2}$, can lead us to determine the density of the vapours of combustible substances, or at least to approximate closely to that determination. For if we suppose all combustible substances to be in the gaseous state, a specified volume of each would absorb an equal volume of oxygen, or twice as much, or else half; and as we know the proportion of oxygen taken up by each combustible substance in the solid or liquid state, it is sufficient to convert the oxygen into volumes and also the combustible, under the condition that its vapour shall be equal to the volume of oxygen, or else double or half this value. For example, mercury is susceptible of two degrees of oxidation, and we may compare the first one to nitrous oxide. Now, according to MM. Fourcoy and Thenard, 100 parts of mercury absorb 4·16, which reduced to gas would occupy a space of 8·20. These 100 parts of mercury reduced to vapour should therefore occupy twice the space, viz., 16·40. We thence conclude that the density of mercury vapour is 12·01 greater than that of oxygen, and that the metal on passing from the liquid to the gaseous state assumes a volume 961 times as great.

I shall not discuss more of these determinations, because they are only based on analogies, and it is besides easy to multiply them. I shall conclude this memoir by examining if compounds are formed in constant or variable proportions, as the experiments of which I have just given an account lead me to the discussion of these two opinions.

According to Dalton's ingenious idea, that combinations are formed from atom to atom, the various compounds which two substances can form would be produced by the union of one molecule of the one with one molecule of the other, or with two, or with a greater number, but always without intermediate compounds. Thomson and Wollaston have indeed described experiments which appear to confirm this theory. Thomson has found that super-oxalate of potash contains twice as much acid as is necessary to saturate the alkali; and Wollaston, that the sub-carbonate of potash contains, on the other hand, twice as much alkali as is necessary to saturate the acid.

The numerous results I have brought forward in this Memoir are also very favourable to the theory. But M. Berthollet, who thinks that combinations are made continuously, cites in proof of his opinion the acid sulphates, glass, alloys, mixtures of various liquids – all of which are compounds with very variable proportions, and he insists principally on the identity of the force which produces chemical compounds and solutions.

Each of these two opinions has, therefore, a large number of facts in its favour; but although they are apparently utterly opposed, it is easy to reconcile them.

We must first of all admit, with M. Berthollet, that chemical action is exercised indefinitely in a continuous manner between the molecules of substances, whatever their number and ratio may be, and that in general we can obtain compounds with very variable proportions. But then we must admit at the same time that – apart from insolubility, cohesion, and elasticity, which tend to produce compounds in fixed proportions – chemical action is exerted more powerfully when the elements are in simple ratios or in multiple proportions among themselves, and that compounds are thus produced which separate out more easily. In this way we reconcile the two opinions, and maintain the great chemical law, that whenever two substances are in the presence of each other they act in their sphere of activity according to their masses, and give rise in general to compounds with very variable proportions, unless these proportions are determined by special circumstances.

§ *Conclusion*

I have shown in this Memoir that the compounds of gaseous substances with each other are always formed in very simple ratios, so that representing one of the terms by unity, the other is 1, or 2, or at most 3. These ratios by volume are not observed with solid or liquid substances, nor when we consider weights, and they form a new proof that it is only in the gaseous state that substances are in the same circumstances and obey regular laws. It is remarkable to see that ammonia gas neutralizes exactly its own volume of gaseous acids; and it is probable that if all acids and alkalis were in the elastic state, they would all combine in equal volumes to produce neutral salts. The capacity of saturation of acids and alkalis measured by volume would then be the same, and this might perhaps be the true manner of determining it. The apparent contraction of volume suffered by gases on combination is also very simply related to the volume of one of them, and this property likewise is peculiar to gaseous substances.

# AMEDEO AVOGADRO
## 1776–1856

### THE DISTINCTION BETWEEN AN ATOM
### AND A MOLECULE

LORENZO ROMANO AMEDEO CARLO AVOGADRO was
born in Turin and trained as a lawyer. He became interested
in physics and mathematics, and in 1809 was appointed to
a professorship at the Royal College at Vercelli. In 1811 he
published his hypothesis, which, now famous, was rejected
by his contemporaries.

Avogadro's hypothesis consists of two basic assumptions.
The first is that equal volumes of different gases, under the
same conditions of temperature and pressure, contain the
same number of molecules. The actual number of molecules
present in a given volume was not known to Avogadro, but
in the twentieth century the number of molecules present in
a gram molecular weight of any substance was determined.
This is known as Avogadro's number; the accepted value at
present is $6 \cdot 02 \times 10^{23}$.

The second assumption is that the smallest particle of a
gaseous element such as hydrogen or oxygen consists not of
one atom but of two atoms chemically combined and constituting a molecule. Avogadro thus introduced the modern
concept of the molecule as the smallest particle of a gaseous
substance that can have independent existence and retain
its chemical properties. It is a pity, however, that he used
the term 'solitary elementary molecules' for what we now
call atoms, though he was consistent in its use. Dalton, of
course, used the term 'compound atoms' for what we now
call molecules.

Avogadro's hypothesis was incorporated in the Essay published by the *Journal de Physique* in 1811. Extracts are reprinted here from the Alembic Club translation (Reprint
No. 4).

After the publication of this essay, Avogadro turned to other problems in physical chemistry. In 1820 he was appointed to a chair of mathematical physics at the University of Turin. The University, however, was closed as a result of political upheavals, and Avogadro was given a pension of about twenty pounds per annum. For ten years he returned to the practice of law, but continued to study science. Then with the re-opening of the University, he returned to his chair, which he occupied for a further twenty years.

\*

This book is primarily concerned with the moments of original discovery in science. Here, however, we must include a reference to an incident of re-discovery which for the chemical world of the time must have had the force of something completely new. Avogadro's hypothesis had virtually been neglected by chemists. It was brought to their attention again by his fellow-countryman, Cannizzaro, who at the time held the Chair of Chemistry in the University of Genoa.

Cannizzaro published a paper in *Il nuovo cimento* which was a 'Sketch of a Course in Chemical Philosophy'. (An English translation is found in No. 18 of the Alembic Club Reprints.) It set out the substance of a course of lectures to his students, which began with a historical summary of the reasons for the neglect of Avogadro's hypothesis and then a demonstration of its value. He went further by showing how the hypothesis could be used to derive probable atomic weights of elements (Cannizzaro's method) which could be checked by reference to the law of specific heats (Dulong and Petit).

His views were put forward at a Congress held in Carlsruhe two years later. Lothar Meyer recorded that at this meeting 'it was as though scales fell from my eyes, doubt vanished, and was replaced by a feeling of peaceful certainty'. Not all of the chemists present at the congress were so percipient, but recognition of the value of his work gradually came. As early as 1862 the British chemists made him an Honorary Member of the Chemical Society. For the rest of his long life (1826–1910) he was as much honoured as Avogadro had been neglected.

---

¶ *Essay on A Manner of Determining the Relative Masses of the Elementary Molecules of Bodies and the Proportions in which they enter into these Compounds*

I

M. Gay-Lussac has shown in an interesting Memoir (*Mémoires de la Société d'Arcueil,* Tome II) that gases always unite in a very simple proportion by volume, and that when the result of the union is a gas, its volume also is very simply related to those of its components. But the quantitative proportions of substances in compounds seem only to depend on the relative number of molecules which combine, and on the number of composite molecules which result. It must then be admitted that very simple relations also exist between the volumes of gaseous substances and the numbers of simple or compound molecules which form them. The first hypothesis to present itself in this connexion, and apparently even the only admissible one, is the supposition that the number of integral molecules in any gases is always the same for equal volumes, or always proportional to the volumes. Indeed, if we were to suppose that the number of molecules contained in a given volume were different for different gases, it would scarcely be possible to conceive that the law regulating the distance of molecules could give in all cases relations so simple as those which the facts just detailed compel us to acknowledge between the volume and the number of molecules. On the other hand, it is very well conceivable that the molecules of gases being at such a distance that their mutual attraction cannot be exercised, their varying attraction for caloric may be limited to condensing a greater or smaller quantity around them, without the atmosphere formed by this fluid having any greater extent in the one case than in the other, and, consequently, without the distance between the molecules varying; or, in other words, without the number of molecules contained in a given volume being different. Dalton, it is true, has proposed a hypothesis directly opposed to this, namely, that the quantity of caloric is always the same for the molecules of all bodies whatsoever in the gaseous state, and that the greater or less attraction for caloric only results in producing a greater or less condensation of this quantity around the molecules, and thus varying the distance between the molecules themselves. But in our present ignorance of the manner in which this attraction of the molecules for caloric is exerted, there is nothing to decide us *a priori* in favour of the one of these hypotheses rather than the other; and we should rather be inclined to adopt a neutral hypothesis, which would make the distance between the molecules and the quantities of caloric vary according to unknown laws, were it not that the hypothesis we have just proposed is based on that simplicity of relation between the volumes of gases on combination, which would appear to be otherwise inexplicable.

Setting out from this hypothesis, it is apparent that we have the means of determining very easily the relative masses of the molecules of substances obtainable in the gaseous state, and the relative number of these molecules in compounds; for the ratios of the masses of the molecules are then the same as those of the densities of the different gases at equal temperature and pressure, and the relative number of molecules in a compound is given at once by the ratio of the volumes of the gases that form it. For example, since the numbers 1·10359 and 0·07321 express the densities of the two gases oxygen and hydrogen compared to that of atmospheric air as unity, and the ratio of the two numbers consequently represents the ratio between the masses of equal volumes of these two gases, it will also represent on our hypothesis the ratio of the masses of their molecules. Thus the mass of the molecule of oxygen will be about 15 times that of the molecule of hydrogen, or, more exactly, as 15·074 to 1. In the same way the mass of the molecule of nitrogen will be to that of hydrogen as 0·96913 to 0·07321, that is, as 13, or more exactly 13·238, to 1. On the other hand, since we know that the ratio of the volumes of hydrogen and oxygen in the formation of water is 2 to 1, it follows that water results from the union of each molecule of oxygen with two molecules of hydrogen. Similarly, according to the proportions by volume established by M. Gay-Lussac for the elements of ammonia, nitrous oxide, nitrous gas, and nitric acid, ammonia will result from the union of one molecule of nitrogen with three of hydrogen, nitrous oxide from one molecule of oxygen with three of hydrogen, nitrous oxide from one molecule of oxygen with two of nitrogen, nitrous gas from one molecule of nitrogen with one of oxygen, and nitric acid from one of nitrogen with two of oxygen.

## II

There is a consideration which appears at first sight to be opposed to the admission of our hypothesis with respect to compound substances. It seems that a molecule composed of two or more elementary molecules should have its mass equal to the sum of the masses of these molecules; and that in particular, if in a compound one molecule of one substance unites with two or more molecules of another substance, the number of compound molecules should remain the same as the number of molecules of the first substance. Accordingly, on our hypothesis when a gas combines with two or more times its volume of another gas, the resulting compound, if gaseous, must have a volume equal to that of the first of these gases. Now, in general, this is not actually the case. For instance, the volume of water in the gaseous state is, as M. Gay-Lussac has shown, twice as great as the volume of oxygen which enters into it, or, what comes to the same thing, equal to that of the hydrogen instead of being equal to that of the oxygen. But a means of explaining facts of this type in conformity with our hypothesis presents itself naturally enough: we suppose, namely, that the constituent molecules of any simple gas whatever (*i.e.*, the molecules which are at such a distance from each other that they cannot exercise their mutual action) are not formed of a solitary elementary molecule, but are made up of a certain number of these molecules united by attraction to form a single one; and further, that when molecules of another substance unite with the former to form a compound molecule, the integral molecule which should result splits up into two or more parts (or integral molecules) composed of half, quarter, etc., the number of elementary molecules going to form the constituent molecule of the first substance, combined with half, quarter, etc., the number of constituent molecules of the second substance that ought to enter into combination with one constituent molecule of the first substance (or, what comes to the same thing, combined with a number equal to this last of half-molecules, quarter-molecules, etc., of the second substance); so that the number of integral molecules of the compound becomes double, quadruple, etc., what it would have been if there had been no splitting-up, and exactly what is necessary to satisfy the volume of the resulting gas.*

On reviewing the various compound gases most generally known, I only find examples of duplication of the volume relatively to the volume of that one of the constituents which combines with one or more volumes of the other. We have already seen this for water. In the same way, we know that the volume of ammonia gas is twice that of the nitrogen which enters into it. M. Gay-Lussac has also shown that the volume of nitrous oxide is equal to that of the nitrogen which forms part of it, and consequently is twice that of the oxygen. Finally, nitrous gas, which contains equal volumes of nitrogen and oxygen, has a volume equal to the sum of the two constituent gases, that is to say, double that of each of them. Thus, in all these cases there must be a division of the molecule into two; but it is possible that in other cases the division might be into four, eight, etc. The possibility of this division of compound molecules might have been conjectured *a priori*; for otherwise the integral molecules of bodies composed of several substances with a relatively large num-

---

*Thus, for example, the integral molecule of water will be composed of a half-molecule of oxygen with one molecule, or, what is the same thing, two half-molecules of hydrogen.

ber of molecules, would come to have a mass excessive in comparison with the molecules of simple substances. We might therefore imagine that nature has some means of bringing them back to the order of the latter, and the facts have pointed out to us the existence of such means. Besides, there is another consideration which would seem to make us admit in some cases the division in question; for how could one otherwise conceive a real combination between two gaseous substances uniting in equal volumes without condensation, such as takes place in the formation of nitrous gas? Supposing the molecules to remain at such a distance that the mutual attraction of those of each gas could not be exercised, we cannot imagine that a new attraction could take place between the molecules of one gas and those of the other. But on the hypothesis of division of the molecule, it is easy to see that the combination really reduces two different molecules to one, and that there would be contraction by the whole volume of one of the gases if each compound molecule did not split up into two molecules of the same nature. M. Gay-Lussac clearly saw that, according to the facts, the diminution of volume on the combination of gases cannot represent the approximation of their elementary molecules. The division of molecules on combination explains to us how these two things may be made independent of each other.

### III

Dalton, on arbitrary suppositions as to the most likely relative number of molecules in compounds, has endeavoured to fix ratios between the masses of the molecules of simple substances. Our hypothesis, supposing it well-founded, puts us in a position to confirm or rectify his results from precise data, and, above all, to assign the magnitude of compound molecules according to the volumes of the gaseous compounds, which depend partly on the division of molecules entirely unsuspected by this physicist.

Thus Dalton supposes* that water is formed by the union

*In what follows I shall make use of the exposition of Dalton's ideas given in Thomson's *System of Chemistry*.

of hydrogen and oxygen, molecule to molecule. From this, and from the ratio by weight of the two components, it would follow that the mass of the molecule of oxygen would be to that of hydrogen as $7\frac{1}{2}$ to 1 nearly, or according to Dalton's evaluation, as 6 to 1. This ratio on our hypothesis is, as we saw, twice as great, namely, as 15 to 1. As for the molecule of water, its mass ought to be roughly expressed by $15 + 2 = 17$ (taking for unity that of hydrogen), if there were no division of the molecule into two; but on account of this division it is reduced to half, $8\frac{1}{2}$, or more exactly $8 \cdot 537$, as may also be found directly by dividing the density of aqueous vapour $0 \cdot 625$ (Gay-Lussac) by the density of hydrogen $0 \cdot 0732$. This mass only differs from 7, that assigned to it by Dalton, by the difference in the values for the composition of water; so that in this respect Dalton's result is approximately correct from the combination of two compensating errors, – the error in the mass of the molecule of oxygen, and his neglect of the division of the molecule.

Dalton supposes that in nitrous gas the combination of nitrogen and oxygen is molecule to molecule; we have seen on our hypothesis that this is actually the case. Thus Dalton would have found the same molecular mass for nitrogen as we have, always supposing that of hydrogen to be unity, if he had not set out from a different value for that of oxygen, and if he had taken precisely the same value for the quantities of the elements in nitrous gas by weight. But by supposing the molecule of oxygen to be less than half what we find, he has been obliged to make that of nitrogen also equal to less than half the value we have assigned to it, viz., 5 instead of 13. As regards the molecule of nitrous gas itself, his neglect of the division of the molecule again makes his result approach ours; he has made it $6 + 5 = 11$, whilst according to us it is about

$$\frac{15 + 13}{2} = 14,$$

or more exactly

$$\frac{15 \cdot 074 + 13 \cdot 238}{2} = 14 \cdot 156,$$

as we also find by dividing $1 \cdot 03636$, the density of nitrous gas according to Gay-Lussac, by $0 \cdot 07321$. Dalton has likewise fixed in the same manner as the facts given us, the relative number of molecules in nitrous oxide and in nitric acid, and in the first case the same circumstance has rectified his result for the magnitude of the molecule. He makes it $6 + 2 \times 5 = 16$, whilst according to our method it should be

$$\frac{15 \cdot 074 + 2 \times 13 \cdot 238}{2} = 20 \cdot 775,$$

a number which is also obtained by dividing $1 \cdot 52092$, Gay-Lussac's value for the density of nitrous oxide, by the density of hydrogen.

In the case of ammonia, Dalton's supposition as to the relative number of molecules in its composition is on our hypothesis entirely at fault. He supposes nitrogen and hydrogen to be united in it molecule to molecule, whereas we have seen that one molecule of nitrogen unites with three molecules of hydrogen. According to him the molecule of ammonia would be $5 + 1 = 6$: according to us it should be

$$\frac{13 + 3}{2} = 8,$$

or more exactly $8 \cdot 119$, as may also be deduced directly from the density of ammonia gas. The division of the molecule, which does not enter into Dalton's calculations, partly corrects in this case also the error which would result from his other suppositions.

All the compounds we have just discussed are produced by the union of one molecule of one of the components with one or more molecules of the other. In nitrous acid we have another compound of two of the substances already spoken of, in which the terms of the ratio between the number of molecules both differ from unity. From Gay-Lussac's experiments (*Société d'Arcueil*, same volume), it appears that this acid is formed from 1 part by volume of oxygen and 3 of nitrous gas, or, what comes to the same thing, of 3 parts of nitrogen and 5 of oxygen; whence it would follow, on our hypothesis, that its molecule should be composed of 3 molecules of nitrogen and 5 of oxygen, leaving the possibility of division out of account. But this mode of combination can be referred to the preceding simpler forms by considering it as the result of the union of 1 molecule of oxygen with 3 of nitrous gas, *i.e.*, with 3 molecules, each composed of a half-molecule of oxygen and a half-molecule of nitrogen, which thus already includes the division of some of the molecules of oxygen which enter into that of nitrous acid. Supposing there to be no other division, the mass of this last molecule would be 57·542, that of hydrogen being taken as unity, and the density of nitrous acid gas would be 4·21267, the density of air being taken as unity. But it is probable that there is at least another division into two, and consequently a reduction of the density to half: we must wait until this density has been determined by experiment.

IV

We may now look at a few more compounds, which on our hypothesis can give us at least conjectural information concerning the relative masses of the molecules and their number in these compounds, and compare our results with the supposition of Dalton.

M. Gay-Lussac has shown that if we assume that dry sulphuric acid is composed of 100 parts of sulphur and 138 of oxygen by weight, as the most recent work of chemists has established, and that the density of sulphurous acid gas is 2·265 referred to air as unity (Kirwan's determination), and if we admit, as the result of Gay-Lussac's experiments, that sulphuric acid is composed of two parts by volume of sulphurous acid gas and one of oxygen, then the volume of sulphurous acid is nearly equal to that of the oxygen which entered into it; and this equality would be exact if the bases on which the calculation rests were the same. If we suppose

Kirwan's determination to be exact, throwing the whole error on the analysis of sulphuric acid, we find that in sulphurous acid 100 parts of sulphur take 95·02 of oxygen, and consequently in sulphuric acid

$$95 \cdot 02 + \frac{95 \cdot 02}{2} = 142 \cdot 53,$$

instead of 138. If, on the contrary, we suppose the analysis of sulphuric acid to be exact, it follows that sulphuric acid contains 92 of oxygen for 100 of sulphur, and that its specific gravity should be 2·30314, instead of 2·265.

One consideration would appear to weigh in favour of the first assumption, until the density of sulphurous acid gas has been confirmed or rectified by fresh experiments – namely, that there must have been in the determination of the composition of sulphuric acid, a source of error tending to increase the quantity of the radical, or, what is the same thing, diminish the quantity of oxygen. The determination was made from the quantity of dry sulphuric acid produced. Now it seems almost certain that ordinary sulphur contains hydrogen; the weight of this hydrogen, which must have been converted into water in the operation, has therefore been added to the true weight of the radical. I shall therefore assume sulphurous acid to be composed of 95·02* of oxygen to 100 of sulphur, or rather of sulphuric radical, instead of 92.†

In order now to determine the mass of the molecule of the sulphuric radical, it would be necessary to know what proportion by volume this radical in the gaseous state would bear to the oxygen in the formation of sulphurous acid. The analogy with other combinations already discussed, where

*[Erroneously 92.02 in the original.]

† This was written before I had seen the Memoir of Davy on oxymuriatic acid, which also contains new experiments on sulphur and phosphorus. In it he determines the density of sulphurous acid gas, and finds it to be only 2·0967, which gives new force to the above considerations. If we adopt this density, we find that in sulphurous acid 100 parts by weight of sulphur take 111 of oxygen, and in sulphuric acid 167 instead of 138; but perhaps this density of sulphurous acid, according to Davy, is somewhat too low.

there is in general a doubling of the volume or halving of the molecule, leads us to suppose that it is the same in this case also, i.e., that the volume of the sulphur as gas is half that of the sulphurous acid, and consequently also half that of the oxygen with which it combines. On this supposition the density of sulphur gas will be to that of oxygen as 100 to

$$\frac{95 \cdot 02}{2},$$

or 47·51; which gives 2·323 for the density of gaseous sulphur, taking that of air as unity. The masses of the molecules being according to our hypothesis in the same ratio as the densities of the gases to which they belong, the mass of the molecule of the sulphuric radical will be to that of hydrogen as 2·323 to 0·07321, or as 31·73 to 1. One of these molecules combined, as we have said, with two of oxygen, will form sulphurous acid (division of the molecule being left out of account), and combined with yet another molecule of oxygen, will form sulphuric acid. Accordingly, sulphurous acid should be analogous to nitric acid, with regard to the relative number of molecules of its constituents, sulphuric acid having no analogue amongst the nitrogen compounds. The molecule of sulphurous acid, having regard to division, will be equal to

$$\frac{31 \cdot 73 + 2 \times 15 \cdot 074}{2},$$

or 30·94, as would also be obtained directly by dividing the density 2·265 of sulphurous acid gas by that of hydrogen gas. As for the molecule of sulphuric acid, it cannot be determined, for we do not know whether there is further division of the molecule on its formation, or not.*

Dalton had supposed that sulphuric acid was composed of

* Davy, in the Memoir alluded to, has made the same suppositions as to the relative number of molecules of oxygen and radical in sulphurous and sulphuric acids. From his determination of the density of sulphurous acid gas, the density of the sulphuric radical would be 1·9862, and its molecule 27·13, that of hydrogen being taken as unity. Davy, by a similar calculation, fixes it at about half, viz. 13·7, because he supposes

two molecules of oxygen to one of radical and sulphurous acid of one molecule of oxygen to one of sulphur. These two assumptions are incompatible, for according to Gay-Lussac's results the quantities of oxygen in these two acids, for a given quantity of radical, are represented by 1 and $1\frac{1}{2}$. Besides, in his determination of the molecule he set out from a wrong value for the composition of sulphuric acid, and it is only by chance that the mass 15 which he assigns to it, bears to his value for the mass of the oxygen molecule a ratio which approaches that presented by these two substances on our hypothesis.

Phosphorus has so much analogy with sulphur that we might apparently assume that phosphoric acid also is

---

the molecule of oxygen to be equal to about half our molecule, using Dalton's hypothesis with respect to water.

He finds nearly the same mass, viz. 13·4, by taking as his starting-point the density of sulphuretted hydrogen, which his experiments make equal to 1·0645, a result only slightly different from Kirwan's, and by assuming that this gas (which contains, as we know, its own volume of hydrogen combined with sulphur) is composed of one molecule of sulphur and one of hydrogen. As we suppose the molecule of sulphur to be nearly twice as great, we must assume that this gas is the product of the union of one molecule of the radical with at least two of hydrogen, and that its volume is twice that of the gaseous radical, as in so many other cases. I say *at least* with two molecules of hydrogen, for if there were hydrogen already in ordinary sulphur, as known experiments on this substance indicate, its quantity also must be added. If, for instance, ordinary sulphur were composed of one molecule of sulphuric radical and one of hydrogen, sulphuretted hydrogen would be composed of three molecules of hydrogen and one of radical. This could be decided by the comparison of the specific gravities of sulphuretted hydrogen and sulphurous acid gas, if both were known exactly. For example, supposing Davy's determination for sulphuretted hydrogen to be exact, the molecule of the sulphuric radical, on the supposition of only two molecules of hydrogen, would be 27·08, that of hydrogen being taken as unity; but on the supposition of three molecules of hydrogen, 27·08 would be the sum of one molecule of radical and one of hydrogen, so that the former would be reduced to 26·08. If the exact density of sulphurous acid gas confirmed one or other of these results, it would confirm by that means one or other of these hypotheses; but we are not sufficiently agreed about these densities to be able to draw any conclusion in this respect from the determinations hitherto existing.

composed of three molecules of oxygen to one of radical, and phosphorous acid of only two of oxygen to one of radical. On this assumption we may calculate approximately the mass of the molecule of the phosphoric radical. Rose found by a method analogous to that which had been employed for sulphuric acid, that phosphoric acid contains about 115 parts by weight of oxygen to 100 of phosphorus. There ought to be a little more oxygen in it if we suppose that phosphorus, like sulphur, contains hydrogen. As an approximation we can make this increase in the same proportion as we have seen holds good for sulphuric acid, in accordance with the specific gravity of sulphurous acid, and thus bring the quantity of oxygen up to 120. We then find from our hypotheses that the mass of the molecule of the phosphoric radical is about 38, that of hydrogen being taken as unity. Dalton also has adopted for phosphorous and phosphoric acids, hypotheses analogous to those he had made for sulphurous and sulphuric acids; but since he used different values for the elements of these acids by weight, he arrived at a determination of the molecule of phosphorus, which does not bear the same ratio to his determination of the molecule of sulphur as ought to exist, according to us, between these molecules: he has fixed that of phosphorus as 8, hydrogen being unity. *

Let us now see what conjecture we may form as to the mass of the molecule of a substance which plays in nature a far greater part than sulphur or phosphorus, namely, that of carbon. As it is certain that the volume of carbonic acid is equal to that of the oxygen which enters into it, then, if we admit that the volume of carbon, supposed gaseous,

* Davy has adopted the same suppositions as ourselves for the number of molecules of oxygen and radical in phosphorous and phosphoric acids; and by still taking the molecule of oxygen nearly half ours, he finds 16·5 for the molecule of phosphorus, which would give about 33 on our evaluation of the molecule of oxygen, instead of 38. The difference arises from Davy having taken from his own experiments 34 parts to 25, *i.e.* 136 to 100 of phosphorus, as the quantity of oxygen in phosphoric acid, instead of 120 as we have assumed. Further experiments will clear up this point.

which forms the other element, is doubled by the division of its molecules into two, as in several combinations of that sort, it will be necessary to suppose that this volume is the half of that of the oxygen with which it combines, and that consequently carbonic acid results from the union of one molecule of carbon and two of oxygen, and is therefore analogous to sulphurous and phosphorous acids, according to the preceding suppositions. In this case we find from the proportion by weight between the oxygen and the carbon, that the density of carbon as gas would be 0·832 with respect to that of air as unity, and the mass of its molecule 11·36 with respect to hydrogen. There is, however, one difficulty in this supposition, for we can give to the molecule of carbon a mass less than that of nitrogen and oxygen, whereas one would be inclined to attribute the solidity of its aggregation at the highest temperatures to a higher molecular mass, as is observed in the case of the sulphuric and phosphoric radicals. We might avoid this difficulty by assuming a division of the molecule into four, or even into eight, on the formation of carbonic acid; for in that way we should have the molecule of carbon twice or four times as great as that we have just fixed. But such a composition would not be analogous to that of the other acids; and, besides, according to other known examples, the assumption or not of the gaseous state does not appear to depend solely on the magnitude of the molecule, but also on some other unknown property of substances. Thus we see sulphurous acid in the form of a gas at the ordinary temperature and pressure of the atmosphere notwithstanding its large molecule, which is almost equal to that of the solid sulphuric radical. Oxygenated muriatic acid gas has a density, and consequently a molecular mass, still more considerable. Mercury, which as we shall see further on, should have an extremely large molecule, is nevertheless gaseous at a temperature infinitely lower than would be necessary to vaporize iron, the molecule of which is smaller. Thus there is nothing to prevent us from regarding carbonic acid to be composed in the manner indicated above, – and therefore analogous to nitric, sulphuric, and phosphoric acids, – and the molecule of carbon to have a mass expressed by 11·36.

Dalton has made the same supposition as we have done regarding the composition of carbonic acid, and has consequently been led to attribute to carbon a molecule equal to 4·4, which is almost in the same ratio to his value for that of oxygen as 11·36 is to 15, the mass of the molecule of oxygen according to us.

Assuming the values indicated for the mass of the molecule of carbon and the density of its gas, carbonic oxide will be formed, according to the experiments of M. Gay-Lussac, of equal parts by volume of carbon gas and oxygen gas; and its volume will be equal to the sum of the volumes of its constituents: it will accordingly be formed of carbon and oxygen united molecule to molecule, with subsequent halving – all in perfect analogy to nitrous gas.

The mass of the molecule of carbonic acid will be –

$$\frac{11 \cdot 36 + 2 \times 15 \cdot 074}{2} = 20 \cdot 75 = \frac{1 \cdot 5196}{0 \cdot 07321},$$

and that of carbonic oxide will be –

$$\frac{11 \cdot 36 + 15 \cdot 074}{2} = 13 \cdot 22 = \frac{0 \cdot 96782}{0 \cdot 07321}.$$

\*

## VI

Let us now apply our hypothesis to some metallic substances. M. Gay-Lussac assumes that mercurous oxide, in the formation of which 100 parts by weight of mercury absorb 4·16 of oxygen, according to Fourcroy and Thenard, is analogous to nitrous oxide, i.e., that the mercury, supposed gaseous, is combined in it with half its volume of oxygen gas, which on our hypothesis is to say that one molecule of oxygen combines with two molecules of mercury. Supposing this to be the case, the density of mercury gas ought to be to that of oxygen as 100 to 8·32, which would give 13·25 as its density taking that of air as unity, and for the mass of the molecule of mercury 181 taking as unity that of hydrogen. On this supposition mercuric oxide, which contains twice as much oxygen, should be formed of mercury and oxygen united molecule to molecule; but some reasons lead me to think that it is mercurous oxide which represents this last case, and that in mercuric oxide one molecule of mercury combines with two of oxygen. Then the density of mercury gas, and the mass of its molecule, would be double what they are on the preceding hypothesis, viz., 26½ for the first, and 362 for the second. In this assumption I am supported by analogies drawn from other metals, and particularly from iron. It follows from the experiments of different chemists, carefully discussed by Hassenfratz, that the two best known oxides of iron, the black oxide and the red oxide, are composed respectively of 31·8 and 45 parts by weight of oxygen to 100 of iron. We see that the second of these two quantities of oxygen is nearly half as great again as the first, so that we are naturally led to suppose that in the first oxide one molecule of iron combines with two molecules of oxygen, and in the second with three. If that is so, and if we admit the proportion for the black oxide to be the more exact, the proportion for the red oxide would be 47·7 for 100 of iron, which comes very near the proportion found directly by Proust, viz. 48. The mass of a molecule of iron will therefore be to the mass of a molecule of oxygen as 100 to 15·9, which gives about 94 with regard to hydrogen as unity. It would appear from this that there should be another oxide of iron which would contain 15·9 of oxygen to 100 of iron, and this is perhaps the white oxide, although the experiments hitherto performed point to this substance containing a greater proportion of oxygen. Now the two oxides of mercury of which we have spoken, one of which contains twice as much oxygen as the other, should apparently be analogous to this last oxide of iron and to the black oxide, the red oxide having no analogue in the case of mercury.

In the same way the other metals present for the most

part two oxides in which the quantities of oxygen are as 1 to 2, so that from the proportions of their elements, by weight, we may determine in the same manner the mass of their molecules. I find for example, 206 for the molecule of lead, 198 for that of silver, 123 for copper, etc.*

\*

## VIII

It will have been in general remarked on reading this Memoir that there are many points of agreement between our special results and those of Dalton, although we set out from a general principle, and Dalton has only been guided by considerations of detail. This agreement is an argument in favour of our hypothesis, which is at bottom merely Dalton's system furnished with a new means of precision from the connexion we have found between it and the general fact established by M. Gay-Lussac. Dalton's system supposes that compounds are made in general in fixed proportions, and this is what experiment shows with regard to the more stable compounds and those most interesting to the chemist. It would appear that it is only combinations of this sort that can take place amongst gases, on account of the enormous size of the molecules which would result from ratios expressed by larger numbers, in spite of the division of the molecules, which is in all probability confined within narrow limits. We perceive that the close packing of the molecules in solids and liquids, which only leaves between the integral molecules distances of the same order as those between the elementary molecules, can give rise to more complicated ratios, and even to combinations in all proportions; but these compounds will be so to speak of a different type from those with which we have been concerned, and this distinction may serve to reconcile M. Berthollet's ideas as to compounds with the theory of fixed proportions.

———

\* Avogadro here adds a footnote about potassium.

# DMITRI IVANOVICH MENDELEEV
## 1834–1907

### THE PERIODIC TABLE OF THE ELEMENTS

As elements were progressively discovered during the nineteenth century, regularities in their physical and chemical properties were noticed, and chemists began to group them together. Many schemes were put forward, one of the most promising being suggested by Newlands in 1865. He had noticed that if the elements were listed in order of atomic weight, every eighth element resembled the element seven places earlier (the inert gases had not been discovered at that time); he emphasized, incidentally, that this regularity became apparent only if Cannizzaro's atomic weights were used. His ideas were ridiculed when he first put them forward, perhaps because he referred to them as the Law of Octaves and the musical analogy seemed too far-fetched for chemists to take seriously. The great unifying scheme was put forward by Mendeleev in 1869, though Lothar Meyer, in Germany, published a similar scheme almost at the same time.

Mendeleev was born in Tobolsk, the fourteenth child of a teacher who became blind soon after Dmitri's birth. Mendeleev's mother took responsibility for the family, reviving a glass-works, which her family had founded, in order to augment her husband's small pension. She travelled to Moscow in an attempt to secure her son's admission to the University, which the officials denied to a Siberian. He was, however, admitted to the Central Pedagogic Institute in St Petersburg (Leningrad), a short time before his mother died.

The Periodic Table was put forward in 1869, three years after Mendeleev had been appointed Professor of General Chemistry in the University of St Petersburg. He had realized that the properties of the sixty-three elements then known were a periodic function of their atomic weights, so that they could be grouped into distinct families.

A property which he emphasized was the valency of the element. Frankland in 1852 had noted the tendency for an atom of nitrogen, phosphorus, arsenic or antimony to combine with either three or five equivalents of other elements. '... No matter what the characters of the uniting atoms may be, the combining power of the attracting element ... is always satisfied by the same number of these atoms.' The 'combining power' was later called 'quantivalence', which became 'valence' in America and 'valency' in Britain.

The most remarkable feature of the Periodic Table was the realization that the discovery of elements was incomplete, and that gaps should be left for undiscovered elements within the Table, not merely after the heaviest known member (at that time uranium). Moreover, he predicted the properties which would be possessed by the elements which he expected to fit into these empty positions. His predictions were verified remarkably well during his own lifetime by the discovery of gallium, scandium, and germanium.

In some ways his greatest insight was shown in assigning tellurium and iodine to their present positions in the Table on the basis of their chemical properties, although their atomic weights placed them in the reverse order. He suggested that the atomic weight of tellurium might be found to be in error. This was not so, and it was not until the isotopic composition of the two elements was established, after Mendeleev's death, that the situation was completely explained.

The Periodic Table proved to be the great unifying scheme of inorganic chemistry, and is no less useful today than it was when first put forward. The gaps were gradually filled in by the discovery of further elements. Only within the last twenty years has it been extended, by the preparation, rather than the discovery, of the new post-uranium elements. Some of their properties, too, could be predicted by reference to the Periodic Table, and this proved of great value in identifying the minute quantities available. This help was recognized by naming one of the new elements mendelevium.

The selection that follows appeared originally in the *Journal of the Russian Chemical Society*, Vol. 1 (1869). The translation is taken from *Selected Readings in Natural Science* (University of Chicago Press, 1947).

⸻

¶ *The Relations between the Properties of Elements and their Atomic Weights*

During the course of the development of our science, the systematic arrangement of elements has undergone manifold and repeated changes. The most frequent classification of elements into metals and non-metals is based upon physical differences, as they are observed for many simple bodies, as well as upon differences in character of the oxides and of the compounds corresponding to them. However, what at first acquaintance with the subject-matter appeared to be completely clear, lost its importance entirely when more detailed knowledge was obtained. Ever since it became known that an element such as phosphorus could appear in non-metallic as well as in metallic form, it became impossible to found a classification on physical differences. Even the formation of basic and acid oxides does not provide a reliable guarantee since, between the definitely basic and definitely acid oxides, a series of transitional forms exists among which the oxides of bismuth, antimony, arsenic, gold, platinum, titanium, boron, tin, and of many other elements must be counted. Moreover, the analogy of compounds of metals such as bismuth, vanadium, antimony, and arsenic with the compounds of phosphorus and nitrogen, of tellurium with selenium and sulphur, as well as of silicon, titanium, and zirconium with tin no longer permits a distinction between metals and non-metals for the classification of simple bodies. The investigations concerning metal-organic compounds which demonstrated that sulphur, phosphorus, and arsenic form compounds of the same kind as do mercury, zinc, lead, and bismuth, confirm the validity of the above point conclusively.

Those systems which are based upon the behaviour of elements with respect to hydrogen and oxygen, likewise show many uncertainties and separate elements that, without doubt, exhibit great similarity. So far, bismuth has not been compounded with hydrogen as have the elements similar to it; nitrogen which resembles phosphorus forms extraordinarily unstable oxides and, in contrast to phosphorus, does not oxidize directly. Iodine and fluorine are clearly distinguished from each other by the fact that the first very easily forms compounds with oxygen but with hydrogen only under extreme conditions. The latter, however, has not yet been compounded with oxygen; on the contrary, it displaces oxygen, but does form a very stable compound with hydrogen. Magnesium, zinc, and cadmium which form such a natural group of elements would belong, according to this system, to different groups, as would also copper and silver. For the same reason, thallium would be separated from the alkali metals similar to it, and lead from the related barium, strontium, and calcium; even the most natural groups of elements, palladium, rhodium, ruthenium, on the one hand, and osmium, iridium, and platinum on the other hand, would have to take widely separated places in this system.

The ordering of the elements according to their electrochemical sequence is considered by the history of chemistry to be as unfortunate an attempt as is the ordering according to their relative resemblance. Because of the diversity of relations existing between elements, one cannot think of representing their system in the form of a continuous series, since the mutual relations of the bodies are extraordinarily diverse. If the bodies are ordered according to their resemblance or according to the electrical sequence, then involuntarily one leaves out of consideration the reversal of reactions which represents an essential property of chemical behaviour. If zinc decomposes water (forming zinc oxide and releasing hydrogen), then hydrogen also decomposes zinc oxide; chlorine displaces oxygen, but oxygen does the same with chlorine as we see from the synthesis of chlorine, for this reaction consists in the oxidation of hydrochloric acid. This fact is left out from consideration completely by all who desire to arrange the elements in a continuous series.

In recent times the majority of chemists is inclined to achieve a correct ordering of the elements on the basis of their valency. There are many uncertainties involved in such an attempt. ... Elements such as vanadium, molybdenum, tungsten, manganese, chromium, uranium, arsenic, antimony, and the elements of the platinum group form compounds with different valencies, which are so characteristic and which resemble so little the ideas we gain from the acquaintance with organic compounds that, at least for the present, it is impossible to think that we can make use of the strict concept of valency in order to understand the compounds of these elements. For aluminium, compounds which contain one atom of this element are totally unknown; for copper and mercury the sub-oxides, in which these elements are univalent, represent, in many regards, far more stable compounds than do the oxides; thus, these elements – similar to silver – are univalent elements with respect to the salts of their sub-oxides, but with respect to the salts of their oxides, they are bi-valent. Lead appears in its metal-organic compounds as a four-valent element, while its mineral compounds lead us to regard it as a bi-valent element; iodine is a tri-valent element in a certain sense, phosphorus is three- and five-valent. For the determination of the valency of elements one has to come to a conclusion on the basis of the molecular composition of arbitrarily chosen compounds. If, for example, for the case of copper, cupric chloride is chosen as the saturated compound, then it appears that this saturated copper compound is a very unstable body which easily changes into an unsaturated compound, namely cuprous chloride, in which copper is a univalent element. But when one chooses the highest, even though less stable, compounds as a measure for valency, then doubts regarding even the valency of hydrogen may arise; for the peroxide of hydrogen is analogous to the higher copper- or mercury-oxides. In this event arsenic, phosphorus, and nitrogen, antimony and others have to be regarded as five-valent and even as seven-valent elements; iodine (because of its compounds with chlorine) must be considered as a three- or five-valent element, and perhaps of even still higher valency. Then it is nearly impossible to determine the valency of elements such as manganese and aluminium. The analogy between potassium permanganate and potassium hyperchlorate is of such importance in the problem of valency that either manganese appears as univalent as is chlorine, or chlorine must be accepted as a two-, four-, or six-valent element similar to manganese. . . .

That it is correct to consider the principle of valency in its application to the system of elements as uncertain can also be seen from the fact that, so far, not a single strict system has been constructed in this direction, and also from the fact that for this system elements such as silicon and boron have to be widely separated, as must be the case for silver, copper and mercury, antimony and bismuth, thallium and caesium. . . . As far as the changes of the doctrine of the valency of elements are concerned in the direction that it recognizes the variability of the valency, it can only serve as the best proof that the doctrine is untenable. If carbon may be four- or two-valent, if copper and mercury may occur as bi-valent and uni-valent, if phosphorus may be five-, three-, two-valent, why should one not admit, then, that hydrogen and chlorine can also be one-, two-, three-, etc. valent; in this case, no difficulties at all would arise, naturally, regarding the explanation for the existence and structure of any arbitrary compound, but, of course, there would also be no firm basis to judge it.

Thus, there does not exist yet a single universal principle which can withstand criticism, that could serve as guide to judge the relative properties of elements, and that would permit their arrangement in a more or less strict system.

Only with respect to some groups of elements there are no doubts that they form a whole and represent a natural order of similar manifestations of matter. Such groups are: the halogens (F, Cl, Br, I), the alkaline earth metals (Ca, Sr, Ba), the nitrogen group (N, P, As, Sb, Bi), partially also the sulphur group (S, Se, Te), the companions of platinum (Pt, Os, Ir), the companions of cerium, and a few others. Already there exist numerous experiments to show the regularities in those relations that have been noticed within the series of elements belonging to a single group. Thus, repeatedly, there have been noted the parallels which exist, e.g., between Li, K, and Na on the one hand; Ca, Sr, and Ba as well as Cl, I, and Br on the other hand – also between O, S, Se, Te, and N, P, As, and Sb. . . .

The discovery of rubidium, caesium, and thallium gave rise to the reflection that our knowledge of the elements is very limited; and the attempt to construct a system appears to be premature as long as there exists no hypothetical basis which could serve as the foundation of a strict system.

The investigations regarding the simple relations of atomic weights have caused many, in particular, Dumas, Pettenkofer, and Sokolow, to point out the numerical relations between the atomic weights of those elements which form a group; but, so far as I know, they have not led to a systematic arrangement of all known elements. I know only of an attempt by Lenssen to satisfy this requirement that seems so natural. However, this system of triads of single bodies suffers from a certain ambiguity, since it possesses no definite principle as a basis. Lenssen endeavours to support his classification of elements into triads with the help of the relations between atomic weights (in every triad the atomic weight of the in-between element is equal to half the sum of the atomic weights of the two outside elements, as was done first by Kremers and others); further, he claims support in chemical similarity and the colour of compounds. However, the classification according to the latter principle becomes uncertain as a result of the differences noted in the colours of Co – , Cr – , Cu – , and many other compounds according to the external conditions they have undergone or according to the form of combination in which they are found. Yet there are natural groups to be found in Lenssen's system which agree quite frequently with our general concepts, such as, e.g., K, Na, and Li; Ba, Sr, and Ca; Mg, Zn, and Cd; Ag, Pb, and Hg; S, Se, and Te; P, As, and Sb; Os, Pt, and Ir; Pd, Ru, and Rh; W, V, and Mo; Ta, Sn, and Ti, and others. But to place into one group Si, B, and F; O, N, and C; Cr, Ni, and Cu; Be, Zr, and U as Lenssen does, is hardly possible, after all. Moreover in his system the tendency appears to be implicit to subjugate the natural grouping of elements to the triads, which scarcely correspond to nature, and this is also not consonant with the certainty that the known series of elements are incomplete. If space could be found in his system to accommodate elements which are still to be discovered, this would result in the destruction of groups considered to be complete up to this time.

When I undertook to write a handbook of chemistry entitled 'Foundations of Chemistry', I had to make a decision in favour of some system of elements in order not to be guided in their classification by accidental, or instinctive reasons, but by some exact, definite principle. In what has been said above we have seen the nearly complete absence of numerical relations in the construction of systems of elements; every system, however, that is based upon exactly observed numbers is to be preferred of course to other systems not based upon numbers because then only little margin is left to arbitrariness. The numerical data available regarding elements are limited at this time. Even if the physical properties of some of them have been determined accurately, this is true only of a very small number of elements. Properties, such as the optical and even the electrical or magnetic ones, cannot serve as basis for the system naturally, since one and the same body, according to the state in which it happens to be at the moment, may show enormous differences in this regard. With respect to this fact, it is sufficient to remember graphite and diamond, ordinary and red phosphorus. The vapour density which enables us to know the molecular weight of bodies is not only unknown for most elements but it is subject also to changes which agree completely with the polymeric transformations as they have been observed for compound bodies. Oxygen and sulphur furnish unambiguous proof for this fact; the relations between nitrogen, phosphorus, and arsenic provide another confirmation, in so far as these similar elements possess the molecular weights $N_2$, $P_4$, $As_4$ which are unequal to each other with respect to the number of atoms. But there is no doubt that the polymerization of an element must go hand in hand with the change of a number of its properties. One cannot be certain whether for any arbitrarily chosen element, e.g., for platinum, another state would become known and that therefore, the place of a given element in the system would have to be changed according to its physical properties. However, everybody does understand that in all changes of properties of elements, something remains unchanged, and that when elements go into compounds this material something represents the (common) characteristics of compounds the given element can form. In this regard only a numerical value is known, and this is the atomic weight appropriate to the element. The magnitude of the atomic weight, according to the actual, essential nature of the concept, is a quantity which does not refer to the momentary state of an element but belongs to a material part of it, a part which it has in common with the free element and with all its compounds. The atomic weight does not belong to coal and to the diamond but to carbon. The procedure, according to which *Gerhardt* and *Cannizzaro* have determined the atomic weights of elements, is based upon such unshakeable and indubitable methods that for the majority of bodies and, in particular, for those elements whose heat capacity in the free state was already determined, there exist no longer any doubts about the atomic weight of the element. These doubts still existed a few years earlier when the atomic weight was so often confused with the equivalent weight and when it was determined according to different, even contradictory, principles.

For this reason I have endeavoured to found the system upon the quantity of the atomic weight.

The first attempt I undertook in this direction was the following: I selected the bodies with the smallest atomic weight and ordered them according to the magnitude of their atomic weights. Thereby it appeared that there exists a periodicity of properties, and that even according to valency, one element follows the other in the order of an arithmetical sequence:

| | | | | | | |
|---|---|---|---|---|---|---|
| Li = 7 | Be = 9·4 | B = 11 | C = 12 | N = 14 | O = 16 | F = 19 |
| Na = 23 | Mg = 24 | Al = 27·4 | Si = 28 | P = 31 | S = 32 | Cl = 35·3 |
| K = 39 | Ca = 40 | ....... | Ti = 50 | V = 51 | ...... | ...... |

In the division of elements with an atomic weight greater than 100 we encounter a completely analogous series:

Ag = 108 Cd = 112 U = 116 Sn = 118 Sb = 122 Te = 128 I = 127

It is seen that Li, Na, K, Ag show the same relationship to one another as do N, P, V, Sb, etc. Immediately the idea arose in me whether it was not possible to express the properties of elements by their atomic weights and whether one could not base a system upon this? In the following, the attempt at such a system is described.

In the proposed system, the atomic weight of an element serves to determine its place. Collecting the groups of elements known up to now, according to their atomic weight, leads to the conclusion that the method of ordering elements according to their atomic weight does not contradict the natural similarity existing among the elements but, on the contrary, points directly toward it. In this regard the collection of the following six groups is sufficient:

| | | | | |
|---|---|---|---|---|
| | Ca = 40 | Sr = 87·6 | Ba = 137 | |
| Na = 23 | K = 39 | Rb = 85·4 | Cs = 133 | |
| F = 19 | Cl = 35·5 | Br = 80 | I = 127 | |
| O = 16 | S = 32 | Se = 79·4 | Te = 128 | |
| N = 14 | P = 31 | As = 75 | Sb = 122 | |
| C = 12 | Si = 28 | ...... | Sn = 118 | |

These six groups show clearly that there exist certain, definite relations between the natural properties of elements and the magnitudes of their atomic weights. However, one should not imagine that such relations represent a picture of homology; this is not the case for the reason that, in those elements whose atomic weights are known with accuracy, no genuine homologous differences exist. Even though the difference in atomic weights of sodium and potassium, fluorine and chlorine, oxygen and sulphur, carbon and silicon amounts to 16, the difference between the atomic weights of nitrogen and phosphorus is 17, however, and – what is still more important – the differences between calcium and strontium, potassium and rubidium, chlorine and bromine, etc. are unequal; and the deviation, in the first place, exhibits a certain regularity and, secondly it is much larger than the difference which could be ascribed to experimental error. In the collections indicated above the strict regularity is striking in the change of atomic weights within the horizontal rows and the vertical columns. Only the atomic weight of tellurium is out of place in the series; but this could easily be the case because it has not been determined accurately, and if we assume the atomic weight 126–124 instead of 128, then the system fits completely.

Thus the group of fluorine possesses elements which combine, preferentially, with a single atom of hydrogen, the group of oxygen with two, of nitrogen with three, of carbon with four atoms of hydrogen. Thus, in this respect, the naturalness of the group-classification, in an arrangement defined according to the numbers expressing the atomic weight, does not suffer any disturbance but, on the contrary, is suggested in advance.

In the first arrangement, we have seven columns (perhaps the most natural ones also), of which Li and F are univalent and are most widely separated with respect to electrochemical behaviour; Be and O which succeed them are bi-valent, then come B and N – tri-valent, and in the middle the quadri-valent carbon has its place. If we consider the distance of Na and Cl, Ag and I, and similar aspects, we notice that the arrangement of elements according to magnitude (of atomic weights) corresponds in a certain degree to the valency and to the concept of similarity.

All comparisons carried out by me in this direction led me to the conclusion that the magnitude of the atomic weight determines the character of the element just as the molecular weight determines the properties and many reactions of a compound body. As soon as this assertion is verified in the further application of the proposed principle to the study of elements, then we shall approach the epoch where we understand conceptually the essential differences – and the reasons for the similarity, of the elements.

I state in advance that the law proposed by me does not contradict the general tendency in natural science and that, so far, it has not been proved, although suggestions of this kind did exist already. From now on, it appears to me, new interest will be awakened for the determination of atomic weights, for the discovery of new elements, and for the finding of new analogies among the elements.

I shall now present one of the many systems of elements which are based upon the atomic weight. They form but one attempt to represent the results which can be achieved in this direction. I am quite conscious of the fact that this attempt is not final,* but it appears to me to express quite clearly already the applicability of my proposed principle to all elements whose atomic weight is determined with

---

* Perhaps it may be more rational to arrange the proposed table in the following way:

| | | | | | | |
|---|---|---|---|---|---|---|
| above | Li | Na | K | Rb | Cs | Tl |
| | — | — | — | Sr | Ba | Pb |
| then follows | — | — | Cr | Mo | — | — |
| | — | — | V | Nb | Ta | etc. |
| but below | O | S | Se | Te | — | — |
| | F | Cl | Br | I | — | — |

This would possess the advantage that elements which are sharply distinguished, as are Cl and Na, form the most outside rows, between which the elements have to be placed having a chemical character with less pronounced distinction. However, in this case the centre of the table would be nearly empty, and, moreover, it would be of a rather doubtful

some reliability. Above all I was interested to find out a general system of elements. The attempt is as follows:

```
                        Ti =50   Zr = 90    ?  =180
                        V  =51   Nb = 94    Ta =182
                        Cr =52   Mo = 96    W  =186
                        Mn =55   Rh =104·4  Pt =197·4
                        Fe =56   Ru =104·4  Ir =198
                   Ni=Co =59     Pd =106·6  Os =199
H =1                    Cu =63·4  Ag =108   Hg =200
     Be = 9·4 Mg =24    Zn =65·2 Cd =112
     B  =11   Al =27·4   ?  =68   Ur =116   Au =197?
     C  =12   Si =28     ?  =70   Sn =118
     N  =14   P  =31     As =75   Sb =122   Bi =210
     O  =16   S  =32     Se =79·4 Te =128?
     F  =19   Cl =35.5   Br =80   I  =127
Li=7 Na=23    K  =39     Rb =85·4 Cs =133   Tl =204
              Ca =40     Sr =87·6 Ba =137   Pb =207
              ?  =45     Ce =92
              ?Er =56    La =94
              ?Yt =60    Di =95
              ?In =75·6  Th =118?
```

The table above has convinced me of the possibility that the atomic weight of elements may be used as the basis of the system. Initially, I had ordered the elements into an uninterrupted sequence according to the magnitude of their atomic weights; but I noticed immediately that in the series of elements thus obtained some discontinuities are

kind; while in the present arrangement the centre is indubitable and possesses many representatives; and all less known elements are placed above and below at the edges. ...

The two following sketches may show how diverse the arrangement can be to the fundamental principle stated in this essay.

| Li | Na | K | Cu | Rb | Ag | Cs | — | Tl |
|----|----|----|----|----|----|----|----|----|
| 7 | 23 | 39 | 63·4 | 85·4 | 108 | 133 | — | 204 |
| Be | Mg | Ca | Zn | Sr | Cd | Ba | — | Pb |
| B | Al | — | — | — | Ur | — | — | Bi? |
| C | Si | Ti | — | Zr | Sn | — | — | — |
| N | P | V | As | Nb | Sb | — | Ta | — |
| O | S | — | Se | — | Te | — | W | — |
| F | Cl | — | Br | — | I | — | — | — |
| 19 | 35.5 | 58 | 80 | 100 | 127 | 160 | 190 | 220 |

present. If one starts, e.g., with $H = 1$, then until $Na = 23$ there are present at least eight elements, and nearly the same number is found between elements with atomic weights from 23 to 56, from 63 to 90, from 100 to 140, from 180 to 210, and in these particular groups of elements alone, the analogy is apparent by arranging them according to their atomic weights. In many cases there exist strong doubts still regarding the place of such elements which are not yet sufficiently investigated and which are placed close to the edges of the system as, e.g., vanadium; according to the investigation of *Roscoe* it should be ascribed a place in the nitrogen group, but on the grounds of its atomic weight (51) it should be placed between phosphorus and arsenic. The physical properties equally support this position of vanadium; thus vanadium oxychloride, $VOCl_3$, is a liquid, having at $14°$ the specific weight of $1·841$ and boiling at $127°$, by

---

Hereby the row Cr, Mn, Fe, Ni, Co must supply the transition (the atomic weights of 52–59) from the lower part of the third column (where we have K, Ca, V) to the upper part of the fourth column (i.e. up to Cu); and, similarly, Mo, Rh, Ru, Pd form the transition from the fifth to the sixth column (up to Ag), as well as Au, Pt, Os, Ir, Hg from the eighth to the ninth column. In this manner a system of spiral form is obtained, in which the similarity in the number of the alternate rows is particularly noticeable, e.g., in the second row with Be, Ca, Sr, Ba, Pb, and also with Mg, Zn, Cd. The difference in atomic weights, in this case, is nearly equal for each vertical and horizontal row. If one separates from this system the members which resemble each other most, one obtains a system of the following type:

Above there will be

| Li | K | Rb | Cs |
|----|----|----|----|
| Be | Ca | Sr | Ba |

in the middle there would stand

| O | — | — | — |
|----|----|----|----|
| F | — | — | — |
| Na | Cu | Ag | — |
| Mg | Zn | Cd | — |

but below

| S | Se | Te | — |
|----|----|----|----|
| Cl | Br | I | — |

Similar arrangements can be imagined in great numbers, but they do not change the essentials of the system.

which properties it approaches the corresponding phosphorus compound and places itself somewhat higher than the latter. If one assigns vanadium its place between phosphorus and arsenic, then we have to include in our table above a special column for vanadium and for the elements corresponding to it. In this column then, in the row containing carbon, a place will be opened up also for titanium. Titanium is related, according to this system, to silicon and tin just as vanadium is to phosphorus and antimony. Among these, in the succeeding row, which contains oxygen and sulphur, chromium is to be placed, perhaps; for chromium exhibits the same behaviour toward sulphur and tellurium, as titanium does toward carbon and tin. In this case, we would have to place manganese, $Mn = 55$, between chlorine and bromine.

Thus, this part of the table would be composed as follows:

| | | |
|---|---|---|
| Si $=28$ | Ti $=50$ | ? $=70$ |
| P $=31$ | V $=51$ | As $=75$ |
| S $=32$ | Cr $=52$ | Se $=79$ |
| Cl $=35.5$ | Mn $=55$ | Br $=80$ |

Evidently thereby, the natural connexion between members of a horizontal row is disrupted, although manganese does show some similarity to chlorine, as does chromium to sulphur.

On top of this, however, it would be necessary to introduce another column between arsenic and antimony in order to include in this group, niobium, $Nb = 94$, which represents the analogue of vanadium and antimony. Within the group magnesium, zinc, and cadmium in this column, it appears that indium ($In = 75.6$?) has to be placed provided it really belongs to this row (it is less volatile than Zn and Cd). Further, one would have to place zirconium in the row of carbon and tin, actually next to the latter, as the atomic weight of Zr is smaller than that of tin but larger than that of titanium. In this manner, there would be a vacant place in this horizontal row, for an element whose position would be between titanium and zirconium.

All the same, I decided not to construct the columns mentioned above, and this because analogies belonging indubitably to different rows would be left unconsidered. It suffices to point out that Mg, Zn, and Cd exhibit many analogies with Ca, Sr, and Ba, but to unite these bodies into one group: Mg = 24, Ca = 40, Zn = 65, Sr = 87·6, Cd = 112, Ba = 137, would, in my opinion, mean the destruction of the natural similarity of the elements.

For elements with small atomic weight, such as lithium and hydrogen, the first column is reserved, and in this way six columns would be obtained, or eight if we take special columns for Ti and Zr, over which all elements are distributed in horizontal rows whose members possess chemical similarity. Only the one row of lithium and sodium has representatives in all columns, the other rows have representatives only in a few columns, so that vacant places occur for elements which, perhaps, shall be discovered in the course of time.

It must be remarked here that all elements occurring more frequently in nature possess atomic weights between 1 and 60, and these elements are H, C, N, O, Na, Al, Fe, Ca, K, Cl, S, P, Si, Mg; the higher atomic weights belong to elements that are rarely encountered in nature, which do not form large deposits, and which, therefore, have been studied relatively little.

With respect to the position of some elements, there exists, quite understandably, complete uncertainty. In particular, this holds for those elements that are little investigated and whose atomic weight has hardly been determined correctly. Among these elements are, for example, yttrium, thorium, and indium.

It must be remarked, moreover, that the upper members of the fourth column (Mn, Fe, Co, Ni, Zn) form the transition to the lower members of the (third) column in which Ca, K, Cl and similar elements are found; thus, cobalt and nickel, chromium, manganese, and iron represent, in their properties and with respect to atomic weight, the transition from copper and zinc to calcium and potassium. Perhaps their position may have to be changed for this reason; and if they were to be placed in the lower rows instead of the upper rows, then there would be three columns here which in many respects exhibit similarities; namely, one column comprising cobalt, nickel, chromium, manganese, and iron, a second column with:– cerium, lanthanum, and didymium, palladium, rhodium, ruthenium; finally a third column which contains platinum, iridium, and osmium.

The system of elements proposed here is, of course, not to be considered as completely closed, but it appears to me to be based upon such data and such natural approximations, that its existence can hardly be regarded as doubtful; for the numbers confirm the similarities which result from the study of the compounds of the elements. A number of questions will arise when all elements are arranged into one whole, but the most interesting problem appears to me to be the arrangement of groups of similar elements, such as those of iron, cerium, palladium, and platinum since, in this case, elements close to each other in their nature also exhibit approximately the same atomic weights, a circumstance not to be observed in other rows, for in the latter similar elements possess different atomic weights. It may be that the system of elements arranged in groups will, in consequence of the study of these groups, be changed in such a manner that in certain parts of the system, the similarity between members of horizontal rows has to be considered, but in other parts, the similarity between members of the vertical columns. In any event, it appears to be certain when we look at the proposed table, that in some rows the corresponding members are missing; this appears especially clearly, e.g., for the row of calcium; in which there are missing the members analogous to sodium and lithium; magnesium represents, to a certain degree, the analogue of sodium, but magnesium cannot be placed in the row of calcium, strontium, and barium. This is proved not only by the properties of some compounds of these elements but also by those physical properties which are attributed to the metals themselves.

I cannot but direct attention to the fact that in the comparison of the lower members of the row with the upper there is noticeable a sharply distinct difference in properties and reactions. This is analogous to what we perceive in the series of organic homologues: in the upper members of the homologous series some of the characteristics belonging to the series are weakened; thus, for example, paraffin which was assigned, at first, to the ethylene series, can be taken with the same (and naturally stronger) justification to belong to the series of marsh gas, since for such high homologues distinct characteristics cannot be expected in either this or that series. Similarly, characteristics of simple bodies, that show up strongly in the first column, become weakened in the last column formed by the heaviest elements. Lead, thallium, bismuth, gold, mercury, platinum, iridium, osmium, and tungsten are not only less energetic elements, but at the same time they are heavy elements, from which in many respects one single group could even be constructed without thereby destroying the foremost requirements of analogy. Thallium and bismuth are more widely separated in this relation, however, than lead and thallium, or bismuth and gold, mercury and platinum. At the same time, the elements standing lower than the halogen row possess oxides which exhibit basic properties rather than acid ones and which are the best representatives of the metals; while those elements which stand higher than the row of halogens possess either complete acid character or show transitional characteristics which lie between acid and base. For the latter reason also I could not persuade myself to put the iron-group with the erbium-group in the lower part of the table.

Hydrogen has not yet been assigned a definite position because of its small atomic weight; it appears to me to be the most natural to place it in the row of copper, silver, and mercury, although it is possible that it belongs in some unknown row lower than that of copper.

If it is permitted to express a wish when looking at the proposed table, then it is that the number of elements should be completed which stand closer to hydrogen. Those elements which form the transition from hydrogen to boron and carbon, would represent, naturally, the most important scientific achievement that may be expected upon acquaintance with bodies yet to be discovered.

With regard to the bodies of the second (vertical) row it would be most promising, in my view, to subject beryllium and boron to an exact study and I shall endeavour to carry this out as soon as possible. In general, the elements with low atomic weight deserve greater scientific interest, to judge from what has been said previously, than those elements whose atomic weight is high. Considering the characteristics of the system, the remark has still to be made that some analogies are clearly visible from the table. Thus, C, B, Si, Al stand together, as well as Ba, Pb, Tl, or V, Cr, Nb, Mo, Ta, W; others can be guessed in advance so to speak. Thus, there is no doubt that for uranium (but not for gold which, perhaps, has to be placed in the row of iron) a place has to be made in the row of boron and of aluminium, and, indeed, between these elements no little similarity exists. Thus, e.g., turmeric is turned brown by the action of uranium oxide as well as by boric acid; the composition of borax, $Na_2B_4O_7$, is analogous to that of the uranium compound $K_2U_4O_7$. The compounds which aluminium oxide forms with a base have been little studied so far, and this question, which has interested me already for some time, is going to form the subject-matter of one of my next communications.

In conclusion I do not deem it superfluous to summarize the results of what has been said above:

1. The elements, if arranged according to their atomic weights, show a distinct periodicity of their properties.

2. Elements exhibiting similarities in their chemical behaviour have atomic weights which are approximately equal (as in the case of Pt, Ir, Os) or they possess atomic weights which increase in a uniform manner (as in the case of K, Rb, Cs). The uniformity of such an increase in the various groups remained hidden to previous observers since in their calculations they did not make use of the conclusions drawn by Gerhardt, Regnault, Cannizzaro, and others, by which

conclusions the true magnitude of the atomic weights of the elements was determined.

3. The arrangement of elements or of groups of elements according to the magnitude of their atomic weights corresponds to their so-called valencies, as well as, to some extent, to their distinctive chemical properties, a fact which can be clearly seen from the row: Li, Be, B, C, N, O, F and which also occurs in the other rows.

4. The bodies most abundantly found in nature possess a small atomic weight; but all elements of small atomic weight are characterized by their distinct properties and are, therefore, typical elements. Hydrogen, being the lightest element, is reasonably to be chosen as the most typical element of all.

5. The magnitude of the atomic weight determines the character of the element, just as the magnitude of the molecule determines the properties of a compound body; it is therefore necessary in the study of compounds to direct attention not only towards the properties and number of the elements as well as to their mutual behaviour, but also towards their atomic weight. Thus, the compounds, e.g., of S and Te, Cl and I, and of others, present, in spite of all their resemblance, distinct differences.

6. The discovery of numerous unknown elements is still to be expected, for instance, of elements similar to Al and Si having atomic weights from 65–75.

7. The atomic weight of an element will have to be corrected, eventually, when its analogues become known. Thus, must not the atomic weight of tellurium be 123–126, and not 128?

## II

# THE EMERGENCE OF ORGANIC
# CHEMISTRY

DURING the nineteenth century, chemistry became differentiated into separate branches. Berzelius had distinguished between organic chemistry and inorganic chemistry, by defining the first as the chemistry of substances produced by living matter, whereas inorganic was concerned with non-living or mineral substances (and is still '*la chimie minérale*' in France). At the time, this distinction was a fundamental one, but it disappeared later and was replaced by a second distinction based rather more on convenience; organic chemistry was concerned with the compounds of carbon, inorganic chemistry with the remaining elements and their compounds.

Early 'Vegetable Chemistry' and 'Animal Chemistry' dealt with some simple compounds, such as alcohol and glycerol, but also with such complex materials as gums, tannin, india-rubber, gelatin, blood, oils, and bitter principles, 'like a primeval forest of the tropics' wrote Wöhler in 1835, 'full of the most remarkable things'. The fundamental difference between these substances and the minerals was that the former were supposed to be formed only through the operation of a 'Vital Force'. This idea disappeared only gradually. One important experiment which led to its being questioned was Wöhler's preparation of urea in a test-tube, instead of through the medium of a kidney. This was not a complete synthesis, i.e. a synthesis of the compound from its elements, nor a preparation entirely from inorganic substances (his cyanic acid ultimately was derived from an organic source). A complete synthesis of an organic compound was that of trichloracetic acid by Kolbe in 1844. Nevertheless the old idea of a vital force began to decline in 1828.

Later, Cannizzaro's 'Sketch' showed that the laws relating to atomic and molecular weights applied equally to organic and inorganic compounds. In this sense a unification of chemistry came about. In another sense, diversification took place as the interests of individual chemists came to lead them to investigations in one or other field, either the discovery of new elements and the elucidation of their chemistry (inorganic chemistry) or the development of the chemistry of organic substances.

Organic chemistry prospered, partly because laboratory synthesis (*in vitro*) became a recognized possibility, partly because the growing ability of chemists to represent chemical change in terms of chemical formulae helped to make synthesis more purposive. Allied to this was the replacement of Berzelius's dualistic theory by the theory of structural types which had greater relevance in organic chemistry. In the field of inorganic chemistry, Berzelius regarded salts as compounds of acids and bases; an acid, according to Lavoisier, was formed from oxygen and a radical, whereas a base, according to Davy, was formed from oxygen and a metal. Berzelius found that, on electrolysis, salts were split up into positive and negative components. Hence he came to regard acids as electronegative oxides, and bases as electropositive oxides.

This idea, when refined, became of great value in inorganic chemistry. Its universal application was, however, soon challenged by reference to organic substances. Dumas regarded the properties of organic substances as being due to their structure, which is a function of the whole molecule, not of its parts. Dumas was thus propounding a unitary theory to replace the dualistic theory. For example, the replacement of three out of the four hydrogen atoms in acetic acid by chlorine did not make the product (trichloracetic acid) violently different from the starting material; it remained qualitatively similar, as we can now see from its structure.

Dumas' ideas were developed by Gerhardt and by Laurent, who realized that many organic compounds had common features in their structures and could be regarded as belonging to the same type or class of compound. This theory of types proved to be of great value in rationalizing organic chemistry, but like the dualistic theory, was valuable within limitations. Our continued use of the terms alcohols, ethers, amines, ketones, esters, etc. indicates its success.

Although the theory of types was to prove of great value in the field of synthesis, a chance discovery initiated an advance into an enormous new field of organic chemistry. In a sense, it came about because the theory could not at the time be adequately applied. Perkin attempted to synthesize quinine using only molecular formulae as a guide to the reactions required. In terms of structural formulae, his method would have been seen to be quite inappropriate. He failed completely in his object, but succeeded in preparing a substance, mauveine, which he recognized as a potential dyestuff. All dyestuffs in use at that time were obtained from natural sources. Mauveine proved to be remarkably effective by the standards of the time, and so became the first synthetic dyestuff to be used commercially. Perkin lost no time in exploiting his discovery and quite quickly, as further discoveries were made, an important industry grew up. It depended for its materials on coal-tar products, coal-tar itself being a by-product of the manufacture of coal-gas, which had been introduced earlier in the century.

When structural formulae were later introduced, they were of immense value in the development of synthetic dyestuff chemistry. Kekulé played an important part in this advance, first in recognizing that carbon is tetravalent (as did Couper independently) and then in showing that if carbon atoms were regarded as forming bonds to each other as well as to the atoms of other elements, it was possible to explain the structures of many organic compounds. Later he made a second major contribution in putting forward a structure for the benzene molecule which had appeared not to fit into his simpler scheme. Yet this was important, because benzene and other, related, 'aromatic' compounds were available as components of coal-tar and were being extensively investigated, so leading progressively to a vast range of substances of economic importance. So much research was undertaken in the field of organic chemistry at this time that even the greater organic chemists could be mentioned only in a more detailed treatment.

The theme of structure is taken one stage further by the representation of molecules in three dimensions, as opposed to the two dimensions of a formula written on a blackboard or printed on the page of a book. With a carbon atom at the centre of a tetrahedron, its four valency bonds were regarded as pointing to the four corners. At once it was possible to explain Pasteur's earlier observation that two forms of sodium ammonium tartrate could be produced, identical in chemical composition, but one with crystals 'hemihedral to the right' and the other with crystals 'hemihedral to the left'; the two forms caused deviations in opposite directions to the plane of polarized light. Van't Hoff and le Bel explained this behaviour in terms of molecular structure. Once the structures were represented in three dimensions, it could be seen that two possibilities existed for tartaric acid, and that these were related as mirror-images. This idea of 'the third dimension in chemistry' has grown increasingly important not only in organic but also in inorganic chemistry.

These themes, which form the basis of classical organic chemistry, were applied widely to relatively simple organic substances. Many naturally-occurring compounds, however, were seen to be very complex and thus to present a challenge. As the nineteenth century ended, the challenge had been taken up, notably by Emil Fischer, who first analysed the products which could be obtained by partial breakdown of such substances as carbohydrates and proteins, and later initiated the first steps towards their synthesis. This task has led to the development of the chemistry of polymers (natural and synthetic, organic and inorganic) which is very prominent in chemistry today.

# FRIEDRICH WÖHLER
1800–1882

## UREA IS PREPARED *IN VITRO*

Two of the great German chemists of the nineteenth century were Friedrich Wöhler and Justus von Liebig (1803–1873). Wöhler was born in Escherheim, near Frankfurt-am-Main. He studied first under Gmelin, and then for a year under Berzelius in Stockholm. While working in Berzelius' laboratory, he prepared silver cyanate. A little later Liebig prepared silver fulminate, which, on analysis, proved to have the same composition as that claimed by Wöhler for silver cyanate, though its properties were quite different. Liebig wrote to Wöhler about this apparent contradiction, which was resolved when Berzelius suggested that it might well be possible for two different substances to have the same composition, and suggested the term 'isomerism' for the phenomenon.

Wöhler later met Liebig on returning to Germany; the two men became friends and subsequently worked together.

In 1828 Wöhler announced that on evaporating a solution containing ammonium cyanate (formed in the reaction between potassium cyanate and ammonium sulphate), he had obtained urea. After he had established this without doubt, he wrote to Berzelius 'I must tell you that I can prepare urea without requiring a kidney of an animal, either man or dog.' When the relevance of this discovery to the 'Vital Force' theory is being considered, it is sometimes overlooked that this is another case of isomerism – between urea and ammonium cyanate.

Wöhler became Professor of Chemistry at Göttingen in 1836. In his later life he turned to inorganic chemistry which he had seen practised in Berzelius' laboratory, and studied methods of obtaining pure forms of aluminium and the less familiar metals, beryllium, yttrium, and titanium. His method of obtaining aluminium in globules was developed at the same time as that of Sainte Claire Deville (1818–81), a Frenchman, under whose name the process became standard until 1886 when Hall in America and Heroult in France introduced the electrolytic method, which became the basis of the modern industrial process. As previously with Liebig, Wöhler sought friendship with Deville and achieved collaboration in research rather than sterile controversy over priority.

Wöhler's account of urea appeared in Poggendorff's *Annalen der Physik und Chemie* in 1828. The translation is from Leicester and Klickstein, *A Source Book in Chemistry* (Harvard, 1952).

---

### ¶ On the Artificial Production of Urea

In a brief earlier communication, printed in Volume III of these Annals, I stated that by the action of cyanogen on aqueous ammonia, besides several other products, there are formed oxalic acid and a crystallizable white substance which is certainly not cyanate of ammonia, but which one nevertheless always obtains when one attempts to combine cyanic acid with ammonia, for instance by so-called double decomposition. The fact that in the union of these substances they appear to change their nature, and give rise to a new body, drew my attention anew to this subject, and research gave the unexpected result that by the combination of cyanic acid with ammonia, urea is formed, a fact that is the more noteworthy inasmuch as it furnishes an example of the artificial production of an organic, indeed a so-called animal substance, from inorganic materials.

I have already stated that the above-mentioned white crystalline substance is best obtained by the decomposition of cyanate of silver with sal ammoniac solution or of cyanate of lead by aqueous ammonia. In the latter way I prepared for myself the not unimportant amounts employed in this research. I obtained it in colourless, clear crystals often more than an inch long in the form of slender four-sided, dull-pointed prisms.

With caustic potash or chalk this substance evolved no trace of ammonia; with acids it showed none of the break-down phenomena of cyanic acid salts, namely, evolution of carbonic acid and cyanic acid; neither would it precipitate lead and silver salts as genuine cyanic acid salts do; it could, therefore, contain neither cyanic acid nor ammonia as such. Since I found that by the last-named method of preparation no other product was formed and that the lead oxide was separated in a pure form, I imagined that an organic substance might arise by the union of cyanic acid with ammonia, possibly a substance like a vegetable salifiable base [an alkaloid]. I therefore made some experiments from this point of view on the behaviour of the crystalline substance with acids. It was, however, indifferent to them, nitric acid excepted; this, when added to a concentrated solution of the substance, produced at once a precipitate of glistening scales. After these had been purified by several recrystalliza-tions, they showed a very acid character, and I was already inclined to take the compound for a peculiar acid, when I found that after neutralization with bases it gave salts of nitric acid, from which the crystallizable substance could be extracted again with alcohol, with all the characteristics it had before the addition of nitric acid. This similarity to urea in behaviour induced me to carry out comparative experi-ments with completely pure urea isolated from urine, from which it was plainly apparent that urea and this crystalline substance, or cyanate of ammonia, if one can so call it, are completely identical compounds.

I will describe the properties of this artifical urea no fur-ther, since it coincides perfectly with that of urea from urine, according to the accounts of Proust, Prout, and others, to be found in their writings, and I will mention only the fact, not specified by them, that both natural and artificial urea, on distillation, evolve first large amounts of carbonate of am-monia, and then give off to a remarkable extent the sharp, acetic acid-like odour of cyanic acid, exactly as I found in the distillation of cyanate of mercury or uric acid, and especially of the mercury salt of uric acid. In the distillation of urea, another white, apparently distinct, substance also appears, with the examination of which I am still occupied.

But if the combination of cyanic acid and ammonia actually gives merely urea, it must have exactly the composition allotted to cyanate of ammonia by calculation from my formula for the cyanates; and this is, in fact, the case if one atom of water is added to cyanate of ammonia, as all ammonium salts contain water, and if Prout's analysis of urea is taken as the most correct.

According to him urea consists of:

|          |        | ATOMS |
|----------|--------|-------|
| Nitrogen | 46·650 | 4     |
| Carbon   | 19·975 | 2     |
| Hydrogen | 6·670  | 8     |
| Oxygen   | 26·650 | 2     |
|          | 99·875 |       |
|          | [*sic*] |      |

But cyanate of ammonia would consist of 56·92 cyanic acid, 28·14 ammonia, and 14·74 water, which for the separate elements gives:

|          |         | ATOMS |
|----------|---------|-------|
| Nitrogen | 46·78   | 4     |
| Carbon   | 20·19   | 2     |
| Hydrogen | 6·59    | 8     |
| Oxygen   | 26·24*  | 2     |
|          | 99·80   |       |

One would have been able to reckon beforehand that cyanate of ammonia with one atom of water has the same composition as urea, without having discovered by experiment the formation of urea from cyanic acid and ammonia.

*The new atomic weights of Berzelius are used as a basis; accordingly N = 88·518, C = 76·437, H = 6·2398, O = 100·000, water (Ḣ) = 112·479, cyanate of ammonia = NH³ + C̶N̶O̶, and urea = NH³ + C̶N̶O̶ + Ḣ. [A bar through the symbol of an element indicates the presence of two atoms; a dot above the symbol of an element indicates the presence of an atom of oxygen. — Editor.]

By the combustion of cyanic acid with copper oxide one obtains two volumes of carbonic acid and one volume of nitrogen, but by the combustion of cyanate of ammonia one must obtain equal volumes of these gases, which proportion also holds for urea, as Prout actually found.

I refrain from all the considerations which so naturally offer themselves, particularly those bearing upon the composition relations of organic substances, upon the like elementary and quantitative composition of compounds of very different properties, as for example fulminic acid and cyanic acid, a liquid hydrocarbon and olefiant gas. The deduction of a general law awaits further experiment on several similar cases.

# CHARLES GERHARDT
## 1816–1856

## TYPES OF ORGANIC COMPOUND

GERHARDT was born in Strasbourg and studied with Liebig and other German chemists before returning to spend the rest of his short life in French universities. He helped to modernize the formulae of organic compounds by halving most of them. Many organic reactions involve the elimination of water, ammonia, or carbon dioxide. If the organic formulae were halved, these substances could be represented as eliminated in the form of single and not double molecules. This involved essentially a return to Berzelius' table of atomic weights, though Gerhardt did not express it in this way. It was, however, useful to have the formula of acetic acid as $C_2H_4O_2$, and not $C_4H_8O_4$ (or even, with the atomic weight of carbon as 6) $C_8H_4O_2 + H_4O_2$.

Gerhardt is represented here as expressing very clearly the combination of the unitary theory, which owed much to Dumas and Laurent, and the idea of organic radicals. He acknowledged the similar function possessed by the radicals methyl ($CH_3$), ethyl ($C_2H_5$), propyl ($C_3H_7$), etc. in combining with the hydroxyl radical (OH) to form substances all of one type (the alcohols) by referring to such series as 'homologous series'.

Gerhardt introduced his ideas in the face of considerable opposition and courted enmity by his dogmatic manner, although he had been warned against this by Liebig. Only shortly before he died did recognition come to him.

The extract below is taken from his paper on acid anhydrides published in 1853 in *Annales de chemie et de physique*. The translation appears in Leicester and Klickstein, *A Source Book in Chemistry* (Harvard, 1952).

## ¶ Groups of Atoms in Organic Reactions

To arrange organic compounds in series, that is, to determine the laws according to which the properties in a given type are modified by substitution of an element or group of elements for other elements, this is the constant purpose of the chemist philosopher. These thousands of compounds which he produces in his laboratory are for him, however, the terms which serve him to construct his series. Today, in the imperfect state of the science, there is still need for many terms; but later, knowledge of certain series will eliminate direct study of many other terms whose properties he will be able to predict with the same certainty as he predicts today the properties of propionic or valeric alcohols, even though he has not yet obtained these alcohols.

In the state of the science, organic compounds can be related to three or four types, each capable of giving series which resemble those represented by formic and stearic acids, potash, and sulphuric acid; these types are:

| | |
|---|---|
| Water | $H^2O$ |
| Hydrogen | $H^2$ |
| Hydrochloric acid | $HCl$ |
| Ammonia | $H^3N$ |

By exchanging their hydrogens among certain groups, these types give rise to acids, to alcohols, to ethers, to hydrides, to radicals, to organic chlorides, to acetones, to alkalis.

The series formed by each type has its extremes, which can be called the positive, or left, side and the negative, or right, side. An organic group substituting for hydrogen which places itself on the positive side will produce compounds placed on the same side; the groups ethyl $CH^3$, methyl $C^2H^3$,* amyl $C^5H^{11}$, for example, will give by this substitution alcohols resembling water, aldehydes or radicals resembling hydrogen, ethers resembling hydrochloric acid, alkalis resembling ammonia. The groups of which I

*[These are obviously misprints.]

speak resemble, in fact, potash or other reputedly electropositive metals; the oxides (the alcohols) and the alkalis to which they give rise behave like bases, in that they can combine with acids placed at the other extreme of the series.

Other organic groups, for example cyanogen CN, acetyl $C^2H^3O$, benzoyl $C^7H^5O$, on substituting for the hydrogen of the types mentioned give rise to those compounds which are farther removed than the preceding from compounds formed with hydrogen, to compounds which are placed more to the right, toward the negative extreme. The oxides formed by these groups resemble sulphuric acid more than potash.
. . .

The *water* type, changing half its hydrogen for a hydrocarbon group $CH^3$, $C^2H^5$, etc., gives rise to an alcohol; changing all its hydrogen for a similar group, it produces the corresponding ether.

The same type, in changing half its hydrogen for a group containing at once carbon, hydrogen, and oxygen, produces a hydrated monobasic acid, resembling acetic acid. When the substitution is effected by the same group on the two atoms of hydrogen of water, the product is the corresponding acid and anhydride; Mr Williamson has already made the same comparison, and its exactitude seems to me today to be perfectly demonstrated by my experiments. Finally, when the substitution of the two hydrogen atoms of water is made half by a hydrocarbon group like ethyl or methyl and half by an oxygenated group resembling that which is found in a monobasic acid, the ester of this acid is obtained.

The *hydrogen* type can undergo the same substitutions as the water type and produce as many combinations.

The compounds resembling marsh gas, known as *hydrides,* are evidently related to hydrogen as alcohols are to water; the ethyl and methyl radicals correspond to the ethers of these alcohols. Aldehydes are to hydrogen as monobasic acids are to water; acetyl, benzoyl, and other oxygenated radicals correspond to acid anhydrides; the acetones, finally, as M. Chancel has already remarked, represent the esters of the aldehydes and consequently are to hydrogen as the esters of monobasic acids are to water.

The *hydrochloric acid* type gives rise, on the one hand, to hydrochloric ethers, that is, to chlorides resembling chloride of potassium or chlorides of electropositive elements, when the substitution is effected by hydrocarbon groups; and, on the other hand, to electronegative chlorides corresponding to monobasic acids, like acetyl chloride or benzoyl chloride, when the same substitution is effected by groups contained in these monobasic acids.

Finally, the *ammonia* type produces alkalis able to combine with acids, or amides able to combine with bases (oxide of silver, mercury, copper, etc.), according to whether the substitution on the hydrogens of the ammonia is effected by groups which give rise to bases (alcohols, organic oxides), or by groups which produce organic acids. The bodies resembling the hydrate of oxide of ammonia are represented at the other end of the series by acid amides.

It can be seen by this rapid summary how the application of the notion of series permits simplification of the general theory of organic compounds. They no longer terrify by their number and variety, for instead of being formulated by special theories which lack any connexion, as they are called ethers, amides, alkalis, or acids, they become simply terms whose properties can be predicted according to the place they occupy in the series. And what certainly adds to the advantage of such a system is the similarity of method of formation or decomposition which it expresses for all the bodies which it contains. Experiment shows, in fact, that organic compounds are almost all the result of *double decompositions* resembling those which we effect in mineral chemistry.

# WILLIAM HENRY PERKIN,
## SENIOR
### 1838–1907

## THE DISCOVERY OF MAUVEINE

LIEBIG came to have a considerable influence in agricultural chemistry, and when he visited England in 1842 made a great impression not only with influential agriculturalists but also with the Prime Minister. Following this, he was consulted when a Royal College of Chemistry was founded in London under the presidency of the Prince Consort. He was asked to advise on the appointment of a professor and nominated one of his pupils, August von Hofmann (1818–92), who took up his post in 1845. In Giessen he had started to investigate coal-tar, and continued this work in London.

In 1853, at the age of fifteen, Perkin was admitted to the College to study under Hofmann, and later to undertake research. On the basis of his research he was promoted to the staff. Perkin's enthusiasm went beyond the work he could do at the College, and he fitted up a laboratory at his father's house, where he worked in the evenings and during vacations.

It was in this laboratory, in the Easter vacation of 1856, that Perkin attempted a synthetic preparation of quinine, working from an early suggestion of Hofmann's. Organic chemistry at that time was very much concerned with the preparation of crystalline compounds; if a product was both amorphous and coloured it was usually taken as a sign that the object of the research had failed. Perkin certainly failed in his object of preparing quinine, but had the insight to see a potentially valuable substance in the dark-coloured precipitate formed in the reaction. With confirmation from J. Pullar and Son of Perth that the material he isolated was potentially a useful dyestuff, he patented it and determined to manufacture it on a commercial scale. He was, not unnaturally, advised against this by Hofmann, but he was determined. With help from his father, who advanced most of his life's savings, he built a factory and was selling 'Aniline Purple' or 'Tyrian Purple' in 1858 before he had reached the age of twenty. The name 'mauve' was given to the dyestuff in France.

He remained an industrial chemist until 1874, but continued to publish research papers, not all of which were concerned with dyestuffs. One of his papers concerned the 'artificial production of coumarin', a preparation from a coal-tar product of a vegetable perfume. By selling his factory after eighteen years, he became financially independent and continued work in other fields (notably in that of magnetic rotation), in which his publications far outweighed those on the chemistry of dyestuffs.

Perkin's three sons were all chemists; William Henry Perkin, junior, became Professor of Chemistry at Manchester and then at Oxford.

The account of the discovery of mauve is taken from Perkin's *Hofmann Memorial Lecture* delivered to the Chemical Society in 1893.

_____

At this period much interest was taken in the artificial formation of natural organic substances; but at the time I was at the Royal College of Chemistry, although the theory of compound radicals, the doctrine of substitution, etc., were occupying much attention, very little was known of the internal structure of compounds, and the conceptions as to the method by which one compound might be formed from another was necessarily very crude.

Thus, in the Report of the Royal College of Chemistry, published in 1849, Hofmann refers to the artificial formation of quinine as a great *desideratum*, and then states: 'It is a remarkable fact that naphthalene, the beautiful hydrocarbon of which immense quantities are annually produced in the manufacture of coal-gas, when subjected to a series of chemical processes, may be converted into a crystalline alkaloid. This substance, which has received the name of naphthalidine, contains 20 equivalents of carbon, 9 equivalents of hydrogen, and 1 equivalent of nitrogen.' (C=6, O=8.) '... Now if we take 20 equivalents of carbon, 11 equivalents of hydrogen, 1 equivalent of nitrogen, and 2 equivalents of oxygen, as the composition of quinine, it will be obvious that naphthalidine, differing only by the elements of 2 equivalents of water, might pass into the former alkaloid simply by an assumption of water. We cannot, of course, expect to induce the water to enter merely by placing it in contact, but a happy experiment may attain this end by the discovery of an appropriate metamorphic process.'

In fact there was but little other ground to work upon in many instances than this kind of speculation.

As a young chemist I was ambitious enough to wish to work on this subject of the artificial formation of natural organic compounds. Probably from reading the above remarks on the importance of forming quinine, I began to think how it might be accomplished, and was led by the then popular additive and subtractive method to the idea that it might be formed from toluidine by first adding to its composition $C_3H_4$ by substituting allyl for hydrogen, thus forming allyltoluidine, and then removing two hydrogen atoms and adding two atoms of oxygen, thus

$$2(\underbrace{C_{10}H_{13}N}_{\text{Allyltoluidine}}) + 3O = \underbrace{C_{20}H_{21}N_2O_2}_{\text{Quinine}} + H_2O$$

The allyltoluidine having been prepared by the action of allyl iodide on toluidine, was converted into a salt and treated with potassium dichromate; no quinine was formed, but only a dirty reddish-brown precipitate. Unpromising though this result was, I was interested in the action, and thought it desirable to treat a more simple base in the same manner. Aniline was selected, and its sulphate was treated with potassium dichromate; in this instance a black precipitate was obtained, and, on examination, this precipitate was found to contain the colouring matter since so well known as *aniline purple* or *mauve,* and by a number of other names. All these experiments were made during the Easter vacation of 1856 in my rough laboratory at home. Very soon after the discovery of this colouring matter, I found that it had the properties of a dye, and that it resisted the action of light remarkably well.

After the vacation, experiments were continued in the evenings when I had returned from the Royal College of Chemistry, and combustions were made of the colouring matter. I showed it to my friend Church, with whom I had been working, on his visiting my laboratory, and who, from his artistic tastes, had a great interest in colouring matters, and he thought it might be valuable and encouraged me to continue to work upon it; but its evident costliness and the difficulties of preparing aniline on a large scale, made the probability of its proving of practical value appear very doubtful. Through a friend, I then got an introduction to Messrs Pullar, of Perth, and sent them some specimens of dyed silk. On 12 June, 1856, I received the following reply:

'If your discovery does not make the goods too expensive, it is decidedly one of the most valuable that has come out for a very long time. This colour is one which has been very much wanted in all classes of goods, and could not be obtained fast on silks, and only at great expense on cotton yarns. I enclose you a pattern of the *best* lilac we have on cotton – it is dyed only by one house in the United Kingdom, but even this is not quite fast, and does not stand the test that yours does, and fades by exposure to air. On silk the colour has always been fugitive: it is done with cudbear or archil, and then blued to shade.'

This somewhat lengthy extract is quoted because it gives a glimpse at the state of the dyeing trade in reference to this shade of colour at that period.

This first report was very satisfactory; the 'if' with which it commenced was, however, a doubtful point.

During the summer vacation, however, the preparation of the colouring matter on a very small, technical scale was undertaken, my brother (the late T. D. Perkin) assisted me in the operations, and, after preparing a few ounces of product, the results were thought sufficiently promising to make it desirable to patent the process for the preparation of this colouring matter. This was done on 26 August 1856 (Patent No. 1984). A visit was then made to Messrs Pullar's, and experiments on cotton dyeing were made, but, as no suitable mordants were known for this colouring matter, only the pale shades of colour, produced by the natural affinity of the dye for the vegetable fibre, were obtained; these, however, were admired. Experiments on calico printing were also made at some print works, but fears were entertained that it would be too dear, and, although it proved to be one of the most serviceable colours as regards fastness, yet the printers were not satisfied with it because it would not resist the action of chloride of lime like madder purple.

Although the results were not so encouraging as could be wished, I was persuaded of the importance of the colouring matter, and the result was that, in October, I sought an interview with my old master, Hofmann, and told him of the discovery of this dye, showing him patterns dyed with it, at the same time saying that as I was going to undertake its manufacture, I was sorry that I should have to leave the Royal College of Chemistry. At this he appeared much annoyed, and spoke in a very discouraging manner, making me feel that perhaps I might be taking a false step which might ruin my future prospects. I have sometimes thought that, appreciating the difficulties of producing such compounds as aniline and this colouring matter on the large scale, Hofmann perhaps anticipated that the undertaking would be a failure, and was sorry to think that I should be so foolish as to leave my scientific work for such an object, especially as I was then but a lad of eighteen years of age; and I must confess that one of my great fears on entering into technical work was that it might prevent my continuing research work, but I determined that, as far as possible, this should not be the case.

Still, having faith in the results I had obtained, I left the College of Chemistry and continued my experiments, and found that not only aniline, but also toluidine, xylidine, and cumidine gave a purple colouring matter when oxidized.

The following is a copy of the principal part of the complete specification of the patent I took out at this time:

§ *'Dyeing Fabrics*

'The nature of my invention consists in producing a new colouring matter for dyeing with a lilac or purple colour stuffs or silk, cotton, wool, and other materials in the manner following:

'I take a cold solution of sulphate of aniline, or a cold solution of sulphate of toluidine, or a cold solution of sulphate of xylidine, or a cold solution of sulphate of cumidine, or a mixture of any one of such solutions with any others or other of them, and as much of a cold solution of a soluble bichromate as contains base enough to convert the sulphuric acid in any of the above-mentioned solutions into a neutral sulphate. I then mix the solutions and allow them to stand for ten or twelve hours, when the mixture will consist of a black powder and a solution of a neutral sulphate. I then throw this mixture upon a fine filter, and wash it with water till free from the neutral sulphate. I then dry the substance thus obtained at a temperature of 100°C, or 212°F, and digest it repeatedly with coal-tar naphtha, until it is free from a brown substance which is extracted by the naphtha. Any other substance than coal-tar naphtha may be used in which the brown substance is soluble and the colouring matter is not soluble. I then free the residue from the naphtha by evaporation, and digest it with methylated spirit, or any other liquid in which the colouring matter is soluble, which dissolves out the new colouring matter. I then separate the methylated spirit from the colouring matter by distillation, at a temperature of 100°C or 212°F.'

Fresh quantities of colouring matter were prepared and taken to Scotland, and, although the method of applying it by means of lacterine (casein) was then found to give very good results, yet the printers who tried it did not show any great enthusiasm; and even Messrs Pullar began to fluctuate in their opinion as to the advisability of erecting plant for its manufacture, and wrote: 'Should it appear that it will not be of service to printers, it will be questionable whether it would be wise to erect works for the quantity dyers alone will require.' In January 1867, Mr R. Pullar, however, advised me to see Mr Thos Keith, a silk dyer of Bethnal Green, London, and, after making a few experiments with the colouring matter, and exposing the specimens he dyed to the light for some time, he was much pleased with the result, and encouraged me to go on with its production.

I was then joined in the undertaking by my father – who was a builder, and had sufficient faith in the project to risk the necessary capital – and also by my brother, who also had a good knowledge of building, and, as he had taken part in the preliminary experiments on the preparation of the dye, his assistance proved most valuable, especially as he was possessed of good business capabilities. Plans were prepared and a site obtained at Greenford Green, near Harrow, and in June 1857, the building of the works was commenced.

# FRIEDRICH AUGUST KEKULÉ
## 1829–96

## THE VALENCY OF CARBON AND THE
## STRUCTURE OF BENZENE

KEKULÉ, although having a French-sounding name, was a German (by contrast, Wurtz, who helped to spread Gerhardt's ideas, was French). He studied architecture at the University of Giessen, but while there came under the influence of Liebig, and became a chemist. He gained further experience in Paris, Coire (Switzerland), and London before becoming Privatdozent at Heidelberg. In 1858 he became a professor of chemistry at Ghent, to which University many German students were attracted to study under him. Nine years later he returned to Germany to the Chair of Chemistry at Bonn.

Without acknowledging reference to Frankland's ideas on 'combining power', Kekulé pondered on the problem of the valency of carbon. When he realized that carbon was tetravalent, he was able to rationalize the formulae of the very considerable number of aliphatic compounds which had already been discovered. (The term 'aliphatic' is due to Hofmann.)

Unlike most chemists, Kekulé has left an account of the genesis of two of his most important ideas. So few other chemists have done likewise that it is difficult to say whether Kekulé is typical; one rather doubts it. The germ of his idea of the way in which carbon atoms combined with others to form compounds occurred to him while he was in London. 'One fine summer evening I was returning by the last omnibus, "outside" as usual, through the deserted streets of the metropolis, which are at other times so full of life. I fell into a reverie, and lo, the atoms were gambolling before my eyes! Whenever hitherto, these diminutive beings had appeared to me, they had always been in motion; but up to that time I had never been able to discern the nature of their motion. Now, however, I saw how, frequently, two smaller atoms united to form a pair; how a larger one embraced two smaller ones; how still larger ones kept hold of three or even four of the smaller, whilst the whole kept whirling in a giddy dance. I saw how the larger ones formed a chain, dragging the smaller ones after them, but only at the ends of the chain.... The cry of the conductor "Clapham Road" awakened me from my dreaming; but I spent part of the night in putting on paper at least sketches of these dream forms. This was the origin of the *Struktur-theorie*.'

The first of the two passages below is from the *Annalen der Chemie* for 1858. It shows how the formulae of the paraffins can be generalized as $C_nH_{2n+2}$. Kekulé, however, clearly recognized the difficulty of representing, structurally, the formulae of the aromatic compounds (his term), which seemed to contain a minimum of six carbon atoms, but in benzene, only six hydrogen atoms. Again he explains how the important idea came to him, this time in Ghent: 'I was sitting, writing at my text-book; but the work did not progress; my thoughts were elsewhere. I turned my chair to the fire and dozed. Again the atoms were gambolling before my eyes. This time the smaller groups kept modestly in the background. My mental eye, rendered more acute by repeated visions of the kind, could now distinguish larger structures, of manifold conformation: long rows, sometimes more closely fitted together; all twining and twisting in snake-like motion. But look! What was that? One of the snakes had seized hold of its own tail, and the form whirled mockingly before my eyes. As if by a flash of lightning, I awoke; and this time also I spent the rest of the night in working out the consequences of the hypothesis.

'Let us learn to dream, gentlemen, then perhaps we shall find the truth ... but let us beware of publishing our dreams before they have been put to the proof by the waking understanding.'

The second passage is from the *Annalen der Chemie* for 1865.

The translations of both passages are from Leicester and Klickstein, *A Source Book in Chemistry* (Harvard, 1952).

⸻

¶ *The Constitution and the Metamorphoses of Chemical Compounds and the Chemical Nature of Carbon*

§ *Constitution of Radicals. Nature of Carbon*

It has often been pointed out that radicals are not groups of atoms closely bound together but only atoms located near each other, which in certain reactions do not separate, while in others they break apart. It depends on the nature of the atoms which are located together and on the nature of the reacting substance whether or not an atom group plays the part of a so-called 'radical' directly; whether it is a more or less stable radical. In general, it can be said that the greater the difference in the nature of the individual atoms, the more easily will an atom group, a radical, break apart.

It will not be necessary to extend these considerations further: I will give only one example to show how this association of atoms can occur. The radical of sulphuric acid $SO_2$ contains three atoms, each of which is diatomic, thus representing two affinity units. By joining together, one affinity unit of one atom combines with one of the other. Of the six affinity units, four are thus used to hold the three atoms themselves together: two remain over, and the group appears to be diatomic; it unites, e.g., with two atoms of a monatomic element:

Sulphuryl radical　　　　Sulphuryl chloride

$$\ddot{S}\left\{\begin{array}{c} \Theta \\ \Theta \end{array}\right. \qquad\qquad \ddot{S}\left\{\begin{array}{c} Cl \\ \Theta \\ \Theta \\ Cl \end{array}\right.$$

If the sulphuryl chloride acts on water, two HCl split off, the residue remains combined, and the resulting product can be considered as two molecules of $H_2\Theta$ in which two atoms of H are replaced by the group $SO_2$. (It can easily be seen that the group $S\Theta$, which under certain conditions plays the part of a radical, must also be diatomic. The sulphurous acid (as a hydrate), which according to one view contains the same radical as sulphuric acid and belongs to the intermediate type $H_2 + H_2\Theta$, is, according to another, one of the compounds of the radical $S\Theta$, which belongs to the type $2H_2\Theta$. Both expressions are certainly synonymous.)

In a similar way the manner in which the atoms are associated can be shown for all radicals, including those which contain carbon. To do this, it is only necessary to form a picture of the nature of carbon.

If only the simplest compounds of carbon are considered (marsh gas, methyl chloride, carbon tetrachloride, chloroform, carbonic acid, phosgene gas, carbon disulfide, prussic acid, etc.), it is striking that the amount of carbon which the chemist has known as the least possible, as the *atom*, always combines with four atoms of a monatomic, or two atoms of a diatomic, element; that generally, the sum of the chemical unities of the elements which are bound to one atom of carbon is equal to four. This leads to the view that carbon is *tetratomic* (or tetrabasic).*

Accordingly, carbon stands with the three groups of elements mentioned earlier as the only representative yet known of the tetratomic group (the compounds of boron and silicon are still too little known). Its simplest combinations with elements of the three other groups are

$$IV + 4I \qquad\qquad IV + 2II$$
$$IV + (1I + 2I) \qquad\qquad IV + (III + I)$$

or, in examples,

$$\mathtext{C}H_4 \qquad \mathtext{C}\Theta Cl^2 \qquad \mathtext{C}\Theta_2 \qquad CNH$$
$$\mathtext{C}Cl_4 \qquad\qquad\qquad \mathtext{C}S_2$$
$$\mathtext{C}H_3Cl$$
$$\mathtext{C}HCl_3$$

For substances which contain more atoms of carbon, it

---

*If carbon is introduced among the types as a *tetratomic radical*, proportionally simple formulae are obtained for some of the well-known compounds. It would lead too far to go further into this.

must be assumed that at least part of the atoms are held just by the affinity of carbon and that the carbon atoms themselves are joined together, so that naturally a part of the affinity of one for the other will bind an equally great part of the affinity of the other.

The simplest, and therefore the most obvious, case of such linking together of two carbon atoms is this, that one affinity unit of one atom is bound to one of the other. Of the $2 \times 4$ affinity units of the two carbon atoms, two are thus used to hold both atoms themselves together; there still remain six extra which can be bound by the atoms of other elements. In other words, one group of two atoms of carbon $= C_2$ will be hexatomic, it will form compounds with six atoms of a monatomic element, or in general, with so many atoms that the sum of their chemical unities is 6 (e.g., ethyl hydride, ethyl chloride, elayl chloride, $1\frac{1}{2}$ carbon tetrachloride, aceto-nitrile, cyanogen, aldehyde, acetyl chloride, glycol, etc.).

If we put more than two carbon atoms together in the same way, then for each further one added, the basicity of the carbon group will be raised by two units. The number of hydrogen atoms (chemical units) which is bound with n atoms of carbon joined together in this way, e.g., will be expressed by

$$n(4 - 2) + 2 = 2n + 2$$

For $n = 5$, the basicity is thus $= 12$ (amyl hydride, amyl chloride, amylene chloride, valeronitrile, valeraldehyde, valeryl oxide, angelic acid, pyrotartaric acid anhydride, etc.). Until now it has been assumed that all the atoms linked on the carbon are held by the affinity of carbon. However, it is equally possible to think that in the polyatomic elements (O, N, etc.) only a part of their affinity, only one of the two units of oxygen for example, or only one of the three units of nitrogen, is bound to the carbon, so that thus, of the two affinity units of oxygen, one, and of the three affinity units of nitrogen, two, are still left over and can be bound to other elements. These other elements are thus only indirectly bound to carbon, which is expressed by the type method of writing formulae,

$$\left.\begin{array}{c}C_2H_5\\H\end{array}\right\}\Theta \qquad \left.\begin{array}{c}C_2H_5\\H\\H\end{array}\right\}N \qquad \left.\begin{array}{c}C_2H_3\Theta\\C_2H_5\end{array}\right\}O \qquad \left.\begin{array}{c}C_2H_5\\C_2H_5\\C_2H_5\end{array}\right\}N$$

In the same way different carbon groups are held together through the oxygen or the nitrogen.

When such compounds are actually considered in regard to those atoms which are linked thus to the carbon group, then the carbon group appears to be a radical, and it is said that the radical replaces one atom of H of the type, because instead of its one atom of H the affinity of O or N would be saturated in its place.

When comparisons are made between compounds which have an equal number of carbon atoms in the molecule and which can be changed into each other by simple transformations (e.g., alcohol, ethyl chloride, aldehyde, acetic acid, glycolic acid, oxalic acid, etc.) the view is reached that the carbon atoms are arranged in the same way and only the atoms held to the carbon skeleton are changed.

When the homologous bodies are then considered, the view is reached that in them the carbon atoms (regardless of how many are held in a molecule) are arranged together in the same way, according to the same laws of symmetry. In deeper decompositions, in which the carbon skeleton itself is attacked and broken into fragments, each fragment shows the same arrangement of carbon atoms, so that each fragment of the compound is homologous with the starting substance or with a substance which can be obtained from the homologous body by a simple transformation (e.g., replacement of hydrogen by oxygen).

In a great many organic compounds such a 'simplest' arrangement of carbon atoms can be assumed. Others contain so many carbon atoms in the molecule that for them a denser arrangement of carbons must be assumed.*

Benzene, for example, and all its derivatives, like the hydrocarbons homologous with it, shows such a high carbon content as to differentiate these bodies characteristically

---

* It is easy to be convinced that the formulae of these compounds can be constructed through the 'next simplest' arrangement of carbon atoms.

from all the substances resulting from the transformation of ethyl.

Naphthalene contains still more carbon. It must be assumed that in it carbon is arranged in a still denser form, that is, the individual atoms are still more closely bound to one another.

When these carbon-rich hydrocarbons, benzene and its homologues and naphthalene, are compared with the hydrocarbons of the alcohol group (elayl and its homologues), with which they show analogies in many respects, they show:

| Ethylene | Propylene | Butylene | Amylene |
|----------|-----------|----------|---------|
| $C_2H_4$ | $C_3H_6$ | $C_4H_8$ | $C_5H_{10}$ |
| | Benzene | Toluene | Xylene |
| | $C_6H_6$ | $C_7H_8$ | $C_8H_{10}$ |
| | | Naphthalene | |
| | | $C_{10}H_8$ | |

Comparing the hydrocarbons of the second row with those of the first, it is found that with an equal hydrogen content, they contain three more carbons. Between naphthalene and toluene the same relation occurs. It thus seems as if here the same sort of denser arrangement of carbon atoms is repeated and as if there were three classes of carbon-containing compounds differentiated from each other by the type of arrangement of carbon atoms.

¶ *Studies on Aromatic Compounds*

The theory of the atomicity of the elements, and especially the knowledge of carbon as a tetratomic element, has made possible in recent years in a very satisfactory way the explanation of the atomistic constitution of a great many carbon compounds, particularly those which I have called *fatty bodies*. Until now, so far as I know, no one has attempted to apply these views to the aromatic compounds. When I developed my views on the tetratomic nature of carbon, seven years ago, I indicated in a note that I had already formed an opinion on this subject, but I had not considered it suitable to develop the idea further. Most chemists who have since written on theoretical questions have left this subject untouched; some stated directly that the composition of aromatic compounds could not be explained by the theory of atomicity; others assumed the existence of a hexatomic group formed by six carbon atoms, but they did not try to find the method of combination of these carbon atoms, nor to give an account of the conditions under which this group could bind six monatomic atoms. . . .

In order to give an account of the atomistic constitution of aromatic compounds, it is necessary to take into consideration the following facts:

1. All aromatic compounds, even the simplest, are proportionally richer in carbon than the analogous compounds in the class of the fatty bodies.

2. Among the aromatic compounds, just as in the fatty bodies, there are numerous homologous substances, i.e., those whose differences of composition can be expressed by n $CH_2$.

3. The simplest aromatic compound contains at least six atoms of carbon.

4. All alteration products of aromatic substances show a certain family similarity, they belong collectively to the group of 'aromatic compounds.' In more deeply acting reactions, it is true, one part of carbon is often eliminated, but the chief product contains at least six atoms of carbon (benzene, quinone, chloranil, carbolic acid, hydroxyphenic acid, picric acid, etc.). The decomposition stops with the formation of these products if complete destruction of the organic group does not occur.

These facts obviously lead to the conclusion that in all aromatic substances there is contained one and the same atom group, or, if you wish, a common nucleus which consists of six carbon atoms. Within this nucleus the carbon atoms are certainly in close combination or in more compact arrangement. To this nucleus, then, more carbon atoms can add and, indeed in the same way and according to the same laws as in the case of the fatty bodies.

It is next necessary to give an account of the atomic constitution of this nucleus. Now this can be done very easily by the following hypothesis, which, on the now generally accepted view that carbon is tetratomic, explains in such a simple manner that further development is scarcely necessary.

If many carbon atoms can unite with one another, then it can also happen that *one* affinity unit of one atom can bind *one* affinity unit of the neighbouring atom. As I have shown earlier, this explains homology and in general the constitution of the fatty bodies.

It can now be further assumed that many carbon atoms are thus linked together, that they are always bound through two affinity units; it can also be assumed that the union occurs *alternately* through first *one* and then *two* affinity units. The first and the last of these views could be expressed by somewhat the following periods:

$$1/1, \; 1/1, \; 1/1, \; 1/1 \text{ etc.}$$
$$1/1, \; 2/2, \; 1/1, \; 2/2 \text{ etc.}$$

The first law of symmetry of union of the carbon atoms explains the constitution of the fatty bodies, as already mentioned; the second leads to an explanation of the constitution of aromatic substances, or at least of the nucleus which is common to all these substances.

If it is accepted that *six* carbon atoms are linked together according to this law of symmetry, a group is obtained which, if it is considered as an *open chain*, still contains *eight* nonsaturated affinity units. If another assumption is made, that the two carbon atoms which end the chain are linked together by one affinity unit, then there is obtained a *closed chain*\* (a symmetrical ring) which still contains *six* free affinity units.

From this *closed chain* now follow all the substances which are usually called *aromatic compounds*. The *open chain* occurs in quinone, in chloranil, and in the few substances which stand

* In the group of fatty bodies, the hydrocarbons of the ethylene series can be considered as closed chains. It should be clear that ethylene is the starting member of this series and that the hydrocarbon $CH_2$ (methylene) does not exist, for it cannot be believed that two affinities which belong to the same carbon atom should be able to link themselves together.

in close relation to both. I leave these bodies here without further consideration; they are proportionately easy to explain. It can be seen that they stand in close relation with the aromatic substances, but they still cannot truly be counted with the group of aromatic substances.

In all aromatic substances there can be assumed to be a common nucleus; it is the closed chain $C_6A_6$ (where A means an unsaturated affinity or affinity unit).

The six affinity units of this nucleus can be saturated by six monatomic elements. They can also all, or at least in part, be saturated by an affinity of a polyatomic element, but this latter must then be joined to other atoms, and so one or more *side chains* are produced, which can be further lengthened by linking themselves with other elements.

A saturation of two affinity units of the nucleus by an atom of a diatomic element or a saturation of three affinity units by an atom of a triatomic element is not possible in theory. Compounds of the molecular formula $C_6H_4O$, $C_6H_4S$, $C_6H_3N$ are thus unthinkable; if bodies of these compositions exist, and if the theory is correct, the formulae of the first two must be doubled, that of the third tripled.*

* I remember, however, the compound $C_6H_4O$ which Limpricht obtained along with phenol by dry distillation of salicyclic anhydride. The molecular formula of this substance is obviously

$$C_{12}H_8O_2 \;=\; \left.\begin{array}{l} C_6H_4 \\ C_6H_4 \end{array}\right\} OO$$

Its formation is explained by the equation

$$2\,C_{14}H_{10}O_5 = C_{12}H_8O_2 + 2C_6H_6O + 2CO_2 + 2CO$$

# JACOBUS HENRICUS VAN'T HOFF
1852–1911

# JOSEPH ACHILLE LE BEL
1847–1930

## STEREOCHEMISTRY

THE molecular architecture which Kekulé had created needed to be taken one stage further to complete the classical basis of molecular structure. The addition was made in 1874 by two chemists who, although known to one another, had worked independently.

Van't Hoff was born in Rotterdam and educated first in Delft and then at the University of Leiden. He was attracted to Bonn by the fame of Kekulé. There, although he found Kekulé unsympathetic, he became interested in Kekulé's ideas of chemical constitution. Later he moved to Paris to gain further experience under Wurtz. Le Bel was working in the same laboratory. Only a few months after van't Hoff had returned to Holland, each published a paper on the theme of stereochemistry (or *Chemistry in Space* as the French version of van't Hoff's paper was entitled). Van't Hoff made it clear that they had not communicated with each other on the subject.

The importance of their work lies essentially in putting two existing ideas together. The idea of a tetrahedral carbon atom (one in which the four bonds radiated from the central atom towards the corners of a tetrahedron) had been used by Kekulé. The idea that asymmetric optical activity of some pairs of substances was due to their molecular asymmetry was suggested by Pasteur. Van't Hoff and le Bel showed that the tetrahedral carbon atom provided a basis for proposing precise asymmetric molecular structures for the substances which exhibited optical activity. If four different atoms (or groups of atoms) were attached to a carbon atom tetrahedrally, two structures could be produced which were not identical. They were related as mirror-images, or as the left and right hands. Van't Hoff went on to show that a further kind of isomerism (geometrical isomerism) could exist in certain compounds containing a double bond.

Van't Hoff's interests were very wide and he made notable contributions to the development of physical chemistry, dealing with reversible reactions, transition points in heterogeneous equilibria, and the theory of dilute solutions.

The two passages on stereochemistry are printed here for comparison. Van't Hoff's on p. 134ff., which was the more influenced by Kekulé, appeared as a pamphlet published in Utrecht; le Bel's, on p. 143ff., which was the more influenced by Pasteur, in the *Bulletin de la Société chimique de France*. The translations are from Leicester and Klickstein, *A Source Book in Chemistry* (Harvard, 1952).

---

¶ *A Suggestion Looking to the Extension into Space of the Structural Formulae at Present Used in Chemistry. And a Note upon the Relation between the Optical Activity and the Chemical Constitution of Organic Compounds*

I desire to introduce some remarks which may lead to discussion and hope to avail myself of the discussion to give my ideas more definiteness and breadth. Since the starting-point for the following communication is found in the chemistry of the carbon compounds, I shall for the present do nothing more than state the points having reference to it.

It appears more and more that the present constitutional formulae are incapable of explaining certain cases of isomerism; the reason for this is perhaps the fact that we need a more definite statement about the actual positions of the atoms.

If we suppose that the atoms lie in a plane, as for example with isobutyl alcohol where the four affinities are represented by four lines in this plane occupying two directions perpendicular to one another, then methane ($CH_4$) (to start with the simplest case) will give the following siomeric modifications (the different hydrogen atoms being replaced one after the other by univalent groups $R'R''$ etc.):

One   for $CH_3(R')$   and for   $CH(R')_3$
Two   for $CH_2R'_2$ (Figures II and III) or for
      $CH_2R'R''$,   and for   $CHR'_2R''$
Three for $CHR'R''R'''$   and for   $CR'R''R'''R''''$

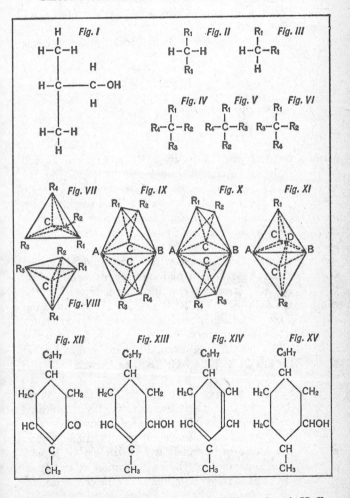

Figures to illustrate the stereochemical ideas of van't Hoff.

numbers that are clearly greater than the numbers actually known thus far.

The theory is brought into accord with the facts if we consider the affinities of the carbon atom directed towards the corners of a tetrahedron of which the carbon atom itself occupies the centre.

The numbers of isomers is then reduced and will be as follows:

One for $CH_3R'$, $CH_2R'_2$, $CH_2R'R''$, $CHR'_3$,
and $CHR'_2R''$ but
Two for $CHR'R''R'''$ or more general, for $CR'R''R'''R''''$.

If one imagines oneself in the line $R'R'''$ in Figures VII and VIII with head towards $R'$ and looking towards the line $R''R'''$ then $R''$ may be on the right or on the left of the observer; in other words: *When the four affinities of the carbon atom are satisfied by four univalent groups differing among themselves, two and not more than two different tetrahedrons are obtained, one of which is the reflected image of the other, they cannot be superposed; that is, we have here to deal with two structural formulae isomeric in space.* According to this hypothesis the combination $CR'R''R'''R''''$ presents a condition not presented by the combinations $CR'_2R''R'''$, $CR'_3R''$, or $CR'_4$, a condition not expressed by the ordinary mode of representation. According to the present mode there would be between $CR'R''R'''R''''$ and $CR'_2R''R'''$ a difference quite as great as between $CR'_2R''R'''$ and $CR'_3R''$, or between $CR'_3R''$ and $CR'_4$.

Submitting the first result of this hypothesis to the control of facts, I believe that it has been thoroughly established that some combinations which contain a carbon atom combined with four different univalent groups (such carbon atoms will henceforth be called asymmetric carbon atoms) present some anomalies in relation to isomerism and other characteristics which are not indicated by the constitutional formulae thus far used.

§ FIRST PART – I. *Relation between the asymmetric carbon and the property of optical activity:*

(a) *All of the compounds of carbon which in solution rotate the plane of polarized light possess an asymmetric carbon atom.*

In order to convince oneself of the justice of these remarks it is necessary to run through the following list of optically active compounds in the formula of which the asymmetric carbon is indicated by $C$:

Ethylidene lactic acid, $CH_3C.H.OH.COOH$.
Aspartic acid, $COOH\ C.H.NH_2.(CH_2COOH)$.
Asparagine, $COOH\ C.H.NH_2.(CH_2CONH_2)$.
Malic acid, $COOH\ C.OH.H.(CH_2COOH)$.
Glutaric acid (Itamalic acid), $CH_2OH\ C.H.COOH.(CH_2COOH)$.
Tartaric acid, $COOH\ C.H.OHC.H.OH.COOH$.
Dextrose, Laevulose, Galactose, Maltose.
Sorbin, Eucalyn, etc., $CH_2OH.C.H.OH.(C_4H_7O_4)$.
Mannite, Quercite, Pinite: $(C_4H_9O_4).C.H.OH.CH_2OH$.

Cane sugar, milk sugar, Melezitose, Melitose, Parasaccharose, and Trehalose; Starch, Inuline, Glycogen, Dextrine, and Arabin all contain the asymmetric carbon atom that was present in the previous compounds inasmuch as they are compound ethers of the previous compounds.

Camphor, according to Kekulé (Figure XII).
Borneol, according to the same (Figure XIII).
Camphoric acid, according to the same.
   $COOH\ CH(C_8H_{14}O.)$.
Terpinolene which apparently has the structure shown in Figure XIV and Menthol which perhaps has the structure shown in Figure XV.

Concerning the active alkaloids, albumens, etc., too little is as yet known of their structure to permit of any conclusion being reached in regard to the relation between their structures and the rotatory power.

The sole definite exception to this rule that I have been able to find is the active propyl alcohol of Chancell, but, according to a private communication of Henniger, this relatively small rotatory power is due to the presence of an impurity.

(b) *The derivatives of optically active compounds lose their rotatory power when the asymmetry of all the carbon atoms disappears; in the contrary case they do not usually lose this power.*

A few examples will be sufficient here:

Inactive malonic, fumaric, and maleïc acids from the active malic acid; inactive succinic and tartronic acids from the active tartaric acid; inactive cymene from active camphor, etc.

In the contrary case there are:

Active malic acid from active tartaric acid;

Active tartaric acid from active lactose;

Active glucose from active glucosides;

Active nitro-mannite from active mannite;

Active camphoric acid and Borneol from active camphor;

Active salts and esters from active acids, etc.

(c) *If one makes a list of compounds which contain an asymmetric carbon atom it is then seen that in many cases the converse of (a) is not true, that is, not every compound with such an atom has an influence upon polarized light.*

This may be ascribed to three causes:

1. The compounds consist of an inactive mixture of two isomers with equal but opposite optical power, which owing to their close agreement in all other properties can be separated with great difficulty, and which have not up to the present been separated.

2. The study of the rotatory power has been imperfect, either on account of the slight solubility of the compounds or on account of the slight specific rotatory power of many compounds, as for example, in the case of mannite.

3. The asymmetric carbon atom may not in itself be sufficient to cause optical activity, the latter may not depend solely upon the mutual diversity of the groups which are in combination with the carbon atom, but may also be dependent upon their character.

However the case may be, the facts noted indicate a probable relation between constitution and active power which may be made use of in the following cases when more convincing arguments fail:

1. A compound which rotates the plane of polarized light probably possesses an asymmetric carbon atom; which gives a means of choosing between possible structures in the case of compounds where the structure is not completely determined.

For example, active amyl alcohol with an asymmetric carbon atom can have only the formula:

$$\begin{matrix} CH_3 \\ C_2H_5 \end{matrix} CHCH_2OH$$

a formula which has also been suggested by Erlenmeyer but upon altogether different grounds.

2. A compound which up the the present has shown no physical isomers acting upon polarized light in all probability contains no asymmetric carbon atom; this fact also may be of service in choosing between possible structural formulae; as for example, citric acid, which on account of its transformation into aconitic acid and tricarballylic acids must have one of the two formulae:

$$\begin{matrix} C.H.OH.COOH \\ | \\ CH.COOH \\ | \\ CH_2COOH \end{matrix} \quad or \quad \begin{matrix} CH_2COOH \\ | \\ C.OH.COOH \\ | \\ CH_2COOH \end{matrix}$$

its inactivity gives preference to the second formula; the first, however, contains an asymmetric carbon atom for which reason I hope to be able to produce the acid named by following the method of Frankland and Duppa from oxalic acid and iodo-acetic acid esters by the aid of zinc.

3. Finally the limits of the rotatory power can be stated with some measure of probability, that is to say, the simplest combinations which will show active power can be indicated; for example, the simplest active monatomic alcohol will be:

$$CH_3.C.H.OH.CH_2CH_3.$$

The simplest active monobasic acid:

$$CH_3.C.H.COOH.CH_2CH_3.$$

The simplest active diatomic alcohol:

$$CH_3CHOH\ CH_2OH.$$

The simplest active saturated hydrocarbon:

$$\begin{matrix} CH_3 \\ C_2H_5 \end{matrix} CHC_3H_7.$$

The simplest active aromatic hydrocarbon:

$$\begin{matrix} CH_3 \\ C_2H_5 \end{matrix} CHC_6H_5\ \text{etc.}$$

At the same time it is probable that some series will be excluded from active power, as for example:

| The normal hydrocarbons | $CH_3(CH_2)_nCH_3$ |
| The normal alcohols | $CH_3(CH_2)_nCH_2OH$ |
| The normal acids | $CH_3(CH_2)_nCOOH$ etc. |

It is more noteworthy that in consequence of the assumptions made, the compound CHBrClI can probably be split up into two isomers which will act upon polarized light. . . .

§ SECOND PART

Thus far we have considered the influence of the hypothesis upon compounds in which the carbon atoms are united by a single affinity only (leaving out some aromatic bodies); there remains now to be considered:

*The influence of the new hypothesis upon compounds containing doubly linked carbon atoms.* Double linking is represented by two tetrahedrons with one edge in common (Figure IX) in which A and B represent the union of the two carbon atoms, and R′R″R‴R⁗ represent the univalent groups which saturate the remaining free affinities of the carbon atoms.

If R′R″R‴R⁗ all represent the same group, then but one form is conceivable, and the same is true if R′ and R″ or R‴ and R⁗ are identical, *but if R′ differs from R″ and at the same time R‴ differs from R⁗, which does not preclude R′ and R‴, R″ and R⁗ from being equal, then two figures become possible shown in Figures IX and X, which differ from one another in regard to the positions of R′ and R″ with respect to R‴ and R⁗. The dissimilarity of these figures, which are limited to two, indicates a case of isomerism not shown by the ordinary formulae.*

Turning to the facts, I believe that I have met with such cases among organic compounds.

1. Maleïc and fumaric acids, all explanations of the isomerism between these have made shipwreck (I count here also the assumption of a bivalent carbon atom since this can exist alone in the case of carbon monoxide and the carbylamines, for evident reasons, without doubling of the molecule); as a matter of fact these acids realize the conditions outlined above: *Two doubly-linked carbon atoms each carrying two unlike univalent groups, H and COOH.*

2. Brom and isobrom maleïc acid, the explanation of the isomerism here is entirely the same as before, one has only to replace an H in the fumaric and maleïc acid by a Br.

3. Citra-, ita-, and mesaconic acids. With the adoption of

$$CH_3CHCOOHCH_2COOH$$

for pyrotartaric acid there remain for the acids mentioned only the formulae

$$CH_2=C.COOH.CH_2COOH$$
$$CH_3C\ COOH=CHCOOH,$$

and if the latter does not contain two isomers (probably ita- and citraconic acids) in accordance with my hypothesis, no plausible explanation can be given.

4. Solid and liquid crotonic acids. The constitution of the solid crotonic acid according to Kekulé is without doubt

$$CH_3CH=CHCOOH,$$

for the liquid crotonic acid there remains therefore (thus it is held) only the formula

$$CH_2=CHCH_2COOH$$

to explain their lack of identity.

But if we take into consideration the following facts with regard to this acid:

(a) Fused with KOH it gives, according to M. Hemilian, acetic acid only.

(b) Oxidizing agents, according to the same authority, convert it into acetic and oxalic acids, and indirectly from oxalic acid into carbonic acid.

(c) At 170–180°, also according to Hemilian, it goes over

into the solid crotonic acid. Thus there is nothing in favour of the formula $CH_2=CHCH_2COOH$ and everything in favour of the isomer $CH_2CH=CHCOOH$, exactly like fumaric and maleïc acids. The formula $CH_3CH=CHCOOH$ really satisfies the conditions exacted by my hypothesis for the possibility of two isomers: two doubly-linked carbon atoms, the free affinities of each of which are saturated by two unlike univalent groups, in this case H and $CH_3$, H and COOH.

Geuther's chlorcrotonic acid and chlorisocrotonic acid, the isomerism of which has hitherto been expressed by the formulae

$$CH_2=CClCH_2COOH$$

and

$$CH_3CCl=CHCOOH,$$

according to Froelich give with nascent hydrogen the acids treated under (4) whence the constitution of both becomes

$$CH_3CCl=CHCOOH$$

and this case of isomerism strengthens my hypothesis.

§ THIRD PART

There remain now to be treated carbon atoms which are united by a triple union as in acetylene; this combination is represented by two tetrahedrons with three summits in common or with one of their faces in common (Figure XI). ACB is the triple union, R' and R'' are the univalent groups which saturate the two remaining affinities of the carbon atoms. The new hypothesis does not in this case lead to any discordance with the views previously held.

In closing, I wish to remark that:

1. The new hypothesis leaves nothing unexplained that is clearly set forth by the previous conceptions.

2. Certain properties and isomers not explained by the usual theories receive some light from this point of view.

3. Finally my remarks about active compounds in solu-

tion, that is, active molecules, are related to the views of Rammelsberg upon active crystals.

Extending the observations of Herschel and Pasteur, Rammelsberg maintains that the property of acting upon the plane of polarization in the solid state (that is the active condition of crystals with inactive molecules as well as the inactive condition of crystals with active molecules) coincides with the appearance of two crystal forms, one of which is the reflected image of the other.

It is evident that we have here to deal with an arrangement of the molecules in the active crystal altogether similar to the arrangement of the groups of atoms in the active molecule according to my hypothesis; an arrangement in which neither the crystal mentioned by Rammelsberg nor the active molecules represented in a general way by Figures VII and VIII have a plane of symmetry.

¶ *On the Relations which exist between the Atomic Formulae of Organic Compounds and the Rotatory Power of their Solutions*

Up to the present time we do not possess any certain rule which enables us to foresee whether or not the solution of a substance has rotatory power. We know only that the derivatives of an active substance are in general also active; nevertheless we often see the rotatory power suddenly disappear in the most immediate derivatives, while in other cases, it persists in very remote derivatives. By considerations, purely geometrical, I have been able to formulate a rule of a quite general character.

Before giving the reasoning which has led me to this law I shall give the facts upon which it rests, and then shall conclude with a discussion of the confirmation of the law offered by the present state of our chemical knowledge.

The labours of Pasteur and others have completely established the correlation which exists between molecular asymmetry and rotatory power. If the asymmetry exists only in the crystalline molecule, the crystal alone will be active; if, on the contrary, it belongs to the chemical molecule, the solution will show rotatory power, and often the crystal also if the structure of the crystal allows us to perceive it, as in the case of the sulphate of strychnine and the alum of amyl amine.

There are, moreover, mathematical demonstrations of the necessary existence of this correlation, which we may consider a perfectly ascertained fact.

In the reasoning which follows, we shall ignore the asymmetries which might arise from the arrangement in space possessed by the atoms and univalent radicals; but shall consider them as spheres or material points, which will be equal if the atoms or radicals are equal, and different if they are different. This restriction is justified by the fact that, up to the present time, it has been possible to account for all the cases of isomerism observed without recourse to such arrangement, and the discussion at the end of the paper will show that the appearance of the rotatory power can be equally well foreseen without the aid of the hypothesis of which we have just spoken.

*First general principle*: Let us consider a molecule of a chemical compound having the formula $MA_4$; M being a simple or complex radical combined with four univalent atoms, A capable of being replaced by substitution. Let us replace three of them by simple or complex univalent radicals differing from one another and from M; the body obtained will be asymmetric.

Indeed, the group of radicals R, R′, R″, A when considered as material points differing among themselves form a structure which is enantiomorphous with its reflected image, and the residue, M, cannot re-establish the symmetry. In general then, it may be stated that if a body is derived from the original type $MA_4$ by the substitution of three different atoms or radicals for A, its molecules will be asymmetric, and it will have rotatory power.

But there are two exceptional cases, distinct in character.

(1) If the molecular type has a plane of symmetry containing the four atoms A, the substitution of these by radicals (which we must consider as not capable of changing their

position) can in no way alter the symmetry with respect to this plane, and in such cases the whole series of substitution products will be inactive.

(2) The last radical substituted for A may be composed of the same atoms that compose all the rest of the group into which it enters, and these two equal groups may have a neutralizing effect upon polarized light, or they may increase the activity; when the former is the case the body will be inactive. Now this arrangement may present itself in a derivative of an active asymmetric body where there is but slight difference in constitution, and later we shall see a remarkable instance of this.

*Second general principle*: If, in our fundamental type we substitute but two radicals, R, R', it is possible to have symmetry or asymmetry according to the constitution of the original type MA$_4$. If this molecule originally had a plane of symmetry passing through the two atoms A which have been replaced by R and R', this plane will remain a plane of symmetry after the substitution; the body obtained will then be inactive. Our knowledge of the constitution of certain simple types will enable us to assert that certain bodies derived from them by two substitutions will be inactive.

Again, if it happens not only that a single substitution furnished but one derivative, but also that two and even three substitutions give only one and the same chemical isomer, we are obliged to admit that the four atoms A occupy the angles of a regular tetrahedron, whose planes of symmetry are identical with those of the whole molecule MA$_4$; in this case also no bisubstitution product can have rotatory power.

*Theorem*: When an asymmetric body is formed in a reaction where there are present originally only unsymmetric bodies, the two isomers of inverse symmetry will be formed in equal quantities.

We know that the general principle of the calculation of probabilities consists in this:

When any phenomenon whatever can take place in two ways only, and there is no reason why it should take place in one of the ways in preference to the other, if the phenomenon has taken place m times in one manner and m' times in the other manner, the ratio m/m' approaches unity as the sum m + m' approaches infinity.

When an asymmetric body has been formed by substitution from a symmetric one, the asymmetry has been introduced by one of the substitutions which has taken place; let us consider this point carefully. The radical or the atom, the substitution of which introduced the asymmetry, had formerly a homologue which was symmetrical to it by its connexion with a point or a plane of symmetry; these radicals being in similar dynamic and geometrical considerations, if m and m' represent the number of times that each one of them is substituted, m'/m ought to approach unity as the number of these substitutions grows beyond a measurable unit.

Now if the substitution of these similar radicals produces a dextro-body, then the other will produce the laevo-body; both will in consequence be formed in equal proportions.

It is the same for asymmetric bodies formed by addition; indeed the body which destroys the symmetry of a symmetrical molecule by adding itself to it, would be able to occupy an identical place situated on the other side of the point or plane of symmetry; the preceding reasoning therefore can be applied equally well to this case.

This is not necessarily true of asymmetric bodies formed in the presence of other active bodies, or traversed by circularly polarized light, or, in short, when submitted to any cause whatever which favours the formation of one of the asymmetric isomers. Such conditions are exceptional; and generally in the case of bodies prepared synthetically those which are active will escape the observation of the chemist unless he endeavours to separate the mixed isomeric products, the combined action of which upon polarized light is neutral.

We have a striking example of this in tartaric acid, for neither the dextro- nor the laevo-tartaric acid has ever been obtained directly by synthesis, but the inactive racemic acid, which is a combination of equal parts of the dextro and laevo acids, is always obtained.

# III

## THE ELECTROMAGNETIC SYNTHESIS

THE progress of scientific thought is marked by the degree of unification which has been achieved amongst an apparently diverse collection of physical facts. Indeed, if the scientist is conscious of a final aim in his work it must be the search for just such unifying principles, in terms of which the various phenomena displayed by the physical world are seen to fall into a coherent pattern, each fact taking its alloted place and clearly displaying its relation to all other facts.

Despite the undoubted and impressive successes of the physical sciences we must admit to being far from the completion of this programme. The ever-increasing range of investigation continually presents the theoretician with fresh challenges and demands conceptual schemes of greater and greater generality. Nevertheless, this vital theme of unification is well illustrated by past achievement, and perhaps nowhere better than in the developments to be illustrated in this section.

As we have seen in an earlier section, classical Newtonian physics was to a large extent born out of speculation inspired by astronomical observation. Such observation, in its turn, was dependent upon the essentially practical skills of the optical instrument maker. Indeed, many of the greatest thinkers were, at the same time, designers and constructors of considerable talent. It is hardly surprising, therefore, that this preoccupation with the practical aspects of the behaviour of light should have given rise to questions concerning the nature of light itself. The story of this problem runs like a dominant theme throughout the history of modern physics. The seventeenth and eighteenth centuries witnessed considerable speculation on this issue, leading to an apparent resolution of the problem. Yet the opening of the twentieth century brought with it further doubts and the demand for a drastic reassessment of the problem.

It is a story of great fascination, and while space does not permit us to give more than limited reference to it, the later extracts will clearly show the presence of this recurring theme. The earlier controversies divided the physicists into two camps, and the two extracts given here represent the views of the chief protagonists.

Newton's demonstration of the composite nature of white light, by passing sunlight through a glass prism, must be familiar to all. This simple experiment was one of a sequence of careful observations covering a wide range of optical phenomena, and formed the subject matter of his great book *Opticks*, first published in 1704. As a result of this work Newton formed the opinion that light consisted of minute 'corpuscles', in terms of which he sought to explain the behaviour of light as revealed by experiment.

The rival hypothesis considered light to have an essentially wave-like nature, and was presented with great power and elegance by Christian Huygens. The great authority of Newton may well have contributed to the fact that, although the English physicist's theory was the subject of attack by his contemporaries, the alternative views offered by Huygens suffered from comparative neglect, and it was not until the later experimental work of such men as Thomas Young (1773–1829) and Augustin Fresnel (1788–1827) that the wave theory of light received due attention, and finally came to be accepted as the correct theory.

And yet it is one of the most startling features of this story, that with the radically new theories of the twentieth century, the corpuscular theory of light was once more reinstated as an essential feature of physical theory. To claim this turn of events as a vindication of the essential correctness of Newton's views would hardly be a fair assessment of the situation. The theories we accept today are based on a wealth of knowledge of the physical world which was completely unknown to Newton and his contemporaries.

We turn now to topics which bear no apparent relation

to the nature of light. To the familiar magnet, for example. The simple properties of magnetic materials were known long before the Christian era, and the use of magnets as an aid to navigation is an early example of applied science.

Another phenomenon with a history almost as old as that of magnetism is the ability of a material like amber to attract light particles when rubbed with a cloth – to become electrically charged, as we should now say. This curious property, in some ways reminiscent of the behaviour of magnetic lodestone, was thought to be a characteristic of the amber itself. Both phenomena excited much extravagant speculation but it was not until the more disciplined inquiries of later centuries that careful and controlled observation were to reveal the significance of these 'curiosities', and to lay the foundations of the subjects of electricity and magnetism which we know today.

The first step along this path was principally due to William Gilbert, and in the extract in this section we learn not only of the results of his own researches but something of his opinion of the earlier speculators. Gilbert's work was followed by an awakening interest in these subjects and the seventeenth and eighteenth centuries were to witness a growing understanding of the underlying principles. A single extract must suffice to represent this period and in the work of Benjamin Franklin we have a good example of the expanding scope of scientific inquiry as a link is established between a familiar aspect of the everyday world and the more circumscribed phenomena of the scientist's laboratory.

A decisive step in the history of a scientific theory is the passage from the purely descriptive, verbal, stage to the quantitative, numerical, stage. It is at this point that a theory 'comes of age', and the logical links which lead from hypothesis to consequence, and prediction, are revealed and the sharp cutting edge of mathematics severely tests the soundness of the theory.

Towards the end of the eighteenth century several attempts were made to determine, in quantitative form, the laws of force governing electric and magnetic phenomena, and the precise experiments of Charles-Augustin Coulomb, represented here, laid the foundations for the quantitative theories which were to follow. The development of such theories was favoured by the fact that, in mathematical expression if not in physical significance, the laws of force were similar in form to that earlier proposed by Newton for the gravitational force, with the result that much of the earlier mathematical work could be carried over into the new field of study. Led by the work of men such as Laplace (whose cosmological theories we have already met) and Siméon Poisson (1781–1840) elegant theories of magnetic and electrical phenomena grew up to take their place beside the older theories, such as that of gravitation.

A new advance was the demonstration of the existence of the electric current by Volta at the end of the eighteenth century. This important development, illustrated by the extract in this section, enormously broadened the scope of electrical science.

The twin subjects of electricity and magnetism had grown up side by side. Indeed, there were certain obvious similarities between the two subjects; but, at the same time, no fundamental link had been established. The existence of such a connexion was revealed by the observations of Hans Oersted (1777–1851) that electric currents gave rise to magnetic effects, apparently indistinguishable from those due to the familiar magnetic materials. This work was extended, as shown in the extract in this section, by Ampère whose mathematical abilities, allied to his experimental skills, enabled him to build up a coherent theory of the magnetic phenomena associated with electric currents and thus to forge a permanent link between the two fields of study.

Michael Faraday was to make many important contributions to the development of the subject, but perhaps none more fundamental than his famous law of electro-magnetic induction, a law which revealed a deeper and wider relation between electricity and magnetism and pointed to a more comprehensive theory – electromagnetism – of which the theories of electricity and magnetism were but two aspects.

The final unification was achieved in 1865, when Maxwell published his *Dynamical Theory of the Electromagnetic Field.* The heart of this theory was a set of equations governing all electrical and magnetic phenomena, containing within them all the laws of the earlier investigators, and clearly displaying the close and symmetrical relationship between electrical and magnetic effects. Yet Maxwell's achievement was greater. On the basis of his equations Maxwell was led to predict the existence of electromagnetic waves, capable of travelling through empty space, with a constant velocity. From an estimate of the magnitude of this velocity Maxwell realized that the velocity he had obtained was the same as that which had previously been measured for the velocity of visible light. His conclusion, that light was simply a form of electromagnetic radiation, revealed to the full the enormous power of his unifying scheme, embracing as it did the diverse phenomena of electricity, magnetism, and optics within the bounds of a single comprehensive theory.

One of the most astounding chapters in the history of physics was brought to an appropriate close when, some twenty years later, Heinrich Hertz was able to demonstrate experimentally the existence of the electromagnetic waves that Maxwell had predicted. This was a triumphant vindication of Maxwell's work, and at the same time these brilliant experiments were to lay the foundations of radio-telegraphy, and in so doing point the way ahead to further achievements.

# ISAAC NEWTON
## 1642–1727

### THE COMPOSITE NATURE OF WHITE
### LIGHT IS DEMONSTRATED

NEWTON published as his first scientific paper a study of
the phenomenon of light; and his general work on the subject of optics would alone justify the fame accorded to him.
Although Descartes had accurately described the rainbow,
and successfully applied mathematics to the measurement of
the angle of the bow, Newton's experiments with prisms
greatly extended the knowledge of the subject. These experiments showed that white light is a composite of many colours of light which are refracted unequally in passing through
the prism. Newton's explanation of the propagation of light
as due to the emission of 'small Bodies' from 'shining Substances' was, as we have seen, only part of the explanation.
In practical applications, Newton, by his invention of the
reflecting telescope, successfully overcame the problem
caused by the chromatic aberration due to the unequal
refraction of different colours of light through the lenses of
the telescope.

Newton's great achievement was in obtaining his explanations by controlled experiment and in his ability to present
the results in precise language. The selection which follows
provides a good example of both aspects of his skill. The
language may be archaic by modern standards, but there is
no doubt, at any point, as to what he means and as to how
he conducted his experiments.

The following selection, taken from W. F. Magie's *A
Sourcebook in Physics,* originally appeared in *Philosophical
Transactions, Abridged,* Vol. I (1672).

## ¶ *Dispersion of Light*

In the year 1666 (at which time I applied myself to the grinding of optick glasses of other figures than spherical) I procured me a triangular glass prism, to try therewith the celebrated phaenomena of colours. And in order thereto, having darkened my chamber, and made a small hole in my window-shuts, to let in a convenient quantity of the sun's light, I placed my prism at its entrance, that it might be thereby refracted to the opposite wall. It was at first a very pleasing divertisement, to view the vivid and intense colours produced thereby; but after a while applying myself to consider them more circumspectly, I became surprised, to see them in an oblong form; which, according to the received laws of refraction, I expected should have been circular. They were terminated at the sides with straight lines, but at the ends, the decay of light was so gradual that it was difficult to determine justly, what was their figure; yet they seemed semicircular.

Comparing the length of this colour'd Spectrum with its breadth, I found it about five times greater, a disproportion so extravagant, that it excited me to a more than ordinary curiosity to examining from whence it might proceed. I could scarce think, that the various thicknesses of the glass, or the termination with shadow or darkness, could have any influence on light to produce such an effect; yet I thought it not amiss, first to examine those circumstances, and so try'd what would happen by transmitting light through parts of the glass of divers thicknesses, or through holes in the window of diverse bignesses, or by setting the prism without, so that the light might pass through it, and be refracted, before it was terminated by the hole: But I found none of those circumstances material. The fashion of the colours was in all these cases the same.

Then I suspected, whether by any unevenness in the glass or other contingent irregularity, these colours might be thus dilated. And to try this, I took another prism like the former, and so placed it, that the light passing through them both might be refracted contrary ways, and so by the latter returned into that course from which the former had diverted it. For by this means I thought the regular effects of the first prism would be destroyed by the second prism, but the irregular ones more augmented, by the multiplicity of refractions. The event was, that the light, which by the first prism was diffused into an oblong form, was by the second reduced into an orbicular one, with as much regularity as when it did not at all pass through them.

\*

Then I began to suspect, whether the rays, after their trajection through the prism, did not move in curve lines, and according to their more or less curvity tend to divers parts of the wall. And it increased my suspicion, when I remembered that I had often seen a tennis ball struck with an oblique racket, describe such a curve line. For, a circular as well as a progressive motion being communicated to it by that stroke, its parts on that side where the motions conspire, must press, and beat the contiguous air more violently than on the other, and there excite a reluctancy and reaction of the air proportionably greater. And for the same reason, if the rays of light should possibly be globular bodies, and by their oblique passage out of one medium into another, acquire a circulating motion, they ought to feel the greater resistance from the ambient ether, on that side, where the motions conspire, and thence be continually bowed to the other. But notwithstanding this plausible ground of suspicion, when I came to examine it, I could observe no such curvity in them. And besides (which was enough for my purpose) I observed, that the difference 'twixt the length of the image, and the diameter of the hole, through which the light was transmitted, was proportionable to their distance.

The gradual removal of these suspicions at length led me to the *Experimentum Crucis*, which was this: I took two boards, and placed one of them close behind the prism at the window, so that the light might pass through a small hole, made in it for the purpose, and fall on the other board, which I placed at about twelve feet distance, having first made a small hole in it also, for some of the incident light to pass through. Then I placed another prism behind this second board, so that the light trajected through both the boards might pass through that also, and be again refracted before it arrived at the wall. This done, I took the first prism in my hand, and turned it to and fro slowly about its axis, so much as to make the several parts of the image cast, on the second board, successively pass through the hole in it, that I might observe to what places on the wall the second prism would refract them. And I saw by the variation of those places, that the light, tending to that end of the image, towards which the refraction of the first prism was made, did in the second prism suffer a refraction considerably greater than the light tending to the other end. And so the true cause of the length of that image was detected to be no other, than that light is not similar or homogenial, but consists of *Difform Rays, some of which are more Refrangible than others*; so that without any difference in their incidence on the same medium, some shall be more Refracted than others; and therefore that, according to their *particular Degrees of Refrangibility*, they were transmitted through the prism to divers parts of the opposite wall.

Now I shall proceed to acquaint you with another more notable *Difformity* in its rays, wherein the origin of colours is unfolded: concerning which I shall lay down the doctrine first, and then for its examination give you an instance or two of the experiments, as a specimen of the rest.

The doctrine you will find comprehended and illustrated in the following propositions:

1. As the rays of light differ in degrees of refrangibility so they also differ in their disposition to exhibit this or that particular colour. Colours are not qualifications of light, derived from refractions, or reflections of natural bodies (as 'tis generally believed) but original and connate properties, which in divers rays are divers. Some rays are disposed to exhibit a red colour and no other; some a yellow and no other, some a green and no other, and so of the rest. Nor are

there only rays proper and particular to the more eminent colours, but even to all their intermediate gradations.

2. To the same degree of refrangibility ever belongs the same colour, and to the same colour ever belongs the same degree of refrangibility. The least refrangible rays are all disposed to exhibit a red colour, and contrarily those rays which are disposed to exhibit a red colour, are all the least refrangible: so the most refrangible rays are all disposed to exhibit a deep violet colour, and contrarily those which are apt to exhibit such a violet colour are all the most refrangible. And so to all the intermediate colours in a continued series belong intermediate degrees of refrangibility. And this Analogy 'twixt colours and refrangibility is very precise and strict; the rays always either exactly agreeing in both, or proportionally disagreeing in both.

3. The species of colour, and degree of refrangibility proper to any particular sort of rays, is not mutable by refraction, nor by reflection from natural bodies, nor by any other cause that I could yet observe. When any one sort of rays hath been well parted from those of other kinds, it hath afterwards obstinately retained its colour, notwithstanding my utmost endeavours to change it. I have refracted it with prisms, and reflected it with bodies, which in daylight were of other colours; I have intercepted it with the coloured film of air, interceded two compressed plates of glass; transmitted it through coloured mediums, and through mediums irradiated with other sorts of rays, and diversely terminated it; and yet could never produce any new colour out of it. It would by contracting or dilating become more brisk, or faint, and by the loss of many rays, in some cases very obscure and dark; but I could never see it changed *in specie*.

4. Yet seeming transmutations of colours may be made, where there is any mixture of divers sorts of rays. For in such mixtures, the component colours appear not, but, by their mutual allaying each other, constitute a middling colour. And therefore, if by refraction, or any other of the aforesaid causes, the difform rays, latent in such a mixture, be separated, there shall emerge colours different from the colour of

the composition. Which colours are not new generated, but only made apparent by being parted; for if they be again entirely mixt and blended together, they will again compose that colour, which they did before separation. And for the same reason, transmutations made by the convening of divers colours are not real; for when the difform rays are again severed, they will exhibit the very same colours which they did before they entered the composition; as you see blue and yellow powders, when finely mixed, appear to the naked eye, green, and yet the colours of the component corpuscles are not thereby really transmuted, but only blended. For when viewed with a good microscope they still appear blue and yellow interspersedly.

5. There are therefore two sorts of colours. The one original and simple, and the other compounded of these. The original or primary colours are red, yellow, green, blue, and a violet-purple, together with orange, indico, and an indefinite variety of intermediate gradations.

6. The same colours *in specie* with these primary ones, may be also produced by composition. For a mixture of yellow and blue makes green; of red and yellow makes orange; of orange and yellowish green makes yellow. And in general, if any two colours be mixed, which in the series of those generated by the prism are not too far distant one from another, they by their mutual alloy compound that colour, which in the said series appeareth in the midway between them. But those which are situated at too great a distance, do not so. Orange and indico produce not the intermediate green, nor scarlet and green the intermediate yellow.

7. But the most surprising, and wonderful composition was that of whiteness. There is no one sort of rays which alone can exhibit this. 'Tis ever compounded, and to its composition, are requisite all the aforesaid primary colours, mixed in a due proportion. I have often with admiration beheld that all the colours of the prism being made to converge, and thereby to be again mixed, as they were in the light before it was incident upon the prism, reproduced

light, entirely and perfectly white, and not at all sensibly differing from a direct light of the sun, unless when the glasses, I used, were not sufficiently clear; for then they would a little incline it to their colour.

8. Hence therefore it comes to pass, that whiteness is the usual colour of light; for light is a confused aggregate of rays indued with all sorts of colours, as they were promiscuously darted from the various parts of luminous bodies. And of such a confused aggregate, as I said, is generated whiteness, if there be a due proportion of the ingredients; but if any one predominate, the light must incline to that colour; as it happens in the blue flame of brimstone; the yellow flame of a candle; and the various colours of the fixed stars.

9. These things considered, the manner how colours are produced by the prism is evident. For, of the rays, constituting the incident light, since those which differ in colour proportionally differ in refrangibility, they by their unequal refractions must be severed and dispersed into an oblong form in an orderly succession, from the least refracted scarlet, to the most refracted violet. And for the same reason it is, that objects when looked upon through a prism, appear coloured. For the difform rays, by their unequal refractions, are made to diverge towards several parts of the Retina, and these express the images of things coloured, as in the former case they did the sun's image upon a wall. And by this inequality of refractions, they become not only coloured, but also very confused and indistinct.

10. Why the colours of the rainbow appear in falling drops of rain, is also from hence evident. For those drops which refract the rays, disposed to appear purple, in greatest quantity to the spectator's eye, refract the rays of other sorts so much less, as to make them pass beside it; and such are the drops on the inside of the primary bow, and on the outside of the secondary or exterior one. So those drops, which refract in greatest plenty the rays, apt to appear red, toward the spectator's eye, refract those of other sorts so much more, as to make them pass beside it; and such are the drops on

the exterior part of the primary, and interior part of the secondary bow.

11. The odd phaenomena of an infusion of *Lignum Nephriticum*, leaf-gold, fragments of coloured glass, and some other transparently coloured bodies, appearing in one position of one colour, and of another in another, are on these grounds no longer riddles. For those are substances apt to reflect one sort of light, and transmit another; as may be seen in a dark room, by illuminating them with familiar or uncompounded light. For then they appear of that colour only, with which they are illuminated, but yet in one position more vivid and luminous than in another, accordingly as they are disposed more or less to reflect or transmit the incident colour.

12. From hence also is manifest the reason of an unexpected experiment which Mr *Hook*, somewhere in his *Micrography* relates to have made with two wedge-like transparent vessels, filled the one with a red, the other with a blue liquor: namely, that though they were severally transparent enough, yet both together became opake; for if one transmitted only red, and the other only blue, no rays could pass through both.

13. I might add more instances of this nature, but I shall conclude with this general one. That the colours of all natural bodies have no other origin than this, that they are variously qualified, to reflect one sort of light in greater plenty than another. And this I have experimented in a dark room, by illuminating those bodies with uncompounded light of diverse colours. For by that means any body may be made to appear of any colour. They have there no appropriate colour, but ever appear of the colour of the light cast upon them, but yet with this difference, that they are most brisk and vivid in the light of their own daylight colour. Minium appeareth there of any colour indifferently, with which it is illustrated, but yet most luminous in red, and so bise appeareth indifferently of any colour, but yet most luminous in blue. And therefore minium reflecteth rays of any colour, but most copiously those endowed with red, and

consequently when illustrated with daylight; that is, with all sorts of rays promiscuously blended, those qualified with red shall abound most in the reflected light, and by their prevalence cause it to appear of that colour. And for the same reason bise, reflecting blue most copiously, shall appear blue by the excess of those rays in its reflected light; and the like of other bodies. And that this is the entire and adequate cause of their colours, is manifest, because they have no power to change or alter the colours of any sort of rays incident apart, but put on all colours indifferently, with which they are enlighted.

These things being so, it can be no longer disputed, whether there be colours in the dark, or whether they be the qualities of the objects we see, no nor perhaps, whether light be a body. For, since colours are the qualities of light, having its rays for their entire and immediate subject, how can we think those rays qualities also, unless one quality may be the subject of, and sustain another; which in effect is to call it substance. We should not know bodies for substances; were it not for their sensible qualities, and the principal of those being now found due to something else, we have as good reason to believe that to be a substance also.

Besides, who ever thought any quality to be a heterogeneous aggregate, such as light is discovered to be? But to determine more absolutely what light is, after what manner refracted, and by what modes or actions it produceth in our minds the phantasms of colours, is not so easie; and I shall not mingle conjectures with certainties.

# CHRISTIAN HUYGENS
## 1629–95

### THE WAVE THEORY OF LIGHT
### IS SET FORTH

ALTHOUGH he was born in the Netherlands, Huygens was a close associate of a number of men with whom we are already familiar. A correspondent of Newton's, he was elected to membership of the Royal Society at the age of thirty-four and was thus given official recognition of his association with Newton, Halley, Boyle, and the rest of this most interesting group.

Huygens began his scientific work with the study of lenses, for the grinding and polishing of which he discovered better methods. As a result of this improvement, he was able to detect a satellite of Saturn and to observe more accurately the constellation of Orion. His studies in optics were paralleled by his work on the pendulum. Huygens determined the relation between the length of the pendulum and its period of vibration and developed the theory of evolutes. He applied his discovery about the pendulum to the regulation of clocks, making possible, for the first time, the construction of accurate time pieces. His theory of centrifugal forces in circular motion was of great help to Newton in the formulation of the latter's concepts of gravity. Huygens rejected Newton's theory of gravitation as a universal quality of matter, though he accepted his contemporary's explanation of planetary motions.

After some years of work in France, under the patronage of Louis XIV, Huygens returned to Holland and published the results of his studies on light. He made lenses of very great focal length and, like Newton, studied the refraction of light through prisms. As a result of his investigations, he evolved the wave theory of light. This theory presented Huygens with the problem of explaining shadows and the propagation of light in straight lines, which Newton achieved by resorting to a corpuscular theory. For this reason, and perhaps because of the greater prestige of Newton, Huygens's theory was ignored for a hundred years or so, until the study of his work by Thomas Young and Augustin Jean Fresnel revived interest in it. As work on the quantum theory was to show later, both Newton's and Huygens's theories were necessary to a full explanation of light.

In the following selection will be found a reference to Roemer (1644–1710). There was, at this time, uncertainty as to whether light had a finite velocity, and Roemer had made experiments in 1676, the results of which were not immediately accepted, which showed that light was not instantaneous but required time in which to travel. Roemer had observed the eclipses of the moons of Jupiter in two cases: when the earth was between the sun and Jupiter and when the earth was on the other side of the sun. The difference in the times observed was as much as fifteen minutes, which, if the moon's motions were uniform, would clearly indicate the time taken by light to travel the greater distance. These observations were used by Huygens in support of his wave theory, which stated that light was propagated in a pulse movement which could be subjected to mathematical analysis.

As a mathematical physicist, Huygens is considered as second only to Newton. Evidently, each owed much to each other, if only for the values derived from that scepticism of another's results which is the essence of scientific controversy.

The selection is from Huygens's *Traité de la lumière*, composed in France in 1678 but published in Holland in 1690 and translated by S. P. Thompson as *Treatise on Light* (1912).

---

§ *Preface*

I wrote this treatise during my sojourn in France twelve years ago, and I communicated it in the year 1678 to the learned persons who then composed the Royal Academy of

Science, to the membership of which the King had done me the honour of calling me. Several of that body who are still alive will remember having been present when I read it, and above the rest those amongst them who applied themselves particularly to the study of Mathematics; of whom I cannot cite more than the celebrated gentlemen Cassini, Römer, and De la Hire. And although I have since corrected and changed some parts, the copies which I had made of it at that time may serve for proof that I have yet added nothing to it save some conjectures touching the formation of Iceland Crystal, and a novel observation on the refraction of Rock Crystal. I have desired to relate these particulars to make known how long I have meditated the things which now I publish, and not for the purpose of detracting from the merit of those who, without having seen anything that I have written, may be found to have treated of like matters: as has in fact occurred to two eminent Geometricians, Messieurs Newton and Leibnitz, with respect to the Problem of the figure of glasses for collecting rays when one of the surfaces is given.

One may ask why I have so long delayed to bring this work to the light. The reason is that I wrote it rather carelessly in the Language in which it appears, with the intention of translating it into Latin, so doing in order to obtain greater attention to the thing. After which I proposed to myself to give it out along with another Treatise on Dioptrics, in which I explain the effects of Telescopes and those things which belong more to that Science. But the pleasure of novelty being past, I have put off from time to time the execution of this design, and I know not when I shall ever come to an end of it, being often turned aside either by business or by some new study. Considering which I have finally judged that it was better worth while to publish this writing, such as it is, than to let it run the risk, by waiting longer, of remaining lost.

There will be seen in it demonstrations of those kinds which do not produce as great a certitude as those of Geometry, and which even differ much therefrom, since whereas

the Geometers prove their Propositions by fixed and incon-
testable Principles, here the Principles are verified by the
conclusions to be drawn from them; the nature of these
things not allowing of this being done otherwise. It is always
possible to attain thereby to a degree of probability which
very often is scarcely less than complete proof. To wit, when
things which have been demonstrated by the Principles that
have been assumed correspond perfectly to the phenomena
which experiment has brought under observation; especially
when there are a great number of them, and further, principally, when one can imagine and foresee new phenomena
which ought to follow from the hypotheses which one employs, and when one finds that therein the fact corresponds
to our pre-vision. But if all these proofs of probability are met
with in that which I propose to discuss, as it seems to me
they are, this ought to be a very strong confirmation of the
success of my inquiry; and it must be ill if the facts are not
pretty much as I represent them. I would believe then that
those who love to know the Causes of things and who are
able to admire the marvels of Light, will find some satisfaction in these various speculations regarding it, and in the
new explanation of its famous property which is the main
foundation of the construction of our eyes and of those great
inventions which extend so vastly the use of them. I hope
also that there will be some who by following these beginnings will penetrate much further into this question than I
have been able to do, since the subject must be far from
being exhausted. This appears from the passages which I
have indicated where I leave certain difficulties without
having resolved them, and still more from matters which I
have not touched at all, such as Luminous Bodies of several
sorts, and all that concerns Colours; in which no one until
now can boast of having succeeded. Finally, there remains
much more to be investigated touching the nature of Light
which I do not pretend to have disclosed, and I shall owe
much in return to him who shall be able to supplement that
which is here lacking to me in knowledge. The Hague. The
8 January 1690.

¶ CHAPTER I *On Rays Propagated in Straight Lines*

As happens in all the sciences in which Geometry is applied to matter, the demonstrations concerning Optics are founded on truths drawn from experience. Such are that the rays of light are propagated in straight lines; that the angles of reflection and of incidence are equal; and that in refraction the ray is bent according to the law of sines, now so well known, and which is no less certain than the preceding laws.

The majority of those who have written touching the various parts of Optics have contented themselves with presuming these truths. But some, more inquiring, have desired to investigate the origin and the causes, considering these to be in themselves wonderful effects of Nature. In which they advanced some ingenious things, but not however such that the most intelligent folk do not wish for better and more satisfactory explanations. Wherefore I here desire to propound what I have meditated on the subject, so as to contribute as much as I can to the explanation of this department of Natural Science, which, not without reason, is reputed to be one of its most difficult parts. I recognize myself to be much indebted to those who were the first to begin to dissipate the strange obscurity in which these things were enveloped, and to give us hope that they might be explained by intelligible reasoning. But, on the other hand I am astonished also that even here these have often been willing to offer, as assured and demonstrative, reasonings which were far from conclusive. For I do not find that any one has yet given a probable explanation of the first and most notable phenomena of light, namely why it is not propagated except in straight lines, and how visible rays, coming from an infinitude of diverse places, cross one another without hindering one another in any way.

I shall therefore essay in this book, to give, in accordance with the principles accepted in the Philosophy of the present day, some clearer and more probable reasons, firstly of these properties of light propagated rectilinearly; secondly of light which is reflected on meeting other bodies. Then I shall explain the phenomena of those rays which are said to suffer refraction on passing through transparent bodies of different sorts; and in this part I shall also explain the effects of the refraction of the air by the different densities of the Atmosphere.

Thereafter I shall examine the causes of the strange refraction of a certain kind of Crystal which is brought from Iceland. And finally I shall treat of the various shapes of transparent and reflecting bodies by which rays are collected at a point or are turned aside in various ways. From this it will be seen with what facility, following our new Theory, we find not only the Ellipses, Hyperbolas, and other curves which Mr Des Cartes has ingeniously invented for this purpose; but also those which the surface of a glass lens ought to possess when its other surface is given as spherical or plane, or of any other figure that may be.

It is inconceivable to doubt that light consists in the motion of some sort of matter. For whether one considers its production, one sees that here upon the Earth it is chiefly engendered by fire and flame which contain without doubt bodies that are in rapid motion, since they dissolve and melt many other bodies, even the most solid; or whether one considers its effects, one sees that when light is collected, as by concave mirrors, it has the property of burning as a fire does, that is to say it disunites the particles of bodies. This is assuredly the mark of motion, at least in the true Philosophy, in which one conceives the causes of all natural effects in terms of mechanical motions. This, in my opinion, we must necessarily do, or else renounce all hopes of ever comprehending anything in Physics.

And as, according to this Philosophy, one holds as certain that the sensation of sight is excited only by the impression of some movement of a kind of matter which acts on the nerves at the back of our eyes, there is here yet one reason more for believing that light consists in a movement of the matter which exists between us and the luminous body.

Further, when one considers the extreme speed with which light spreads on every side, and how, when it comes from different regions, even from those directly opposite, the rays traverse one another without hindrance, one may well understand that when we see a luminous object, it cannot be by any transport of matter coming to us from this object, in the way in which a shot or an arrow traverses the air; for assuredly that would too greatly impugn these two properties of light, especially the second of them. It is then in some other way that light spreads; and that which can lead us to comprehend it is the knowledge which we have of the spreading of Sound in the air.

We know that by means of the air, which is an invisible and impalpable body, Sound spreads around the spot where it has been produced, by a movement which is passed on successively from one part of the air to another; and that the spreading of this movement, taking place equally rapidly on all sides, ought to form spherical surfaces ever enlarging and which strike our ears. Now there is no doubt at all that light also comes from the luminous body to our eyes by some movement impressed on the matter which is between the two; since, as we have already seen, it cannot be by the transport of a body which passes from one to the other. If, in addition, light takes time for its passage – which we are now going to examine – it will follow that this movement, impressed on the intervening matter, is successive; and consequently it spreads, as Sound does, by spherical surfaces and waves: for I call them waves from their resemblance to those which are seen to be formed in water when a stone is thrown into it, and which present a successive spreading as circles, though these arise from another cause, and are only in a flat surface.

To see then whether the spreading of light takes time, let us consider first whether there are any facts of experience which can convince us to the contrary. As to those which can be made here on the Earth, by striking lights at great distances, although they prove that light takes no sensible time to pass over these distances, one may say with good reason that they are too small, and that the only conclusion to be drawn from them is that the passage of light is extremely rapid. Mr Des Cartes, who was of opinion that it is instantaneous, founded his views, not without reason, upon a better basis of experience, drawn from the Eclipses of the Moon; which, nevertheless, as I shall show, is not at all convincing. I will set it forth, in a way a little different from his, in order to make the conclusion more comprehensible.

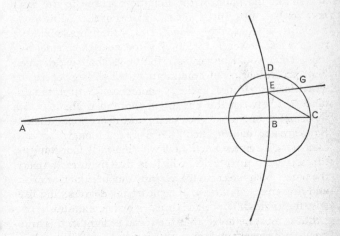

Fig.1

Let *A* be the place of the sun, *BD* a part of the orbit or annual path of the Earth: *ABC* a straight line which I suppose to meet the orbit of the Moon, which is represented by the circle *CD*, at *C*.

Now if light requires time, for example one hour, to traverse the space which is between the Earth and the Moon, it will follow that the Earth having arrived at *B*, the shadow which it casts, or the interruption of the light, will not yet have arrived at the point *C*, but will only arrive there an hour after. It will then be one hour after, reckoning from the moment when the Earth was at *B*, that the Moon, arriving at *C*, will be obscured: but this obscuration or interruption of the light will not reach the Earth till after another hour. Let us suppose that the Earth in these two hours will have arrived at $E$. The Earth then, being at $E$, will see the Eclipsed Moon at $C$, which it left an hour before, and at the same time will see the sun at $A$. For it being immovable, as I suppose with Copernicus, and the light moving always in straight lines, it must always appear where it is. But one has always observed, we are told, that the eclipsed Moon appears at the point of the Ecliptic opposite to the Sun; and yet here it would appear in arrear of that point by an amount equal to the angle $GEC$, the supplement of $AEC$. This, however, is contrary to experience, since the angle $GEC$ would be very sensible, and about 33 degrees. Now according to our computation, which is given in the Treatise on the causes of the phenomena of Saturn, the distance $BA$ between the Earth and the Sun is about twelve thousand diameters of the Earth, and hence four hundred times greater than $BC$ the distance of the Moon, which is 30 diameters. Then the angle $ECB$ will be nearly four hundred times greater than $BAE$, which is five minutes; namely, the path which the earth travels in two hours along its orbit; and thus the angle $BCE$ will be nearly 33 degrees; and likewise the angle $CEG$, which is greater by five minutes.

But it must be noted that the speed of light in this argument has been assumed such that it takes a time of one hour to make the passage from here to the Moon. If one supposes that for this it requires only one minute of time, then it is manifest that the angle $CEG$ will only be 33 minutes; and if it requires only ten seconds of time, the angle will be less than six minutes. And then it will not be easy to perceive anything of it in observations of the Eclipse; nor, consequently, will it be permissible to deduce from it that the movement of light is instantaneous.

It is true that we are here supposing a strange velocity that would be a hundred thousand times greater than that of Sound. For Sound, according to what I have observed, travels about 180 Toises in the time of one Second, or in about one beat of the pulse. But this supposition ought not to seem an impossibility; since it is not a question of the transport of a body with so great a speed, but of a successive movement which is passed on from some bodies to others. I have then made no difficulty, in meditating on these things, in supposing that the emanation of light is accomplished with time, seeing that in this way all its phenomena can be explained, and that in following the contrary opinion everything is incomprehensible. For it has always seemed to me that even Mr Des Cartes, whose aim has been to treat all the subjects of Physics intelligibly, and who assuredly has succeeded in this better than anyone before him, has said nothing that is not full of difficulties, or even inconceivable, in dealing with Light and its properties.

But that which I employed only as a hypothesis, has recently received great seemingness as an established truth by the ingenious proof of Mr Römer which I am going here to relate, expecting him himself to give all that is needed for its confirmation. It is founded as is the preceding argument upon celestial observations, and proves not only that Light takes time for its passage, but also demonstrates how much time it takes, and that its velocity is even at least six times greater than that which I have just stated.

For this he makes use of the Eclipses suffered by the little planets which revolve around Jupiter, and which often enter his shadow: and see what is his reasoning. Let $A$ be the Sun, $BCDE$ the annual orbit of the Earth, $F$ Jupiter, $GN$ the orbit of the nearest of his Satellites, for it is this one which is more apt for this investigation than any of the other three, because of the quickness of its revolution. Let $G$ be this Satellite entering into the shadow of Jupiter, $H$ the same Satellite emerging from the shadow.

Let it be then supposed, the Earth being at $B$ some time before the last quadrature, that one has seen the said Satellite emerge from the shadow; it must needs be, if the Earth remains at the same place, that, after $42\frac{1}{2}$ hours, one would again see a similar emergence, because that is the time in which it makes the round of its orbit, and when it would come again into opposition to the Sun. And if the Earth, for instance, were to remain always at $B$ during 30 revolutions of this Satellite, one would see it again emerge from the

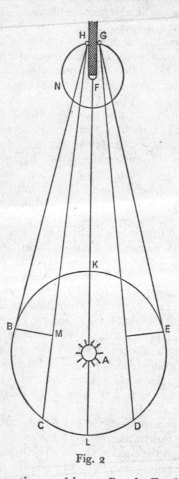

Fig. 2

shadow after 30 times 42½ hours. But the Earth having been carried along during this time to *C*, increasing thus its distance from Jupiter, it follows that if Light requires time for its passage the illumination of the little planet will be perceived later at *C* than it would have been at *B*, and that there must be added to this time of 30 times 42½ hours that which the Light has required to traverse the space *MC*, the difference of the spaces *CH*, *BH*. Similarly at the other quadrature when the earth has come to *E* from *D* while approaching toward Jupiter, the immersions of the Satellite ought to be observed at *E* earlier than they would have been seen if the Earth had remained at *D*.

Now in quantities of observations of these Eclipses, made during ten consecutive years, these differences have been found to be very considerable, such as ten minutes and more; and from them it has been concluded that in order to traverse the whole diameter of the annual orbit *KL*, which is double the distance from here to the sun, Light requires about 22 minutes of time.

The movement of Jupiter in his orbit while the Earth passed from *B* to *C*, or from *D* to *E*, is included in this calculation; and this makes it evident that one cannot attribute the retardation of these illuminations or the anticipation of the eclipses, either to any irregularity occurring in the movement of the little planet or to its eccentricity.

If one considers the vast size of the diameter *KL*, which according to me is some 24 thousand diameters of the Earth, one will acknowledge the extreme velocity of Light. For, supposing that *KL* is no more than 22 thousand of these diameters, it appears that being traversed in 22 minutes this makes the speed a thousand diameters in one minute, that is 16⅔ diameters in one second or in one beat of the pulse, which makes more than eleven hundred times a hundred thousand toises; since the diameter of the Earth contains 2,865 leagues, reckoned at 25 to the degree, and each league is 2,282 Toises, according to the exact measurement which Mr Picard made by order of the King in 1669. But Sound, as I have said above, only travels 180 toises in the same time of one second: hence the velocity of Light is more than six hundred thousand times greater than that of Sound. This, however, is quite another thing from being instantaneous, since there is all the difference between a finite thing and an infinite. Now the successive movement of Light being confirmed in this way, it follows, as I have said, that it spreads by spherical waves, like the movement of Sound.

But if the one resembles the other in this respect, they differ in many other things; to wit, in the first production of the movement which causes them; in the matter in which the movement spreads; and in the manner in which it is propagated. As to that which occurs in the production of Sound, one knows that it is occasioned by the agitation undergone by an entire body, or by a considerable part of one, which shakes all the contiguous air. But the movement of the Light must originate as from each point of the luminous object, else we should not be able to perceive all the different parts of that object, as will be more evident in that which follows. And I do not believe that this movement can be better explained than by supposing that all those of the luminous bodies which are liquid, such as flames, and apparently the sun and the stars, are composed of particles which float in a much more subtle medium which agitates them with great rapidity, and makes them strike against the particles of the ether which surrounds them, and which are much smaller than they. But I hold also that in luminous solids such as charcoal or metal made red hot in the fire, this same movement is caused by the violent agitation of the particles of the metal or of the wood; those of them which are on the surface striking similarly against the ethereal matter. The agitation, moreover, of the particles which engender the light ought to be much more prompt and more rapid than is that of the bodies which cause sound, since we do not see that the tremors of a body which is giving out a sound are capable of giving rise to Light, even as the movement of the hand in the air is not capable of producing Sound.

Now if one examines what this matter may be in which the movement coming from the luminous body is propagated, which I call Ethereal matter, one will see that it is not the same that serves for the propagation of Sound. For one finds that the latter is really that which we feel and which we breathe, and which being removed from any place still leaves there the other kind of matter that serves to convey Light. This may be proved by shutting up a sounding body in a glass vessel from which the air is withdrawn by the machine which Mr Boyle has given us, and with which he has performed so many beautiful experiments. But in doing this of which I speak, care must be taken to place the sounding body on cotton or on feathers, in such a way that it cannot communicate its tremors either to the glass vessel which encloses it, or to the machine; a precaution which has hitherto been neglected. For then after having exhausted all the air one hears no Sound from the metal, though it is struck.

One sees here not only that our air, which does not penetrate through glass, is the matter by which Sound spreads; but also that it is not the same air but another kind of matter in which Light spreads; since if the air is removed from the vessel the Light does not cease to traverse it as before.

And this last point is demonstrated even more clearly by the celebrated experiment of Torricelli, in which the tube of glass from which the quicksilver has withdrawn itself, remaining void of air, transmits Light just the same as when air is in it. For this proves that a matter different from air exists in this tube, and that this matter must have penetrated the glass or the quicksilver, either one or the other, though they are both impenetrable to the air. And when, in the same experiment, one makes the vacuum after putting a little water above the quicksilver, one concludes equally that the said matter passes through glass or water, or through both.

As regards the different modes in which I have said the movements of Sound and of Light are communicated, one may sufficiently comprehend how this occurs in the case of Sound if one considers that the air is of such a nature that it can be compressed and reduced to a much smaller space than that which it ordinarily occupies. And in proportion as it is compressed the more does it exert an effort to regain its volume; for this property along with its penetrability, which remains notwithstanding its compression, seems to prove that it is made up of small bodies which float about and which are agitated very rapidly in the ethereal matter composed of much smaller parts. So that the cause of the spreading of Sound is the effort which these little bodies make in collisions with one another, to regain freedom when they are a little more squeezed together in the circuit of these waves than elsewhere.

But the extreme velocity of Light, and other properties which it has, cannot admit of such a propagation of motion, and I am about to show here the way in which I conceive it must occur. For this, it is needful to explain the property which hard bodies must possess to transmit movement from one to another.

When one takes a number of spheres of equal size, made of some very hard substance, and arranges them in a straight line, so that they touch one another, one finds, on striking with a similar sphere against the first of these spheres, that the motion passes as in an instant to the last of them, which separates itself from the row, without one's being able to perceive that the others have been stirred. And even that one which was used to strike remains motionless with them. Whence one sees that the movement passes with an extreme velocity which is the greater, the greater the hardness of the substance of the spheres.

But it is still certain that this progression of motion is not instantaneous, but successive, and therefore must take time. For if the movement, or the disposition to movement, if you will have it so, did not pass successively through all these spheres, they would all acquire the movement at the same time, and hence would all advance together; which does not happen. For the last one leaves the whole row and acquires the speed of the one which was pushed. Moreover there are experiments which demonstrate that all the bodies which we reckon of the hardest kind, such as quenched steel, glass, and agate, act as springs and bend somehow, not only when extended as rods but also when they are in the form of spheres or of other shapes. That is to say they yield a little in themselves at the place where they are struck, and immediately regain their former figure. For I have found that on striking with a ball of glass or of agate against a large and quite thick piece of the same substance which had a flat surface, slightly soiled with breath or in some other way, there remained round marks, of smaller or larger size according as the blow had been weak or strong. This makes it evident that these substances yield where they meet, and spring back: and for this time must be required.

*

I have then shown in what manner one may conceive Light to spread successively, by spherical waves, and how it is possible that this spreading is accomplished with as great a velocity as that which experiments and celestial observations demand. Whence it may be further remarked that although the particles are supposed to be in continual movement (for there are many reasons for this) the successive propagation of the waves cannot be hindered by this; because the propagation consists nowise in the transport of those particles but merely in a small agitation which they cannot help communicating to those surrounding, notwithstanding any movement which may act on them causing them to be changing positions amongst themselves.

But we must consider still more particularly the origin of these waves, and the manner in which they spread. And, first, it follows from what has been said on the production of Light, that each little region of a luminous body, such as the Sun, a candle, or a burning coal, generates its own waves of which that region is the centre. Thus in the flame of a candle, having distinguished the points $A$, $B$, $C$, concentric circles described about each of these points represent the waves which come from them. And one must imagine the same about every point of the surface and of the part within the flame.

But as the percussions at the centres of these waves possess no regular succession, it must not be supposed that the waves themselves follow one another at equal distances:

and if the distances marked in the figure appear to be such, it is rather to mark the progression of one and the same wave at equal intervals of time than to represent several of them issuing from one and the same centre.

After all, this prodigious quantity of waves which traverse one another without confusion and without effacing one another must not be deemed inconceivable; it being certain that one and the same particle of matter can serve for many waves coming from different sides or even from contrary directions, not only if it is struck by blows which follow one another closely but even for those which act on it at the same instant. It can do so because the spreading of the movement is successive. This may be proved by the row of equal spheres of hard matter, spoken of above. If against this row there are pushed from two opposite sides at the same time two similar spheres A and D, one will see each of them rebound with the same velocity which it had in striking, yet the whole row will remain in its place, although the movement has passed along its whole length twice over. And if these contrary movements happen to meet one another at the middle sphere, B, or at some other such as C, that sphere will yield and act as a spring at both sides, and so will serve at the same instant to transmit these two movements.

But what may at first appear full strange and even incredible is that the undulations produced by such small movements and corpuscles, should spread to such immense distances; as for example from the Sun or from the Stars to us. For the force of these waves must grow feeble in proportion as they move away from their origin, so that the action of each one in particular will without doubt become incapable of making itself felt to our sight. But one will cease to be astonished by considering how at a great distance from the luminous body an infinitude of waves, though they have issued from different points of this body, unite together in such a way that they sensibly compose one single wave only, which, consequently, ought to have enough force to make itself felt. Thus this infinite number of waves which originate at the same instant from all points of a fixed star, big it may be as the Sun, make practically only one single wave which may well have force enough to produce an impression on our eyes. Moreover from each luminous point there may come many thousands of waves in the smallest imaginable time, by the frequent percussion of the corpuscles which strike the Ether at these points: which further contributes to rendering their action more sensible.

# WILLIAM GILBERT

## 1540–1603

## THE SCIENCE OF ELECTRICITY AND MAGNETISM IS INITIATED

WHILE Francis Bacon was developing his ideas about the virtues of the experimental method, William Gilbert was actually laying its foundations by intensive experimentation. Gilbert's researches began in medicine, in which he was distinguished enough to be a member of the committee appointed to prepare a pharmacopoeia (published in 1618, after his death) and to be Court Physician to Queen Elizabeth I.

Gilbert's major work, *De magnete* (from which this selection has been taken, translated by E. F. Mottelay), published in 1600, did more than show the usefulness of experiment; it established magnetism and electricity as sciences, influencing thought on these subjects down to the time of Michael Faraday (1791–1867). The magnetic needle, which was invented by the Chinese in the eleventh century and introduced to Western navigation by Mediterranean sailors in the twelfth century, may have stimulated Gilbert's inquiries and experiments. He had first to overcome the superstitions which were associated with the lodestone and provide a reasonable explanation for magnetic phenomena. He detected the poles of a magnet and discovered the magnetic field of force. From these ideas and his experiments with a spherical magnet (a *terella*), Gilbert arrived at the hypothesis that the earth itself is a gigantic magnet, a hypothesis which would explain the tendency of the compass needle to turn towards the north. In some of this work, Gilbert was, in fact, reviving some thirteenth-century studies of Peter Peregrinus, who described the 'poles' of strongest attraction which attracted needles. Moreover, in his application of this idea to explain the planetary motions,

Gilbert followed the general theories of Giordano Bruno (1547–1600).

Gilbert distinguished between electricity and magnetism, but his explanation was inaccurate and took him into metaphysics; for him electricity was a force binding the particles of matter together. He made many experiments based on a fact which had been observed even in antiquity: that when a piece of amber was rubbed in the proper way it developed the power to attract objects to it. Thus Gilbert introduced the word *electricity* into our language (from the Greek word meaning amber). He observed the differences between what we now call conductors and insulators, though he got no further than describing the two types of material as *electrics* and *non-electrics*.

Gilbert accepted the Copernican theory and tried to explain the rotation of the earth as the result of its magnetic character. However, it is as an experimenter that we read Gilbert today, impressed by his great skill and imagination.

¶ *The Loadstone Possesses Parts Differing in Their Natural Powers, And Has Poles Conspicuous For Their Properties*

The many qualities exhibited by the loadstone itself, qualities hitherto recognized yet not well investigated, are to be pointed out in the first place, to the end the student may understand the powers of the loadstone and of iron, and not be confused through want of knowledge at the threshold of the arguments and demonstrations. In the heavens, astronomers give to each moving sphere two poles; thus do we find two natural poles of excelling importance even in our terrestrial globe, constant points related to the movement of its daily revolution, to wit, one pole pointing to Arctos (Ursa) and the north; the other looking towards the opposite part of the heavens. In like manner the loadstone has from nature its two poles, a northern and a southern; fixed, definite points in the stone, which are the primary termini of the movements and effects, and the limits and regulators of the several actions and properties. It is to be understood, however, that not from a mathematical point does the force of the stone emanate, but from the parts themselves; and all these parts in the whole – while they belong to the whole – the nearer they are to the poles of the stone, the stronger virtues do they acquire and pour out on other bodies. These poles look towards the poles of the earth, and move towards them, and are subject to them. The magnetic poles may be found in every loadstone, whether strong and powerful (male, as the term was in antiquity) or faint, weak, and female; whether its shape is due to design or to chance, and whether it be long, or flat, or four-square, or three-cornered, or polished; whether it be rough, broken-off, or unpolished: the loadstone ever has and ever shows its pole. . . .

¶ *One Loadstone Appears to Attract Another In The Natural Position; But In The Opposite Position Repels It And Brings It To Rights*

First we have to describe in popular language the potent and familiar properties of the stone; afterwards, very many subtle properties, as yet recondite and unknown, being involved in obscurities, are to be unfolded; and the causes of all these (nature's secrets being unlocked) are in their place to be demonstrated in fitting words and with the aid of apparatus. The fact is trite and familiar, that the loadstone attracts iron; in the same way, too, one loadstone attracts another. Take the stone on which you have designated the poles, *N.* and *S.*, and put it in its vessel so that it may float; let the poles lie just in the plane of the horizon, or at least in a plane not very oblique to it; take in your hand another stone the poles of which are also known, and hold it so that its south pole shall lie towards the north pole of the floating stone, and near it alongside; the floating loadstone will straightway follow the other (provided it be within the range and dominion of its powers), nor does it cease to move nor does it quit the other till it clings to it, unless by moving your hand away, you manage skilfully to prevent the conjunction.

In like manner, if you oppose the north pole of the stone in your hand to the south pole of the floating one, they come together and follow each other. For opposite poles attract opposite poles. But, now, if in the same way you present *N.* to *N.* or *S.* to *S.*, one stone repels the other; and as though a helmsman were bearing on the rudder it is off like a vessel making all sail, nor stands nor stays as long as the other stone pursues. One stone also will range the other, turn the other around, bring it to right about, and make it come to agreement with itself. But when the two come together and are conjoined in nature's order, they cohere firmly. For example, if you present the north pole of the stone in your hand to ... any point between the equator and the south pole: immediately the floating stone turns round and so places itself that its south pole touches the north pole of the other and is most closely joined to it.

In the same way you will get like effect at the other side of the equator by presenting pole to pole; and thus by art and contrivance we exhibit attraction and repulsion, and motion in a circle towards the concordant position, and the same movements to avoid hostile meetings. Furthermore, in one same stone we are thus able to demonstrate all this: but also we are able to show how the self-same part of one stone may by division become either north or south. Take the oblong stone *ad* in which *a* is the north pole and *d* the south. Cut the stone in two equal parts, and put part *a* in a vessel and let it float in water.

You will find that *a*, the north point, will turn to the south* as before; and in like manner the point *d* will move to the north, in the divided stone, as before division. But *b* and *c*, before connected, now separated from each other, are not what they were before, *b* is now south while *c* is north; *b* attracts *c*, longing for union and for restoration of the original continuity. They are two stones made out of one,

* [Today we name the poles the other way. The 'north pole' of a magnet is the 'north-seeking' pole.]

and on that account the *c* of one turning towards the *b* of the other, they are mutually attracted, and being freed from all impediments and from their own weight, borne as they are on the surface of the water, they come together and into conjunction. But if you bring the part or point *a* up to *c* of the other, they repel one another and turn away; for by such a position of the parts nature is crossed and the form of the stone is perverted: but nature observes strictly the laws it has imposed upon bodies: hence the flight of one part from the undue position of the other, and hence the discord unless everything is arranged exactly according to nature. And nature will not suffer an unjust and inequitable peace, or agreement, but makes war and employs force to make bodies acquiesce fairly and justly. Hence, when rightly arranged the parts attract each other, i.e., both stones, the weaker and the stronger, come together and with all their might tend to union: a fact manifest in all loadstones, and not, as Pliny supposed, only in those from Ethiopia.

The Ethiopic stones if strong, and those brought from China, which are all powerful stones, show the effect most quickly and most plainly, attract with most force in the parts nighest the pole, and keep turning till pole looks straight on pole. The pole of a stone has strongest attraction for that part of another stone which answers to it (the *adverse* as it is called); e.g., the north pole of one has strongest attraction for, has the most vigorous pull on, the south part of another; so too it attracts iron more powerfully, and iron clings to it more firmly, whether previously magnetized or not. Thus it has been settled by nature, not without reason, that the parts nigher the pole shall have the greatest attractive force; and that in the pole itself shall be the seat, the throne as it were, of a high and splendid power; and that magnetic bodies brought near thereto shall be attracted most powerfully and relinquished with most reluctance. So, too, the poles are readiest to spurn and drive away what is presented to them amiss, and what is inconformable and foreign. ...

¶ *Of Magnetic Coition; And, First, Of The Attraction Exerted By Amber, or More Properly The Attachment of Bodies to Amber*

Great has ever been the fame of the loadstone and of amber in the writings of the learned: many philosophers cite the loadstone and also amber whenever, in explaining mysteries, their minds become obfuscated and reason can no farther go. Over-inquisitive theologians, too, seek to light up God's mysteries and things beyond man's understanding by means of the loadstone as a sort of Delphic sword and as an illustration of all sorts of things. Medical men also (at the bidding of Galen), in proving that purgative medicines exercise attraction through likeness of substance and kinships of juices (a silly error and gratuitous!), bring in as a witness the loadstone, a substance of great authority and of noteworthy efficiency, and a body of no common order.

Thus in very many affairs persons who plead for a cause the merits of which they cannot set forth, bring in as masked advocates the loadstone and amber. But all these, besides sharing the general misapprehension, are ignorant that the causes of the loadstone's movements are very different from those which give to amber its properties; hence they easily fall into errors, and by their own imaginings are led farther and farther astray. For in other bodies is seen a considerable power of attraction, differing from that of the loadstone – in amber, for example. Of this substance a few words must be said, to show the nature of the attachment of bodies to it, and to point out the vast difference between this and the magnetic actions; for men still continue in ignorance, and deem that inclination of bodies to amber to be an attraction, and comparable to the magnetic coition. . . .

The ancients as well as moderns tell (and their report is confirmed by experience) that amber attracts straws and chaff. The same is done by jet, a stone taken out of the earth in Britain, Germany, and many other regions: it is a hard concretion of black bitumen – a sort of transformation of bitumen to stone. Many modern authors have written about amber and jet as attracting chaff and about other facts unknown to the generality, or have copied from other writers; with the results of their labours booksellers' shops are crammed full. Our generation has produced many volumes about recondite, abstruse, and occult causes and wonders, and in all of them amber and jet are represented as attracting chaff; but never a proof from experiments, never a demonstration do you find in them. The writers deal only in words that involve in thicker darkness subject-matter; they treat the subject esoterically, miracle-mongeringly, abstrusely, reconditely, mystically.

Hence such philosophy bears no fruit; for it rests simply on a few Greek or unusual terms – just as our barbers toss off a few Latin words in the hearing of the ignorant rabble in token of their learning, and thus win reputation – bears

A blacksmith pounds a glowing iron bar which is held so that its ends point north (*septentrio*) and south (*auster*). In this way the bar is magnetized. From William Gilbert's *De Magnete*, London, 1600.

no fruit, because few of the philosophers themselves are investigators, or have any first-hand acquaintance with things; most of them are indolent and untrained, add nothing to knowledge by their writings, and are blind to the things that might throw a light upon their reasonings. For not only do amber and jet, as they suppose attract light substances: the same is done by diamond, sapphire, carbuncle, iris stone, opal, amethyst, vincentina, Bristol stone, beryl, rock crystal. Like powers of attracting are possessed by glass, especially clear, brilliant glass; by artificial gems made of (paste), glass, or rock crystal, antimony glass, many fluor-spars, and belemnites. Sulphur also attracts, and likewise mastich, and sealing-wax (of lac), hard resin, orpiment (weakly). Feeble power of attraction is also possessed in favouring dry atmosphere by sal gemma [native chloride of sodium], mica, rock alum. This we may observe when in mid winter the atmosphere is very cold, clear, and thin; when the electrical effluvia of the earth offers less impediment, and electric bodies are harder: of all this later. These several bodies (electric) not only draw to themselves straws and chaff, but all metals, wood, leaves, stones, earths, even water and oil; in short, whatever things appeal to our senses or are solid: yet we are told that it attracts nothing but chaff and twigs. Hence Alexander Aphrodiseus incorrectly declares the question of amber to be unsolvable, because that amber does attract chaff, yet not the leaves of basil; but such stories are false, disgracefully inaccurate.

Now in order clearly to understand by experience how such attraction takes place, and what those substances may be that so attract other bodies (and in the case of many of these electrical substances, though the bodies influenced by them lean towards them, yet because of the feebleness of the attraction they are not drawn clean up to them, but are easily made to rise), make yourself a rotating-needle (electroscope – *versorium*) of any sort of metal, three or four fingers long, pretty light, and poised on a sharp point after the manner of a magnetic pointer. Bring near to one end of it a piece of amber or a gem, lightly rubbed, polished, and shining: at once the instrument revolves. Several objects are seen to attract not only natural objects, but things artificially prepared, or manufactured, or formed by mixture. Nor is this a rare property possessed by one object or two (as is commonly supposed), but evidently belongs to a multitude of objects, both simple and compound, e.g., sealing-wax and other unctuous mixtures. But why this inclination and what these forces – on which points a few writers have given a very small amount of information, while the common run of philosophers give us nothing – these questions must be considered fully. . . .

———

# BENJAMIN FRANKLIN
## 1706–90

### THE FAMOUS KITE EXPERIMENT
### IS DESCRIBED

IT is worth remembering, in these days of international science, that Benjamin Franklin, a leader in the struggle for the independence of the United States, was, for most of his life, an international scientist. Most of his discoveries were communicated, through his friend Peter Collinson, to the Royal Society in London and so to the world. The Royal Society honoured him with its Copley medal in 1753 and three years later elected him to a fellowship.

Franklin began his career as a printer's apprentice in Philadelphia, worked as a compositor in London, and later became a successful publisher in the United States. His interest in scientific matters was concentrated in the period before 1737, for after that date he became too involved in political affairs to have much time for scientific pursuits.

Franklin's experimentation with electricity arose during a period of intense excitement over the effects which could be produced by the so-called electrical machines. These reproduced, in effect, the events caused by rubbing a glass rod with silk – or by rubbing an ebonite rod with fur: in either case, light particles of matter would be attracted to the charged rod. What puzzled the earlier experimenters in their attempts to explain the nature of electricity was the phenomenon we now describe as positive or negative charge. Two glass rods charged by rubbing would repel each other; as would two ebonite rods after rubbing with fur; but if brought into proximity, a glass rod and an ebonite one, both charged, would attract each other. This could be accounted for only by assuming that there were two kinds of electricity, the one distinct and opposite from the other. Franklin, on the other hand, came to the conclusion that there was but a single 'electric fluid'. This was found in all bodies but in varying quantities, a body having an excess quantity being positively charged; one with a relatively smaller quantity being negatively charged. There were 'extremely subtle' particles of electrical matter and also of common matter. The former repelled each other but were attracted by common matter, which was capable of absorbing electrical particles until it reached a state in which the electrical matter lay on the surface of the body as an 'electrical atmosphere'. Franklin used his theory to explain the functioning of the Leyden jar and the condenser.

Franklin's later and best known work was concerned with explaining the similarity between static electricity (as developed by the primitive machines of the period) and lightning. Franklin's suggestion of the lightning conductor (which was first applied experimentally by French readers of Franklin's communications to the Royal Society) was followed by the direct experiment described in the reading that follows. Though he was not the first to see the connexion between the electric 'shock' and the 'thunderbolt', Franklin was the first to offer formal evidence on the subject. After the experiment here described, taken from his *Experiments and Observations on Electricity*, he discovered that the charge in a thunder cloud can sometimes be positive and sometimes negative.

¶ *The Kite Experiment*

PETER COLLINSON, ESQ., F. R. S. LONDON
16 Oct. 1752

SIR:

As frequent mention is made in public papers from Europe of the success of the Philadelphia experiment for drawing the electric fire from clouds by means of pointed rods of iron erected on high buildings, etc., it may be agreeable to the curious to be informed that the same experiment has succeeded in Philadelphia, though made in a different and more easy manner, which is as follows:

Make a small cross of two light strips of cedar, the arms so long as to reach the four corners of a large thin silk handkerchief when extended; tie the corners of the handkerchief to the extremities of the cross, so you have the body of a kite; which being properly accommodated with a tail, loop, and string, will rise in the air, like those made of paper; but this being of silk is fitter to bear the wet and wind of a thunder gust without tearing. To the top of the upright stick of the cross is to be fixed a very sharp pointed wire, rising a foot or more above the wood. To the end of the twine, next the hand, is to be tied a silk ribbon, and where the silk and twine join, a key may be fastened. This kite is to be raised when a thunder gust appears to be coming on, and the person who holds the string must stand within a door or window, or under some cover, so that the silk ribbon may not be wet; and care must be taken that the twine does not touch the frame of the door or window. As soon as any of the thunder clouds come over the kite, the pointed wire will draw the electric fire from them, and the kite, with all the twine, will be electrified, and the loose filaments of the twine will stand out every way, and be attracted by an approaching finger. And when the rain has wet the kite and twine, so that it can conduct the electric fire freely, you will find it stream out plentifully from the key on the approach of your knuckle. At this key the phial may be charged; and from electric fire thus obtained, spirits may be kindled, and all the other electric experiments be performed, which are usually done by the help of a rubbed glass globe or tube, and thereby the sameness of the electric matter with that of lightning completely demonstrated.

B. FRANKLIN

# CHARLES AUGUSTIN COULOMB
## 1736–1806

### THE ELECTRIC AND MAGNETIC
### FORCES ARE MEASURED

CHARLES AUGUSTIN COULOMB was born in Angoulême, in the south of France, and studied science and mathematics in Paris. On completing his studies he entered a technical branch of the army, and during his service he spent nine years in Martinique supervising the building of fortifications there. Failing health forced him to return to France and his new-found leisure was devoted to scientific investigation. His range of interests was wide, and in addition to electricity and magnetism, he made important contributions to the study of the elasticity of materials and to the subject of friction. There followed a rise to eminence in the French academic world, but with the great social upheavals which accompanied the French Revolution Coulomb retired to his estate, near Blois, and pursued his research in peace. With the restoration of social order he returned to Paris to resume his former posts and worked there until his death at the age of seventy.

Coulomb's famous measurements on the forces between electrically charged bodies, and between magnetic bodies, are distinguished not by historical priority, but rather for the precision of his techniques. There are several claimants to the title of the discoverer of the force between two charged bodies. Certainly Coulomb had been anticipated by the great English physicist and chemist Henry Cavendish (1731–1810) who obtained the same law in 1771, fourteen years before Coulomb announced his results. Cavendish, however, had failed to publish his work and it was not until the investigation of his posthumous papers that his achievement came to light.

Coulomb's claim to fame is nonetheless well founded. The

accuracy of his work provided a firm foundation for the mathematical theories which rapidly transformed a subject which had more than its share of confusion into an important and growing branch of physics. The success of these experiments, which are described in the following reading taken from Magie's *A Sourcebook in Physics* (McGraw-Hill Book Co., 1935) and which first appeared in the Mémoires de l'Académie Royale des Sciences for 1785, was due to the fact that Coulomb was able to use a sensitive torsion balance, an instrument of his own construction, the principles of which were based on his earlier work on the twisting of wires.

The greatness of Coulomb's work was to receive appropriate recognition when, in later years, the unit of electric charge was named the 'coulomb'.

———

§ LAW OF ELECTRIC FORCE – *Construction and use of an electric balance based on the properties of metallic wires, having a force of reaction of torsion proportional to the angle of torsion.*

*Experimental determination of the law according to which the elements of bodies electrified with the same kind of electricity repel each other.*

In a memoir presented to the Academy in 1784, I determined by experiment the laws of the force of torsion of a metallic wire, and I found that this force was in a ratio compounded of the angle of torsion, of the fourth power of the diameter of the suspended wire, and of the reciprocal of its length, all being multiplied by a constant coefficient which depends on the nature of the metal and which is easy to determine by experiment.

I showed in the same memoir that by using this force of torsion it was possible to measure with precision very small forces, as for example, a ten thousandth of a grain. I gave in the same memoir an application of this theory, by attempting to measure the constant force attributed to adhesion in the formula which expresses the friction of the surface of a solid body in motion in a fluid.

I submit today to the Academy an electric balance constructed on the same principle; it measures very exactly the state and the electric force of a body however slightly it is charged.

## § *Construction of Balance*

Although I have learned by experience that to carry out several electric experiments in a convenient way I should correct some defects in the first balance of this sort which I have made; nevertheless as it is so far the only one that I have used I shall give its description, simply remarking that its form and size may be and should be changed according to the nature of the experiments that one is planning to make. The first figure represents this balance in perspective and the details of it are as follows:

On a glass cylinder *ABCD* (Fig. I) 12 inches in diameter and 12 inches high is placed a glass plate 13 inches in diameter, which entirely covers the glass vessel; this plate is pierced with two holes of about twenty lines in diameter, one of them in the middle, at *f*, above which is placed a glass tube 24 inches high; this tube is cemented over the hole *f* with the cement ordinarily used in electrical apparatus: at the upper end of the tube at *h* is placed a torsion micrometer which is seen in detail in figure 2. The upper part, No. 1, carries the milled head *b*, the index *io*, and the clamp *q*; this piece fits into the hole *G* of the piece No. 2; this piece No. 2 is made up of a circle *ab* divided on its edge into 360 degrees and of a copper tube *Φ* which fits into the tube *H*, No. 3, sealed to the interior of the upper end of the glass tube or column *fh* of figure 1. The clamp *q* (Fig. I, 2, No. 1), is shaped much like the end of a solid crayon holder, which is closed by means of the ring *q*. In this holder is clamped the end of a very fine silver wire; the other end of the silver wire (Fig. I, 3) is held at *P* in a clamp made of a cylinder *Po* of copper or iron with a diameter of not more than a line, whose upper end *P* is split so as to form a clamp which is

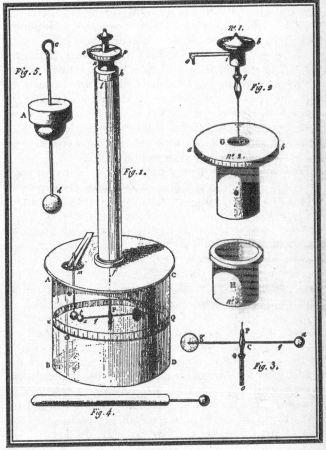

Fig. 5.

Fig. 1.

Fig. 2.

n° 1.

n° 2.

H

n°

Fig. 3.

Fig. 4.

Fig. I

closed by means of the sliding piece $\Phi$. This small cylinder is enlarged at $C$ and a hole bored through it, in which can be inserted (Fig. I, 1) the needle $ag$: the weight of this little cylinder should be sufficiently great to keep the silver wire stretched without breaking it. The needle that is shown (Fig. I, 1) at $ag$ suspended horizontally about half-way up in the large vessel which encloses it, is formed either of a silk thread soaked in Spanish wax or of a straw likewise soaked in Spanish wax and finished off from $q$ to $a$ for eighteen lines of its length by a cylindrical rod of shellac; at the end $a$ of this needle is carried a little pith ball two or three lines in diameter; at $g$ there is a little vertical piece of paper soaked in terebinth, which serves as a counterweight for the ball $a$ and which slows down the oscillations.

We have said that the cover $AC$ was pierced by a second hole at $m$. In this second hole there is introduced a small cylinder $m\Phi t$, the lower part of which $\Phi t$ is made of shellac; at $t$ is another pith ball; about the vessel, at the height of the needle, is described a circle $zQ$ divided into 360 degrees: for greater simplicity I use a strip of paper divided into 360 degrees which is pasted around the vessel at the height of the needle.

To arrange this instrument for use I set on the cover so that the hole $m$ practically corresponds to the first division of the circle $zoQ$ traced on the vessel. I place the index $oi$ of the micrometer on the point $o$ or the first division of this micrometer; I then turn the micrometer in the vertical tube $fh$ until, by looking past the vertical wire which suspends the needle and the centre of the ball, the needle $ag$ corresponds to the first division of the circle $zoQ$. I then introduce through the hole $m$ the other ball $t$ suspended by the rod $m\Phi t$ in such a way that it touches the ball $a$ and that by looking past the suspension wire and the ball $t$ we encounter the first division $o$ of the circle $zoQ$. The balance is then in condition to be used for all our operations; as an example we go on to give the method which we have used to determine the fundamental law according to which electrified bodies repel each other.

¶ FUNDAMENTAL LAW OF ELECTRICITY – *The repulsive force between two small spheres charged with the same sort of electricity is in the inverse ratio of the squares of the distances between the centres of the two spheres.*

§ *Experiment*

We electrify a small conductor (Fig. I, 4) which is simply a pin with a large head insulated by sinking its point into the end of a rod of Spanish wax; we introduce this pin through the hole *m* and with it touch the ball *t*, which is in contact with the ball *a*; on withdrawing the pin the two balls are electrified with electricity of the same sort and they repel each other to a distance which is measured by looking past the suspension wire and the centre of the ball *a* to the corresponding division of the circle *zoQ*; then by turning the index of the micrometer in the sense *pno* we twist the suspension wire *lp* and exert a force proportional to the angle of torsion, which tends to bring the ball *a* nearer to the ball *t*. We observe in this way the distance through which different angles of torsion bring the ball *a* toward the ball *t*, and by comparing the forces of torsion with the corresponding distances of the two balls we determine the law of repulsion. I shall here only present some trials which are easy to repeat and which will at once make evident the law of repulsion.

*First Trial.* Having electrified the two balls by means of the pin head while the index of the micrometer points to *o*, the ball *a* of the needle is separated from the ball *t* by 36 degrees.

*Second Trial.* By twisting the suspension wire through 126 degrees as shown by the pointer *o* of the micrometer, the two balls approach each other and stand 18 degrees apart.

*Third Trial.* By twisting the suspension wire through 567 degrees the two balls approach to a distance of 8 degrees and a half.

## § *Explanation and Result of This Experiment*

Before the balls have been electrified they touch, and the centre of the ball *a* suspended by the needle is not separated from the point where the torsion of the suspension wire is zero by more than half the diameters of the two balls. It must be mentioned that the silver wire *lp* which formed this suspension was twenty-eight inches long and was so fine that a foot of it weighed only 1/16 grain. By calculating the force which is needed to twist this wire by acting on the point *a* four inches away from the wire *lp* or from the centre of suspension, I have found by using the formulae explained in a memoir on the laws of the force of torsion of metallic wires, printed in the Volume of the Academy for 1784, that to twist this wire through 360 degrees the force that was needed when applied at the point *a* so as to act on the lever *an* four inches long was only 1/340 grains: so that since the forces of torsion, as is proved in that memoir, are as the angles of torsion, the least repulsive force between the two balls would separate them sensibly from each other.

We found in our first experiment, in which the index of the micrometer is set on the point *o*, that the balls are separated by 36 degrees, which produces a force of torsion of 36° = 1/3400 of a grain; in the second trial the distance between the balls is 18 degrees, but as the micrometer has been turned through 126 degrees it results that at a distance of 18 degrees the repulsive force was equivalent to 144 degrees; so at half the first distance the repulsion of the balls is quadruple.

In the third trial the suspension wire was twisted through 567 degrees and the two balls are separated by only 8 degrees and a half. The total torsion was consequently 576 degrees, four times that of the second trial, and the distance of the two balls in this third trial lacked only one-half degree of being reduced to half of that at which it stood in the second trial. It results then from these three trials that the repulsive action which the two balls exert on each other when they are electrified similarly is in the inverse ratio of the square of the distances.*

¶ SECOND MEMOIR ON ELECTRICITY AND MAGNETISM, *in which there are determined the laws according to which the magnetic fluid as also the electric fluid act either by repulsion or by attraction.*†

§ *Second experimental method to determine the law with which a sphere one or two feet in diameter attracts a small body charged with electricity of a different sort from its own.*

The method which we shall follow is analogous to that which we have used in the seventh volume of the *Savans étrangers* to determine the magnetic force of a steel plate in relation to its length, its thickness, and its width. It consists in suspending a needle horizontally, of which the end only is electrified and which, when brought to a certain distance from a sphere, electrified with the other sort of electricity, is attracted and oscillates because of the action of the sphere: we determine then by calculation from the number of oscillations in a given time the attractive force at different distances, just as we determine the force of gravity by the oscillations of an ordinary pendulum.

* [In the remarks which Coulomb adds to this account he points out first that when the very fine wire which he describes is used there is some uncertainty about the natural position of the zero. This uncertainty can be corrected by a suitable modification of the method of observation but he suggests that it is generally better to use a thicker wire. He also calls attention to the possible loss of electricity during the experiment, and suggests a way by which this can be observed and allowed for. He also points out that the repulsive action actually takes place along the chord of the arc by which the distances are measured, but shows that the errors introduced by measuring the distance by the degrees at least partly compensate each other, and that the errors are unimportant when the deflections do not exceed 25 to 30 degrees. He also shows how the instrument can be used to detect exceedingly small quantities of electricity.]

† [The first section of this memoir calls attention to the difficulties encountered in the use of the torsion balance when the electrical force is attractive, and describes the precautions which it was found necessary to take in order to obtain satisfactory results. The law of inverse squares was found to hold also in the case of attraction.]

We shall first consider some observations which have guided us in the experiments which are to follow: A silk fibre taken from a cocoon which can sustain 80 grains without breaking yields so readily to torsion that if we suspend horizontally to such a fibre three inches long in vacuum a small circular plate of which the weight and diameter are known we shall find from the period of oscillation of this little plate, using the formulae explained in a memoir on the force of torsion printed in the Volume of the Academy for 1784, that when we use a lever of 7 or 8 lines long to twist the fibre about its axis of suspension we shall need for a complete rotation to use usually not more than the force of a sixty thousandth of a grain; and if the suspended fibre is twice as long there will be needed only a hundred-and-twenty-thousandth of a grain. Therefore if we suspend a needle horizontally on this fibre, when the needle has come to rest and the fibre is entirely untwisted, and if by means of any force we set the needle in oscillations whose amplitude does not depart from the line in which the torsion is zero by more than 20 or 30 degrees, the force of torsion will have no sensible effect on the period of the oscillation, even when the force that produces the oscillations is not more than a hundredth of a grain. Premising this much, let us see how we proceed to determine the law of electrical attraction.

We suspend (Fig. II, 2) a needle $lg$ made of shellac by a silk thread $sc$ 7 to 8 inches long of a single fibre such as is drawn from the cocoon; at the end $l$ we fix perpendicularly to the needle a little disc eight or ten lines in diameter, made very light and cut from a sheet of gilt paper; the silk thread is attached at $s$ to the lower end of a little rod $st$ dried in a furnace and coated with shellac or with Spanish wax; this rod is held at $t$ by a clamp which slides along a ruled rod $oE$ and can be placed anywhere we desire by means of the screw $V$.

$G$ is a globe of copper or of cardboard covered with tin. It is carried on four uprights of glass coated with Spanish wax, and terminated, in order to make the insulation more

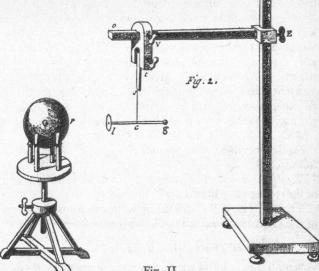

Fig. II

perfect, by four rods of Spanish wax, three or four inches long, The lower ends of these four uprights are set in a base which is placed on a little moveable table that, as the figure shows, can be set at the height which is most convenient for the experiment; the rod *Eo* may also, by means of the screw *E*, be set at a convenient height.

When everything is ready we adjust the globe *G* in such a way that its horizontal diameter *Gr* is opposite the centre of the plate *l*, which is some inches away from it. We give an electric spark to the sphere from a Leyden jar; we then touch the plate *l* with a conductor and the action of the electrified sphere on the electric fluid of the unelectrified plate gives to the plate a charge of the other sort from that of the sphere; so that when the conducting body is removed the sphere and the plate act on each other by attraction.

§ *Experiment*

The sphere *G* was a foot in diameter; the plate *l* was seven

lines in diameter; the shellac needle *lg* was fifteen lines long;
the suspension fibre *sc* was a silk fibre taken from the cocoon
and eight lines long; when the slider was at the point *o*
the plate *l* touched the sphere at *r*, and as the slider was
moved toward *E* the plate was removed from the centre of
the sphere by the quantity given by the divisions 0, 3, 6, 9,
12 inches, and when the sphere was electrified with what is
called positive electricity and the plate with negative
electricity by the method which has been described, we had:

*Trial 1* – The plate *l* being at 3 inches from the surface of
the sphere or nine inches from its centre gave fifteen oscillations in 20″.

*Trial 2* – The plate *l* distant by 18 inches from the centre
of the sphere gave fifteen oscillations in 40″.

*Trial 3* – The plate *l* distant by 24 inches from the centre
of the sphere gave fifteen oscillations in 60″.

## § *Explanation of This Experiment and Its Result*

When all the points of a spherical surface act by an attractive or repulsive force which varies inversely as the square of
the distance on a point placed at any distance from this
surface, it is known that the action is the same as if all the
spherical surface were concentrated at the centre of the
sphere.

As in our experiment the plate *l* was only seven lines in
diameter and as in the trials its least distance from the centre
of the sphere was nine inches, we may, without sensible
error, suppose that all the lines which are drawn from the
centre of the sphere to a point of the plate are parallel and
equal; and in consequence the total action of the plate can
be supposed to be united at its centre just as in the case of
the sphere; so that for the small oscillations of the needle,
the action which makes the needle oscillate will be a constant quantity for a given distance and will act along the
line which joins the two centres. Therefore if we call the
force $\phi$ and the time of a certain number of oscillations $T$
we shall have $T$ proportional to $1/\sqrt{\phi}$, but if $d$ is the distance
*Gl* from the centre of the sphere to the centre of the plate

and if the attractive forces are proportional to the reciprocal of the square of the distances or to $1/d^2$, it follows that $T$ will be proportional to $d$ or to the distance; so that when we make our trials and change the distance, the time of the same number of oscillations ought to be proportional to the distance from the centre of the plate to the centre of the sphere: let us compare this theory with experiment.

*Trial 1* – Distance between centres 9 inches, 15 oscillations in 20″.

*Trial 2* – Distance between centres 18 inches, 15 oscillations in 41″.

*Trial 3* – Distance between centres 24 inches, 15 oscillations in 60″.

The distances are as the numbers 3, 6, 8.

The times of the same number of oscillations 20, 41, 60.

By theory they ought to have been 20, 40, 54.

Thus in these three trials the difference between theory and experiment is 1/10 for the last trial compared with the first, and almost nothing for the second trial compared with the first; but it should be remarked that it took almost four minutes to make the three trials; that although the electricity held pretty well on the day this experiment was tried, it nevertheless lost 1/40 of its amount each minute. We shall see, in a memoir which will follow the one which I am presenting today, that when the electric density is not very great, the electric action of two electrified bodies diminishes in a given time exactly as the electric density or as the intensity of the action; therefore, since our trials lasted four minutes and since the electric action lost 1/40 each minute from the first to the last trial, the action arising from the intensity of the electric density independently of the distance should be diminished by almost a tenth; consequently, to have the corrected time of the fifteen oscillations in the last trial, we must set $\sqrt{(10)} : \sqrt{(9)} :: 60″$: the quantity required, which will be found to be 57 seconds, which differs only by 1/20 from the sixty seconds found by experiment.

We have thus come, by a method absolutely different from the first, to a similar result; we may therefore conclude that the mutual attraction of the electric fluid which is called positive on the electric fluid which is ordinarily called negative is in the inverse ratio of the square of the distances; just as we have found in our first memoir, that the mutual action of the electric fluid of the same sort is in the inverse ratio of the square of the distance.

¶ LAW OF MAGNETIC FORCE – *Experiments to determine the law according to which the magnetic fluid acts whether by attraction or by repulsion.**

§ *The magnetic fluid acts by attraction or repulsion in a ratio compounded directly of the density of the fluid and inversely of the square of the distance of its molecules.*

The first part of this proposition does not need to be proved; let us pass to the second.

We have seen that the magnetic fluid in our steel wire twenty-five inches long was concentrated at its ends in a length of two or three inches; that the centre of action of each half of this needle was about ten lines from its ends: therefore, by setting up some inches away from our steel wire a very short needle, in which as we shall see in the sequel, the magnetic fluid may be supposed to be concentrated in one or two lines at its ends, we may calculate the mutual action of the wire on the needle and of the needle on the wire by supposing the magnetic fluid in the wire concentrated at a point ten lines from its ends and in a needle an inch long at a point one or two lines from its end. These reflections have directed us in the experiment which follows:

§ *Fourth Experiment*

We suspended a steel wire weighing 70 grains and an inch

* [Several experiments were tried by which it was proved that the centre of action in each half of a magnetized wire is very near the end of the wire; so that in a steel wire twenty-five inches long we may, without sensible error, suppose that all the magnetic fluid is condensed near the end of the wire in two or three inches of its length.]

in length, magnetized by the method of double touch, by a silk thread three lines long made of a single fibre taken from a cocoon; we allowed it to come to rest in the magnetic meridian, we then placed vertically in the meridian at different distances a steel wire 25 inches long, in such a way that its end was always ten lines below the level of the suspended needle: in each trial we changed the distance, and then by oscillating the suspended needle we counted the number of oscillations which it made in the same number of seconds. The following is the result of these experiments:

*Trial 1* – The free needle oscillating because of the action of the earth makes 15 oscillations in 60″.

*Trial 2* – The wire placed at 4 inches from the centre of the needle, 41 in 60″.

*Trial 3* – The wire placed 8 inches from the centre of the needle, 24 in 60″.

*Trial 4* – The wire placed 16 inches from the centre of the needle, 17 in 60″.

§ *Explanation of This Experiment and Its Result*

When a pendulum is freely suspended and acted on by forces in a given direction, which make it oscillate, the forces are measured by the inverse ratio of the square of the time of the same number of oscillations, or, what comes to the same thing, by the direct ratio of the square of the number of oscillations made in the same time.

In the preceding experiment, the needle oscillates because of two different forces; the one is the magnetic force of the earth, the other is the action of all the points of the wire on the points of the needle. In our experiment all the forces are in the plane of the magnetic meridian, and since the needle is suspended horizontally the true force which makes it oscillate depends on those parts of all these forces which are resolved in the horizontal direction. Now we have seen from the three preceding experiments that since the magnetic fluid is concentrated in the ends of our wire, it may be supposed to be all brought together at a point ten lines from the end of the wire. And, since the suspended needle is an inch long, that the boreal end is attracted at a distance of 3 inches and a half, and that the austral end is repelled by the lower pole of the needle, which is distant from it $4\frac{1}{2}$ inches; it may be supposed without sensible error that the mean distance at which the lower end of the steel wire exerts its action on the two poles of the needle is 4 inches. Consequently if the action of the magnetic fluid was in the inverse ratio of the square of the distances, the action of the lower pole of the steel wire on the needle should be proportional to $\frac{1}{4^2}, \frac{1}{8^2}, \frac{1}{16^2}$; or to $1, \frac{1}{4}, \frac{1}{16}$.

Now since the horizontal forces which make the needle oscillate are proportional to the square of the number of oscillations made in the same time, and since because of the magnetic force of the earth alone, the free needle makes 15 oscillations in 60″, this force can be measured by the square of these 15 oscillations or by $15^2$. In the second trial the combined forces of the earth and of the steel wire make the needle make 41 oscillations in 60″; therefore, these forces combined are measured by $41^2$, and the force resulting from the action of the magnetized steel wire alone is consequently measured by the difference of these two squares; it is thus proportional to $41^2 - 15^2$. We shall then have for the action of the wire on the needle:

| Distance | Force depending on the magnetic action of the steel wire |
|---|---|
| In *Trial 2* – At 4 inches | $41^2 - 15^2 = 1456.$ |
| *Trial 3* – At 8 inches | $24^2 - 15^2 = 351.$ |
| *Trial 4* – At 16 inches | $17^2 - 15^2 = 64.$ |

The second and third trials, in which the distances are as 1:2, give very approximately for the forces the inverse ratio of the square of the distance. The fourth trial gives a number which is a little too small; but it may be remarked that in this fourth trial the distance of the lower pole of the steel wire from the centre of the needle is 16 inches; and that the distance of the upper pole from the centre of the needle is about $\sqrt{(16^2 + 23^2)}$: thus if we represent the action of the lower pole by $1/16^2$ the horizontal action of the upper pole will be

$$\frac{16}{(16^2 + 23^2)^{\frac{1}{2}}};$$

so that the action of the lower pole is to that of the upper pole about as 100:19; from which it follows that since the oscillations of the needle are caused by the action of these two poles, and since the action of the upper pole is opposed in sense to that of the lower pole, the square of the oscillations which the action of the lower pole of the magnetized wire alone would produce is diminished by 19/100 by the opposite action of the upper end of the same wire; and so to have the action of the lower part of the wire alone, we must, if we represent the true value of this force by $x$, set $(x — 19/100x) = 64$, from which $x = 79$. If we substitute this quantity in the result of the fourth trial we shall find

*Trial 2* – 4 inches of distance, the force 1456.
*Trial 3* – 8 inches of distance, the force 351.
*Trial 4* – 16 inches of distance, the force 79.

These forces are very approximately as the numbers 16, 4, 1, or are in the inverse ratio of the square of the distance.

I have repeated this experiment several times by suspending needles two or three inches long and I have always found that when I have made the necessary corrections, which I have just explained, the action of the magnetic fluid, whether repulsive or attractive, was inversely as the square of the distances.

[*The same law of attraction or repulsion was determined by a method in which the torsion balance was used.*]

# ALESSANDRO VOLTA
## 1745–1827

### THE VOLTAIC PILE AND THE VOLTAIC
### BATTERY ARE DEVELOPED

ALESSANDRO VOLTA became a professor of physics before he was thirty, occupying the chairs at Como, Pavia, and finally at Padua in northern Italy. Most of our information about his experimental work comes from his letters to his scientific friends.

The work of Volta must be considered in relation to that of another Italian, Luigi Galvani (1737–98). The latter's observation of the muscular reactions of a frog's leg in contact with two dissimilar metals was ascribed by him to the presence of electricity in the organism of the animal itself. When Galvani's *Commentaries*, describing his experiments, was published in 1791, Volta had already established himself in the field of electrical studies by his work on the electrometer, with which the amount of an electrical charge could be measured.

The publication of Galvani's ideas stimulated Volta's interest and, having repeated the experiments, Volta set out to find the explanation for the phenomena. He extended the experiment from frog's legs to himself, finding, for example, that if he placed a piece of tinfoil on the upper surface of the tongue and a silver coin on the lower, and connected them with copper wire, he experienced a sour taste. This and similar experiments led to the conclusion that the metals were not only acting as conductors; they were actually generating electricity themselves. It was now possible for Volta to reject Galvani's animal electricity in favour of *metallic electricity*.

This was the beginning of a long series of experiments from which Volta was eventually able to demonstrate, in 1797, the phenomenon of current electricity. Volta had, in fact, shown the existence of an electric current as contrasted with static electricity.

The importance of Volta's 'pile', as it came to be called, lay in the consequences. It was described in a letter addressed to the President of the Royal Society of London, Sir Joseph Banks (and reproduced below from the translation in Magie's *A Sourcebook in Physics*, Harvard University Press, 1935). Banks showed Volta's letter – or, at least, part of it – to a London surgeon, Sir Anthony Carlisle, who built a pile out of silver coins and zinc and proceeded to experiment with it. He and William Nicholson, whose *Journal* was a well-known scientific periodical of the time, showed that the silver end of the pile was negatively charged and the zinc end positively charged. In pursuing this observation, they detected a gas (hydrogen) emanating from the silver side when the current was passed through water, the negative electrodes becoming tarnished and black. Thus the electrolysis of water was effected for the first time: water was decomposed into hydrogen and oxygen and the relative quantities of the constituent gases determined in the approximate proportion of 1:2 by volume. Thus electrochemistry was introduced as a fundamental tool of chemical research, much exploited, as we have seen, by Humphry Davy.

Volta was less interested in the chemical than in the purely electrical results of his discovery. He made many important improvements in the techniques of measurement of electric currents, for which he is commemorated in the name given in 1893 to the standard unit of electromotive force.

¶ *The Voltaic Pile*

Como, in the Milanais
20 March 1800

After a long silence, which I do not attempt to excuse, I have the pleasure of communicating to you, Sir, and through you to the Royal Society, some striking results to which I have come in carrying out my experiments on electricity excited by the simple mutual contact of metals of different sorts, and even by the contact of other conductors, also different among themselves, whether liquids or containing some liquid, to which property they owe their conducting power. The most important of these results, which includes practically all the others, is the construction of an apparatus which, in the effects which it produces, that is, in the disturbances which it produces in the arms etc., resembles Leyden jars; or better still electric batteries feebly charged, which act unceasingly or so that their charge after each discharge re-establishes itself; which in a word provides an unlimited charge or imposes a perpetual action or impulsion on the electric fluid; but which otherwise is essentially different from these, both because of this continued action which is its property and because, instead of being made, as are the ordinary jars and electric batteries, of one or more insulating plates in thin layers of those bodies which are thought to be the only electric bodies, coated with conductors or bodies called non-electrics, this new apparatus is formed altogether of several of these latter bodies, chosen even among the best conductors and therefore the most remote, according to what has always been believed, from the electric nature. Yes! the apparatus of which I speak, and which will doubtless astonish you, is only an assemblage of a number of good conductors of different sorts arranged in a certain way. 30, 40, 60, pieces or more of copper, or better of silver, each in contact with a piece of tin, or what is much better, of zinc and an equal number of layers of water or some other liquid which is a better conductor than pure water, such as salt-water or lye and so forth, or pieces of cardboard or of leather, etc. well soaked with these liquids; when such layers are interposed between each couple or combination of the two different metals, such an alternative series of these three sorts of conductors always in the same order, constitutes my new instrument; which imitates, as I have said, the effects of Leyden jars or of electric batteries by giving the same disturbances as they;

which in truth, are much inferior to these batteries when highly charged in the force and noise of their explosions, in the spark, in the distance through which the charge can pass, etc., and equal in effect only to a battery very feebly charged, but a battery nevertheless of an immense capacity; but which further infinitely surpasses the power of these batteries in that it does not need, as they do, to be charged in advance by means of an outside source; and in that it can give the disturbance every time that it is properly touched, no matter how often.

*

I proceed to give a more detailed description of this apparatus and of some other analogous ones, as well as the most remarkable experiments made with them.

I provided myself with several dozen small round plates or discs of copper, of brass, or better of silver, an inch in diameter more or less (for example, coins) and an equal number of plates of tin, or which is much better, of zinc, approximately of the same shape and size; I say approximately because precision is not necessary, and in general the size as well as the shape of the metallic pieces is arbitrary: all that is necessary is that they may be arranged easily one above the other in a column. I further provided a sufficiently large number of discs of cardboard, of leather, or of some other spongy matter which can take up and retain much water, or the liquid with which they must be well soaked if the experiment is to succeed. These pieces, which I will call the moistened discs, I make a little smaller than the metallic discs or plates, so that when placed between them in the way that I shall soon describe, they do not protrude.

Now having in hand all these pieces in good condition, that is to say, the metallic discs clean and dry, and the other non-metallic ones well soaked in water, or which is much better, in brine, and afterwards slightly wiped so that the liquid does not come out in drops, I have only to arrange them in the proper way; and this arrangement is simple and easy.

I place horizontally on a table or base one of the metallic plates, for example, one of the silver ones, and on this first plate I place a second plate of zinc; on this second plate I lay one of the moistened discs; then another plate of silver, followed immediately by another of zinc, on which I place again a moistened disc: I thus continue in the same way coupling a plate of silver with one of zinc, always in the same sense, that is to say, always silver below and zinc above or vice versa, according as I began, and inserting between these couples a moistened disc: I continue, I say, to form from several of these steps a column as high as can hold itself up without falling.

*

Coming back to the mechanical construction of my apparatus, which admits of several variations, I proceed to describe here not all those which I have thought out and constructed either on a large or small scale, but some only which are either more curious, or more useful, or which present some real advantage, such as being easier or quicker to construct, more certain in their effects, or keeping in good condition longer. To begin with one of these which unites almost all of these advantages, which in its form differs the most from the columnar apparatus described before but which has the disadvantage of being a much larger apparatus, I present this new apparatus which I call the crown of cups in the next figure [p. 215].

We set up a row of several cups or bowls made of any material whatever except the metals, cups of wood, of shell, of clay, or better of crystal (small drinking glasses or goblets are very suitable) half-full of pure water, or better of brine or of lye; and we join them all together in a sort of chain by means of metallic arcs of which one arm $Aa$ or only the end $A$ which is placed in one of the goblets is of red or yellow copper, or better of silvered copper, and the other Z, which is placed in the next goblet is of tin or better of zinc. I may observe here in passing that lye and the other alkaline liquids are preferable when one of the metals which is immersed in them is tin; brine is preferable when it is zinc.

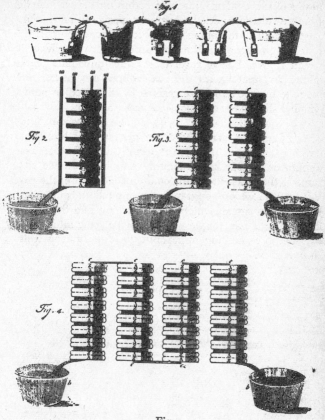

Fig.

The two metals of which each arc is composed are soldered together somewhere above the part which is immersed in the liquid and which ought to touch it with a sufficiently large surface: for this purpose it is suitable that this part should be an inch square or very little less; the rest of the arc may be as much narrower as we please, and may even be a simple metallic wire. It may also be made of a third metal different from the two which are immersed in the liquid of the goblets; since the action on the electric fluid which results from all the contacts of several metals which are in immediate contact, the force with which this fluid is driven at the end, is the same absolutely or nearly as that which it would have received by the immediate contact of the first metal with the last without any of the intermediate metals, as I have verified by direct experiment, of which I shall have occasion to speak elsewhere.

Now then a train of 30, 40, 60 of these goblets joined up in this manner and arranged either in a straight line or in a curve or set round in any way forms the whole of this new apparatus, which fundamentally and in substance is the same as the other one of the column tried before; the essential feature, which consists in the immediate connexion of the different metals which form each pair and the mediate connexion of one couple with another by the intermediary of a damp conductor, appears in this apparatus as well as in the other.

# ANDRÉ MARIE AMPÈRE
## 1775–1836

### THE FOUNDATION OF ELECTRODYNAMICS

OERSTED'S discovery, in 1820, that an electric current gave rise to magnetic effects, was a key event in the history of electricity and magnetism, and an indication of the great synthesis which was to follow. Yet the full significance of this result was not to be seen against the background of a subject which was still in a comparatively early stage of development. It was the great achievement of André Marie Ampère to reveal to his contemporaries the fundamental import of this new discovery. With his clear insight into the nature of the phenomenon Ampère was able, not only to clarify the situation, but to develop important consequences, and, in so doing, found the subject of electrodynamics.

Ampère was born in Lyons, and, whilst still a young boy, showed unmistakable signs of an extraordinary intellect, particularly in the field of mathematics. At the age of eighteen he suffered a personal tragedy when his father became a victim of the French Revolution. Declared an aristocrat by the revolutionaries, his father was murdered in the name of the Revolution. For a year Ampère could not work, overcome by the loss, but gradually his interest in science returned and his great abilities brought him increasing success and advancement.

The announcement of Oersted's discovery inspired Ampère to his greatest work, work which was to place him in the front rank of men of science. In developing the implications of the original observation Ampère realized that if an electric current passing through a wire could behave like a magnet, then two adjacent wires, with currents passing through them, should either attract or repel one another, as do two magnets. This result he was able to verify by means of ingenious experiments; moreover, Ampère was able to express his results in the form of a quantitative physical law, thus laying the foundations of a new field of electrical theory.

The reading which follows, describing this work, is taken from Magie's *A Sourcebook in Physics* (McGraw-Hill Book Co., 1935).

---

❡ *New Names*\*

The word '*electromagnetic*', which is used to characterize the phenomena produced by the conducting wires of the voltaic pile, could not suitably describe them except during the period when the only phenomena which were known of this sort were those which M. Oersted discovered, exhibited by an electric current and a magnet. I have determined to use the word *electrodynamic* in order to unite under a common name all these phenomena, and particularly to designate those which I have observed between two voltaic conductors. It expresses their true character, that of being produced by electricity in motion: while the electric attractions and repulsions, which have been known for a long time, are *electrostatic* phenomena produced by the unequal distribution of electricity at rest in the bodies in which they are observed.

❡ *Actions between Currents*

§ *1. On the Mutual Action of Two Electric Currents*

1. Electromotive action is manifested by two sorts of effects which I believe I should first distinguish by precise definitions.

I shall call the first *electric tension*, the second *electric current*.

The first is observed when two bodies, between which this action occurs, are separated from each other by non-conducting bodies at all the points of their surfaces except those where it is established; the second occurs when the

\* [The paragraph given here is a note attached to the title.]

bodies make a part of a circuit of conducting bodies, which are in contact at points on their surface different from those at which the electromotive action is produced. In the first case the effect of the electromotive action is to put the two bodies, or the two systems of bodies, between which it exists, in two states of tension, of which the difference is constant when this action is constant, when, for example, it is produced by the contact of two substances of different sorts; this difference may be variable, on the contrary, with the cause which produces it, if it results from friction or from pressure.

The first case is the only one which can arise when the electromotive action develops between different parts of the same non-conducting body; tourmaline is an example of this when its temperature changes.

In the second case there is no longer any electric tension, light bodies are not sensibly attracted and the ordinary electrometer can no longer be of service to indicate what is going on in the body; nevertheless the electromotive action continues; for if, for example, water, or an acid, or an alkali, or a saline solution forms part of the circuit, these bodies are decomposed, especially when the electromotive action is constant, as has been known for some time; and furthermore as M. Oersted has recently discovered, when the electromotive action is produced by the contact of metals, the magnetic needle is turned from its direction when it is placed near any portion of the circuit; but these effects cease, water is no longer decomposed, and the needle comes back to its ordinary position as soon as the circuit is broken, when the tensions are re-established and light bodies are again attracted. This proves that the tensions are not the cause of the decomposition of water, or of the changes of direction of the magnetic needle discovered by M. Oersted. This second case is evidently the only one which can occur if the electromotive action is developed between the different parts of the same conducting body. The consequences deduced in this memoir from the experiments of M. Oersted will lead us to recognize the existence of this condition in the only case where there is need as yet to admit it.

2. Let us see in what consists the difference of these entirely different orders of phenomena, one of which consists in the tension and attractions or repulsions which have been long known, and the other, in decomposition of water and a great many other substances, in the changes of direction of the needle, and in a sort of attractions and repulsions entirely different from the ordinary electric attractions and repulsions; which I believe I have first discovered and which I have named *voltaic attractions* and *repulsions* to distinguish them from the others. When there is not conducting continuity from one of the bodies, or systems of bodies, in which the electromotive action develops, to the other, and when these bodies are themselves conductors, as in Volta's pile, we can only conceive this action as constantly carrying positive electricity into the one body and negative electricity into the other: in the first moment, when there is nothing opposed to the effect that it tends to produce, the two electricities accumulate, each in the part of the whole system to which it is carried, but this effect is checked as soon as the difference of electric tensions gives to their mutual attraction, which tends to reunite them, a force sufficient to make equilibrium with the electromotive action. Then everything remains in this state, except for the leakage of electricity, which may take place little by little across the non-conducting body, the air, for example, which interrupts the circuit; for it appears that there are no bodies which are perfect insulators. As this leakage takes place the tension diminishes, but since when it diminishes, the mutual attraction of the two electricities no longer makes equilibrium with the electromotive action, this last force, in case it is constant, carries a new positive electricity on one side and negative electricity on the other, and the tensions are re-established. It is this state of a system of electromotive and conducting bodies that I called *electric tension*. We know that it exists in the two halves of this system when we separate them or even in case they remain in contact after

the electromotive action has ceased, provided that then it arose by pressure or friction between bodies which are not both conductors. In these two cases the tension is gradually diminished because of the leakage of electricity of which we have recently spoken.

But when the two bodies or the two systems of bodies between which the electromotive action arises are also connected by conducting bodies in which there is no other electromotive action equal and opposite to the first, which would maintain the state of electrical equilibrium, and consequently the tensions which result from it, these tensions would disappear or at least would become very small and the phenomena occur which have been pointed out as characterizing this second case. But as nothing is otherwise changed in the arrangement of the bodies between which the electromotive action develops, it cannot be doubted that it continues to act, and as the mutual attraction of the two electricities, measured by the difference in the electric tensions, which has become nothing or has considerably diminished, can no longer make equilibrium with this action, it is generally admitted that it continues to carry the two electricities in the two senses in which it carried them before; in such a way that there results a double current, one of positive electricity, the other of negative electricity, starting out in opposite senses from the points where the electromotive action arises, and going out to reunite in the parts of the circuit remote from these points. The currents of which I am speaking are accelerated until the inertia of the electric fluids and the resistance which they encounter because of the imperfection of even the best conductors make equilibrium with the electromotive force, after which they continue indefinitely with constant velocity so long as this force has the same intensity, but they always cease on the instant that the circuit is broken. It is this state of electricity in a series of electromotive and conducting bodies which I name, for brevity, the *electric current*; and as I shall frequently have to speak of the two opposite senses in which the two electricities move, I shall understand every time that the question arises, to avoid tedious repetition, after the words *'sense of the electric current'* these words, *of positive electricity*; so that if we are considering, for example, a voltaic pile, the expression: *direction of the electric current in the pile*, will designate the direction from the end where hydrogen is disengaged in the decomposition of water to that end where oxygen is obtained; and this expression, *direction of the electric current in the conductor which makes connexion between the two ends of the pile*, will designate the direction which goes, on the contrary, from the end where oxygen appears to that where the hydrogen develops. To include these two cases in a single definition we may say that what we may call the direction of the electric current is that followed by hydrogen and the bases of the salts when water or some saline substance is a part of the circuit, and is decomposed by the current, whether, in the voltaic pile, these substances are a part of the conductor or are interposed between the pairs of which the pile is constructed. *

3. The ordinary electrometer indicates tension and the intensity of the tension; there was lacking an instrument which would enable us to recognize the presence of the electric current in a pile or a conductor and which would indicate the energy and the direction of it. This instrument now exists; all that is needed is that the pile, or any portion of the conductor, should be placed horizontally, approximately in the direction of the magnetic meridian, and that an apparatus similar to a compass, which, in fact, differs from it only in the use that is made of it, should be placed above the pile or either above or below a portion of the conductor. So long as the circuit is interrupted, the magnetic needle remains in its ordinary position, but it departs from this position as soon as the current is established, so much the more as the energy is greater, and it determines the direction of the current from this general fact, that if one places oneself in thought in the direction of the current in such a way that it is directed from the feet to the head of the

* [The paragraphs in which it is pointed out that the electric tensions cannot be the cause of chemical or magnetic actions are omitted.]

observer and that he has his face turned towards the needle; the action of the current will always throw towards the left that one of the ends of the needle which points towards the north and which I shall always call the austral pole of the magnetic needle, because it is the pole similar to the southern pole of the earth. I express this more briefly by saying, that the austral pole of the needle is carried to the left of the current which acts on the needle. I think that to distinguish this instrument from the ordinary electrometer we should give it the name of *galvanometer* and that it should be used in all experiments on electric currents, as we habitually use an electrometer on electric machines, so as to see at every instant if a current exists and what is its energy.

The first use that I have made of this instrument is to employ it to show that the current in the voltaic pile, from the negative end to the positive end, has the same effect on the magnetic needle as the current in the conductor which goes on the contrary from the positive end to the negative end.

It is well to have for this experiment two magnetic needles, one of them placed on the pile and the other above or below the conductor; we see the austral pole of each needle move to the left of the current near which it is placed; so that when the second is above the conductor it is turned to the opposite side from that towards which the needle turns which has been placed on the pile, because the currents have opposite directions in these two portions of the circuit; the two needles, on the contrary are turned towards the same side, remaining nearly parallel with each other, when the one is above the pile and the other below the conductor. As soon as the circuit is broken they come back at once in both cases to their ordinary position.

4. Such are the differences already recognized in the effects produced by electricity in the two states which I have described, of which the one consists, if not in rest, at least in a movement which is slow and only produced because of the difficulty of completely insulating the bodies in which the electric tension exhibits itself, the other, in a double

current of positive and negative electricity along a continuous circuit of conducting bodies. In the ordinary theory of electricity, we suppose that the two fluids of which we consider it composed are unceasingly separated one from the other in a part of a circuit and carried rapidly in contrary senses into another part of the same circuit, where they are continually reunited. Although the electric current thus defined can be produced with an ordinary machine by arranging it in such a way as to develop the two electricities and by joining by a conductor the two parts of the apparatus where they are produced, we cannot, unless we use a very large machine, obtain the current with an appreciable energy except by the use of the voltaic pile, because the quantity of electricity produced by a frictional machine remains the same in a given time whatever may be the conducting power of the rest of the circuit, whereas that which the pile sets in motion during a given time increases indefinitely as we join the two extremities by a better conductor.

But the differences which I have recalled are not the only ones which distinguish these two states of electricity. I have discovered some more remarkable ones still by arranging in parallel directions two straight parts of two conducting wires joining the ends of two voltaic piles; the one was fixed and the other, suspended on points and made very sensitive to motion by a counterweight, could approach the first or move from it while keeping parallel with it. I then observed that when I passed a current of electricity in both of these wires at once they attracted each other when the two currents were in the same sense and repelled each other when they were in opposite senses. Now these attractions or repulsions of electric currents differ essentially from those that electricity produces in the state of repose; first, they cease, as chemical decompositions do, as soon as we break the circuit of the conducting bodies; secondly, in the ordinary electric attractions and repulsions the electricities of opposite sort attract and those of the same name repel; in the attractions and repulsions of electric currents we have precisely the contrary; it is when the two conducting wires are placed parallel in such a way that their ends of the same name are on the same side and very near each other that there is attraction, and there is repulsion when the two conductors, still always parallel, have currents in them in opposite senses, so that the ends of the same name are as far apart as possible. Thirdly, in the case of attraction, when it is sufficiently strong to bring the movable conductor into contact with the fixed conductor, they remain attached to one another like two magnets and do not separate after a while, as happens when two conducting bodies which attract each other because they are electrified, one positively and the other negatively, come to touch. Finally, and it appears that this last circumstance depends on the same cause as the preceding, two electric currents attract or repel in vacuum as in air, which is contrary to that which we observe in the mutual action of two conducting bodies charged with ordinary electricity. It is not the place here to explain these new phenomena; the attractions and repulsions which occur

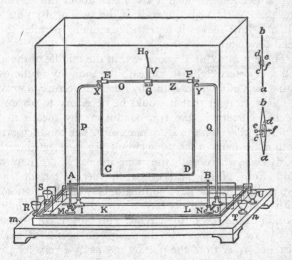

Fig.

between two parallel currents, according as they are directed in the same sense or in opposite senses, are facts given by an experiment which is easy to repeat. It is necessary in this experiment, in order to prevent the motions which would be given to the movable conductor by agitation of the air, to place the apparatus under a glass cover within which we introduce, through the base which carries it, those parts of the conductors which can be joined to the two ends of the pile. The most convenient arrangement of these conductors is to place one of them on two supports in a horizontal position in which it is fixed, and to hang up the other by two metallic wires, which are joined to it, on a glass rod which is above the first conductor and which rests on two other metal supports by very fine steel points; these points are soldered to the two ends of the metallic wires of which I have spoken, in such a way that connexion is established through the supports by the aid of these points.

The two conductors are thus parallel and one beside the other in a horizontal plane; one of them is movable because of the oscillations which it can make about the horizontal line passing through the ends of the two steel points and when it thus moves it necessarily remains parallel to the fixed conductor.

There is introduced above and in the middle of the glass rod a counterweight, to increase the mobility of the oscillating part of the apparatus, by raising its centre of gravity.

I first thought that it would be necessary to set up the electric current in the two conductors by means of two different piles; but this is not necessary. The conductors may both make parts of the same circuit; for the electric current exists everywhere with the same intensity. We may conclude from this observation that the electric tensions of the two ends of the pile have nothing to do with the phenomena with which we are concerned; for there is certainly no tension in the rest of the circuit. This view is confirmed by our being able to move the magnetic needle at a great distance away from the pile by means of a very long conductor, the middle of which is curved over in the direction of the magnetic meridian above or below the needle. This experiment was suggested to me by the illustrious savant to whom the physico-mathematical sciences owe so much of the great progress that they have made in our time: it has fully succeeded.

Designate by $A$ and $B$ the two ends of the fixed conductor, by $C$ the end of the movable conductor which is on the side of $A$ and by $D$ that of the same conductor which is on the side of $B$; it is plain that if one of the ends of the pile is joined to $A$, $B$ to $C$, and $D$ to the other end of the pile, the electric current will be in the same sense in the two conductors; then we shall see them attract each other; if on the other hand, while $A$ always is joined to one end of the pile, $B$ is joined to $D$ and $C$ to the other end of the pile, the current will be in opposite senses in the two conductors and then they repel each other. Further, we may recognize that since the attractions and repulsions of electric currents act at all points in the circuit we may, with a single fixed conductor, attract and repel as many conductors and change the direction of as many magnetic needles as we please. I propose to have made two movable conductors within the same glass case so arranged that by making them parts of the same circuit, with a common fixed conductor, they may be alternately both attracted or both repelled, or one of them attracted and the other repelled at the same time, according to the way in which the connexions are made. Following up the success of the experiment which was suggested to me by the Marquis de Laplace, by employing as many conducting wires and magnetized needles as there are letters, by fixing each letter on a different magnet, and by using a pile at a distance from these needles, which can be joined alternately by its own ends to the ends of each conductor, we may form a sort of telegraph, by which we can write all the matters which we may wish to transmit, across whatever obstacles there may be, to the person whose duty it is to observe the letters carried by the needles. By setting up above the pile a key-board of which the keys carry the same letters and by making connexion by pressing them down, this method of correspondence could be managed easily and would take no more time than is necessary to touch the keys at one end and to read off each letter at the other.

If the movable conductor, instead of being adjusted so as to move parallel to the fixed conductor, can only turn in a plane parallel to the fixed conductor about a common perpendicular passing through their centres, it is clear, from the law that we have discovered of the attractions and repulsions of electric currents, that each half of the two conductors will attract or repel at the same time, according as the currents are in the same sense or in opposite senses; and consequently that the movable conductor will turn until it becomes parallel to the fixed conductor; in such a way that the currents are directed in the same sense: from which it follows that in the mutual action of two electric currents the directive action and the attractive or repulsive action depend on the same principle and are only different effects of one and the same action. It is no longer necessary, therefore, to set up between these two effects the distinction which it is so important to make, as we shall see very soon, when we are dealing with the mutual action of an electric current and of a magnet considered, as we ordinarily do, with respect to its axis, because in this action the two bodies tend to place themselves perpendicular to each other.

We now turn to the examination of this last action and of the action of two magnets on each other and we shall see that they both come under the law of the mutual action of two electric currents, if we conceive one of these currents as set up at every point of a line drawn on the surface of a magnet from one pole to the other, in planes perpendicular to the axis of the magnet, so that from the simple comparison of facts it seems to me impossible to doubt that there are really such currents about the axis of a magnet, or rather that magnetization consists in a process by which we give to the particles of steel the property of producing, in the sense of the currents of which we have spoken, the same electromotive action as is shown by the voltaic pile, by the oxidized zinc of the mineralogists, by heated tourmaline, and even in a pile made up of damp cardboard and discs of the same metal at two different temperatures. However, since this electromotive action is set up in the case of a magnet between the different particles of the same body, which is a good conductor, it can never, as we have previously remarked, produce any electric tension, but only a continuous current similar to that which exists in a voltaic pile re-entering itself in a closed curve. It is sufficiently evident from the preceding observations that such a pile cannot produce at any of its points either electric tensions or attractions or repulsions or chemical phenomena, since it is then impossible to insert a liquid in the circuit; but that the current which is immediately established in this pile will act to direct it or to attract or repel it either by another electric current or by a magnet, which, as we shall see, is only an assemblage of electric currents.

It is thus that we come to this unexpected result, that the phenomena of the magnet are produced by electricity and that there is no other difference between the two poles of a magnet than their positions with respect to the currents of which the magnet is composed, so that the austral pole is that which is to the right of these currents and the boreal pole that which is to the left.*

* [The rest of the memoir in the same volume of the *Annales* contains descriptions of more elaborate experiments by which the discoveries announced in the first part of the memoir are confirmed.]

# MICHAEL FARADAY
## 1791–1867

## ELECTROMAGNETIC INDUCTION IS
## DESCRIBED

MICHAEL FARADAY is a classic example of the rise to scientific eminence from obscure origins. The son of a blacksmith, and thus born into a world in which hard work and poverty seemed inevitable, this bookbinder's apprentice celebrated his coming of age by attending the lectures of Sir Humphry Davy at the Royal Institution. He then attempted to enter the 'amiable and liberal' company of scientists by the bold and simple step of writing to Davy to ask for a job. Faraday backed his application with his notes of the lecture he had attended, written out 'more fairly in a quarto volume'! As a result, Davy gave him the position of assistant in the laboratory.

Soon after Faraday's appointment in 1813, Davy made an eighteen-month tour of Europe (in the midst of the Napoleonic wars) and took his young apprentice with him as his 'assistant in experiments and in writing'. Faraday soon showed his adaptability to the disciplines of science. By the age of thirty he was superintendent of the laboratory of the Royal Institution and at thirty-three he was elected to the Royal Society.

Faraday made great contributions in many fields, both in physics and chemistry (an extract from his chemical researches appears in the following section), but it is his work on electricity with which we are concerned here. His achievements in this sphere were to play a monumental part in the development of this rapidly growing subject and together with such men as Ampère (who is represented in this section), Oersted, Henry, and Ohm, he helped to lay the foundations of a subject which, in its many ramifications, plays an integral and increasing part in modern life.

In the reading that follows (taken from Faraday's 'Experimental Researches' in Magie's *A Sourcebook in Physics*, Harvard University Press, 1935) Faraday describes the process in which the motion of a wire, arranged in a closed circuit, through the field of force of a magnet leads to the induction of an electric current – a simple principle which introduced the concept of alternating current and, in effect, provided the basis for the construction of dynamos and electric motors.

For nearly fifty years Faraday lived and worked at the Royal Institution, continuing Davy's public lectures but, for the most part, living only for scientific research. He was one of the first scientists to receive government support, for his small salary from the Royal Institution was, after 1835, supplemented by a pension from the state.

¶ *Induced Currents*

1. The power which electricity of tension possesses of causing an opposite electrical state in its vicinity has been expressed by the general term Induction; which, as it has been received into scientific language, may also, with propriety, be used in the same general sense to express the power which electrical currents may possess of inducing any particular state upon matter in their immediate neighbourhood, otherwise indifferent. It is with this meaning that I purpose using it in the present paper.

2. Certain effects of the induction of electrical current have already been recognized and described: as those of magnetization; Ampère's experiments of bringing a copper disc near to a flat spiral; his repetition with electro-magnets of Arago's extraordinary experiments, and perhaps a few others. Still it appeared unlikely that these could be all the effects which induction by currents could produce; especially as, upon dispensing with iron, almost the whole of them disappear, whilst yet an infinity of bodies, exhibiting definite phenomena of induction with electricity of tension, still

remain to be acted upon by the induction of electricity in motion.

3. Further: Whether Ampère's beautiful theory were adopted, or any other, or whatever reservation were mentally made, still it appeared very extraordinary, that as every electric current was accompanied by a corresponding intensity of magnetic action at right angles to the current, good conductors of electricity, when placed within the sphere of this action, should not have any current induced through them, or some sensible effect produced equivalent in force to such a current.

4. These considerations, with their consequence, the hope of obtaining electricity from ordinary magnetism, have stimulated me at various times to investigate experimentally the inductive effect of electric currents. I lately arrived at positive results, and not only had my hopes fulfilled, but obtained a key which appeared to me to open out a full explanation of Arago's magnetic phenomena, and also to discover a new state, which may probably have great influence in some of the most important effects of electric currents.

5. These results I purpose describing, not as they were obtained, but in such a manner as to give the most concise view of the whole.

## § 1. Induction of Electric Currents

6. About twenty-six feet of copper wire one twentieth of an inch in diameter were wound round a cylinder of wood as a helix, the different spires of which were prevented from touching by a thin interposed twine. This helix was covered with calico, and then a second wire applied in the same manner. In this way twelve helices were superposed, each containing an average length of wire of twenty-seven feet, and all in the same direction. The first, third, fifth, seventh, ninth, and eleventh of these helices were connected at their extremities end to end, so as to form one helix; the others were connected in a similar manner; and thus two principal helices were produced, closely interposed, having the same

direction, not touching anywhere, and each containing one hundred and fifty-five feet in length of wire.

7. One of these helices was connected with a galvanometer, the other with a voltaic battery of ten pairs of plates four inches square, with double coppers and well charged; yet not the slightest sensible deflection of the galvanometer needle could be observed.

8. A similar compound helix, consisting of six lengths of copper and six of soft iron wire, was constructed. The resulting iron helix contained two hundred and fourteen feet of wire, the resulting copper helix two hundred and eight feet; but whether the current from the trough was passed through the copper or the iron helix, no effect upon the other could be perceived at the galvanometer.

9. In these and many similar experiments no difference in action of any kind appeared between iron and other metals.

10. Two hundred and three feet of copper wire in one length were coiled round a large block of wood; other two hundred and three feet of similar wire were interposed as a spiral between the turns of the first coil, and metallic contact everywhere prevented by twine. One of these helices was connected with a galvanometer, and the other with a battery of one hundred pairs of plates four inches square, with double coppers, and well charged. When the contact was made, there was a sudden and very slight effect at the galvanometer, and there was also a similar slight effect when the contact with the battery was broken. But whilst the voltaic current was continuing to pass through the one helix, no galvanometrical appearances nor any effect like induction upon the other helix could be perceived, although the active power of the battery was proved to be great, by its heating the whole of its own helix, and by the brilliancy of the discharge when made through charcoal.

11. Repetition of the experiments with a battery of one hundred and twenty pairs of plates produced no other effects; but it was ascertained, both at this and the former time, that the slight deflection of the needle occurring at the moment of completing the connexion, was always in one

direction, and that the equally slight deflection produced when the contact was broken, was in the other direction; and also, that these effects occurred when the first helices were used (6, 8).

12. The results which I had by this time obtained with magnets led me to believe that the battery current through one wire, did, in reality, induce a similar current through the other wire, but that it continued for an instant only, and partook more of the nature of the electrical wave passed through from the shock of a common Leyden jar than of the current from a voltaic battery, and therefore might magnetize a steel needle, although it scarcely affected the galvanometer.

13. This expectation was confirmed: for on substituting a small hollow helix, formed round a glass tube, for the galvanometer, introducing a steel needle, making contact as before between the battery and the inducing wire (7, 10), and then removing the needle before the battery contact was broken, it was found magnetized.

14. When the battery contact was first made, then an unmagnetized needle introduced into the small indicating helix (13), and lastly the battery contact broken, the needle was found magnetized to an equal degree apparently as before; but the poles were of the contrary kind.

15. The same effects took place on using the large compound helices first described (6, 8).

16. When the unmagnetized needle was put into the indicating helix, before contact of the inducing wire with the battery, and remained there until the contact was broken, it exhibited little or no magnetism; the first effect having been nearly neutralized by the second (13, 14). The force of the induced current upon making contact was found always to exceed that of the induced current at breaking of contact; and if therefore the contact was made and broken many times in succession, whilst the needle remained in the indicating helix, it at last came out not unmagnetized, but a needle magnetized as if the induced current upon making contact had acted alone on it. This effect may be due to the

accumulation (as it is called) at the poles of the unconnected pile, rendering the current upon first making contact more powerful than what it is afterwards, at the moment of breaking contact.

17. If the circuit between the helix or wire under induction and the galvanometer or indicating spiral was not rendered complete *before* the connexion between the battery and the inducing wire was completed or broken, then no effects were perceived at the galvanometer. Thus, if the battery communications were first made, and then the wire under induction connected with the indicating helix, no magnetizing power was there exhibited. But still retaining the latter communications, when those with the battery were broken, a magnet was formed in the helix, but of the second kind (14), i.e. with poles indicating a current in the same direction to that belonging to the battery current, or to that always induced by that current at its cessation.

18. In the preceding experiments the wires were placed near to each other, and the contact of the inducing one with the battery made when the inductive effect was required; but as the particular action might be supposed to be exerted only at the moments of making and breaking contact, the induction was produced another way. Several feet of copper wire were stretched in wide zigzag forms, representing the letter, *W*, on one surface of a broad board; a second wire was stretched in precisely similar forms on a second board, so that when brought near the first, the wire should everywhere touch, except that a sheet of thick paper was interposed. One of these wires was connected with the galvanometer, and the other with a voltaic battery. The first wire was then moved towards the second, and as it approached, the needle was deflected. Being then removed, the needle was deflected in the opposite direction. By first making the wires approach and then recede, simultaneously with the vibrations of the needle, the latter soon became very extensive; but when the wires ceased to move from or towards each other, the galvanometer-needle soon came to its usual position.

19. As the wires approximated, the induced current was in the *contrary* direction to the inducing current. As the wires receded, the induced current was in the *same* direction as the inducing current. When the wires remained stationary, there was no induced current.

20. When a small voltaic arrangement was introduced into the circuit between the galvanometer (10) and its helix or wire, so as to cause a permanent deflection of 30° or 40°, and then the battery of one hundred pairs of plates connected with the inducing wire, there was an instantaneous action as before (11); but the galvanometer-needle immediately resumed and retained its place unaltered, notwithstanding the continued contact of the inducing wire with the trough: such was the case in whichever way the contacts were made (33).

21. Hence it would appear that collateral currents, either in the same or in opposite directions, exert no permanent inducing power on each other, affecting their quantity or tension.

22. I could obtain no evidence by the tongue, by spark, or by heating fine wire or charcoal, of the electricity passing through the wire under induction; neither could I obtain any chemical effects, though the contacts with metallic and other solutions were made and broken alternately with those of the battery, so that the second effect of induction should not oppose or neutralize the first (13, 16).

23. This deficiency of effect is not because the induced current of electricity cannot pass fluids, but probably because of its brief duration and feeble intensity; for on introducing two large copper plates into the circuit on the induced side (20), the plates being immersed in brine, but prevented from touching each other by an interposed cloth, the effect at the indicating galvanometer or helix occurred as before. The induced electricity could also pass through a voltaic trough (20). When, however, the quantity of interposed fluid was reduced to a drop, the galvanometer gave no indication.

24. Attempts to obtain similar effects by the use of wires

conveying ordinary electricity were doubtful in the results. A compound helix similar to that already described, containing eight elementary helices (6), was used. Four of the helices had their similar ends bound together by wire, and the two general terminations thus produced connected with the small magnetizing helix containing an unmagnetized needle (13). The other four helices were similarly arranged, but their ends connected with a Leyden jar. On passing the discharge, the needle was found to be a magnet; but it appeared probable that a part of the electricity of the jar had passed off to the small helix, and so magnetized the needle. There was indeed no reason to expect that the electricity of a jar possessing as it does great tension, would not diffuse itself through all the metallic matter interposed between the coatings.

25. Still it does not follow that the discharge of ordinary electricity through a wire does not produce analogous phenomena to those arising from voltaic electricity; but as it appears impossible to separate the effects produced at the moment when the discharge begins to pass, from the equal and contrary effects produced when it ceases to pass (16), inasmuch as with ordinary electricity these periods are simultaneous, so there can be scarcely any hope that in this form of the experiment they can be perceived.

26. Hence it is evident that currents of voltaic electricity present phenomena of induction somewhat analogous to those produced by electricity of tension, although, as will be seen hereafter, many differences exist between them. The result is the production of other currents (but which are only momentary), parallel, or tending to parallelism, with the inducing current. By reference to the poles of the needle formed in the indicating helix (13, 14) and to the deflections of the galvanometer-needle (11), it was found in all cases that the induced current, produced by the first action of the inducing current, was in the contrary direction to the latter, but that the current produced by the cessation of the inducing current was in the same direction (19). For the purpose of avoiding periphrasis, I propose to call this action of

the current from the voltaic battery *volta-electric induction*. The properties of the second wire, after induction has developed the first current, and whilst the electricity from the battery continues to flow through its inducing neighbour (10, 18), constitute a peculiar electric condition, the consideration of which will be resumed hereafter. All these results have been obtained with a voltaic apparatus consisting of a single pair of plates.

## § 2. *Evolution of Electricity from Magnetism*

27. A welded ring was made of soft round bar-iron, the metal being seven eighths of an inch in thickness, and the ring six inches in external diameter. Three helices were put round one part of this ring, each containing about twenty-four feet of copper wire one twentieth of an inch thick; they were insulated from the iron and each other, and superposed in the manner before described (6), occupying about nine inches in length upon the ring. They could be used separately or conjointly; the group may be distinguished by the letter *A*. On the other part of the ring about sixty feet of similar copper wire in two pieces were applied in the same manner, forming a helix *B*, which had the same common direction with the helices of *A*, but being separated from it at each extremity by about half an inch of the uncovered iron.

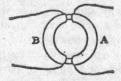

28. The helix *B* was connected by copper wires with a galvanometer three feet from the ring. The helices of *A* were connected end to end so as to form one common helix, the extremities of which were connected with a battery of ten pairs of plates four inches square. The galvanometer was immediately affected, and to a degree far beyond what has been described when with a battery of tenfold power helices

*without iron* were used (10); but though the contact was continued, the effect was not permanent, for the needle soon came to rest in its natural position, as if quite indifferent to the attached electromagnetic arrangement. Upon breaking the contact with the battery, the needle was again powerfully deflected, but in the contrary direction to that induced in the first instance.

29. Upon arranging the apparatus so that B should be out of use, the galvanometer be connected with one of the three wires of A (27), and the other two made into a helix through which the current from the trough (28) was passed, similar but rather more powerful effects were produced.

30. When the battery contact was made in one direction, the galvanometer-needle was deflected on the one side; if made in the other direction, the deflection was on the other side. The deflection on breaking the battery contact was always the reverse of that produced by completing it. The deflection on making a battery contact always indicated an induced current in the opposite direction to that from the battery; but on breaking the contact the deflection indicated an induced current in the same direction as that of the battery. No making or breaking of the contact at B side, or in any part of the galvanometer circuit, produced any effect at the galvanometer. No continuance of the battery current caused any deflection of the galvanometer-needle. As the above results are common to all these experiments, and to similar ones with ordinary magnets to be hereafter detailed, they need not be again particularly described.

31. Upon using the power of one hundred pairs of plates (10), with this ring, the impulse at the galvanometer, when contact was completed or broken, was so great as to make the needle spin round rapidly four or five times, before the air and terrestrial magnetism could reduce its motion to mere oscillation.

32. By using charcoal at the ends of the B helix, a minute *spark* could be perceived when the contact of the battery with A was completed. This spark could not be due to any diversion of a part of the current of the battery through the

iron to the helix $B$; for when the battery contact was continued, the galvanometer still resumed its perfectly indifferent state (28). The spark was rarely seen on breaking contact. A small platina wire could not be ignited by this induced current; but there seems every reason to believe that
the effect would be obtained by using a stronger original
current or a more powerful arrangement of helices.

33. A feeble voltaic current was sent through the helix $B$
and the galvanometer, so as to deflect the needle of the
latter 30° or 40°, and then the battery of one hundred pairs
of plates connected with $A$; but after the first effect was over,
the galvanometer-needle resumed exactly the position due
to the feeble current transmitted by its own wire. This
took place in whichever way the battery contacts were made,
and shows that here again (20) no permanent influence of
the currents upon each other, as to their quantity and tension, exists.

34. Another arrangement was then employed connecting
the former experiments on volta-electric induction (6–26)
with the present. A combination of helices like that already
described (6) was constructed upon a hollow cylinder of
pasteboard: there were eight lengths of copper wire, containing altogether 220 feet; four of these helices were connected end to end, and then with the galvanometer (7); the
other intervening four were also connected end to end, and
the battery of one hundred pairs discharged through them.
In this form the effect on the galvanometer was hardly sensible (11), though magnets could be made by the induced
current (13). But when a soft iron cylinder seven eighths of an
inch thick, and twelve inches long, was introduced into the
pasteboard tube, surrounded by the helices, then the induced current affected the galvanometer powerfully, and
with all the phenomena just described (30). It possessed also
the power of making magnets with more energy, apparently,
than when no iron cylinder was present.

# JAMES CLERK MAXWELL
## 1831–79

## A DYNAMICAL THEORY OF
## ELECTROMAGNETIC PHENOMENA

IN 1854 Maxwell took up the study of electricity, and two years later he published a paper entitled *On Faraday's Lines of Force*, in which he discussed the concepts which had previously been used to describe the phenomena of electricity and magnetism. Faraday's experimental investigations in the field of electromagnetism have already been discussed. Great as they were, a final assessment of his contribution to the subject would be incomplete without taking into account an achievement of a rather different kind. Faraday conceived a new way of thinking about such phenomena, in which the 'lines of force' played a central role. A charged (or magnetized) body was thought of as exerting an influence over the space surrounding it, in a fashion analogous to the strains induced in a material body by external pressures. The 'lines of force' provided a semi-pictorial means of characterizing this influence.

Faraday's point of view was in sharp contrast to the customary modes of thinking which took as their starting-point the direct interaction between the charged bodies, and Maxwell, in following Faraday in this way of thinking, was moving counter to the prevailing tide of ideas in physics. No doubt for this reason, the significance of Maxwell's discussion was lost on his contemporaries, and the consequences of this new approach were not revealed until, in 1861 and 1862, Maxwell himself published four papers entitled *On Physical Lines of Force* in which he began that synthesis of all the earlier theories of electric and magnetic effects, which culminated in *A Dynamical Theory of the Electromagnetic Field*, as his final memoir was titled.

The reading which follows is taken from this memoir,

which appeared in the *Philosophical Transactions of the Royal Society* (Vol. 155, 1865). It consists of the introduction to the mathematical theory which followed, and provides a lucid survey of the theory and its consequences. Included in this extract are Maxwell's conclusions concerning the electromagnetic nature of light, a feature of the theory which presented the entire subject of optics as a branch of electromagnetism, and thus achieved a tremendous unification of a vast range of physical phenomena.

James Clerk Maxwell was born in Edinburgh. After attending the university in that city he moved to Cambridge, and following his graduation, became a fellow of Trinity College. A return to the north, and a professorship at Aberdeen, led to his being appointed Professor of Physics at King's College, in London. These years, from 1860 to 1865, were highly productive, and it was during this period that Maxwell met Faraday.

Returning to his estate in Scotland he devoted himself to the writing of his great *Treatise on Electricity and Magnetism*. In 1871 Maxwell was persuaded to accept the Chair of Physics at Cambridge, and here he remained until his death at the early age of forty-eight.

In addition to his work on electromagnetism, Maxwell made important contributions to many other subjects, and it is an indication of his genius that his researches on the kinetic theory of gases are rated by many as greater even than his theories of electricity and magnetism.

---

¶ *A Dynamical Theory of the Electromagnetic Field*

(1) The most obvious mechanical phenomenon in electrical and magnetical experiments is the mutual action by which bodies in certain states set each other in motion while still at a sensible distance from each other. The first step, therefore, in reducing these phenomena into scientific form, is to ascertain the magnitude and direction of the force acting between the bodies, and when it is found that this force

depends in a certain way upon the relative position of the bodies and on their electric or magnetic condition, it seems at first sight natural to explain the facts by assuming the existence of something either at rest or in motion in each body, constituting its electric or magnetic state, and capable of acting at a distance according to mathematical laws.

In this way mathematical theories of statical electricity, of magnetism, of the mechanical action between conductors carrying currents, and of the induction of currents have been formed. In these theories the force acting between the two bodies is treated with reference only to the condition of the bodies and their relative position, and without any express consideration of the surrounding medium.

These theories assume, more or less explicitly, the existence of substances the particles of which have the property of acting on one another at a distance by attraction or repulsion. The most complete development of a theory of this kind is that of M. W. Weber, who has made the same theory include electrostatic and electromagnetic phenomena.

In doing so, however, he has found it necessary to assume that the force between two electric particles depends on their relative velocity, as well as on their distance.

This theory, as developed by MM. W. Weber and C. Neumann, is exceedingly ingenious, and wonderfully comprehensive in its application to the phenomena of statical electricity, electromagnetic attractions, induction of currents, and diamagnetic phenomena; and it comes to us with the more authority, as it has served to guide the speculations of one who has made so great an advance in the practical part of electric science, both by introducing a consistent system of units in electrical measurement, and by actually determining electrical quantities with an accuracy hitherto unknown.

(2) The mechanical difficulties, however, which are involved in the assumption of particles acting at a distance with forces which depend on their velocities are such as to prevent me from considering this theory as an ultimate one,

though it may have been, and may yet be useful in leading to the coordination of phenomena.

I have therefore preferred to seek an explanation of the facts in another direction, by supposing them to be produced by actions which go on in the surrounding medium as well as in the excited bodies, and endeavouring to explain the action between distant bodies without assuming the existence of forces capable of acting directly at sensible distances.

(3) The theory I propose may therefore be called a theory of the *Electromagnetic Field*, because it has to do with the space in the neighbourhood of the electric or magnetic bodies, and it may be called a *Dynamical* Theory, because it assumes that in that space there is matter in motion, by which the observed electromagnetic phenomena are produced.

(4) The electromagnetic field is that part of space which contains and surrounds bodies in electric or magnetic conditions.

It may be filled with any kind of matter, or we may endeavour to render it empty of all gross matter, as in the case of Geissler's tubes and other so-called vacua.

There is always, however, enough of matter left to receive and transmit the undulations of light and heat, and it is because the transmission of these radiations is not greatly altered when transparent bodies of measurable density are substituted for the so-called vacuum, that we are obliged to admit that the undulations are those of an aethereal substance, and not of the gross matter, the presence of which merely modifies in some way the motion of the aether.

We have therefore some reason to believe, from the phenomena of light and heat, that there is an aethereal medium filling space and permeating bodies, capable of being set in motion and of transmitting that motion from one part to another, and of communicating that motion to gross matter so as to heat it and affect it in various ways.

(5) Now the energy communicated to the body in heating it must have formerly existed in the moving medium, for the

undulations had left the source of heat some time before they reached the body, and during that time the energy must have been half in the form of motion of the medium and half in the form of elastic resilience. From these considerations Professor W. Thomson has argued, that the medium must have a density capable of comparison with that of gross matter, and has even assigned an inferior limit to that density.

(6) We may therefore receive, as a datum derived from a branch of science independent of that with which we have to deal, the existence of a pervading medium, of small but real density, capable of being set in motion, and of transmitting motion from one part to another with great, but not infinite, velocity.

Hence the parts of this medium must be so connected that the motion of one part depends in some way on the motion of the rest; and at the same time these connexions must be capable of a certain kind of elastic yielding, since the communication of motion is not instantaneous, but occupies time.

The medium is therefore capable of receiving and storing up two kinds of energy, namely, the 'actual' energy depending on the motion of its parts, and 'potential' energy, consisting of the work which the medium will do in recovering from displacement in virtue of its elasticity.

The propagation of undulations consists in the continual transformation of one of these forms of energy into the other alternately, and at any instant the amount of energy in the whole medium is equally divided, so that half is energy of motion, and half is elastic resilience.

(7) A medium having such a constitution may be capable of other kinds of motion and displacement than those which produce the phenomena of light and heat, and some of these may be of such a kind that they may be evidenced to our senses by the phenomena they produce.

(8) Now we know that the luminiferous medium is in certain cases acted on by magnetism; for Faraday discovered that when a plane polarized ray traverses a transparent diamagnetic medium in the direction of the lines of magnetic

force produced by magnets or currents in the neighbourhood, the plane of polarization is caused to rotate.

This rotation is always in the direction in which positive electricity must be carried round the diamagnetic body in order to produce the actual magnetization of the field.

M. Verdet has since discovered that if a paramagnetic body, such as solution of perchloride of iron in ether, be substituted for the diamagnetic body, the rotation is in the opposite direction.

Now Professor W. Thomson has pointed out that no distribution of forces acting between the parts of a medium whose only motion is that of the luminous vibrations, is sufficient to account for the phenomena, but that we must admit the existence of a motion in the medium depending on the magnetization, in addition to the vibratory motion which constitutes light.

It is true that the rotation by magnetism of the plane of polarization has been observed only in media of considerable density; but the properties of the magnetic field are not so much altered by the substitution of one medium for another, or for a vacuum, as to allow us to suppose that the dense medium does anything more than merely modify the motion of the ether. We have therefore warrantable grounds for inquiring whether there may not be a motion of the ethereal medium going on wherever magnetic effects are observed, and we have some reason to suppose that this motion is one of rotation, having the direction of the magnetic force as its axis.

(9) We may now consider another phenomenon observed in the electromagnetic field. When a body is moved across the lines of magnetic force it experiences what is called an electromotive force; the two extremities of the body tend to become oppositely electrified, and an electric current tends to flow through the body. When the electromotive force is sufficiently powerful, and is made to act on certain compound bodies, it decomposes them, and causes one of their components to pass towards one extremity of the body, and the other in the opposite direction.

Here we have evidence of a force causing an electric current in spite of resistance; electrifying the extremities of a body in opposite ways, a condition which is sustained only by the action of the electromotive force, and which, as soon as that force is removed, tends, with an equal and opposite force, to produce a counter current through the body and to restore the original electrical state of the body; and finally, if strong enough, tearing to pieces chemical compounds and carrying their components in opposite directions, while their natural tendency is to combine, and to combine with a force which can generate an electromotive force in the reverse direction.

This, then, is a force acting on a body caused by its motion through the electromagnetic field, or by changes occurring in that field itself; and the effect of the force is either to produce a current and heat the body, or to decompose the body, or, when it can do neither, to put the body in a state of electric polarization – a state of constraint in which opposite extremities are oppositely electrified, and from which the body tends to relieve itself as soon as the disturbing force is removed.

(10) According to the theory which I propose to explain, this 'electromotive force' is the force called into play during the communication of motion from one part of the medium to another, and it is by means of this force that the motion of one part causes motion in another part. When electromotive force acts on a conducting circuit, it produces a current, which, as it meets with resistance, occasions a continual transformation of electrical energy into heat, which is incapable of being restored again to the form of electrical energy by any reversal of the process.

(11) But when electromotive force acts on a dielectric it produces a state of polarization of its parts similar in distribution to the polarity of the parts of a mass of iron under the influence of a magnet, and like the magnetic polarization, capable of being described as a state in which every particle has its opposite poles in opposite conditions.

In a dielectric under the action of electromotive force, we

may conceive that the electricity in each molecule is so displaced that one side is rendered positively and the other negatively electrical, but that the electricity remains entirely connected with the molecule, and does not pass from one molecule to another. The effect of this action on the whole dielectric mass is to produce a general displacement of electricity in a certain direction. This displacement does not amount to a current, because when it has attained to a certain value it remains constant, but it is the commencement of a current, and its variations constitute currents in the positive or the negative direction according as the displacement is increasing or decreasing. In the interior of the dielectric there is no indication of electrification, because the electrification of the surface of any molecule is neutralized by the opposite electrification of the surface of the molecules in contact with it; but at the bounding surface of the dielectric, where the electrification is not neutralized, we find the phenomena which indicate positive or negative electrification.

The relation between the electromotive force and the amount of electric displacement it produces depends on the nature of the dielectric, the same electromotive force producing generally a greater electric displacement in solid dielectrics, such as glass or sulphur, than in air.

(12) Here, then, we perceive another effect of electromotive force, namely, electric displacement, which according to our theory is a kind of elastic yielding to the action of the force, similar to that which takes place in structures and machines owing to the want of perfect rigidity of the connexions.

(13) The practical investigation of the inductive capacity of dielectrics is rendered difficult on account of two disturbing phenomena. The first is the conductivity of the dielectric, which, though in many cases exceedingly small, is not altogether insensible. The second is the phenomenon called electric absorption, in virtue of which, when the dielectric is exposed to electromotive force, the electric displacement gradually increases, and when the electromotive force is

removed, the dielectric does not instantly return to its primitive state, but only discharges a portion of its electrification, and when left to itself gradually acquires electrification on its surface, as the interior gradually becomes depolarized. Almost all solid dielectrics exhibit this phenomenon, which gives rise to the residual charge in the Leyden jar, and to several phenomena of electric cables described by Mr F. Jenkin.

(14) We have here two other kinds of yielding besides the yielding of the perfect dielectric, which we have compared to a perfectly elastic body. The yielding due to conductivity may be compared to that of a viscous fluid (that is to say, a fluid having great internal friction), or a soft solid on which the smallest force produces a permanent alteration of figure increasing with the time during which the force acts. The yielding due to electric absorption may be compared to that of a cellular elastic body containing a thick fluid in its cavities. Such a body, when subjected to pressure, is compressed by degrees on account of the gradual yielding of the thick fluid; and when the pressure is removed it does not at once recover its figure, because the elasticity of the substance of the body has gradually to overcome the tenacity of the fluid before it can regain complete equilibrium.

Several solid bodies in which no such structure as we have supposed can be found, seem to possess a mechanical property of this kind; and it seems probable that the same substances, if dielectrics, may possess the analogous electrical property, and if magnetic, may have corresponding properties relating to the acquisition, retention, and loss of magnetic polarity.

(15) It appears therefore that certain phenomena in electricity and magnetism lead to the same conclusion as those of optics, namely, that there is an aethereal medium pervading all bodies, and modified only in degree by their presence; that the parts of this medium are capable of being set in motion by electric currents and magnets; that this motion is communicated from one part of the medium to another by forces arising from the connexions of those parts;

that under the action of these forces there is a certain yielding depending on the elasticity of these connexions; and that therefore energy in two different forms may exist in the medium, the one form being the actual energy of motion of its parts, and the other being the potential energy stored up in the connexions, in virtue of their elasticity.

(16) Thus, then, we are led to the conception of a complicated mechanism capable of a vast variety of motion, but at the same time so connected that the motion of one part depends, according to definite relations, on the motion of other parts, these motions being communicated by forces arising from the relative displacement of the connected parts, in virtue of their elasticity. Such a mechanism must be subject to the general laws of Dynamics, and we ought to be able to work out all the consequences of its motion, provided we know the form of the relation between the motions of the parts.

(17) We know that when an electric current is established in a conducting circuit, the neighbouring part of the field is characterized by certain magnetic properties, and that if two circuits are in the field, the magnetic properties of the field due to the two currents are combined. Thus each part of the field is in connexion with both currents, and the two currents are put in connexion with each other in virtue of their connexion with the magnetization of the field. The first result of this connexion that I propose to examine, is the induction of one current by another, and by the motion of conductors in the field.

The second result, which is deduced from this, is the mechanical action between conductors carrying currents. The phenomenon of the induction of currents has been deduced from their mechanical action by Helmholtz and Thomson. I have followed the reverse order, and deduced the mechanical action from the laws of induction. I have then described experimental methods of determining the quantities $L$, $M$, $N$, on which these phenomena depend.

(18) I then apply the phenomena of induction and attraction of currents to the exploration of the electromagnetic

field, and the laying down systems of lines of magnetic force which indicate its magnetic properties. By exploring the same field with a magnet, I show the distribution of its equipotential magnetic surfaces, cutting the lines of force at right angles.

In order to bring these results within the power of symbolical calculation, I then express them in the form of the General Equations of the Electromagnetic Field. These equations express –

(*A*) The relation between electric displacement, true conduction, and the total current, compounded of both.

(*B*) The relation between the lines of magnetic force and the inductive coefficients of a circuit, as already deduced from the laws of induction.

(*C*) The relation between the strength of a current and its magnetic effects, according to the electromagnetic system of measurement.

(*D*) The value of the electromotive force in a body, as arising from the motion of the body in the field, the alteration of the field itself, and the variation of electric potential from one part of the field to another.

(*E*) The relation between electric displacement, and the electromotive force which produces it.

(*F*) The relation between an electric current, and the electromotive force which produces it.

(*G*) The relation between the amount of free electricity at any point, and the electric displacements in the neighbourhood.

(*H*) The relation between the increase or diminution of free electricity and the electric currents in the neighbourhood.

There are twenty of these equations in all, involving twenty variable quantities.

(19) I then express in terms of these quantities the intrinsic energy of the Electromagnetic Field as depending partly on its magnetic and partly on its electric polarization at every point.

From this I determine the mechanical force acting, 1st,

on a moveable conductor carrying an electric current; 2ndly, on a magnetic pole; 3rdly, on an electrified body.

The last result, namely, the mechanical force acting on an electrified body, gives rise to an independent method of electrical measurement founded on its electrostatic effects. The relation between the units employed in the two methods is shown to depend on what I have called the 'electric elasticity' of the medium, and to be a velocity, which has been experimentally determined by MM. Weber and Kohlrausch.

I then show how to calculate the electrostatic capacity of a condenser, and the specific inductive capacity of a dielectric.

The case of a condenser composed of parallel layers of substances of different electric resistances and inductive capacities is next examined, and it is shown that the phenomenon called electric absorption will generally occur, that is, the condenser, when suddenly discharged, will after a short time show signs of a *residual* charge.

(20) The general equations are next applied to the case of a magnetic disturbance propagated through a non-conducting field, and it is shown that the only disturbances which can be so propagated are those which are transverse to the direction of propagation, and that the velocity of propagation is the velocity $v$, found from experiments such as those of Weber, which expresses the number of electrostatic units of electricity which are contained in one electromagnetic unit.

This velocity is so nearly that of light, that it seems we have strong reason to conclude that light itself (including radiant heat, and other radiations if any) is an electromagnetic disturbance in the form of waves propagated through the electromagnetic field according to electromagnetic laws. If so, the agreement between the elasticity of the medium as calculated from the rapid alternations of luminous vibrations, and as found by the slow processes of electrical experiments, shows how perfect and regular the elastic properties of the medium must be when not encumbered with any matter denser than air. If the same character of the elasticity is retained in dense transparent bodies, it appears that the square of the index of refraction is equal to the product of the specific dielectric capacity and the specific magnetic capacity. Conducting media are shown to absorb such radiations rapidly, and therefore to be generally opaque.

The conception of the propagation of transverse magnetic disturbances to the exclusion of normal ones is distinctly set forth by Professor Faraday in his *Thoughts on Ray Vibrations*. The electromagnetic theory of light, as proposed by him, is the same in substance as that which I have begun to develop in this paper, except that in 1846 there were no data to calculate the velocity of propagation.

(21) The general equations are then applied to the calculation of the coefficients of mutual induction of two circular currents and the coefficient of self-induction in a coil. The want of uniformity of the current in the different parts of the section of a wire at the commencement of the current is investigated, I believe for the first time, and the consequent correction of the coefficient of self-induction is found.

These results are applied to the calculation of the self-induction of the coil used in the experiments of the Committee of the British Association on Standards of Electric Resistance, and the value compared with that deduced from the experiments.

# HEINRICH HERTZ

## 1857-94

### THE EXISTENCE OF ELECTROMAGNETIC
### WAVES IS EXPERIMENTALLY CONFIRMED

MAXWELL's theory of electromagnetism had led him to predict the existence of electromagnetic waves, capable of travelling through empty space with a velocity equal to that of visible light. This was such an important conclusion from the theory that direct confirmation was highly desirable. Indeed, final acceptance of Maxwell's ideas, as with any physical theory, had to wait upon experimental verification.

Twenty years after Maxwell's monumental theoretical studies had been published, Heinrich Hertz proved experimentally the existence of electromagnetic waves and a mathematical conception thus became another important tool, to be put to practical use some years later by Guglielmo Marconi in the form of radio transmission. Of greater importance to the subsequent development of physics, however, was Hertz's proof that Maxwell's electromagnetic waves were capable of reflection, refraction, and polarization as well as diffraction and interference and so corresponded precisely in this behaviour with the waves of light.

Born in Hamburg, Hertz studied at Berlin under Hermann Helmholtz (1821–94), who made outstanding contributions to medicine, physiology, and psychology as well as to physics and who is distinguished by his mathematical formulation of the theory of the conservation of energy. Hertz's first academic appointment was at Kiel; but his most important work was done at the technical school at Karlsruhe. His stature was such that he was appointed to succeed Clausius at Bonn in 1889, but his brilliant and promising career was ended by his early death before he was able to participate in the great developments which his

254

experiments had stimulated. Had he lived, Hertz would undoubtedly have played an important part in the atomic developments of our own century.

The paper reproduced here describes Hertz's experimental production of electromagnetic waves by means of an oscillating electric current. This translation, by D. E. Jones, is taken from Magie's *A Sourcebook in Physics* (Harvard University Press, 1935).

─────

## ¶ *Electric Radiation*

As soon as I had succeeded in proving that the action of an electric oscillation spreads out as a wave into space, I planned experiments with the object of concentrating this action and making it perceptible at greater distances by putting the primary conductor in the focal line of a large concave parabolic mirror. These experiments did not lead to the desired result, and I felt certain that the want of success was a necessary consequence of the disproportion between the length (4–5 metres) of the waves used and the dimensions which I was able, under the most favourable circumstances, to give to the mirror. Recently I have observed that the experiments which I have described can be carried out quite well with oscillations of more than ten times the frequency, and with waves less than one-tenth the length of those which were first discovered. I have, therefore, returned to the use of concave mirrors, and have obtained better results than I had ventured to hope for. I have succeeded in producing distinct rays of electric force, and in carrying out with them the elementary experiments which are commonly performed with light and radiant heat. The following is an account of these experiments:

## § *The Apparatus*

The short waves were excited by the same method which we used for producing the longer waves. The primary conductor used may be most simply described as follows: Imagine a cylindrical brass body, 3 cm. in diameter and 26 cm. long, interrupted midway along its length by a spark-gap whose poles on either side are formed by spheres of 2 cm. radius. The length of the conductor is approximately equal to the half wave-length of the correponding oscillation in straight wires; from this we are at once able to estimate approximately the period of oscillation. It is essential that the pole-surfaces of the spark-gap should be frequently re-polished, and also that during the experiments they should be carefully protected from illumination by simultaneous side-discharges; otherwise the oscillations are not excited. Whether the spark-gap is in a satisfactory state can always be recognized by the appearance and sound of the sparks. The discharge is led to the two halves of the conductor by means of two gutta-percha-covered wires which are connected near the spark-gap on either side. I no longer made use of the large Ruhmkorff, but found it better to use a small induction-coil by Keiser and Schmidt; the longest sparks, between points, given by this were 4·5 cm. long. It was supplied with current from three accumulators, and gave sparks 1 – 2 cm. long between the spherical knobs of the primary conductor. For the purpose of the experiments the spark-gap was reduced to 3 mm.

Here, again, the small sparks induced in a secondary conductor were the means used for detecting the electric forces in space. As before, I used partly a circle which could be rotated within itself and which had about the same period of oscillation as the primary conductor. It was made of copper wire 1 mm. thick, and had in the present instance a diameter of only 7·5 cm. One end of the wire carried a polished brass sphere a few millimeters in diameter; the other end was pointed and could be brought up, by means of a fine screw insulated from the wire, to within an exceedingly short distance from the brass sphere. As will be readily understood, we have here to deal only with minute sparks of a few hundredths of a millimetre in length; and after a little practice one judges more according to the brilliancy than the length of the sparks.

The circular conductor gives only a differential effect,

and is not adapted for use in the focal line of a concave mirror. Most of the work was therefore done with another conductor arranged as follows: Two straight pieces of wire, each 50 cm. long and 5 mm. in diameter, were adjusted in a straight line so that their near ends were 5 cm. apart. From these ends two wires, 15 cm. long and 1 mm. in diameter, were carried, parallel to one another and perpendicular to the wires first mentioned, to a spark-gap arranged just as in the circular conductor. In this conductor the resonance-action was given up, and indeed it only comes slightly into play in this case. It would have been simpler to put the spark-gap directly in the middle of the straight wire; but the observer could not then have handled and observed the spark-gap in the focus of the mirror without obstructing the aperture. For this reason the arrangement above described was chosen in preference to the other which would in itself have been more advantageous.

## § The Production of the Ray

If the primary oscillator is now set up in a fairly large free space, one can, with the aid of the circular conductor, detect in its neighbourhood on a smaller scale all those phenomena which I have already observed and described as occurring in the neighbourhood of a larger oscillation. The greatest distance at which sparks could be perceived in the secondary conductor was 1·5 metre, or, when the primary spark-gap was in very good order, as much as 2 metres. When a plane reflecting plate is set up at a suitable distance on one side of the primary oscillator, and parallel to it, the action on the opposite side is strengthened. To be more precise: If the distance chosen is either very small, or somewhat greater than 30 cm., the plate weakens the effect; it strengthens the effect greatly at distances of 8–15 cm., slightly at a distance of 45 cm., and exerts no influence at greater distances. We have drawn attention to this phenomenon in an earlier paper, and we conclude from it that the wave in air corresponding to the primary oscillation has a half wave-length of about 30 cm. We may expect to find a still further reinforcement if we replace the plane surface by a concave mirror having the form of a parabolic cylinder, in the focal line of which the axis of the primary oscillation lies. The focal length of the mirror should be chosen as small as possible, if it is properly to concentrate the action. But if the direct wave is not to annul immediately the action of the reflected wave, the focal length must not be much smaller than a quarter wavelength. I therefore fixed on $12\frac{1}{2}$ cm. as the focal length, and constructed the mirror by bending a zinc sheet 2 metres long, 2 metres broad, and $\frac{1}{2}$ mm. thick into the desired shape over a wooden frame of the exact curvature. The height of the mirror was thus 2 metres, the breadth of its aperture 1·2 metre, and its depth 0·7 metre. The primary oscillator was fixed in the middle of the focal line. The wires which conducted the discharge were led through the mirror; the induction-coil and the cells were accordingly placed behind the mirror so as to be out of the way. If we now investigate the neighbourhood of the oscillator with our conductors, we find that there is no action behind the mirror or at either side of it; but in the direction of the optical axis of the mirror the sparks can be perceived up to a distance of 5 – 6 metres. When a plane conducting surface was set up so as to oppose the advancing waves at right angles, the sparks could be detected in its neighbourhood at even greater distances – up to about 9 – 10 metres. The waves reflected from the conducting surface reinforce the advancing waves at certain points. At other points again the two sets of waves weaken one another. In front of the plane wall one can recognize with the rectilinear conductor very distinct maxima and minima, and with the circular conductor the characteristic interference-phenomena of stationary waves which I have described in an earlier paper. I was able to distinguish four nodal points, which were situated at the wall and at 33, 65, and 98 cm. distance from it. We thus get 33 cm. as a closer approximation to the half wave-length of the waves used, and 1·1 thousand-millionth of a second as their period of oscillation, assuming that they travel with the velocity of light. In wires the oscillation gave a wave-length of 29 cm.

Hence it appears that these short waves also have a somewhat lower velocity in wires than in air; but the ratio of the two velocities comes very near to the theoretical value – unity – and does not differ from it so much as appeared to be probable from our experiments on longer waves. This remarkable phenomenon still needs elucidation. Inasmuch as the phenomena are only exhibited in the neighbourhood of the optic axis of the mirror, we may speak of the result produced as an electric ray proceeding from the concave mirror.

I now constructed a second mirror, exactly similar to the first, and attached the rectilinear secondary conductor to it in such a way that the two wires of 50 cm. length lay in the focal line, and the two wires connected to the spark-gap passed directly through the walls of the mirror without touching it. The spark-gap was thus situated directly behind the mirror, and the observer could adjust and examine it without obstructing the course of the waves. I expected to find that, on intercepting the ray with this apparatus, I should be able to observe it at even greater distances; and the event proved that I was not mistaken. In the rooms at my disposal I could now perceive the sparks from one end to the other. The greatest distance to which I was able, by availing myself of a doorway, to follow the ray was 16 metres; but according to the results of the reflection-experiments (to be presently described), there can be no doubt that sparks could be obtained at any rate up to 20 metres in open spaces. For the remaining experiments such great distances are not necessary, and it is convenient that the sparking in the secondary conductor should not be too feeble; for most of the experiments a distance of 6 – 10 metres is most suitable. We shall now describe the simple phenomena which can be exhibited with the ray without difficulty. When the contrary is not expressly stated, it is to be assumed that the focal lines of both mirrors are vertical.

§ *Rectilinear Propagation*

If a screen of sheet zinc 2 metres high and 1 metre broad is placed on the straight line joining both mirrors, and at right angles to the direction of the ray, the secondary sparks disappear completely. An equally complete shadow is thrown by a screen of tinfoil or gold-paper. If an assistant walks across the path of the ray, the secondary spark-gap becomes dark as soon as he intercepts the ray, and again lights up when he leaves the path clear. Insulators do not stop the ray – it passes right through a wooden partition or door; and it is not without astonishment that one sees the sparks appear inside a closed room. If two conducting screens, 2 metres high and 1 metre broad, are set up symmetrically on the right and left of the ray, and perpendicular to it, they do not interfere at all with the secondary spark so long as the width of the opening between them is not less than the aperture of the mirrors, viz., 1·2 metre. If the opening is made narrower the sparks become weaker, and disappear when the width of the opening is reduced below 0·5 metre. The sparks also disappear if the opening is left with a breadth of 1·2 metre, but is shifted to one side of the straight line joining the mirrors. If the optical axis of the mirror containing the oscillator is rotated to the right or left about 10° out of the proper position, the secondary sparks become weak, and a rotation through 15° causes them to disappear.

There is no sharp geometrical limit to either the ray or the shadows; it is easy to produce phenomena corresponding to diffraction. As yet, however, I have not succeeded in observing maxima and minima at the edge of the shadows.

§ *Polarization*

From the mode in which our ray was produced we can have no doubt whatever that it consists of transverse vibrations and is plane-polarized in the optical sense. We can also prove by experiment that this is the case. If the receiving mirror be rotated about the ray as axis until its focal line, and therefore the secondary conductor also, lies in a horizontal plane, the secondary sparks become more and more feeble, and when the two focal lines are at right angles, no sparks whatever are obtained even if the mirrors are moved close up to one another. The two mirrors behave like the polarizer and analyser of a polarization apparatus.

I next had made an octagonal frame, 2 metres high and 2 metres broad; across this were stretched copper wires 1 mm. thick, the wires being parallel to each other and 3 cm. apart. If the two mirrors were now set up with their focal lines parallel, and the wire screen was interposed perpendicularly to the ray and so that the direction of the wires was perpendicular to the direction of the focal lines, the screen practically did not interfere at all with the secondary sparks. But if the screen was set up in such a way that its wires were parallel to the focal lines, it stopped the ray completely. With regard then to transmitted energy, the screen behaves towards our ray as a tourmaline plate behaves towards a plane-polarized ray of light. The receiving mirror was now placed once more so that its focal line was horizontal; under these circumstances, as already mentioned, no sparks appeared. Nor were any sparks produced when the screen was interposed in the path of the ray, so long as the wires in the screen were either horizontal or vertical. But if the frame was set up in such a position that the wires were inclined at 45° to the horizontal on either side, then the interposition of the screen immediately produced sparks in the secondary spark-gap. Clearly the screen resolves the advancing oscillation into two components and transmits only that component which is perpendicular to the direction of its wires. This component is inclined at 45° to the focal line of the second mirror, and may thus, after being again resolved by the mirror, act upon the secondary conductor. The phenomenon is exactly analogous to the brightening of the dark field of two crossed Nicols by the interposition of a crystalline plate in a suitable position.

With regard to the polarization it may be further observed that, with the means employed in the present investigation, we are only able to recognize the electric force. When the primary oscillator is in a vertical position the oscillations of this force undoubtedly take place in the vertical plane through the ray, and are absent in the horizontal plane. But the results of experiments with slowly alternating currents leave no room for doubt that the electric oscillations are accompanied by oscillations of magnetic force which take place in the horizontal plane through the ray and are zero in the vertical plane. Hence the polarization of the ray does not so much consist in the occurrence of oscillations in the vertical plane, but rather in the fact that the oscillations in the vertical plane are of an electrical nature, while those in the horizontal plane are of a magnetic nature. Obviously, then, the question, in which of the two planes the oscillation in our ray occurs, cannot be answered unless one specifies whether the question relates to the electric or the magnetic oscillation. It was Herr Kolacek who first pointed out clearly that this consideration is the reason why an old optical dispute has never been decided.

§ *Reflection*

We have already proved the reflection of the waves from conducting surfaces by the interference between the reflected and the advancing waves, and have also made use of the reflection in the construction of our concave mirrors. But now we are able to go further and to separate the two systems of waves from one another. I first placed both mirrors in a large room side by side, with their apertures facing in the same direction, and their axes converging to a point about 3 metres off. The spark-gap of the receiving mirror naturally remained dark. I next set up a plane vertical wall made of thin sheet zinc, 2 metres high and 2 metres broad, at the point of intersection of the axes, and adjusted it so that it was equally inclined to both. I obtained a vigorous stream of sparks arising from the reflection of the ray by the wall. The sparking ceased as soon as the wall was rotated around a vertical axis through about 15° on either side of the correct position; from this it follows that the reflection is regular, not diffuse. When the wall was moved away from the mirrors, the axes of the latter being still kept converging towards the wall, the sparking diminished very slowly. I could still recognize sparks when the wall was 10 metres away from the mirrors, i.e when the waves had to traverse a distance of 20 metres. This arrangement might be adopted with advantage for the purpose of comparing the rate of propagation, e.g. through cables.

In order to produce reflection of the ray at angles of incidence greater than zero, I allowed the ray to pass parallel to the wall of the room in which there was a doorway. In the neighbouring room to which this door led I set up the receiving mirror so that its optic axis passed centrally through the door and intersected the direction of the ray at right angles. If the plane conducting surface was now set up vertically at the point of intersection, and adjusted so as to make angles of 45° with the ray and also with the axis of the receiving mirror, there appeared in the secondary conductor a stream of sparks which was not interrupted by closing the door. When I turned the reflecting surface about 10° out of the correct position the sparks disappeared. Thus the reflection is regular, and the angles of incidence and reflection are equal. That the action proceeded from the source of disturbance to the plane mirror, and hence to the secondary conductor, could also be shown by placing shadow-giving screens at different points of this path. The secondary sparks then always ceased immediately; whereas no effect was produced when the screen was placed anywhere else in the room. With the aid of the circular secondary conductor it is possible to determine the position of the wave-front in the ray; this was found to be at right angles to the ray before and after reflection, so that in the reflection it was turned through 90°.

Hitherto the focal lines of the concave mirrors were vertical, and the plane of oscillation was therefore perpendicular to the plane of incidence. In order to produce reflection with the oscillations in the plane of incidence, I placed both mirrors with their focal lines horizontal. I observed the same phenomena as in the previous position; and, moreover, I was not able to recognize any difference in the intensity of the reflected ray in the two cases. On the other hand, if the focal line of the one mirror is vertical, and of the other horizontal, no secondary sparks can be observed. The inclination of the plane of oscillation to the plane of incidence is therefore not altered by reflection provided this inclination has one of the two special values referred to; but in general this statement cannot hold good. It is even questionable whether the ray after reflection continues to be plane-polarized. The interferences which are produced in front of the mirror by the intersecting wave-systems, and which, as I have remarked, give rise to characteristic phenomena in the circular conductor, are most likely to throw light upon all problems relating to the change of phase and amplitude produced by reflection.

One further experiment on reflection from an electrically eolotropic surface may be mentioned. The two concave mirrors were again placed side by side, as in the reflection-experiment first described; but now there was placed opposite them, as a reflecting surface, the screen of parallel copper wires which has already been referred to. It was found that the secondary spark-gap remained dark when the wires intersected the direction of the oscillations at right angles, but that sparking began as soon as the wires coincided with the direction of the oscillations. Hence the analogy between the tourmaline plate and our surface which conducts in one direction is confined to the transmitted part of the ray. The tourmaline plate absorbs the part which is not transmitted; our surface reflects it. If in the experiment last described the two mirrors are placed with their focal lines at right angles, no sparks can be excited in the secondary conductor by reflection from an isotropic screen; but I proved to my satisfaction that sparks are produced when the reflection takes place from the eolotropic wire grating, provided this is adjusted so that the wires are inclined at 45° to the focal lines. The explanation of this follows naturally from what has been already stated.

§ *Refraction*

In order to find out whether any refraction of the rays takes place in passing from air into another insulating medium, I had a large prism made of so-called hard pitch, a material like asphalt. The base was an isosceles triangle 1·2 metres in the side, and with a refracting angle of nearly 30°. The refracting edge was placed vertical, and the height of the whole prism was 1·5 metres. But since the prism weighed about 12 cwt., and would have been too heavy to move as a whole, it was built up of three pieces, each 0·5 metre high, placed one above the other. The material was cast in wooden boxes which were left around it, as they did not appear to interfere with its use. The prism was mounted on a support of such height that the middle of its refracting edge was at the same height as the primary and secondary spark-gaps. When I was satisfied that refraction did take place, and had obtained some idea of its amount, I arranged the experiment in the following manner: The producing mirror was set up at a distance of 2·6 metres from the prism and facing one of the refracting surfaces, so that the axis of the beam was directed as nearly as possible towards the centre of mass of the prism, and met the refracting surface at an angle of incidence of 25° (on the side of the normal towards the base). Near the refracting edge and also at the opposite side of the prism were placed two conducting screens which prevented the ray from passing by any other path than that through the prism. On the side of the emerging ray there was marked upon the floor a circle of 2·5 metres radius, having as its centre the centre of mass of the lower end of the prism. Along this the receiving mirror was now moved about, its aperture being always directed towards the centre of the circle. No sparks were obtained when the mirror was placed in the direction of the incident ray produced; in this direction the prism threw a complete shadow. But sparks appeared when the mirror was moved towards the base of the prism, beginning when the angular deviation from the first position was about 11°. The sparking increased in intensity until the deviation amounted to about 22°, and then again decreased. The last sparks were observed with a deviation of about 34°. When the mirror was placed in a position of maximum effect, and then moved away from the prism along the radius of the circle, the sparks could be traced up to a distance of 5 – 6 metres. When an assistant stood either in front of the prism or behind it the sparking invariably ceased, which shows that the action reaches the secondary conductor through the prism and not in any other way. The experiments were repeated after placing both mirrors with their focal lines horizontal, but without altering the position of the prism. This made no difference in the phenomena observed. A refracting angle of 30° and a deviation of 22° in the neighbourhood of the minimum deviation corresponds to a refractive index of 1·69. The refractive index of pitch-like materials for light is given as being between 1·5 and 1·6. We must not attribute any importance to the magnitude or even the sense of this difference, seeing that our method was not an accurate one, and that the material used was impure.

We have applied the term rays of electric force to the phenomena which we have investigated. We may perhaps further designate them as rays of light of very great wavelength. The experiments described appear to me, at any rate, eminently adapted to remove any doubt as to the identity of light, radiant heat, and electro-magnetic wave-motion. I believe that from now on we shall have greater confidence in making use of the advantages which this identity enables us to derive both in the study of optics and of electricity.

# IV

## THE RISE OF PHYSICAL
## CHEMISTRY

THE term 'inorganic chemistry' gradually came to be used in a slightly restricted sense to mean the discovery of new elements and an examination of their compounds. Similarly 'organic chemistry' meant the analysis (in the widest sense of the term) and synthesis of organic substances. Neither term, however, then covered a number of important themes in chemical theory, which were and are common to both inorganic and organic substances. Some obviously lie in the borderland between chemistry and physics – the freezing points of solutions (which differ from those of the pure solvents), the viscosities of liquids, and the properties which have come to be known as the 'kinetic' properties of gases. Others are themes in chemistry which owe much to developments in physics, for example, the electrical properties of matter seen in terms of chemical compounds, or the value to chemistry of considering the spectra of individual chemical substances.

Eventually it proved so profitable to investigate this region of science that a new discipline was recognized, that of physical chemistry. Insofar as the examples quoted seem to belong to the study of properties of matter, the distinctive approach of the physical chemist has been increasingly to deal with these properties in terms of the molecules (or ions, i.e. electrically charged atoms or groups of atoms) of which matter is composed. This has also been true of his interest in chemical reactions, which have been interpreted in terms of molecular change.

Some scientists of the nineteenth century are acknowledged for their contributions both to physics and to chemistry. Faraday is a notable example. Appointed to the Royal Institution where Davy had isolated new metals by electrolysis, Faraday examined the quantitative aspects of this process which are summarized in two laws. The mass of a given substance liberated in an electrolytic decomposition is proportional to the quantity of electricity which has passed through the electrolyte, and the mass of any substance liberated by a given quantity of electricity is proportional to its *chemical* equivalent weight.

These conclusions at once brought chemistry and the new field of electricity into a close relationship. The further implication was not readily accepted by Faraday, who was disinclined to accept the atomic theory. It is that if chemical matter ultimately consists of discrete particles, so also must electricity. This idea became of increasing importance in chemistry as the ionic theory was developed and later, when the nature of the electron was realized, it became essential to the modern electronic theory of chemistry in which such previously diverse subjects as electrolysis, valency, chemical bonding, and the structure of the Periodic Table were all related to the structure of the atom. Again developments in physics were important. However one classifies Becquerel, Thomson, the Curies, and Rutherford, their discoveries had a profound effect on modern chemistry.

Before this had been achieved, however, much had happened in chemistry. The considerable investigations of gases had led to the determination of molecular weights from vapour densities, but many new compounds were being discovered which were not readily vapourized. They could usually be dissolved however, either in water or in a simple organic solvent, so attention was turned to the properties of solutions, and some outstanding work of fundamental importance to physical chemistry was produced. Earlier observations were expanded to the stage at which they would support useful generalizations. Osmotic pressure, vapour pressure, freezing point, and boiling point of solutions were all shown to be determined by the concentration of the molecules of solute, independently of their kind. These 'colligative' properties not only demonstrated a molecular basis for these properties of matter but gave chemists a new method of determining molecular weights. If, from the measurement of a colligative property, the molecular concentration of a solution could be established, then from the weight of substance used to make a given volume of solution, the molecular weight could readily be calculated. Besides the work of Raoult which is represented in this section, that of Pfeffer and van't Hoff on osmotic pressure also constituted a major contribution to the theory of solutions which rapidly emerged in the later part of the nineteenth century.

For organic chemistry, the molecular weight of a substance was an important figure; used in conjunction with the composition by weight, it gave the formula of the molecule. This was the basis for establishing a structural formula, in terms of which the chemical properties of the substance could be understood.

For inorganic chemistry (and for a few organic substances) a full understanding of the nature of dissolved salts was only reached when the results of these experiments were combined with those of electrolysis. To Raoult, non-electrolytic organic solutes had seemed anomalous when compared with salts. The difference was explained by Arrhenius. It had been assumed that ions were produced in a solution only during the actual passage of a current. Arrhenius came to the conclusion that electrolytes normally existed in solution in dissociated (or 'ionized') form, the extent of the dissociation varying, but becoming complete in infinitely dilute solutions. The initial failure of chemists to appreciate the difference between ions and atoms led them to oppose this theory, as it was difficult to understand how sodium and chlorine atoms could exist uncombined in water, which was the way in which they pictured dissociation. Gradually, however, it became clear that the ionic theory could explain not only the earlier work, notably of Hittorf and Kohlrausch on the electrical conductivity of solutions, but also that of Raoult on freezing points, van't Hoff on osmotic pressures, and Arrhenius' own work on the velocity of reactions in solution. Colligative properties were seen to be determined by the concentration of solute particles present, whether ions or undissociated molecules. Sodium chloride, therefore, produced twice the effect which would be due to a molecule (NaCl) because it was present as two ions ($Na^+$ and $Cl^-$). This at once resolved the anomaly between electrolytes and non-electrolytes.

Along with an interest in the state of substances not undergoing chemical reactions went the investigation of chemical change. At the beginning of the nineteenth century it was shown that in some chemical reactions which could be represented by an equation of the type:

$$A + B = C + D,$$

A and B were not wholly converted into C and D. Indeed, as Berthollet showed, a chemical equilibrium is established which can be approached from either side; C and D, when they react together, are not wholly converted into A and B.

The rate at which chemical reactions take place was first measured by Wilhelmy in 1850. He followed the hydrolysis of cane sugar (the 'inversion' of sucrose, i.e., its conversion into glucose and fructose). He found that, for dilute solutions, the rate of hydrolysis of the cane sugar at a given time was proportional to the concentration present in the solution at that time.

The law of mass action takes into account, not only reactions such as this, but also chemical equilibria. These equilibria are regarded as being dynamic. Molecules of A and B are always reacting to form C and D, but C and D are also reacting to form A and B; the two opposing reactions take place at equal rates. In 1888 the effects of temperature and pressure were further considered by le Chatelier. Chemical equilibria were also studied from the stand-point of thermodynamics, a subject important to physicists and engineers, but notably applied to chemistry by the American, Willard Gibbs.

From such beginnings grew the twentieth-century studies of the kinetics of chemical change. Again the molecular basis of chemistry has come to the fore. From sufficiently sophisticated measurements of rates of chemical reaction it is possible to suggest what changes occur to the actual molecules during the reactions. This line of thought became much more fiuitful as the changes described in the next section brought about a more detailed conception of the nature of atoms and molecules.

One further development was the recognition that the rate of chemical reactions could be increased by substances which are not ultimately consumed in the reactions; they are known as catalysts. From the recognition of their essential characteristics, such as are outlined by Ostwald, they have become of intense interest in the present century. In the petrochemical field, we see, *par excellence*, their importance in large-scale industry. In biology, it has become evident that plants and animals can bring about many chemical changes at their own temperatures for which the chemist requires very much higher temperatures. This they do by the use of enzymes which can be regarded as biological catalysts, and which form one of the most important subjects of study today.

# MICHAEL FARADAY
1791–1867

## THE LAWS OF ELECTROLYSIS

FARADAY has been presented above in the company of physicists. Here he is represented drawing a tight connexion between physics and chemistry. He also carried out important work in organic chemistry. It is not always realized that (in 1825) he discovered benzene, which he called 'bicarburet of hydrogen' from its composition ($C_2H$), based on $C = 6$ as the combining weight of carbon. He also prepared colloidal gold and was familiar with some of its special properties.

An extra achievement of Faraday's was the rationalizing of the terms applicable to electrolysis. He introduced, in 1834, a series of new terms, devised with the aid of Whewell, later Master of Trinity College, Cambridge, so that he (and no doubt he hoped that other scientists also) would be able 'to avoid much periphrasis and ambiguity of expression'. Though he is 'aware that names are one thing and science another', an author facilitates the acceptance of new ideas if he provides appropriate terms in which they can be discussed by his fellow-scientists. It is worthwhile, therefore, to examine Faraday's approach to nomenclature, which is set out in the first passage below. The next two describe typical experiments which he used to add support to generalizations which he had already reached by earlier experiments. The fourth passage is typical of his summaries of the progress of his thought up to the time of writing. He frequently refers back to conclusions found in earlier paragraphs by the relevant number, as the paragraphs of all his publications were numbered consecutively.

The passages are taken from Volume 1 of his *Experimental Researches in Electricity* published in 1839 by Richard and John Edward Taylor, 'printers and publishers to the

University of London'. The book consists of papers reprinted from the *Philosophical Transactions of the Royal Society*. The sections printed below appeared in 1834.

## ¶ On Electro-chemical Decomposition

661. The theory which I believe to be a true expression of the facts of electrochemical decomposition, and which I have therefore detailed in a former series of these Researches, is so much at variance with those previously advanced, that I find the greatest difficulty is stating results, as I think, correctly, whilst limited to the use of terms which are current with a certain accepted meaning. Of this kind is the term *pole*, with its prefixes of positive and negative, and the attached ideas of attraction and repulsion. The general phraseology is that the positive pole *attracts* oxygen, acids, etc., or more cautiously, that it *determines* their evolution upon its surface; and that the negative pole acts in an equal manner upon hydrogen, combustibles, metals, and bases. According to my view, the determining force is *not* at the poles, but *within* the body under decomposition; and the oxygen and acids are rendered at the *negative* extremity of that body, whilst hydrogen, metals, etc., are evolved at the positive extremity (518, 524).

662. To avoid, therefore, confusion and circumlocution, and for the sake of greater precision of expression than I can otherwise obtain, I have deliberately considered the subject with two friends, and with their assistance and concurrence in framing them, I purpose henceforward using certain other terms, which I will now define. The *poles*, as they are usually called, are only the doors or ways by which the electric current passes into and out of the decomposing body (556); and they of course, when in contact with that body, are the limits of its extent in the direction of the current. The term has been generally applied to the metal surfaces in contact with the decomposing substance; but whether philosophers generally would also apply it to the

surfaces of air (465, 471) and water (493), against which I have effected electrochemical decomposition, is subject to doubt. In place of the term pole, I propose using that of *Electrode**, and I mean thereby that substance or rather surface, whether of air, water, metal, or any other body, which bounds the extent of the decomposing matter in the direction of the electric current.

663. The surfaces at which, according to common phraseology, the electric current enters and leaves a decomposing body, are most important places of action, and require to be distinguished apart from the poles, with which they are mostly, and the electrodes, with which they are always, in contact. Wishing for a natural standard of electric direction to which I might refer these, expressive of their difference and at the same time free from all theory, I have thought it might be found in the earth. If the magnetism of the earth be due to electric currents passing round it, the latter must be in a constant direction, which, according to present usage of speech, would be from east to west, or, which will strengthen this help to the memory, that in which the sun appears to move. If in any case of electro-decomposition we consider the decomposing body as placed so that the current passing through it shall be in the same direction, and parallel to that supposed to exist in the earth, then the surfaces at which the electricity is passing into and out of the substance would have an invariable reference, and exhibit constantly the same relations of powers. Upon this notion we purpose calling that towards the east the *anode*†, and that towards the west the *cathode;*‡ and whatever changes may take place in our views of the nature of electricity and electrical action, as they must affect the *natural standard* referred to, in the same direction, and to an equal amount with any decomposing substances to which these terms may at any time be applied, there seems no reason to expect that they will lead to confusion, or tend in any way to support false views.

* ἤλεκτρον, and ὁδος a way.
† ἄνω upwards, and ὁδός a way; the way which the sun rises.
‡ κατὰ downwards, and ὁδός way, the way which the sun sets.

The *anode* is therefore that surface at which the electric current, according to our present expression, enters: it is the *negative* extremity of the decomposing body; is where oxygen, chlorine, acids, etc. are evolved; and is against or opposite the positive electrode. The *cathode* is that surface at which the current leaves the decomposing body, and is its *positive* extremity; the combustible bodies, metals, alkalies, and bases, are evolved there, and it is in contact with the negative electrode.

664. I shall have occasion in these Researches, also to class bodies together according to certain relations derived from their electrical actions (822); and wishing to express those relations without at the same time involving the expression of any hypothetical views, I intend using the following names and terms. Many bodies are decomposed directly by the electric current, their elements being set free; these I propose to call *electrolytes*. * Water, therefore, is an electrolyte. The bodies which, like nitric or sulphuric acids, are decomposed in a secondary manner (752, 757), are not included under this term. Then for *electro-chemically decomposed*, I shall often use the term *electrolyzed*, derived in the same way, and implying that the body spoken of is separated into its components under the influence of electricity: it is analogous in its sense and sound to *analyze*, which is derived in a similar manner. The term *electrolytical* will be understood at once: muriatic acid is electrolytical, boracic acid is not.

665. Finally, I require a term to express those bodies which can pass to the *electrodes*, or, as they are usually called, the poles. Substances are frequently spoken of as being *electro-negative*, or *electro-positive*, according as they go under the supposed influence of a direct attraction to the positive or negative pole. But these terms are much too significant for the use to which I should have to put them; for though the meanings are perhaps right, they are only hypothetical, and may be wrong; and then, through a very imperceptible, but still very dangerous, because continual, influence, they do great injury to science, by contracting and limiting the

* ἤλεκτρον and λύω, *solvo*. N. Electrolyte, V. Electrolyze.

habitual views of those engaged in pursuing it. I propose to distinguish such bodies by calling those *anions** which go to the *anode* of the decomposing body; and those passing to the *cathode, cations*;† and when I have occasion to speak of these together, I shall call them *ions*. Thus, the chloride of lead is an *electrolyte*, and when *electrolyzed* evolves the two *ions*, chlorine and lead, the former being an *anion*, and the latter a *cation*.

666. These terms being once well defined, will, I hope, in their use enable me to avoid much periphrasis and ambiguity of expression. I do not mean to press them into service more frequently than will be required, for I am fully aware that names are one thing and science another.‡

667. It will be well understood that I am giving no opinion respecting the nature of the electric current now, beyond what I have done on former occasions (283, 517); and that though I speak of the current as proceeding from the parts which are positive to those which are negative (663), it is merely in accordance with the conventional, though in some degree tacit, agreement entered into by scientific men, that they may have a constant, certain, and definite means of referring to the direction of the forces of that current.

\*

789. In the preceding cases, except the first, the water is believed to be inactive; but to avoid any ambiguity arising from its presence, I sought for substances from which it should be absent altogether; and taking advantage of the law of conduction already developed (380 etc.), I soon found abundance, amongst which *protochloride of tin* was first subjected to decomposition in the following manner. A piece of platina wire had one extremity coiled up into a small knob, and, having been carefully weighed, was sealed hermetically

* ἀνιὼν, *that which goes up* (neuter participle).

† κατιὼν, *that which goes down*.

‡ Since this paper was read, I have changed some of the terms which were first proposed, that I might employ only such as were at the same time simple in their nature, clear in their references, and free from hypothesis.

into a piece of bottle-glass tube, so that the knob should be at the bottom of the tube within. The tube was suspended by a piece of platina wire, so that the heat of a spirit-lamp could be applied to it. Recently fused protochloride of tin was introduced in sufficient quantity to occupy, when melted, about one half of the tube; the wire of the tube was connected with a volta-electrometer (711), which was itself connected with the negative end of a voltaic battery; and a platina wire connected with the positive end of the same battery was dipped into the fused chloride in the tube; being however so bent, that it could not by any shake of the hand or apparatus touch the negative electrode at the bottom of the vessel.

790. Under these circumstances the chloride of tin was decomposed: the chlorine evolved at the positive electrode formed bichloride of tin (779), which passed away in fumes, and the tin evolved at the negative electrode combined with the platina, forming an alloy, fusible at the temperature to which the tube was subjected, and therefore never occasioning metallic communication through the decomposing chloride. When the experiment had been continued so long as to yield a reasonable quantity of gas in the volta-electrometer, the battery connexion was broken, the positive electrode removed, and the tube and remaining chloride allowed to cool. When cold, the tube was broken open, the rest of the chloride and the glass being easily separable from the platina wire and its button of alloy. The latter when washed was then reweighed, and the increase gave the weight of the tin reduced.

791. I will give the particular results of one experiment, in illustration of the mode adopted in this and others, the results of which I shall have occasion to quote. The negative electrode weighed at first 20 grains; after the experiment, it, with its button of alloy, weighed 23·2 grains. The tin evolved by the electric current at the *cathode* weighed therefore 3·2 grains. The quantity of oxygen and hydrogen collected in the volta-electrometer = 3·85 cubic inches. As 100 cubic inches of oxygen and hydrogen, in the proportions to form

water, may be considered as weighing 12·92 grains, the 3·85 cubic inches would weigh 0·49742 of a grain; that being, therefore, the weight of water decomposed by the same electric current as was able to decompose such weight of protochloride of tin as could yield 3·2 grains of metal. Now 0·49742:3·2::9 the equivalent of water is to 57·9, which should therefore be the equivalent of tin, if the experiment had been made without error, and if the electrochemical decomposition *is in this case also definite*. In some chemical works 58 is given as the chemical equivalent of tin, in others 57·9. Both are so near to the result of the experiment, and the experiment itself is so subject to slight causes of variation (as from the absorption of gas in the volta-electrometer (716), etc.), that the numbers leave little doubt of the applicability of the *law of definite action* in this and all similar cases of electrodecomposition.

\*

807. Let us turn to another kind of proof of the *definite chemical action of electricity*. If any circumstances could be supposed to exert an influence over the quantity of the matters evolved during electrolytic action, one would expect them to be present when electrodes of different substances, and possessing very different chemical affinities for such matters, were used. Platina has no power in dilute sulphuric acid of combining with the oxygen at the *anode*, though the latter be evolved in the nascent state against it. Copper, on the other hand, immediately unites with the oxygen, as the electric current sets it free from the hydrogen; and zinc is not only able to combine with it, but can, without any help from the electricity, abstract it directly from the water, at the same time setting torrents of hydrogen free. Yet in cases where these three substances were used as the positive electrodes in three similar portions of the same dilute sulphuric acid, specific gravity 1·336 precisely the same quantity of water was decomposed by the electric current, and precisely the same quantity of hydrogen set free at the *cathodes* of the three solutions.

808. The experiment was made thus. Portions of the dilute

sulphuric acid were put into three basins. Three volta-electrometer tubes were filled with the same acid, and one inverted in each basin (707). A zinc plate, connected with the positive end of a voltaic battery, was dipped into the first basin, forming the positive electrode there, the hydrogen, which was abundantly evolved from it by the direct action of the acid, being allowed to escape. A copper plate, which dipped into the acid of the second basin, was connected with the negative electrode of the *first* basin; and a platina plate, which dipped into the acid of the third basin, was connected with the negative electrode of the *second* basin. The negative electrode of the third basin was connected with a volta-electrometer (711), and that with the negative end of the voltaic battery.

809. Immediately that the circuit was complete, the *electrochemical action* commenced in all the vessels. The hydrogen still rose in, apparently, undiminished quantities from the positive zinc electrode in the first basin. No oxygen was evolved at the positive copper electrode in the second basin, but a sulphate of copper was formed there; whilst in the third basin the positive platina electrode evolved pure oxygen gas, and was itself unaffected. But in *all* the basins the hydrogen liberated at the *negative* platina electrodes was the *same in quantity*, and the same with the volume of hydrogen evolved in the volta-electrometer, showing that in all the vessels the current had decomposed an equal quantity of water. In this trying case, therefore, the *chemical action of electricity* proved to be *perfectly definite*.

810. A similar experiment was made with muriatic acid diluted with its bulk of water. The three positive electrodes were zinc, silver, and platina; the first being able to separate and combine with the chlorine *without* the aid of the current, the second combining with the chlorine only after the current had set it free; and the third rejecting almost the whole of it. The three negative electrodes were, as before, platina plates fixed within glass tubes. In this experiment, as in the former, the quantity of hydrogen evolved at the *cathodes* was

the same for all, and the same as the hydrogen evolved in the volta-electrometer. I have already given my reasons for believing that in these experiments it is the muriatic acid which is directly decomposed by the electricity (764); and the results prove that the quantities so decomposed are *perfectly definite* and proportionate to the quantity of electricity which has passed.

811. In this experiment the chloride of silver formed in the second basin retarded the passage of the current of electricity, by virtue of the law of conduction before described (394), so that it had to be cleaned off four or five times during the course of the experiment; but this caused no difference between the results of that vessel and the others.

812. Charcoal was used as the positive electrode in both sulphuric and muriatic acids (808, 810); but this change produced no variation of the results. A zinc positive electrode, in sulphate of soda or solution of common salt, gave the same constancy of operation.

813. Experiments of a similar kind were then made with bodies altogether in a different state, i.e. with *fused* chlorides, iodides, etc. I have already described an experiment with fused chloride of silver, in which the electrodes were of metallic silver, the one rendered negative becoming increased and lengthened by the addition of metal, whilst the other was dissolved and eaten away by its abstraction. This experiment was repeated, two weighed pieces of silver wire being used as the electrodes, and a volta-electrometer included in the circuit. Great care was taken to withdraw the negative electrode so regularly and steadily that the crystals of reduced silver should not form a *metallic* communication beneath the surface of the fused chloride. On concluding the experiment the positive electrode was reweighed, and its loss ascertained. The mixture of chloride of silver, and metal, withdrawn in successive portions at the negative electrode, was digested in solution of ammonia, to remove the chloride, and the metallic silver remaining also weighed: it was the reduction at the *cathode*, and exactly equalled the solution

at the *anode*; and each portion was as nearly as possible the equivalent to the water decomposed in the volta-electrometer.

\*

821. All these facts combine into, I think, an irresistible mass of evidence, proving the truth of the important proposition which I at first laid down, namely, *that the chemical power of a current of electricity is in direct proportion to the absolute quantity of electricity which passes* (377, 783). They prove, too, that this is not merely true with one substance, as water, but generally with all electrolytic bodies; and, further, that the results obtained with any *one substance* do not merely agree amongst themselves, but also with those obtained from *other substances*, the whole combining together into *one series of definite electro-chemical actions* (505). I do not mean to say that no exceptions will appear: perhaps some may arise, especially amongst substances existing only by weak affinity; but I do not expect that any will seriously disturb the result announced. If, in the well-considered, well-examined, and, I may surely say, well-ascertained doctrines of the definite nature of ordinary chemical affinity, such exceptions occur, as they do in abundance, yet, without being allowed to disturb our minds as to the general conclusion, they ought also to be allowed if they should present themselves at this, the opening of a new view of electrochemical action; not being held up as obstructions to those who may be engaged in rendering that view more and more perfect, but laid aside for a while, in hopes that their perfect and consistent explanation will ultimately appear.

822. The doctrine of *definite electrochemical action* just laid down, and, I believe, established, leads to some new views of the relations and classifications of bodies associated with or subject to this action. Some of these I shall proceed to consider.

823. In the first place, compound bodies may be separated into two great classes, namely, those which are decomposable by the electric current, and those which are not: of the latter, some are conductors, others non-conductors, of vol-

taic electricity.* The former do not depend for their decomposability upon the nature of their elements only; for, of the same two elements, bodies may be formed, of which one shall belong to one class and another to the other class; but probably on the proportions also (697). It is further remarkable, that with very few, if any, exceptions (414, 691), these decomposable bodies are exactly those governed by the remarkable law of conduction I have before described (394); for that law does not extend to the many compound fusible substances that are excluded from this class. I propose to call bodies of this, the decomposable class, *Electrolytes* (664).

824. Then, again, the substances into which these divide, under the influence of the electric current, form an exceedingly important general class. They are combining bodies; are directly associated with the fundamental parts of the doctrine of chemical affinity; and have each a definite proportion, in which they are always evolved during electrolytic action. I have proposed to call these bodies generally *ions*, or particularly *anions* and *cations*, according as they appear at the *anode* or *cathode* (665); and the numbers representing the proportions in which they are evolved *electrochemical equivalents*. Thus hydrogen, oxygen, chlorine, iodine, lead, tin are *ions*; the three former are anions, the two metals are cations, and 1, 8, 36, 125, 104, 58, are their *electrochemical equivalents* nearly.

* I mean here by voltaic electricity, merely electricity from a most abundant source, but having very small intensity.

# FRANÇOIS-MARIE RAOULT
## 1830–1901

### PROPERTIES OF SOLUTIONS

RAOULT was born in Fournes, in the Département du Nord, in France, and seems to have lived a quieter, or at least a less exciting life than many of his contemporaries. He was a student in Paris, but had not the means to complete his course there and obtained a series of teaching posts so that he might earn a living while obtaining his degree in his leisure time. He was successful, and went on to obtain a doctorate in 1863. In 1867 he joined the staff of the chemistry department of the University of Grenoble, and became professor three years later. He remained in Grenoble for the rest of his life.

His most important work concerned the effect of dissolved substances on the freezing-points and vapour pressures of solutions. Blagden had shown, in the previous century, that the freezing-point of water is lowered by the addition of salts, and that, for any given salt, the lowering is proportionnal to the concentration. Raoult found that the same law applied to solutions of organic substances, such as alcohol, but he went further by showing that the same lowering of the freezing-point was produced by a given *molecular* concentration. This immediately proved valuable, as he realized, for it enabled the molecular weights of new substances to be determined, by the cryoscopic method.

In the paper quoted below, Raoult gives the cryoscopic constant for water as 37, whereas the modern value is one-half of that. He had found a value of 18·5 to apply to solutions of organic substances, but not for solutions of inorganic salts. He regarded the organic solutes as abnormal, and suggested that they existed as double molecules in solution. He thought that extreme dilution would break them down, but his experiments failed to achieve this. In the meantime,

Arrhenius' experiments had shown that salts were, in one sense, anomalous for they existed as ions (which might for Raoult's purposes, be regarded as the equivalent of half-molecules). Raoult accepted this explanation.

Guldberg had indicated a connexion between the effects of solutes on freezing-points, boiling-points, and vapour pressures of liquids. Raoult now turned to systematize the vapour pressure relationships as he had done earlier for freezing-point depressions. The regularity he observed is still referred to as Raoult's Law, and a great deal of modern work deals with its extension to concentrated solutions and the departures which are then found from strict adherence to this law.

The two quotations below are taken from papers in *Comptes rendus hebdomadaires des Séances de l'Académie des Sciences* of Paris, in 1882 and 1887, respectively. The translations are from Leicester and Klickstein, *A Source Book in Chemistry* (Harvard, 1952).

---

¶ *General Law of the Freezing of Solutions*

If A is the lowering of the freezing point due to the presence of 1 gram of a substance dissolved in 100 grams of solvent; M the molecular weight of the dissolved substance, supposedly anhydrous, calculated according to the *atomic* formula $H = 1$, $O = 16 \ldots$ ; T its molecular lowering of the freezing point (that is, the lowering of the freezing point caused by one molecule dissolved in 100 gram of liquid), then, if the solutions are dilute,

$$MA = T$$

My previous studies have shown that, in the same liquid, the molecular lowering, T, is a nearly constant number for very numerous groups of compounds of the same type. Since then I have made new experiments using as solvents the following compounds whose freezing points can always be determined with extreme precision.

|  | Freezing Point Degrees |  | Freezing Point Degrees |
|---|---|---|---|
| Water | 0·00 | Ethylene dibromide | 7·92 |
| Benzene | 4·96 | Formic acid | 8·52 |
| Nitrobenzene | 5·28 | Acetic acid | 16·75 |

All these liquids except water contract when solidifying.

Lack of space prevents me from giving details here of the extremely numerous experiments made with these solvents. I will limit myself to giving a summary. Nevertheless, it is possible to judge of the number and variety of dissolved compounds as well as the degree of concordance of the results from the table of 60 analogous experiments made on solutions of organic compounds in water and in benzene published in the *Comptes rendus* of the Academy (5 and 24 June, 1882). My new studies confirm the former and permit the formulation of the *law of freezing of solvents* in a general and complete manner. . . .

*Conclusions.* These experiments, in which more than two hundred compounds have been dissolved in *six* different liquids, are very numerous and agree in establishing the following:

*All bodies, on dissolving in a definite liquid compound which can solidify, lower the freezing point.*

*In all liquids, the molecular lowering of the freezing point due to the different compounds approaches two values, invariable for each liquid, of which one is double the other.* The larger is more often found and constitutes the normal molecular lowering. The lesser corresponds to the case where the molecules of the dissolved body are joined two to two.

*The normal molecular lowering of the freezing point varies with the nature of the solvent*: it is 37 for water, 28 for formic acid, 39 for acetic acid, 49 for benzene, 70·5 for nitrobenzene, and 117 for ethylene dibromide. If each of these numbers is divided by the molecular weight of the solvent to which it relates (which is equivalent to reducing the results to the case where one molecule of dissolved body will be contained in 100 molecules of the solvent), the quotients differ little from each other, except for water. Thus:

| Water | 37:18 = 2·050 | Benzene | 49:78 = 0·628 |
|---|---|---|---|
| Formic acid | 28:46 = 0·608 | Nitrobenzene | 70·5:123 = 0·600 |
| Acetic acid | 39:60 = 0·650 | Ethylene dibromide | 117:188 = 0·623 |

To make water agree with the general rule, it is enough to admit that the physical molecules which compose it are formed from three chemical molecules joined together, at least near the freezing point. Then, indeed, this solvent gives 37:18 × [sic] 3 = 0·685, a number which does not differ much from 0·622 degrees, the mean of the five others. The following law can then be formulated:

*One molecule of any compound dissolved in 100 molecules of any liquid of a different nature lowers the freezing point of this liquid by a nearly constant quantity, close to 0·62 degrees.*

This statement is altogether general if we admit that the physical molecules which act here can be formed of two, and exceptionally, three, chemical molecules.

## ¶ *General Law of the Vapour Pressure of Solvents*

The molecular reduction of the vapour pressure K of a solution, that is to say the relative reduction of pressure produced by 1 molecule of a substance held in 100 grams of a volatile liquid, can be calculated by means of the following formula:

$$K = \frac{f - f'}{fP} \times M$$

in which f is the vapour pressure of the pure solvent, f' the vapour pressure of the solution, M the molecular weight of the dissolved substance, P the weight of this substance in solution in 100 grams of the solvent; if it is admitted that the relative reduction of pressure

$$\frac{f - f'}{f}$$

is proportional to the concentration. As this proportionality is rarely rigorous, even when the solutions are very dilute, I have been obliged in these comparative studies to use solutions which always have nearly the same molecular concentrations and contain four to five molecules of substance held per 100 molecules of volatile solvent. A greater dilution would not allow sufficiently exact measurements. All the experiments were performed by the barometric method and conducted like those I have run in ether solutions. The tubes were plunged in a water bath limited by parallel glasses, constantly agitated, and heated at will.

In each case the temperature was so chosen that the vapour pressure of the pure solvent was about 400 millimetres of mercury. The measurements were made from fifteen to forty-five minutes after agitation of the contents of each tube, the temperature being constant.

I have used 12 different volatile liquids as solvents, namely, water, phosphorus chloride, the sulphide of carbon, the bichloride of carbon ($CCl_4$), chloroform, amylene, benzene, methyl iodide, ethyl bromide, ordinary ether, acetone, methyl alcohol.

*In water* I have dissolved the following organic materials: cane sugar, glucose, tartaric acid, citric acid, urea. All these substances have produced sensibly the same molecular reduction in vapour pressure: K = 0·185. I have, for the present, left the mineral substances to one side; actually, the effect of these substances has been determined by enough conclusive experiments performed by Wüllner, by myself, and recently by M. Tammann.

*In solvents other than water*, I have dissolved materials as little volatile as possible, chosen among the following: oil of turpentine, naphthalene, anthracene, sesquichloride of carbon ($C_2Cl_6$), methyl salicylate, ethyl benzoate, antimonous chloride, mercury ethyl, benzoic, valeric, and trichloroacetic acids, thymol, nitrobenzene, and aniline. The error due to the vapour pressure of these compounds can often be rendered negligible. The vapour pressure of the dissolved substances is, in fact, considerably reduced by their mixture with a great excess of the solvent; and in order that it should not exercise a sensible influence on the results, it is enough that it should not surpass 5 or 6 millimetres at the experimental temperature.

The molecular reductions in vapour pressure caused by

these different bodies in the same solvent are constantly grouped around two values, of which one, which I call *normal*, is double the other. The normal reduction is always produced by simple and chlorinated hydrocarbons and by ethers; the anomalous reduction is almost always produced by acids. There are found, however, solvents in which all the dissolved bodies produce the same molecular reduction of pressure; such are, for example, ether and acetone.

Among the volatile solvents examined there are two, water and benzene, in which I have studied carefully the lowering of freezing point. The comparison of the results obtained shows that *for all solutions made in the same solvent there is a nearly constant relation between the molecular lowering of freezing point and the molecular reduction of vapour pressure.* In water this ratio is equal to 100; in benzene it is equal to 60, nearly 1/20.

If we divide the molecular reduction of vapour pressure K produced in a determined volatile liquid by the molecular weight M′ of the liquid, the quotient obtained K/M′ represents the relative reduction of pressure which will be produced by 1 molecule of substance held in 100 molecules of volatile solvent. In making this calculation for the *normal*

| Solvent | Molecular weight of solvent M′ | Normal molecular reduction of pressure K | Reduction of pressure produced by 1 mol. in 100 mols. K/M′ |
|---|---|---|---|
| Water | 18 | 0·185 | 0·0102 |
| Phosphorus chloride | 137·5 | 1·49 | 0·0108 |
| Sulphide of carbon | 76 | 0·80 | 0·0105 |
| Bichloride of carbon (CCl₄) | 154 | 1·62 | 0·0105 |
| Chloroform | 119·5 | 1·30 | 0·0109 |
| Amylene | 70 | 0·74 | 0·0106 |
| Benzene | 78 | 0·83 | 0·0106 |
| Methyl Iodide | 142 | 1·49 | 0·0105 |
| Ethyl bromide | 109 | 1·18 | 0·0109 |
| Ether | 74 | 0·71 | 0·0096 |
| Acetone | 58 | 0·59 | 0·0101 |
| Methyl alcohol | 32 | 0·33 | 0·0103 |

values of K produced in the various solvents by the organic materials and nonsaline metallic compounds, I have obtained the results given in the above table.

The values of K and M′ assigned in the table vary in the ratio from 1 to 9; in spite of this, the values of K/M′ vary very little and remain always near the mean 0·0105. We can then say,

*One molecule of nonsaline substance (held in the solvent) dissolved in 100 molecules of any volatile liquid decreases the vapour pressure of this liquid by a nearly constant fraction, nearly 0·0105.*

This law is entirely analogous to that which I announced in 1882 relating to the lowering of the freezing point of solvents. The anomalies which it presents are explained for the most part by admitting that, in certain liquids, the dissolved molecules can be formed from two chemical molecules.

---

# SVANTE AUGUST ARRHENIUS
## 1859–1927

### THE IONIC THEORY

THE name of Arrhenius comes from the latinized form of the Swedish village in Arena, from which came the ancestors of Svante August. Arrhenius was a student in the University of Uppsala, and intended to study chemistry. He found the teaching uninspired, however, and turned to physics. When the time came for him to start research, this was impossible for him even in the physics department, so he went to the Swedish Academy in Stockholm, where he was able to investigate the conductivity of electrolytic solutions. He presented a thesis based on this work to his University, but although he was awarded a doctorate, it was considered to be worthy only of a fourth class.

Disappointed by this reception of his theories, he sent copies of his work abroad to Clausius and Lothar Meyer in Germany, from whom he obtained no encouragement, to Oliver Lodge in England, from whom he obtained very little, and to Wilhelm Ostwald, a young Professor of Chemistry at Riga. Ostwald records that on one memorable day he had a bad toothache, one of his daughters was born, and a thesis arrived from an unknown Swedish chemist.

The enthusiasm with which Ostwald read this work led to his championing the cause of Arrhenius for many years. Arrhenius spent several years visiting laboratories in other countries. In Amsterdam he met van't Hoff, who had been investigating the properties (especially the osmotic properties) of dilute solutions. Their ideas on the nature of dilute solutions reinforced one another. It was arranged that papers which each of them had presented to the Swedish Academy should be made more widely known by publishing them in the first volume of the new journal, *Zeitschrift für* *physikalische Chemie*, which Ostwald had just founded in 1887.*

The passage below is taken from the Alembic Club's translation of Arrhenius' paper (Reprint No. 19).

Arrhenius later returned to Stockholm and for many years had to contend with opposition to his theory of ionic dissociation from many of the influential chemists of his day. He was, however, finally recognized by many learned societies and was awarded a Nobel prize. His own country finally appointed him the first director of the Nobel Institute for Physical Chemistry, a post which he accepted in preference to one in Berlin.

---

¶ *On the Dissociation of Substances in Aqueous Solution*

In a memoir submitted to the Swedish Academy of Sciences on 14 October, 1885 van't Hoff established both experimentally and theoretically the following very important generalization of Avogadro's Law.

'*La pression exercée par les gaz à une température determinée si un même nombre de molécules en occupe un volume donné, est égale à la pression osmotique qu'exerce dans les mêmes circonstances la grande majorité des corps, dissous dans les liquides quelconques.*'

This law was proved by van't Hoff so conclusively that little doubt can exist as to its entire accuracy. There remained, however, a certain difficulty to be overcome, namely, that the law was only valid for the 'great majority of substances', a very considerable number of the aqueous solutions examined forming exceptions, since they exert a much higher osmotic pressure than is required by the law.

When a gas shows a similar deviation from Avogadro's Law, the abnormality is explained by assuming that the gas is in a state of dissociation. A well-known example is afforded by the behaviour of chlorine, bromine, and iodine at high temperatures, these substances being regarded under the given conditions as split up into atoms.

The same expedient might be adopted to explain the

* The American *Journal of Physical Chemistry* was first published in 1897.

exceptions to van't Hoff's Law, but so far it has not been used, probably owing to the novelty of the subject, the large number of known exceptions, and the grave objections on the chemical side which might be raised to such an explanation. The object of the present communication is to show that the hypothesis of dissociation of certain substances in aqueous solution is strongly supported by conclusions drawn from their electrical properties, and also that on closer consideration the chemical objections are appreciably lessened.

For the explanation of electrolytic phenomena we must postulate with Clausius that a portion of the molecules of an electrolyte is dissociated into ions which move independently of one another. Since now the 'osmotic pressure' which a substance dissolved in a liquid exerts on the walls of the containing vessel must be attributed, in accordance with modern kinetic conceptions, to the impacts of the ultimate particles of this substance on the boundary walls in the course of their motion, we must in harmony with this assume that the pressure exerted on the walls of the vessel by a molecule dissociated in the above sense will be the same as that exerted by its ions in the free state. If then we could calculate what proportion of the molecules of an electrolyte had undergone dissociation into ions, we could also calculate by van't Hoff's Law the value of the osmotic pressure.

In a previous communication *Sur la conductibilité galvanique des électrolytes* I have called those molecules, whose ions have independent motion, *active molecules,* and those whose ions are firmly bound together, *inactive molecules.* I have likewise emphasized the probability that at the most extreme dilution all the inactive molecules of an electrolyte are converted into active molecules. On this assumption I will base the calculations made in the sequel. The ratio of the number of active molecules to the total number of molecules, active and inactive, I have called the activity coefficient.* The activity

---

* *Le coëfficient d'activité d'un électrolyte est le nombre exprimant le rapport du nombre d'iones qu'il y a réellement dans l'électrolyte, au nombre d'iones qui y seraient renfermées, si l'électrolyte était totalement transformé en molécules électrolytiques simples.*

coefficient of an electrolyte at infinite dilution is thus assumed to be unity. At smaller dilutions it is less than unity, and, on the principles laid down in the work above cited, is equal to the quotient of the actual molecular conductivity of the solution by the limiting value to which the molecular conductivity of the same solution approaches with increasing dilution. This method of calculation is only applicable if the solutions considered are not too concentrated, *i.e.*, to solutions in which disturbing factors, such as internal friction, etc., can be neglected.

If the activity coefficient $\alpha$ is known, we can derive from it, as follows, the value of van't Hoff's coefficient $i$, which is the ratio of the osmotic pressure actually exerted by a substance to the osmotic pressure which it would exert if it consisted entirely of inactive (undissociated) molecules. The coefficient $i$ is obviously equal to the sum of the number of inactive molecules and the number of ions, divided by the total number of molecules, active and inactive. Thus if $m$ is the number of inactive and $n$ the number of active molecules, and if $k$ is the number of ions into which each active molecule is dissociated (*e.g.* for KCl, $k = 2$, viz. K and Cl; for $BaCl_2$ or $K_2SO_4$, $k = 3$, viz. Ba, Cl and Cl, or K, K and $SO_4$), then we have

$$i = \frac{m + kn}{m + n}$$

The activity coefficient $\alpha$ is equal to $\dfrac{n}{m + n}$,

and consequently

$$i = 1 + (k - 1)\alpha,$$

according to which formula the numbers in the last column of the following table have been calculated.

On the other hand the value of $i$ can be calculated by van't Hoff's method from the results of Raoult's experiments on the freezing points of solutions as follows. The depression $t$ of the freezing point of water in degrees centigrade caused by the solution of one gram molecule of the given substance in a litre of water is divided by $18\cdot5$, and the values of $i =$

$t/18\cdot5$ thus obtained are tabulated in the second-last column. All numbers given below are calculated on the assumption that 10 grams of the substance were dissolved in 1 litre of water as was actually the case in Raoult's experiments.

In the following table the first two columns give the name and chemical formula of the substance, the third the value of the activity coefficient (Lodge's dissociation-ratio) and the last two the values of $i$ calculated by the two different methods ($i = t/18\cdot5$ and $i = 1 + (k-1)\alpha$). The substances studied are divided into four main groups: (1) non-conductors, (2) bases, (3) acids, (4) salts.

### I. NON-CONDUCTORS

| Substance | Formula | $\alpha$ | $i=t/18\cdot5$ | $i=1+(k-1)\alpha$ |
|---|---|---|---|---|
| Methyl alcohol | $CH_3OH$ | 0 | 0·94 | 1 |
| Ethyl alcohol | $C_2H_5OH$ | 0 | 0·94 | 1 |
| Butyl alcohol | $C_4H_9OH$ | 0 | 0·93 | 1 |
| Glycerol | $C_3H_5(OH)_3$ | 0 | 0·92 | 1 |
| Mannitol | $C_6H_{14}O_6$ | 0 | 0·97 | 1 |
| Invert Sugar | $C_6H_{12}O_6$ | 0 | 1·04 | 1 |
| Cane sugar | $C_{12}H_{22}O_{11}$ | 0 | 1·00 | 1 |
| Phenol | $C_6H_5OH$ | 0 | 0·84 | 1 |
| Acetone | $C_3H_6O$ | 0 | 0·92 | 1 |
| Ethyl ether | $(C_2H_5)_2O$ | 0 | 0·90 | 1 |
| Ethyl acetate | $C_4H_8O_2$ | 0 | 0·96 | 1 |
| Acetamide | $C_2H_3ONH_2$ | 0 | 0·96 | 1 |

### 2. BASES

| Substance | Formula | $\alpha$ | $i=t/18\cdot5$ | $i=1+(k-1)\alpha$ |
|---|---|---|---|---|
| Baryta | $Ba(OH)_2$ | 0·84 | 2·69 | 2·67 |
| Strontia | $Sr(OH)_2$ | 0·86 | 2·61 | 2·72 |
| Lime | $Ca(OH)_2$ | 0·80 | 2·59 | 2·59 |
| Lithia | $LiOH$ | 0·83 | 2·02 | 1·83 |
| Soda | $NaOH$ | 0·88 | 1·96 | 1·88 |
| Potash | $KOH$ | 0·93 | 1·91 | 1·93 |
| Thallium Hydroxide | $TlOH$ | 0·90 | 1·79 | 1·90 |
| Tetramethyl-ammonium hydroxide | $N(CH_3)_4OH$ | .. | 1·99 | .. |
| Tetraethyl-ammonium hydroxide | $N(C_2H_5)_4OH$ | 0·92 | .. | 1·92 |

## 2. BASES (continued)

| Substance | Formula | $\alpha$ | $i = t/18 \cdot 5$ | $i = 1 + (k-1)\alpha$ |
|---|---|---|---|---|
| Ammonia | $NH_3$ | 0·01 | 1·03 | 1·01 |
| Methylamine | $CH_3NH_2$ | 0·03 | 1·00 | 1·03 |
| Trimethylamine | $(CH_3)_3N$ | 0·03 | 1·09 | 1·03 |
| Ethylamine | $C_2H_5NH_2$ | 0·04 | 1·00 | 1·04 |
| Propylamine | $C_3H_7NH_2$ | 0·04 | 1·00 | 1·04 |
| Aniline | $C_6H_5NH_2$ | 0·00 | 0·83 | 1·00 |

## 3. ACIDS

| Substance | Formula | $\alpha$ | | |
|---|---|---|---|---|
| Hydrochloric | HCl | 0·90 | 1·98 | 1·90 |
| Hydrobromic | HBr | 0·94 | 2·03 | 1·94 |
| Hydriodic | HI | 0·96 | 2·03 | 1·96 |
| Hydrofluosilicic | $H_2SiF_6$ | 0·75 | 2·46 | 1·75 |
| Nitric | $HNO_3$ | 0·92 | 1·94 | 1·92 |
| Chloric | $HClO_3$ | 0·91 | 1·97 | 1·91 |
| Perchloric | $HClO_4$ | 0·94 | 2·09 | 1·94 |
| Sulphuric | $H_2SO_4$ | 0·60 | 2·06 | 2·19 |
| Selenic | $H_2SeO_4$ | 0·66 | 2·10 | 2·31 |
| Phosphoric | $H_3PO_4$ | 0·08 | 2·32 | 1·24 |
| Sulphurous | $H_2SO_3$ | 0·14 | 1·03 | 1·28 |
| Hydrogen sulphide | $H_2S$ | 0·00 | 1·04 | 1·00 |
| Iodic | $HIO_3$ | 0·73 | 1·30 | 1·73 |
| Phosphorous | $H_3PO_3$ | 0·46 | 1·29 | 1·46 |
| Boric | $H_3BO_3$ | 0·00 | 1·11 | 1·00 |
| Hydrocyanic | HCN | 0·00 | 1·05 | 1·00 |
| Formic | HCOOH | 0·03 | 1·04 | 1·03 |
| Acetic | $CH_3COOH$ | 0·01 | 1·03 | 1·01 |
| Butyric | $C_3H_7COOH$ | 0·01 | 1·01 | 1·01 |
| Oxalic | $(COOH)_2$ | 0·25 | 1·25 | 1·49 |
| Tartaric | $C_4H_6O_6$ | 0·06 | 1·05 | 1·11 |
| Malic | $C_4H_6O_5$ | 0·04 | 1·08 | 1·07 |
| Lactic | $C_3H_6O_3$ | 0·03 | 1·01 | 1·03 |

## 4. SALTS

| Substance | Formula | $\alpha$ | | |
|---|---|---|---|---|
| Potassium chloride | KCl | 0·86 | 1·82 | 1·86 |
| Sodium chloride | NaCl | 0·82 | 1·90 | 1·82 |
| Lithium chloride | LiCl | 0·75 | 1·99 | 1·75 |
| Ammonium chloride | $NH_4Cl$ | 0·84 | 1·88 | 1·84 |
| Potassium iodide | KI | 0·92 | 1·90 | 1·92 |

#### 4. SALTS (continued)

| Substance | Formula | $\alpha$ | $i = t/18.5$ | $i = 1 + (k-1)\alpha$ |
|---|---|---|---|---|
| Potassium bromide | KBr | 0·92 | 1·90 | 1·92 |
| Potassium cyanide | KCN | 0·88 | 1·74 | 1·88 |
| Potassium nitrate | $KNO_3$ | 0·81 | 1·67 | 1·81 |
| Sodium nitrate | $NaNO_3$ | 0·82 | 1·82 | 1·82 |
| Ammonium nitrate | $NH_4NO_3$ | 0·81 | 1·73 | 1·81 |
| Potassium acetate | $KC_2H_3O_2$ | 0·83 | 1·86 | 1·83 |
| Sodium acetate | $NaC_2H_3O_2$ | 0·79 | 1·73 | 1·79 |
| Potassium formate | $KCHO_2$ | 0·83 | 1·90 | 1·83 |
| Silver nitrate | $AgNO_3$ | 0·86 | 1·60 | 1·86 |
| Potassium chlorate | $KClO_3$ | 0·83 | 1·78 | 1·83 |
| Potassium carbonate | $K_2CO_3$ | 0·69 | 2·26 | 2·38 |
| Sodium carbonate | $Na_2CO_3$ | 0·61 | 2·18 | 2·22 |
| Potassium sulphate | $K_2SO_4$ | 0·67 | 2·11 | 2·33 |
| Sodium sulphate | $Na_2SO_4$ | 0·62 | 1·91 | 2·24 |
| Ammonium sulphate | $(NH_4)_2SO_4$ | 0·59 | 2·00 | 2·17 |
| Potassium oxalate | $K_2C_2O_4$ | 0·66 | 2·43 | 2·32 |
| Barium chloride | $BaCl_2$ | 0·77 | 2·63 | 2·54 |
| Strontium chloride | $SrCl_2$ | 0·75 | 2·76 | 2·50 |
| Calcium chloride | $CaCl_2$ | 0·75 | 2·70 | 2·50 |
| Cupric chloride | $CuCl_2$ | .. | 2·58 | .. |
| Zinc chloride | $ZnCl_2$ | 0·70 | .. | 2·40 |
| Barium nitrate | $Ba(NO_3)_2$ | 0·57 | 2·19 | 2·13 |
| Strontium nitrate | $Sr(NO_3)_2$ | 0·62 | 2·23 | 2·23 |
| Calcium nitrate | $Ca(NO_3)_2$ | 0·67 | 2·02 | 2·33 |
| Lead nitrate | $Pb(NO_3)_2$ | 0·54 | 2·02 | 2·08 |
| Magnesium sulphate | $MgSO_4$ | 0·40 | 1·04 | 1·40 |
| Ferrous sulphate | $FeSO_4$ | 0·35 | 1·00 | 1·35 |
| Cupric sulphate | $CuSO_4$ | 0·35 | 0·97 | 1·35 |
| Zinc sulphate | $ZnSO_4$ | 0·38 | 0·98 | 1·38 |
| Cupric acetate | $Cu(C_2H_3O_2)_2$ | 0·33 | 1·68 | 1·66 |
| Magnesium chloride | $MgCl_2$ | 0·70 | 2·64 | 2·40 |
| Mercuric chloride | $HgCl_2$ | 0·03 | 1·11 | 1·05 |
| Cadmium iodide | $CdI_2$ | 0·28 | 0·94 | 1·56 |
| Cadmium nitrate | $Cd(NO_3)_2$ | 0·73 | 2·32 | 2·46 |
| Cadmium sulphate | $CdSO_4$ | 0·35 | 0·75 | 1·35 |

The last three entries in the second-last column are not, as are all the others, taken from Raoult's work, but from older data of Rüdorff, who used very large quantities of dissolved material, so that those three values cannot lay claim to great accuracy. The values of $\alpha$ are calculated from the data of Kohlrausch, Ostwald (acids and gases), and a few due to Grotrian and Klein. The values calculated from Ostwald's data are by far the most exact, because both the magnitudes involved in $\alpha$ are here easily determined with great accuracy. The error in $i$ calculated from these values of $\alpha$ can scarcely be more than 5 per cent. The values of $\alpha$ and $i$ calculated from Kohlrausch's data are somewhat less certain, chiefly on account of the difficulty of estimating exactly the maximum value of the molecular conductivity. This is still more difficult for $\alpha$ and $i$ calculated from the experimental data of Grotrian and of Klein, which may in unfavourable cases show an error of 10 or 15 per cent. The degree of accuracy of Raoult's numbers is difficult to estimate: judging from the data themselves for very nearly related substances errors of 5 per cent or even somewhat more are not improbable.

It should be noted that in the above tables there have been included for the sake of completeness *all* substances for which a moderately accurate calculation of $i$ by the two methods has been found possible. When conductivity data for a substance were wanting, *e.g.*, cupric chloride and tetramethylammonium hydroxide, for purposes of comparison the calculation was made from the data for a nearly related substance (zinc chloride and tetra-ethylammonium hydroxide) whose electrical properties could not be notably different from those of the substance in question.

From the values of $i$ which exhibit a very great difference between the two methods of calculation, that for $H_2SiF_6$ should probably at the outset be excluded, for Ostwald has shown that in all probability this acid in aqueous solution partially decomposes into $6HF$ and $SiO_2$, which would explain the high value of $i$ found by Raoult's method.

There is one circumstance which to a small extent tends to invalidate the comparison between the last two columns, namely, that the values in strictness hold good for different temperatures. The values in the second-last column are all for temperatures differing little from o°C. as they have been derived from experiments on slight lowerings of the freezing point of water. On the other hand the values in the last column for acids and bases (Ostwald's experiments) were obtained at 25°C., the others at 18°C. The figures in the last column for non-conductors are of course also valid for o°C., since these substances at this temperature also contain no appreciable quantity of dissociated (active) molecules.

There appears nevertheless on a comparison of the numbers in the last two columns a very marked parallelism between them. This shows *a posteriori* that in all probability the assumptions on which I have based the calculation are in the main correct. These assumptions were:

(1) That van't Hoff's law holds good not merely for the *majority* but for *all* substances, including those formerly regarded as exceptions (electrolytes in aqueous solution).

(2) That every electrolyte in aqueous solution consists in part of molecules electrolytically and chemically active and in part of inactive molecules which, however, on dilution change into active molecules, so that at infinite dilution only active molecules are present.

The objections which may probably be urged from the chemical side, are in the main the same as those raised against Clausius's hypothesis, and these I have already endeavoured to show are completely untenable. A repetition of these objections may therefore be regarded as superfluous. I will emphasize only one point. Although the dissolved substance exerts on the walls of the vessel an osmotic pressure precisely as if it were partly dissociated into ions, yet the dissociation here in question is not quite the same as that, for instance, which is shown by the decomposition of an ammonium salt at a high temperature. In the first case the products of dissociation (the ions) have very large electrical charges of opposite sign, and thus are subject to certain conditions (the incompressibility of electricity), from which it follows that the ions cannot without a great expenditure of energy be separated from each other in any marked degree. In ordinary dissociation, on the other hand, where such conditions do not occur, the products of dissociation can generally be separated from each other.

These two assumptions are of the most far-reaching significance, not only from the theoretical point of view, which will receive discussion below, but also in the highest degree from the practical standpoint. If it can be shown – and I have endeavoured to make it highly probable – that the law of van't Hoff is universally applicable, then the chemist has at hand an extraordinarily convenient means of determining the molecular weight of any substance soluble in a liquid.

I may also draw attention to the fact that the above equation (1) gives the connexion between the two magnitudes $i$ and $\alpha$ which play the chief parts in the two theories recently developed by van't Hoff and by myself.

\*

Most of the properties of dilute salt solutions are of a so-called additive character. In other words, the numerical values of the properties may be regarded as the sum of the properties of the parts of the solution, i.e., of the solvent and of the parts of the dissolved molecules, which in fact coincide with the ions. For example, the conductivity of a salt solution may be regarded as the sum of the conductivities of the solvent (generally zero), of the positive ion, and of the negative ion. In most cases this can be tested by comparing two salts (e.g. of K and Na) of one acid (e.g. HCl) with the corresponding salts of the same metals (K and Na) and another acid (e.g. $HNO_3$). Then the property of the first salt (KCl) minus the property of the second (NaCl) is equal to the property of the third salt ($KNO_3$) minus the property of the fourth ($NaNO_3$). This holds good in most cases for several properties, e.g. conductivity, lowering of the freezing point, refraction equivalent, heat of neutralization, etc., which we shall briefly consider in the sequel, and finds its explanation in the almost complete dissociation of the great majority of salts into their ions. If a salt in aqueous solution is completely split into its ions, it follows naturally that the properties of this salt may in the main be expressed as the sum of the properties of the ions, since the ions are for the most part independent of each other, so that each ion has a characteristic value for the property, whatever be the oppositely charged ion with which it is associated. In the solutions actually investigated complete dissociation is probably never reached, and the above deduction is therefore not strictly accurate, but if we consider salts which are 80 or 90 per cent dissociated, as are almost without exception the salts of strong bases with strong acids, we shall in general commit no very great errors by calculating the values of the properties on the assumption that the salts are completely decomposed into their ions. According to the foregoing table this applies also to the strong bases and acids $Ba(OH)_2$, $Sr(OH)_2$, $Ca(OH)_2$, LiOH, NaOH, KOH, TlOH, and HCl, HBr, HI, $HNO_3$, $HClO_3$, and $HClO_4$. But there is another group of substances which have hitherto in most investigations played a subordinate part and are far removed from complete dissociation, even in dilute solution, as, for example, according to the table, $HgCl_2$ (and other Hg salts), $CdI_2$, $CdSO_4$, $FeSO_4$, $MgSO_4$, $CuSO_4$, and $Cu(C_2H_3O_2)_2$, the weak bases and acids, such as $NH_3$ and the various amines, $H_3PO_4$, $H_2S$, $H_3BO_3$, HCN, formic, acetic, butyric, tartaric, malic and lactic acids. The properties of these substances will not, as a rule, be of the same (additive) nature as those previously considered, as we shall find completely confirmed in the sequel. There exists naturally a number of transitional compounds between these two groups, as may be seen from the table. It should be mentioned here that in consideration of the almost universal occurrence of additive properties in substances of the first group, which are those by far the most frequently studied, several investigators have been led to the assumption of a certain complete dissociation of salts into their ions. Since, however, from the purely chemical point of view no reason could be found why salt molecules should decompose in a perfectly definite way (into their ions), since in addition, for reasons which need not be discussed here, chemists have contested as long as possible the existence of unsaturated radicals (under which rubric ions are included), and since the foundations of such an assumption are somewhat uncertain, the hypothesis of a complete dissociation has till now found little favour. The above table shows also that the reluctance of chemists to accept the complete dissociation demanded is not without a certain justification, inasmuch as at the dilutions actually employed the dissociation is never complete, being indeed for a large number of electrolytes (those of the second group) relatively insignificant.

From these observations we proceed to the special cases in which additive properties occur.

1. *Heat of neutralization in dilute solutions.* In the neutralization of an acid by a base the energies of these two substances are disengaged as heat, but at the same time there is absorbed a certain quantity of heat arising from the energies of the water and salt (ions) which have been formed. We indicate by curved brackets the energies of the substances, for which it is immaterial so far as the deduction is concerned whether they occur as ions or not, and by square brackets those of the ions, the energies taken for them being always those in dilute solution. For example, on the provisional assumption of complete dissociation of the salts, we have for the neutralization of NaOH by $\frac{1}{2}H_2SO_4$ (1) and HCl (2) and of KOH by $\frac{1}{2}H_2SO_4$ (3) and HCl (4) all in equivalent quantities, liberation of the following amounts of heat:

$$(NaOH) + \tfrac{1}{2}(H_2SO_4) - (H_2O) - [Na] - \tfrac{1}{2}[SO_4] \quad (1)$$
$$(NaOH) + \ (HCl) \ - (H_2O) - [Na] - \ [Cl] \quad (2)$$
$$(KOH) \ + \tfrac{1}{2}(H_2SO_4) - (H_2O) - [K] \ - \tfrac{1}{2}[SO_4] \quad (3)$$
$$(KOH) \ + \ (HCl) \ - (H_2O) - [K] \ - \ [Cl] \quad (4)$$

We have obviously (1) — (2) = (3) — (4) if we assume complete dissociation of the salts. As indicated above, this is approximately true for the instances which actually occur. It is all the more the case because the salts which are furthest from complete dissociation – here $Na_2SO_4$ and $K_2SO_4$ – are dissociated approximately to the same extent, whereby the error occurring in the two members of the last equation is

Heats of Formation of some Salts in Dilute Solution.
(From the Data of Thomsen and Berthelot.)

| | HCl, HBr, or HI. | HNO₃. | C₂H₄O₂. | CH₂O₂. |
|---|---|---|---|---|
| NaOH | 13·7 | 13·7 (0·0) | 13·3 (−0·4) | 13·4 (−0·3) |
| KOH | 13·7 | 13·8 (+0·1) | 13·3 (−0·4) | 13·4 (−0·3) |
| NH₃ | 12·4 | 12·5 (+0·1) | 12·0 (−0·4) | 11·9 (−0·5) |
| ½ Ca(OH)₂ | 14·0 | 13·9 (−0·1) | 13·4 (−0·6) | 13·5 (−0·5) |
| ½ Ba(OH)₂ | 13·8 | 13·9 (+0·1) | 13·4 (−0·4) | 13·5 (−0·3) |
| ½ Sr(OH)₂ | 14·1 | 13·9 (−0·2) | 13·3 (−0·8) | 13·5 (−0·6) |

| | ½ (CO₂H)₂. | ½ H₂SO₄. | ½ H₂S. | HCN. | ½ CO₂. |
|---|---|---|---|---|---|
| NaOH | 14·3 (+0·6) | 15·8 (+2·1) | 3·8 (−9·9) | 2·9 (−10·8) | 10·2 (−3·5) |
| KOH | 14·3 (+0·6) | 15·7 (+2·0) | 3·8 (−9·9) | 3·0 (−10·7) | 10·1 (−3·6) |
| NH₃ | 12·7 (+0·3) | 14·5 (+2·0) | 3·1 (−9·3) | 1·3 (−11·1) | 5·3 (−7·1) |
| Ca(OH)₂ | .. | .. | 3·9 (−10·1) | .. | .. |

approximately the same, a circumstance which determines the occurrence of additive properties somewhat more frequently than one might expect. The above short table shows that on the neutralization of strong bases and strong acids the additive properties are clearly apparent. For salts of weak bases with weak acids this is no longer the case, because they are probably partially decomposed by the water.

The numbers in brackets represent the difference between the heat evolution of the salt considered and that of the corresponding chloride. It will be seen if we neglect the last column that they are in each vertical column approximately constant. This is closely connected with the thermo-neutrality of salts; but since I have on a previous occasion treated this subject more particularly and emphasized the close connexion with the Williamson-Clausius hypothesis, I need not here enter into any detailed analysis.

# CATO MAXIMILIAN GULDBERG
1836–1902

## PETER WAAGE
1833–1900

### THE LAW OF MASS ACTION

THE law of Mass Action was first put forward in a series of papers published in the years 1864–7. Guldberg was the Professor of Applied Mathematics and Waage the Professor of Chemistry in the University of Christiana (now Oslo). They followed Berthelot and St Gilles who, in studying the formation of an ester and water by reaction between an acid and an alcohol, had recognized that an equilibrium was set up, and had derived expressions for the velocity of reaction between the acid and the alcohol.

Guldberg and Waage went further and considered the rate of the reverse reaction (between ester and water). The law of mass action is often considered in one of its most useful aspects, that of dealing with dynamic equilibria. Primarily, however, it is concerned with rates of reaction, wherein lies its fundamental importance.

The original statement of the law did not become well known, and the authors subsequently published a restatement in the *Journal für praktische Chemie* for 1879. This gave them an opportunity to comment on further experimental results which supported their law. The section which follows is from the translation in Leicester and Klickstein's *A Source Book in Chemistry* (Harvard, 1952).

———

¶ In the year 1867, we presented a study under the title of *Études sur les affinités chimiques* in which we were concerned chiefly with chemical mass action. We expressed the view that the result of a chemical process depends not only on the substances which enter into the new compound but also on all other substances which are present in the process. The latter we called *foreign substances*, in so far as they exert a noticeable influence, even though they do not themselves undergo any chemical change during the process. The solvent is considered one of these foreign substances.

The chemical forces which come into effect between the substances are dependent on temperature, pressure, the aggregate condition, and the mass ratios.

We differentiate two chief groups of chemical forces: the true affinity forces which bring about the formation of new chemical compounds, and the secondary forces whose action can be referred back to the foreign substances.

The chemical processes which are most suitable for the study of the chemical forces in them are, in our view, those in which an equilibrium state exists between the forces, or, in other words, processes in which the chemical reaction goes equally in two opposite directions. As examples, we will mention

1. A metal is oxidized by water vapour, and the metal oxide under the same conditions is reduced by hydrogen.

2. Dissociation of a body AB, in which both parts A and B and the original substance AB are present at the same time.

3. Two dissolved substances give rise to a double decomposition: thus alcohol and acetic acid go partly into ester and water, and reversibly, ester and water go partly into alcohol and acetic acid.

4. A soluble and an insoluble salt partly exchange their acids; thus potassium sulphate and barium carbonate go partly into potassium carbonate and barium sulphate, and reversibly, potassium carbonate and barium sulphate change partly into potassium sulphate and barium carbonate.

These last classes of chemical compounds were those which we chiefly made the subject of our experimental studies.

From our own experimental studies combined with

already known material, we deduced the law for chemical mass action which we stated as follows:

If two substances A and B change into two new substances A' and B', the chemical strength with which A and B are held together is measured by the mass of new substances A' and B' formed in unit time.

The mass with which a definite substance enters the unit volume of the body in which the chemical process proceeds we have called the *active mass* of the substance.

Actually, we mean by the active mass only the mass of the substance within the sphere of action; under otherwise equal conditions, however, the action sphere can be represented by the unit volume.

The chemical force with which two substances A and B act on each other is equal to the product of their active masses multiplied by the affinity coefficient (see *Études sur l e affinités chimiques,* page 6).

By the affinity coefficient is understood a coefficient which depends on the chemical nature of both substances and on the temperature. If the active masses of A and B are called $p$ and $q$, and $k$ is the affinity coefficient, then the chemical forces acting between A and B are expressed by $kpq$; this expression accordingly represents the mass of A and B which is transformed into A' and B' in unit time.

If in a chemical process A and B are changed to A' and B', and reversibly, A' and B' are changed to A and B, then an equilibrium occurs if the chemical force acting between A and B equals the chemical force acting between A' and B'.

If the active masses of A' and B' are expressed by $p'$ and $q'$ and their affinity coefficient by $k'$, the chemical force which acts between A' and B' is expressed by $k'p'q'$. This expression represents, as above, the masses of A' and B' which are changed to A and B in unit time.

The condition of equilibrium will thus be expressed by the equation

$$kpq = k'p'q'.$$

The above equation comprises in the shortest form the law of mass action and the condition of equilibrium, assuming that the secondary forces are not considered (see *Études*, paragraph 5).

In our work cited above we have verified the law of mass action, and for this, among others, we have especially used the following two types of chemical processes:

1. The action of alkali carbonates on barium sulphate, and the action of alkali sulphates on barium carbonate.

2. Ester formation, see Berthelot and St Gilles, *Ann. chim. phys.*, 1862.

In 1869, J. Thomsen in Copenhagen (see *Pogg. Ann.*, Bd. 138) presented a thermochemical study of the affinity relations between acids and bases in aqueous solution, and the results of this study also establish our law of mass action.

Also, W. Ostwald in Dorpat in 1876 sought to determine the affinity relations between acids and bases with the aid of volume changes (see this Journal [2], **16**, 385), thus furnishing a further confirmation of the results of Thomsen. Ostwald, too, from his studies has deduced a property of the affinity coefficient which can be expressed as follows: the affinity coefficient is the product of two coefficients, one of which relates to substance A and the other to substance B.

In 1877 Horstmann proposed a theory of the combustion of mixtures of carbon monoxide and hydrogen (*Ann. Chem. Pharm.*, 190). Actually, however, this theory is nothing but our law of mass action. If we replace $p$ in the above equation by the amount of hydrogen, $q$ by the amount of carbon dioxide, $p'$ by the amount of water, and $q'$ by the amount of carbon monoxide (all at the conclusion of the combustion), then Horstmann finds in his study that the ratio of $k:k'$ depends on temperature. In the same year (1877), van't Hoff further (*Ber. Berl. chem. Ges.*, 10) expressed ester formation by a formula which agrees completely with our equation. As mentioned above, we had already made this calculation in our work which appeared in 1867.

Since in these ways the law of mass action appears to be

valid for insoluble, soluble, and gaseous substances, we are forced to the assumption that it must be considered a general law which is valid for all chemical processes. In the following part we will try to prove this assumption still more positively, partly by developing the physical meaning of the law still further and partly by indicating its applicability to a series of very different chemical processes.

———

# FRIEDRICH WILHELM OSTWALD
## 1853–1932

## CATALYSIS

It would be difficult not to include Ostwald in a survey of the growth of physical chemistry. His influence, which has already been noted in the introductions to previous passages, was probably the most important in gaining recognition for physical chemistry as a separate branch of the subject. This he did through his own research, and the widespread inspiration of his teaching, by writing textbooks, and by founding and editing journals. His *Lehrbuch der allgemeinen Chemie* (Textbook of General Chemistry) was published in two volumes between 1883 and 1887. The *Zeitschrift für physikalische Chemie* was founded in 1887, not only as a vehicle for the publication of research papers in physical chemistry, but for abstracts of papers published in other journals and for reviews of books. In 1894 he was one of the sponsors of a further journal, the *Zeitschrift für Elektrochemie*.

He was born in Riga, of German parents who had settled in the Baltic province of Livland. His early work was done in the University of Dorpat and the Riga Polytechnicum, but his greatest influence came when he was appointed to the Chair of Physical Chemistry in Leipzig. Here, among his assistants were Arrhenius, Nernst, Bodenstein, and Freundlich, and his laboratories attracted many students from Britain and America.

One of his most important achievements was to apply the law of mass action to the ionic equilibria existing in dilute solutions as pictured by Arrhenius. This gave Ostwald's Dilution Law. His interest in chemical reactivity led him to consider the phenomenon of catalysis. One of his expositions of his theory of catalysis was, rather strangely, stated in an abstract, though, to an editor, this may have seemed a natural opportunity for publishing it. The article abstracted was by Stohmann on the heats of combustion of foodstuffs. The abstract is from the *Zeitschrift für Physikalische Chemie* for 1894, the translation being from Leicester and Klickstein's *A Source Book in Chemistry*, (Harvard, 1952).

It is worth recording that, in spite of his boundless enthusiasm for new ideas, Ostwald had not been convinced of the validity of the atomic theory as late as 1904, though he later came to accept it. One of his sons, Wolfgang, followed in Wilhelm's steps by founding the *Kolloid Zeitschrift* – to do for colloid science as a branch of physical chemistry what Wilhelm had done for physical chemistry as a branch of chemistry.

———

After a historical introduction the author brings together the essential values for the heat of combustion of the most important ingredients of nutrients as determined by him and his students. Some general considerations of this are discussed in which the author points out in a praiseworthy manner the great significance of catalytic phenomena for physiology. After a summary of the views of different investigators on this problem, he formulates his own, in which he defines *catalysis* in the following way:

'Catalysis is a condition of movement of the atoms in a molecule of a labile body which follows the entrance of the energy emitted from one body into another and leads to the formation of more stable bodies with loss of energy.'

The abstractor has several objections to make to this definition. First, the assumption of a 'condition of movement of the atoms in a molecule' is hypothetical and therefore not suitable for purposes of definition. Also, that is plainly not a loss of energy. What is more, in describing characteristic conditions of catalysis, a loss of free energy can follow under conditions even of absolute energy uptake.

If the abstractor were to formulate for himself the problem of characterizing the phenomenon of catalysis in a general way, he would consider the following expression as probably most suitable: Catalysis is the acceleration of a chemical reaction, which proceeds slowly, by the presence of a foreign substance. It would then be necessary to give the following explanations.

There are numerous substances or combinations of substances which in themselves are not stable but undergo slow change and only seem stable to us because their changes occur so slowly that during the usual short period of observation they do not strike us. Such substances or systems often attain an increased reaction rate if certain foreign substances, that is, substances which are not in themselves necessary for the reaction, are added. This acceleration occurs without alteration of the general energy relations, since after the end of the reaction the foreign body can again be separated from the field of the reaction, so that the energy used up by the addition can once more be obtained by the separation, or the reverse. However, these processes, like all natural ones, must always occur in such a direction that the free energy of the entire system is decreased.

It is therefore misleading to consider catalytic action as a force which produces something which would not occur without the substance which acts catalytically; still less can it be assumed that the latter performs work. It will perhaps contribute to an understanding of the problem if I especially mention that time is not involved in the idea of chemical energy; thus if the chemical energy relations are such that a definite process must occur, then it is only the initial and final states, as well as the whole series of intermediate given states which must be passed through, which must occur, but in no way is the time during which the reaction takes place of concern. Time is here dependent on conditions which lie outside the two chief laws of energetics. The only form of energy which contains time in its definition is kinetic energy, which is proportional to the mass and the square of the velocity. All cases in which such energies take a fixed part are therefore completely determined in time if the conditions are given; but all cases in which the vibrational energy does not play this role are independent of time, that is, they can occur without violating the laws of energy in any given time.

Catalytic processes are empirically found to be of the type in which this last property is observed; the existence of catalytic processes is to me therefore a positive proof that chemical processes cannot have a kinetic nature.

# V

# THE BREAKDOWN OF CLASSICAL PHYSICS

In studying the history of the physical sciences in the eighteenth and nineteenth centuries one catches something of the overriding spirit of optimism which was born out of the increasing range of successful advance, a triumphant progress which appeared as a powerful vindication of the essential correctness of the scientist's approach and of the power and precision of his methods. Laplace voiced the spirit of his times with his proud boast: 'An intelligence knowing, at a given instant of time, all forces acting in nature, as well as the momentary positions of all things of which the universe consists, would be able to comprehend the motions of the largest bodies of the world and those of the lightest atoms in one single formula, provided his intellect were sufficiently powerful to subject all data to analysis; to him nothing would be uncertain, both past and future would be present in his eyes.'

Towards the end of the nineteenth century, however, there arose a number of problems which appeared strangely resistant to the repeated attempts to provide a solution. New phenomena emerged which stood in curious contrast to the accepted picture of the physical world. The last decade of the nineteenth century was to witness a growing element of doubt in the attitudes of the more percipient of physicists, a doubt which hardened into criticism, and, with the coming of the twentieth century, gave to scientific thinking a radically new perspective.

Of the many great achievements which grew out of the fertile soil of Newtonian mechanical ideas, none was more impressive, both in range of application and in elegance of concept, than the theory of electromagnetism, which reached its climax in the equations of Maxwell. Yet this self-same theory was to be the source of two developments which called in question the very foundations of the Newtonian outlook – the theory of relativity and the quantum theory.

The story of the development of the theory of relativity would take us outside the scope of this book, but it is of interest to note that the title of Einstein's paper, which founded the subject, was *On the Electrodynamics of Moving Bodies*, a reminder of the fact that it was the emergence of a fundamental incompatibility between Maxwell's theory and Newtonian mechanics which was responsible for this drastic reassessment of the foundations of physics.

Among Faraday's many contributions to the study of electrical phenomena, the investigation of the passage of electric currents through gases is somewhat overshadowed by his other great achievements. When a current flows through a gas at very low pressure a colourful glow results (the neon and sodium street lamps are familiar examples), but prior to Faraday such experiments were a source of entertainment rather than an important topic of research. Yet Faraday's intuition led him to insist on the importance of such phenomena, and in so doing he initiated a series of researches which were destined to play a central role in the establishment of modern physics.

Faraday's own observations were continued by investigators like Johann Hittorf (1824–1914) and William Crookes (1832–1919), and led, in 1895, to the discovery of X-rays by Röntgen. The technological applications of this result hardly need emphasis; for the history of physics the occasion offers an interesting link between past and present. Röntgen's discovery was the outcome of a long series of investigations, yet the full significance of his achievement was only to be seen in the context of the atomic theories of the twentieth century.

This same field of study was to be the scene of even more important advances when, two years later, J. J. Thomson discovered the electron. With this step the problem of the ultimate constituents of matter took on a new meaning. The atom no longer represented the finest sub-division of matter, and itself became a complex construction of more fundamental materials. Today the electron is a humble member of a very large family of 'fundamental' particles whose role in the structure of the physical world still represents one of the greatest problems which challenge the contemporary physicist.

If the experiments of Röntgen and Thomson revealed a link with the past, the discovery of radioactivity, by Becquerel, can claim no such ancestry. In a manner both dramatic and uncompromising the world of the atom revealed an aspect of those bizarre phenomena which were to characterize this new realm of experience.

The elucidation of the nature and origins of radioactivity rapidly became the subject of intense research, and the monumental labours of the Curies, husband and wife, pointed the way to future advance. For physics and chemistry alike these pioneering studies were to lead to fresh insights which transformed earlier conceptions of these subjects. The extract from the work of Rutherford and Soddy, which appears in the following section, represents not only the continuing examination of these perplexing phenomena, but looks forward to the years ahead in which both authors were to contribute directly to the establishment of a rational picture of the inner structure of the atom.

These successes of the future were to require, however, more than experiment, ingenious as it might be; the theoretician was forced to change old-established ways of thinking. The last extract in this book is from the writings of Max Planck. It is, perhaps, a fitting conclusion in that it represents the first glimmering of understanding of the strange new world which experiment had revealed. It signals the end of an era, some of whose triumphs we have witnessed in these pages, and, at the same time, it heralds the birth of a new era, and in so doing serves as a reminder of the continuous, and continuing, growth of the physical sciences.

# WILHELM RÖNTGEN
1845–1923

## X-RAYS ARE DISCOVERED

PATIENCE and persistence are essential to scientific work, but now and again the steady and sometimes slow accumulation of experimental data is spectacularly interrupted by a chance observation or a lucky accident of a kind which dramatically changes the course of development. The search for an understanding of the structure of matter has been helped by a few such fortuitous events – of which one of the most important was Röntgen's discovery of the X-ray.

Faraday and others after him had examined the effects of discharging electric currents through gases in partially evacuated glass tubes. Although such experiments made it possible to observe a number of phenomena, these were limited by the efficiency of the pumps used for evacuating the tubes. Vacuum suction pumps were gradually improved, however, so that by 1895, when Röntgen's discovery took place, the cathode-ray tube was well developed. Within the tube was a negative electrode, the *cathode*, and a positive electrode, the *anode*. When a current was passed between the cathode and the anode while the tube was being progressively exhausted, it caused the glass tube wall near the cathode to emit a spectacular greenish glow or luminescence.

Continued studies of this effect led to the suggestion that a stream of 'rays' called cathode rays produced the luminescence. It was later found that this stream of cathode rays could be deflected by a magnet. The glow which permeated the tube was not finally explained until 1898 (as will be seen in the selection from the work of J. J. Thomson), but Röntgen's discovery, along with that of Becquerel, was to prove of crucial importance to Thomson and others in giving a new direction to the theories of atomic structure.

Röntgen, who was born in Germany, began his studies in

Holland but took his doctor's degree at Zurich under Rudolf Clausius (1822–88), a mathematical physicist and one of the important contributors to theoretical work in thermodynamics. Clausius first presented, in 1857, a *useful* kinetic theory of matter dealing with molecular movement and expressed in mathematical form.

Röntgen held a number of teaching positions before his appointment, in 1885, to the professorship of physics at the University of Würzburg. His interests were broad and included work in light, heat, elasticity, and electricity, and it was while he was working with the cathode-ray tube that Röntgen detected the mysterious effect that he subsequently identified as the result of a form of radiation he named X-rays.

In 1895 Röntgen placed a metal target within the cathode-ray tube at an angle to the path of the cathode rays. When the tube was switched on, it caused a screen covered with a fluorescent salt outside the tube to glow. Since it was known that the cathode rays could not penetrate the walls of the glass tube, some other kind of radiation was obviously being produced. Further experiments showed the unusual character of this radiation: it could pass through barriers of wood and glass and, as we now know so well, through human flesh. The higher the vacuum in the cathode-ray tube, the more penetrating were the X-rays.

Röntgen was awarded the Nobel Prize in physics in 1901 for his discovery. His experiments are described in the following selection, taken from G. Barker's translation in *Harper's Scientific Memoirs*, 1895.

---

¶ *On a new kind of Rays*

(1) If the discharge of a fairly large induction-coil be made to pass through a Hittorf vacuum-tube, or through a Lenard tube, a Crookes' tube, or other similar apparatus, which has been sufficiently exhausted, the tube being covered with thin, black cardboard which fits it with tolerable closeness, and if the whole apparatus be placed in a completely

darkened room, there is observed at each discharge a bright illumination of a paper screen covered with barium platino-cyanide, placed in the vicinity of the induction-coil, the fluorescence thus produced being entirely independent of the fact whether the coated or the plain surface is turned towards the discharge tube. This fluorescence is visible even when the paper screen is at a distance of two metres from the apparatus.

It is easy to prove that the cause of the fluorescence pro-ceeds from the discharge-apparatus, and not from any other point in the conducting circuit.

(2) The most striking feature of this phenomenon is the fact that an active agent here passes through a black card-board envelope which is opaque to the visible and the ultra-violet rays of the sun or of the electric arc; an agent, too, which has the power of producing active fluorescence. Hence we may first investigate the question whether other bodies also possess this property.

We soon discover that all bodies are transparent to this agent, though in very different degrees. I proceed to give a few examples: Paper is very transparent; behind a bound book of about one thousand pages I saw the fluorescent screen light up brightly, the printer's ink offering scarcely a noticeable hindrance. In the same way the fluorescence appeared behind a double pack of cards; a single card held between the apparatus and the screen being almost un-noticeable to the eye. A single sheet of tinfoil is also scarcely perceptible, it is only after several layers have been placed over one another that their shadow is distinctly seen on the screen. Thick blocks of wood are also transparent, pine boards 2 or 3 cm. thick absorbing only slightly. A plate of aluminium about 15 mm. thick, though it enfeebled the action seriously, did not cause the fluorescence to disappear entirely. Sheets of hard rubber several centimetres thick still permit the rays to pass through them.

Glass plates of equal thickness behave quite differently, according as they contain lead (flint glass) or not; the for-mer are much less transparent than the latter. If the hand be held between the discharge-tube and the screen, the darker shadow of the bones is seen within the slightly dark shadow image of the hand itself. Water, carbon disulphide, and various other liquids, when they are examined in mica vessels, seem also to be transparent. That hydrogen is to any considerable degree more transparent than air I have not been able to discover. Behind plates of copper, silver, lead, gold, and platinum, the fluorescence may still be recognized, though only if the thickness of the plates is not too great. Platinum of a thickness of 0·2 mm. is still transparent, the silver and copper plates may even be thicker. Lead of a thickness of 1·5 mm. is practically opaque, and on account of this property this metal is frequently most useful. A rod of wood with a square cross-section (20 by 20 mm.), one of whose sides is painted white with lead paint, behaves differently according as to how it is held between the apparatus and the screen. It is almost entirely without action when the X-rays pass through it parallel to the painted side; whereas the stick throws a dark shadow when the rays are made to traverse it perpendicular to the painted side. In a series similar to that of the metals themselves their salts can be arranged with reference to their transparency, either in the solid form or in solution.

(3) The experimental results which now have been given, as well as others, lead to the conclusion that the transparency of different substances, assumed to be of equal thickness, is essentially conditioned upon their density; no other property makes itself felt like this, certainly to so high a degree.

The following experiments show, however, that the density is not the only cause acting. I have examined, with reference to their transparency, plates of glass, aluminium, calcite, and quartz, of nearly the same thickness; and while these substances are almost equal in density, yet it was quite evident that the calcite was sensibly less transparent than the other substances which appeared almost exactly alike. No particularly strong fluorescence (see No. 6 below) of calcite, especially by comparison with glass, has been noticed.

(4) All substances with increase in thickness become less transparent. In order to find a possible relation between transparency and thickness, I have made photographs in which portions of the photographic plate were covered with layers of tinfoil, varying in the number of sheets superimposed. Photometric measurements of these will be made when I am in possession of a suitable photometer.*

(5) Sheets of platinum, lead, zinc, and aluminium were rolled of such thickness that all appeared nearly equally transparent. The following table contains the absolute thickness of these sheets measured in millimetres, the relative thickness referred to that of the platinum sheet, and their densities.

| THICKNESS | RELATIVE THICKNESS | DENSITY |
|---|---|---|
| Pt 0·018 mm. | 1 | 21·5 |
| Pb 0·05 ,, | 3 | 11·3 |
| Zn 0·10 ,, | 6 | 7·1 |
| Al 3·5 ,, | 200 | 2·6 |

We may conclude from these values that different metals possess transparencies which are by no means equal, even when the product of thickness and density are the same. The transparency increases much more rapidly than this product decreases.

(6) The fluorescence of barium platinocyanide is not the only recognizable effect of the X-rays. It should be mentioned that other bodies also fluoresce; such, for instance, as the phosphorescent calcium compounds, then uranium glass, ordinary glass, calcite, rock salt, and so on.

Of special significance in many respects is the fact that photographic dry plates are sensitive to the X-rays. We are therefore in a condition to determine more definitely many phenomena, and so the more easily to avoid deception; wherever it has been possible, therefore I have controlled, by means of photography, every important observation

* A photometer is a device for comparing the intensities of two beams of light. It can be used to compare the blackening of two portions of a photographic plate, since the blacker portion reflects the lesser amount of light.

which I have made with the eye by means of the fluorescent screen.

In these experiments the property of the rays to pass almost unhindered through thin sheets of wood, paper, and tinfoil is most important. The photographic impressions can be obtained in an undarkened room with the photographic plates either in the holders or wrapped up in paper. On the other hand, from this property it results as a consequence that undeveloped plates cannot be left for a long time in the neighbourhood of the discharge-tube, if they are protected merely by the usual covering of paste-board and paper.

It appears questionable, however, whether the chemical action on the silver salts of the photographic plates is directly caused by the X-rays. It is possible that this action proceeds from the fluorescent light which, as noted above, is produced in the glass plate itself or perhaps in the layer of gelatin. 'Films' can be used as well as glass plates.

I have not yet been able to prove experimentally that the X-rays are able also to produce a heating action; yet we may well assume that this effect is present, since the capability of the X-rays to be transformed is proved by means of the observed fluorescence phenomena. It is certain, therefore, that all the X-rays which fall upon a substance do not leave it again as such.

The retina of the eye is not sensitive to these rays. Even if the eye is brought close to the discharge-tube, it observes nothing although, as experiment has proved, the media contained in the eye must be sufficiently transparent to transmit the rays.

(7) After I had recognized the transparency of various substances of relatively considerable thickness, I hastened to see how the X-rays behaved on passing through a prism, and to find whether they were thereby deviated or not.

Experiments with water and with carbon disulphide enclosed in mica prisms of about 30 degrees refracting angle showed no deviation either with the fluorescent screen or on the photographic plate. For purposes of comparison the deviation of rays of ordinary light under the same conditions was observed; and it was noted that in this case the deviated images fell on the plate about 10 or 20 mm. distant from the direct image. By means of prisms made of hard rubber and of aluminium, also of about 30 degree refracting angle, I have obtained images on the photographic plate in which some small deviation may perhaps be recognized. However, the fact is quite uncertain; the deviation, if it does exist, being so small that in any case the refractive index of the X-rays in the substances named cannot be more than 1·05 at the most. With a fluorescent screen I was also unable to observe any deviation.

Up to the present time experiments with prisms of denser metals have given no definite results, owing to their feeble transparency and the consequently diminished intensity of the transmitted rays.

With reference to the general conditions here involved on the one hand, and on the other to the importance of the question whether the X-rays can be refracted or not on passing from one medium into another, it is most fortunate that this subject may be investigated in still another way than with the aid of prisms. Finely divided bodies in sufficiently thick layers scatter the incident light and allow only a little of it to pass, owing to reflection and refraction, so that if powders are as transparent to X-rays as the same substances are in mass – equal amounts of material being presupposed – it follows at once that neither refraction nor regular reflection takes place to any sensible degree. Experiments were tried with finely powdered rock-salt, with fine electrolytic silver powder, and with zinc-dust, such as is used in chemical investigations. In all these cases no difference was detected between the transparency of the powder and that of the substance in mass, either by observation with the fluorescent screen or with the photographic plate.

From what has now been said it is obvious that the X-rays cannot be concentrated by lenses; neither a large lens of hard rubber nor a glass lens having any influence upon them. The shadow-picture of a round rod is darker in the middle than at the edge; while the image of a tube which is filled with a substance more transparent than its own material is lighter at the middle than at the edge.

(8) The question as to the reflection of the X-rays may be regarded as settled, by the experiments mentioned in the preceding paragraph, in favour of the view that no noticeable regular reflection of the rays takes place from any of the substances examined. Other experiments, which I here omit, lead to the same conclusion.

One observation in this connexion should, however, be mentioned, as at first sight it seems to prove the opposite. I exposed to the X-rays a photographic plate which was protected from the light by black paper, and the glass side of which was turned towards the discharge-tube giving the X-rays. The sensitive film was covered, for the most part, with polished plates of platinum, lead, zinc, and aluminium, arranged in the form of a star. On the developed negative it was seen plainly that the darkening under the platinum, the lead, and particularly the zinc, was stronger than under the other plates, the aluminium having exerted no action at all. It appears, therefore, that these three metals reflect the rays. Since, however, other explanations of the stronger darkening are conceivable, in a second experiment, in order to be sure, I placed between the sensitive film and the metal plates a piece of thin aluminium-foil, which is opaque to ultra-violet rays, but is very transparent to the X-rays. Since the same result substantially was again obtained, the reflection of X-rays from the metals above named is proved.

If we compare this fact with the observation already mentioned that powders are as transparent as coherent masses, and with the further fact that bodies with rough surfaces behave like polished bodies with reference to the passage of the X-rays, as shown also in the last experiment, we are led to the conclusion already stated that regular reflection does not take place, but that bodies behave towards the X-rays as turbid media do towards light.

Since, moreover, I could detect no evidence of refraction of these rays in passing from one medium into another, it would seem that X-rays move with the same velocity in all substances: and, further, that this speed is the same in the medium which is present everywhere in space and in which the particles of matter are imbedded. These particles hinder the propagation of the X-rays, the effect being greater, in general, the more dense the substance concerned.

(9) Accordingly it might be possible that the arrangement of particles in the substance exercised an influence on its transparency; that, for instance, a piece of calcite might be transparent in different degrees for the same thickness, according as it was traversed in the direction of the axis, or at right angles to it. Experiments, however, on calcite and quartz gave a negative result.

(10) It is well known that Lenard came to the conclusion, from the results of his beautiful experiments on the transmission of the cathode rays of Hittorf through a thin sheet of aluminium, that these rays are phenomena of the ether, and that they diffuse themselves through all bodies. We can say the same of our rays.

In his most recent research, Lenard has determined the absorptive power of different substances for the cathode rays, and, among others, has measured it for air from atmospheric pressure to 4·10, 3·40, 3·10, referred to 1 centimetre, according to the rarefaction of the gas contained in the discharge apparatus. Judging from the discharge pressure as estimated from the sparking distance, I have had to do in my experiments for the most part with rarefactions of the same order of magnitude, and only rarely with less or greater ones. I have succeeded in comparing by means of the L. Weber photometer – I do not possess a better one – the intensities, taken in atmospheric air, of the fluorescence of my screen at two distances from the discharge apparatus about 100 and 200 mm., and I have found from three experiments, which agree very well with each other, that the intensities vary inversely as the squares of the distances of the screen from the discharge apparatus. Accordingly, air absorbs a far smaller fraction of the X-rays than of the cathode rays. This result is in entire agreement with the observation mentioned above, that it is still possible to detect the fluorescent light at a distance of 2 metres from the discharge apparatus.

Other substances behave in general like air; they are more transparent to X-rays than to cathode rays.

(11) A further difference, and a most important one, between the behaviour of cathode rays and of X-rays lies in the fact that I have not succeeded, in spite of many attempts, in obtaining a deflection of the X-rays by a magnet, even in very intense fields.

The possibility of deflection by a magnet has, up to the present time, served as a characteristic property of the cathode rays, although it was observed by Hertz and Lenard that there are different sorts of cathode rays, 'which are distinguished from each other by their production of phosphorescence, by the amount of their absorption, and by the extent of their deflection by a magnet'. A considerable deflection, however, was noted in all cases investigated by them; so that I do not think that this characteristic will be given up except for stringent reasons.

(12) According to experiments especially designed to test the question, it is certain that the spot on the wall of the discharge tube which fluoresces the strongest is to be considered as the main centre from which the X-rays radiate in all directions. The X-rays proceed from that spot where, according to the data obtained by different investigators, the cathode rays strike the glass wall. If the cathode rays within the discharge apparatus are deflected by means of a magnet, it is observed that the X-rays proceed from another spot, namely from that which is the new terminus of the cathode rays.

For this reason, therefore, the X-rays, which it is impossible to deflect, cannot be cathode rays simply transmitted or reflected without change by the glass wall. The greater density of the gas outside of the discharge-tube certainly cannot account for the great difference in the deflection, according to Lenard.

I therefore reach the conclusion that the X-rays are not identical with the cathode rays, but that they are produced by the cathode rays at the glass wall of the discharge apparatus.

(13) This production does not take place in glass alone, but, as I have been able to observe in an apparatus closed by a plate of aluminium 2 mm. thick, in this metal also. Other substances are to be examined later.

(14) The justification for calling by the name 'rays' the agent which proceeds from the wall of the discharge apparatus I derive in part from the entirely regular formation of shadows, which are seen when more or less transparent bodies are brought between the apparatus and the fluorescent screen (or the photographic plate).

I have observed, and in part photographed, many shadow pictures of this kind, the production of which has a particular charm. I possess, for instance, photographs of the shadow of the profile of a door which separates the rooms in which, on one side of which the discharge apparatus was placed, on the other the photographic plate; the shadow of the bones of the hand; the shadow of a covered wire wrapped on a wooden spool; of a set of weights enclosed in a box; of a galvanometer in which the magnetic needle is entirely enclosed by metal; of a piece of metal whose lack of homogeneity becomes noticeable by means of the X-rays, etc.

Another conclusive proof of the rectilinear propagation of the X-rays is a pin hole photograph which I was able to make of the discharge-apparatus while it was enveloped in black paper; the picture is weak but unmistakably correct.

(15) I have tried in many ways to detect interference phenomena of the X-rays; but, unfortunately, without success, perhaps only because of their feeble intensity.

(16) Experiments have begun but are not yet finished, to ascertain whether electrostatic forces affect the X-rays in any way.

(17) In considering the question what are the X-rays – which as we have seen, cannot be cathode rays – we may perhaps at first be led to think of them as ultra-violet light,

owing to their active fluorescence and their chemical actions. But in so doing we find ourselves opposed by the most weighty considerations. If the X-rays are ultra-violet light, this light must have the following properties:

(a) On passing from air into water, carbon disulphide, aluminium, rock-salt, glass, zinc, etc., it suffers no noticeable refraction.

(b) By none of the bodies named can it be regularly reflected to any appreciable extent.

(c) It cannot be polarized by any of the ordinary methods.

(d) Its absorption is influenced by no other property of substances so much as by their density.

That is to say, we must assume that these ultra-violet rays behave entirely differently from the ultra-red, visible, and ultra-violet rays which have been known up to this time.

I have been unable to come to this conclusion, and so have sought for another explanation.

There seems to exist some kind of relationship between the new rays and light rays; at least this is indicated by the formation of shadows, the fluorescence, and the chemical action produced by them both. Now, we have known for a long time that there can be in the ether longitudinal vibrations besides the transverse light vibrations, and, according to the views of different physicists, these vibrations must exist. Their existence, it is true, has not been proved up to the present, and consequently their properties have not been investigated by experiment.

Ought not, therefore, the new rays to be ascribed to longitudinal vibrations in the ether?

I must confess that in the course of the investigation I have become more and more confident of the correctness of this idea, and so, therefore, permit myself to announce this conjecture, although I am perfectly aware that the explanation given still needs further confirmation.

¶ *Second Communication on a new kind of Rays*

Since my work must be interrupted for several weeks, I take

the opportunity of presenting in the following paper some new phenomena which I have observed.

(18) It was known to me at the time of my first publication that X-rays can discharge electrified bodies; and I conjecture that in Lenard's experiments it was the X-rays, and not the cathode rays, which had passed unchanged through the aluminium window of his apparatus, which produced the action described by him upon electrified bodies at a distance. I have, however, delayed the publication of my experiments until I could contribute results which are free from criticism.

These results can be obtained only when the observations are made in a space which is protected completely, not only from the electrostatic forces proceeding from the vacuum-tube, from the conducting wires, from the induction apparatus, etc., but is also closed against air which comes from the neighbourhood of the discharge-apparatus.

To secure these conditions, I had a chamber made of zinc plates soldered together, which was large enough to contain myself and the necessary apparatus, which could be closed air-tight, and which was provided with an opening which could be closed by a zinc door. The wall opposite the door was for the most part covered with lead. At a place near the discharge-apparatus, which was set up outside the case, the zinc wall, together with the lining of sheet lead, was cut out for a width of 4 centimetres; and the opening was covered again air-tight with a thin sheet of aluminium. The X-rays penetrated through this window into the observation space.

I observed the following phenomena:

(a) Electrified bodies in air, charged either positively or negatively, are discharged if X-rays fall upon them; and this process goes on the more rapidly the more intense the rays are. The intensity of the rays was estimated by their action on a fluorescent screen or a photographic plate.

It is immaterial in general whether the electrified bodies are conductors or insulators. Up to the present, I have not found any specific difference in the behaviour of different bodies with reference to the rate of discharge; nor as to the behaviour of positive and negative electricity. Yet it is not impossible that small differences may exist.

(b) If the electrified conductor be surrounded not by air but by a solid insulator, e.g. paraffin, the radiation has the same action as would result from exposure of the insulating envelope to a flame connected to the earth.

(c) If this insulating envelope be surrounded by a close-fitting conductor which is connected to the earth and which, like the insulator, is transparent to X-rays, the radiation produces on the inner electrified conductor no action which can be detected by my apparatus.

(d) The observations noted, indicate that air through which X-rays have passed possesses the power of discharging electrified bodies with which it comes in contact.

(e) If this is really the case, and if, further, the air retains this property for some time after it has been exposed to the X-rays, then it must be possible to discharge electrified bodies which have not been themselves exposed to the rays, by conducting to them air which has thus been exposed.

We may convince ourselves in various ways that this conclusion is correct. One method of experiment, although perhaps not the simplest, I shall describe.

I used a brass tube 3 centimetres wide and 45 centimetres long; at a distance of some centimetres from one end a part of the wall of the tube was cut away and replaced by a thin aluminium plate; at the other end, through an air-tight cap, a brass ball fastened to a metal rod was introduced into the tube in such a manner as to be insulated. Between the ball and the closed end of the tube there was soldered a side-tube which could be connected with an exhaust-apparatus; so that when this is in action the brass ball is subjected to a stream of air which on its way through the tube has passed by the aluminium window. The distance from the window to the ball was over 20 centimetres.

I arranged this tube inside the zinc chamber in such a position that the X-rays could enter through the aluminium window of the tube perpendicular to its axis. The insulated ball lay then in the shadow, out of the range of the action of these rays. The tube and the zinc case were connected by a conductor, the ball was joined to a Hankel electroscope.

It was now observed that a charge (either positive or negative) given to the ball was not influenced by the X-rays so long as the air remained at rest in the tube, but that the charge instantly decreased considerably if by exhaustion the air which had been subjected to the rays was drawn past the ball. If by means of storage cells the ball was maintained at a constant potential, and if the modified air was drawn continuously through the tube, an electric current arose just as if the ball were connected to the wall of the tube by a poor conductor.

(f) The question arises, how does the air lose the property which is given it by the X-rays? It is not yet settled whether it loses this property gradually of itself – i.e., without coming in contact with other bodies. On the other hand, it is certain that a brief contact with a body of large surface, which does not need to be electrified, can make the air inactive. For instance, if a thick enough stopper of wadding is pushed into the tube so far that the modified air must pass through it before it reaches the electrified ball, the charge on the ball remains unaffected even while the exhaustion is taking place.

If the wad is in front of the aluminium window, the result obtained is the same as it would be without the wad; a proof that it is not particles of dust which are the cause of the observed discharge.

Wire gratings act like wadding; but the gratings must be very fine, and many layers must be placed over each other if the modified air is to be inactive after it is drawn through them. If these gratings are not connected to the earth, as has been assumed, but are connected to a source of electricity at a constant potential, I have always observed exactly what I had expected, but these experiments are not yet completed.

(g) If the electrified bodies, instead of being in air, are placed in dry hydrogen, they are also discharged by the

X-rays. The discharge in hydrogen seemed to me to proceed somewhat more slowly; yet this is still uncertain on account of the difficulty of obtaining exactly equal intensities of the X-rays in consecutive experiments.

The method of filling the apparatus with hydrogen precludes the possibility that the layer of air which was originally present, condensed on the surface of the bodies, played any important role.

(h) In spaces which are highly exhausted the discharge of a body by the direct incidence of X-rays proceeds much more slowly – in one case about seventy times more slowly – than in the same vessels when filled with air or hydrogen at atmospheric pressure.

(i) Experiments are about to be begun on the behaviour of a mixture of chlorine and hydrogen under the influence of X-rays.

(j) In conclusion I would like to mention that the results of investigations on the discharging action of X-rays in which the influence of the surrounding gas is not taken into account should be received with great caution.

# J. J. THOMSON
## 1856–1940

## THE DISCOVERY OF THE ELECTRON

THE progress of science is marked from time to time by the appearance of an investigator who, by synthesizing existing knowledge, establishes a clear-cut pattern of theory and provides his contemporaries with a new set of guides for future work. His own discoveries and his clear restatement of the problems which have arisen serve to resolve controversies and so to eliminate wasteful mis-direction of research.

Such a man was J. J. Thomson. Born at Manchester, and educated there and at Cambridge, he spent the remainder of his long life at Cambridge, as Cavendish Professor and later as Master of Trinity College. He was responsible for the development of the Cavendish Laboratories, which have become one of the world's great research centres, and it was there, in 1897, that Thomson discovered the electron and thus established the theory of the electrical nature of matter.

Thomson's discovery took place at the peak of the controversy about the nature of the cathode ray. There were, at that time, two schools of thought, one of which regarded the cathode rays as wave-like radiations in the ether, whilst the other school favoured the idea that they were high-velocity, negatively charged, particles. Thomson's experiments clearly vindicated the latter school of thought. Not only did he demonstrate the particle nature of the cathode rays, but he was able to measure the ratio of the charge to the mass of these particles. The magnitude of this ratio indicated that the particles involved were different from the other particles known to physics. With the later determination of the charge of the particles it became apparent that they were some two thousand times lighter than the hydrogen atom. The electron, as the particle was later named, was the first of the 'fundamental' particles to be discovered, and thus was initiated a series of investigations which continue to the present day.

The selection (taken from *The Philosophical Magazine*, Vol. 44, 1897) describes Thomson's original experiments, and in his discussion of the results we find Thomson considering the part played by these 'primordial Atoms', as he called the electrons, in the structure of the atom. This was a problem which was to play a central part in the history of modern physics.

Thomson applied his experiments to the analysis of some of the elements. His methods were later improved by F. W. Aston, and from this work evolved the mass spectrograph, which permits the investigation of isotopes. In the United States, R. A. Millikan (1868–1953) refined Thomson's calculations of the relative mass of the electron, which he stated as $\frac{1}{1830}$ of that of the hydrogen atom.

Thomson's experiments provided the basis for the study of atomic structure. In addition to his own experimental accomplishments, for which he was awarded the Nobel Prize in 1906, Thomson stimulated many other workers who made significant contributions of their own. His influence as a teacher can be judged by the fact that six of his students at the Cavendish Laboratories won the Nobel Prize in physics or chemistry. Moreover, an imposing list of his students became Fellows of the Royal Society and won prizes and medals while they occupied professorial chairs at seventy-five universities throughout the world. This is an unprecedented monument to a single figure in scientific history.

---

¶ *Cathode Rays*

The experiments discussed in this paper were undertaken in the hope of gaining some information as to the nature of the Cathode Rays. The most diverse opinions are held as to these rays; according to the almost unanimous opinion of German physicists they are due to some process in the ether to which – inasmuch as in a uniform magnetic field their course is circular and not rectilinear – no phenomenon hitherto observed is analogous: another view of these rays is that, so far from being wholly aetherial, they are in fact wholly material, and that they mark the paths of particles of matter charged with negative electricity. It would seem at first sight that it ought not to be difficult to discriminate between views so different, yet experience shows that this is not the case, as amongst the physicists who have most deeply studied the subject can be found supporters of either theory.

The electrified-particle theory has for purposes of research a great advantage over the aetherial theory, since it is definite and its consequences can be predicted; with the aetherial theory it is impossible to predict what will happen under any given circumstances, as on this theory we are dealing with hitherto unobserved phenomena in the ether, of whose laws we are ignorant.

The following experiments were made to test some of the consequences of the electrified-particle theory.

## § *Charge carried by the Cathode Rays*

If these rays are negatively electrified particles, then when they enter an enclosure they ought to carry into it a charge of negative electricity. This has been proved to be the case by Perrin, who placed in front of a plane cathode two coaxial metallic cylinders which were insulated from each other: the outer of these cylinders was connected with the earth, the inner with a gold-leaf electroscope. These cylinders were closed except for two small holes, one in each cylinder, placed so that the cathode rays could pass through them into the inside of the inner cylinder. Perrin found that when the rays passed into the inner cylinder the electroscope received a charge of negative electricity, while no charge went to the electroscope when the rays were deflected by a magnet so as no longer to pass through the hole.

This experiment proves that something charged with negative electricity is shot off from the cathode, travelling at right angles to it, and that this something is deflected by a magnet; it is open, however, to the objection that it does not prove that the cause of the electrification in the electroscope has anything to do with the cathode rays. Now the supporters of the aetherial theory do not deny that electrified particles are shot off from the cathode; they deny, however, that these charged particles have any more to do with the cathode

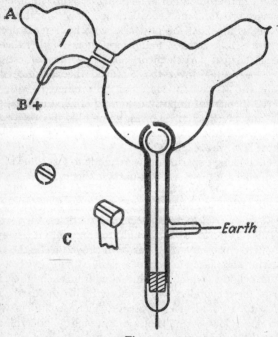

Fig. 1

rays than a rifle-ball has with the flash when a rifle is fired. I have therefore repeated Perrin's experiment in a form which is not open to this objection. The arrangement used was as follows: Two coaxial cylinders (fig. 1) with slits in them are placed in a bulb connected with the discharge-tube; the cathode rays from the cathode A pass into the bulb through a slit in a metal plug fitted into the neck of the tube; this plug is connected with the anode and is put to earth. The cathode rays thus do not fall upon the cylinders unless they are deflected by a magnet. The outer cylinder is connected with the earth, the inner with the electrometer. When the cathode rays (whose path was traced by the phosphorescence on the glass) did not fall on the slit, the electrical charge sent to the electrometer when the induction-coil* producing the rays was set in action was small and irregular; when, however, the rays were bent by a magnet so as to fall on the slit there was a large charge of negative electricity sent to the electrometer. I was surprised at the magnitude of the charge; on some occasions enough negative electricity went through the narrow slit into the inner cylinder in one second to alter the potential of a capacity of 1·5 microfarads by 20 volts. If the rays were so much bent by the magnet that they overshot the slits in the cylinder, the charge passing into the cylinder fell again to a very small fraction of its value when the aim was true. Thus this experiment shows that however we twist and deflect the cathode rays by magnetic forces, the negative electrification follows the same path as the rays, and that this negative electrification is indissolubly connected with the cathode rays.

When the rays are turned by the magnet so as to pass through the slit into the inner cylinder, the deflection of the electrometer connected with this cylinder increases up to a certain value, and then remains stationary although the rays continue to pour into the cylinder. This is due to the fact that the gas in the bulb becomes a conductor of electricity when the cathode rays pass through it, and thus, though the inner cylinder is perfectly insulated when the rays are not passing, yet as soon as the rays pass through the bulb the air between the inner cylinder and the outer one becomes a conductor, and the electricity escapes from the inner cylinder to the earth. Thus the charge within the inner cylinder does not go on continually increasing; the cylinder settles down into a state of equilibrium in which the rate at which it gains negative electricity from the rays is equal to the rate

* Apparatus for producing high voltage.

at which it loses it by conduction through the air. If the inner cylinder has initially a positive charge it rapidly loses that charge and acquires a negative one; while if the initial charge is a negative one, the cylinder will leak if the initial negative potential is numerically greater than the equilibrium value.

### § *Deflection of the Cathode Rays by an electrostatic field*

An objection very generally urged against the view that the cathode rays are negatively electrified particles, is that hitherto no deflection of the rays has been observed under a small electrostatic force and though the rays are deflected when they pass near electrodes connected with sources of large differences of potential, such as induction-coils or electrical machines, the deflection in this case is regarded by the supporters of the aetherial theory as due to the discharge passing between the electrodes, and not primarily to the electrostatic field. Hertz made the rays travel between two

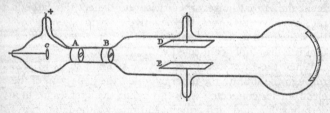

Fig. 2

parallel plates of metal placed inside the discharge-tube, but found that they were not deflected when the plates were connected with a battery of storage-cells; on repeating this experiment I at first got the same result, but subsequent experiments showed that the absence of deflection is due to the conductivity conferred on the rarefied gas by the cathode rays. On measuring this conductivity it was found that it diminished very rapidly as the exhaustion increased; it seemed then that on trying Hertz's experiment at very high exhaustions there might be a chance of detecting the deflection of the cathode rays by an electrostatic force.

The apparatus used is represented in fig. 2.

The rays from the cathode C pass through a slit in the anode A, which is a metal plug fitting tightly into the tube and connected with the earth; after passing through a second slit in another earth-connected metal plug B, they travel between two parallel aluminium plates about 5 cm. long by 2 broad and at a distance of 1·5 cm. apart; they then fall on the end of the tube and produce a narrow well-defined phosphorescent patch. A scale pasted on the outside of the tube serves to measure the deflection of this patch. At high exhaustion the rays were deflected when the two aluminium plates were connected with the terminals of a battery of small storage-cells; the rays were depressed when the upper plate was connected with the negative pole of the battery, the lower with the positive, and raised when the upper plate was connected with the positive, the lower with the negative pole. The deflection was proportional to the difference of potential between the plates, and I could detect the deflection when the potential difference was as small as two volts. It was only when the vacuum was a good one that the deflection took place, but that the absence of deflection is due to the conductivity of the medium is shown by what takes place when the vacuum has just arrived at the stage at which the deflection begins. At this stage there is a deflection of the rays when the plates are first connected with the terminals of the battery, but if this connexion is maintained the patch of phosphorescence gradually creeps back to its undeflected position.

This is just what would happen if the space between the plates were a conductor, though a very bad one, for then the positive and negative ions between the plates would slowly diffuse, until the positive plate became coated with negative ions, the negative plate with positive ones: thus the electric intensity between the plates would vanish and the cathode rays be free from electrostatic force. Another illustration of this is afforded by what happens when the pressure is low enough to show the deflection and a large difference of potential, say 200 volts, is established between the plates; under these circumstances there is a large deflection of the cathode rays, but the medium under the large electromotive force breaks down every now and then and a bright discharge passes between the plates; when this occurs the phosphorescent patch produced by the cathode rays jumps back to its undeflected position. When the cathode rays are deflected by the electrostatic field, the phosphorescent band breaks up into several bright bands separated by comparatively dark spaces; the phenomena are exactly analogous to those observed by Birkeland when the cathode rays are deflected by a magnet, and called by him the magnetic spectrum.

A series of measurements of the deflection of the rays by the electrostatic force under various circumstances will be found later on in the part of the paper which deals with the velocity of the rays and the ratio of the mass of the electrified particles to the charge carried by them. It may, however, be mentioned here that the deflection gets smaller as the pressure diminishes, and when in consequence the potential-difference in the tube in the neighbourhood of the cathode increases.

§ *Magnetic deflection of the Cathode Rays in different gases*

The deflection of the cathode rays by the magnetic field was studied with the aid of the apparatus shown in fig. 3. The cathode was placed in a side-tube fastened on to a bell-jar; the opening between this tube and the bell-jar was closed by a metallic plug with a slit in it; this plug was connected with the earth and was used as the anode. The cathode rays passed through the slit in this plug into the bell-jar, passing in front of a vertical plate of glass ruled into small squares. The bell-jar was placed between two large parallel coils arranged as a Helmholtz galvanometer. The course of the rays was determined by taking photographs of the bell-jar when the cathode rays were passing through it; the divisions on the plate enabled the path of the rays to be determined. Under the action of the magnetic field the narrow beam of cathode rays spreads out into a broad fan-shaped luminosity in the gas. The luminosity in this fan is not uniformly distributed, but is condensed along certain lines. The phosphorescence on the glass is also not uniformly distributed; it is much spread out, showing that the beam consists of rays which are not all deflected to the same extent by the magnet.

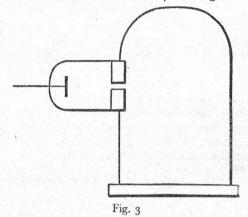

Fig. 3

The luminosity on the glass is crossed by bands along which the luminosity is very much greater than in the adjacent parts. These bright and dark bands are called by Birkeland, who first observed them, the magnetic spectrum. The brightest spots on the glass are by no means always the terminations of the brightest streaks of luminosity in the gas; in fact, in some cases a very bright spot on the glass is not connected with the cathode by any appreciable luminosity, though there may be plenty of luminosity in other parts of the gas. One very interesting point brought out by the photographs is that in a given magnetic field, and with a given mean potential-difference between the terminals, the path of the rays is independent of the nature of the gas. Photographs were taken of the discharge in hydrogen, air, carbonic acid, methyl iodide, *i.e.*, in gases whose densities range from 1 to 70, and yet, not only were the paths of the most deflected rays the same in all cases, but even the details, such as the distribution of the bright and dark spaces, were the same; in fact, the photographs could hardly be distinguished from each other. It is to be noted that the pressures were not the same; the pressures in the different gases were adjusted so that the mean potential-difference between the cathode and the anode were the same in all the gases. When the pressure of a gas is lowered, the potential-difference between the terminals increases, and the deflection of the rays produced by a magnet diminishes, or at any rate the deflection of the rays when the phosphorescence is a maximum diminishes. If an air-break is inserted an effect of the same kind is produced.

In the experiments with different gases, the pressures were as high as was consistent with the appearance of the phosphorescence on the glass, so as to ensure having as much as possible of the gas under consideration in the tube.

As the cathode rays carry a charge of negative electricity, are deflected by an electrostatic force as if they were negatively electrified, and are acted on by a magnetic force in just the way in which this force would act on a negatively electrified body moving along the path of these rays, I can see no escape from the conclusion that they are charges of negative electricity carried by particles of matter. The question next arises, What are these particles? are they atoms, or molecules, or matter in a still finer state of subdivision? To throw some light on this point, I have made a series of measurements of the ratio of the mass of these particles to the charge carried by it. To determine this quantity, I have used two independent methods. The first of these is as follows: Suppose we consider a bundle of homogeneous cathode rays. Let $m$ be the mass of each of the particles, $e$ the charge carried by it. Let N be the number of particles passing across any section of the beam in a given time; then $Q$, the quantity of electricity carried by these particles is given by the equation

$$Ne = Q.$$

We can measure $Q$ if we receive the cathode rays in the

inside of a vessel connected with an electrometer. When these rays strike against a solid body, the temperature of the body is raised, the kinetic energy of the moving particles being converted into heat; if we suppose that all this energy is converted into heat, then if we measure the increase in the temperature of a body of known *thermal capacity* caused by the impact of these rays, we can determine W, the kinetic energy of the particles, and if $v$ is the velocity of the particles,

$$\tfrac{1}{2} Nmv^2 = W.$$

If $\rho$ is the radius of curvature of the path of these rays in a uniform magnetic field H, then

$$\frac{mv^2}{\rho} = Hev$$

$$\frac{mv}{e} = H\rho = I,$$

where I is written for $H\rho$ for the sake of brevity. From these equations we get

$$\frac{mv^2}{2e} = \frac{W}{Q},$$

$$v = \frac{2W}{QI},$$

$$\frac{m}{e} = \frac{I^2Q}{2W}.$$

Thus if we know the values of Q, W, and I, we can deduce the values of v and m/e.

To measure these quantities, I have used tubes of three different types. The first I tried is like that represented in fig. 2, except that the plates E and D are absent, and two coaxial cylinders are fastened to the end of the tube. The rays from the cathode C fall on the metal plug B, which is connected with the earth, and serves for the anode; a horizontal slit is cut in this plug. The cathode rays pass through this slit, and then strike against the two coaxial cylinders at the end of the tube; slits are cut in these cylinders, so that the cathode rays pass into the inside of the inner cylinder. The outer cylinder is connected with the earth, the inner cylinder, which is insulated from the outer one, is connected with an electrometer, the deflection of which measures Q, the quantity of electricity brought into the inner cylinder by the rays. A thermo-electric couple is placed behind the slit in the inner cylinder; this couple is made of very thin strips of iron and copper fastened to very fine iron and copper wires. These wires passed through the cylinders, being insulated from them, and through the glass to the outside of the tube, where they were connected with a low-resistance galvanometer, the deflection of which gave data for calculating the rise of temperature of the junction produced by the impact against it of the cathode rays. The strips of iron and copper were large enough to ensure that every cathode ray which entered the inner cylinder struck against the junction. In some of the tubes the strips of iron and copper were placed end to end, so that some of the rays struck against the iron, and others against the copper; in others, the strip of one metal was placed in front of the other; no difference, however, could be detected between the results got with these two arrangements. The strips of iron and copper were weighed, and the thermal capacity of the junction calculated. In one set of junctions this capacity was $5 \times 10^{-3}$, in another $3 \times 10^{-3}$. If we assume that the cathode rays which strike against the junction give their energy up to it, the deflection of the galvanometer gives us W or $\frac{1}{2} Nmv^2$.

The value of I, *i.e.*, H$\rho$, where $\rho$ is the curvature of the path of the rays in a magnetic field of strength H was found as follows: The tube was fixed between two large circular coils placed parallel to each other, and separated by a distance equal to the radius of either. These coils produce a uniform magnetic field, the strength of which is got by measuring with an ammeter the strength of the current passing through them. The cathode rays are thus in a uniform field, so that their path is circular. Suppose that the rays, when deflected by a magnet, strike against the glass of the tube at

E (fig. 4); then, if $\rho$ is the radius of the circular path of the rays,

$$2\rho = \frac{CE^2}{AC} + AC;$$

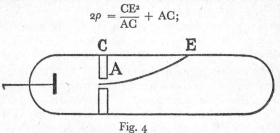

Fig. 4

thus, if we measure CE and AC we have the means of determining the radius of curvature of the path of rays.

The determination of $\rho$ is rendered to some extent uncertain, in consequence of the pencil of rays spreading out under the action of the magnetic field, so that the phosphorescent patch E is several millimetres long; thus values of $\rho$ differing appreciably from each other will be got by taking E at different points of this phosphorescent patch. Part of this patch was, however, generally considerably brighter than the rest; when this was the case, E was taken as the brightest point; when such a point of maximum brightness did not exist, the middle of the patch was taken for E. The uncertainty in the value of $\rho$ thus introduced amounted sometimes to about 20 per cent; by this I mean that if we took E first at one extremity of the patch and then at the other we should get values of $\rho$ differing by this amount.

The measurement of Q, the quantity of electricity, which enters the inner cylinder, is complicated by the cathode rays making the gas through which they pass a conductor, so that though the insulation of the inner cylinder was perfect when the rays were off, it was not so when they were passing through the space between the cylinders; this caused some of the charge communicated to the inner cylinder to leak away so that the actual charge given to the cylinder by the cathode rays was larger than that indicated by the electrometer. To make the error from this cause as small as possible, the inner cylinder was connected to the largest capacity available, 1·5 microfarad, and the rays were only kept on for a short time, about 1 or 2 seconds, so that the alteration in potential of the inner cylinder was not large, ranging from about ·5 to 5 volts in the various experiments. Another reason why it is necessary to limit the duration of the rays to as short a time as possible, is to avoid the correction for the loss of heat from the thermoelectric junction by conduction along the wires; the rise in temperature of the junction was of the order 2°C.; a series of experiments showed that with the same tube and the same gaseous pressure Q and W were proportional to each other when the rays were not kept on too long.

Tubes of this kind gave satisfactory results, the chief drawback being that sometimes in consequence of the charging up of the glass of the tube, a secondary discharge started from the cylinder to the walls of the tube, and the cylinders were surrounded by glow; when this glow appeared, the readings were very irregular; the glow could, however, be got rid of by pumping and letting the tube rest for some time. The results got with this tube are given in the Table under the heading, Tube 1. The second type of tube was like that used for photographing the path of the rays (fig. 3); double cylinders with a thermo-electric junction like those used in the previous tube were placed in the line of fire of the rays, the inside of the bell-jar was lined with copper gauze connected with the earth. This tube gave very satisfactory results; we were never troubled with any glow round the cylinders, and readings were most concordant; the only drawback was that as some of the connexions had to be made with sealing-wax, it was not possible to get the highest exhaustions with this tube, so that the range of pressure for this tube is less than that for tube 1. The results got with this tube are given in the Table under the heading, Tube 2. The third type of tube was similar to the first, except that the openings in the two cylinders were made very much smaller; in this tube the slits in the cylinders were replaced by small holes, about 1·5 mm. in diameter. In consequence of the smallness of the openings the magnitude of the effects was very much reduced, and in order to get measurable results, it was necessary to reduce the capacity of the condenser in

| GAS | VALUE OF w/Q | I | m/e | v |
|---|---|---|---|---|
| | | Tube 1 | | |
| Air | $4·6 \times 10^{11}$ | 230 | $·57 \times 10^{-7}$ | $4 \times 10^9$ |
| Air | $1·8 \times 10^{12}$ | 350 | $·34 \times 10^{-7}$ | $1 \times 10^{10}$ |
| Air | $6·1 \times 10^{11}$ | 230 | $·43 \times 10^{-7}$ | $5·4 \times 10^9$ |
| Air | $2·5 \times 10^{12}$ | 400 | $·32 \times 10^{-7}$ | $1·2 \times 10^{10}$ |
| Air | $5·5 \times 10^{11}$ | 230 | $·48 \times 10^{-7}$ | $4·8 \times 10^9$ |
| Air | $1 \times 10^{12}$ | 285 | $·4 \times 10^{-7}$ | $7 \times 10^9$ |
| Air | $1 \times 10^{12}$ | 285 | $·4 \times 10^{-7}$ | $7 \times 10^9$ |
| Hydrogen | $6 \times 10^{12}$ | 205 | $·35 \times 10^{-7}$ | $6 \times 10^9$ |
| Hydrogen | $2·1 \times 10^{12}$ | 460 | $·5 \times 10^{-7}$ | $9·2 \times 10^9$ |
| Carbonic Acid | $8·4 \times 10^{11}$ | 260 | $·4 \times 10^{-7}$ | $7·5 \times 10^9$ |
| Carbonic Acid | $1·47 \times 10^{12}$ | 340 | $·4 \times 10^{-7}$ | $8·5 \times 10^9$ |
| Carbonic Acid | $3·0 \times 10^{12}$ | 480 | $·39 \times 10^{-7}$ | $1·3 \times 10^{10}$ |
| | | Tube 2 | | |
| Air | $2·8 \times 10^{11}$ | 175 | $·53 \times 10^{-7}$ | $3·3 \times 10^9$ |
| Air | $4·4 \times 10^{11}$ | 195 | $·47 \times 10^{-7}$ | $4·1 \times 10^9$ |
| Air | $3·5 \times 10^{11}$ | 181 | $·47 \times 10^{-7}$ | $3·8 \times 10^9$ |
| Hydrogen | $2·8 \times 10^{11}$ | 175 | $·53 \times 10^{-7}$ | $3·3 \times 10^9$ |
| Air | $2·5 \times 10^{11}$ | 160 | $·51 \times 10^{-7}$ | $3·1 \times 10^9$ |
| Carbonic Acid | $2 \times 10^{11}$ | 148 | $·54 \times 10^{-7}$ | $2·5 \times 10^9$ |
| Air | $1·8 \times 10^{11}$ | 151 | $·63 \times 10^{-7}$ | $2·3 \times 10^9$ |
| Hydrogen | $2·8 \times 10^{11}$ | 175 | $·53 \times 10^{-7}$ | $3·3 \times 10^9$ |
| Hydrogen | $4·4 \times 10^{11}$ | 201 | $·46 \times 10^{-7}$ | $4·4 \times 10^9$ |
| Air | $2·5 \times 10^{11}$ | 176 | $·61 \times 10^{-7}$ | $2·8 \times 10^9$ |
| Air | $4·2 \times 10^{11}$ | 200 | $·48 \times 10^{-7}$ | $4·1 \times 10^9$ |
| | | Tube 3 | | |
| Air | $2·5 \times 10^{11}$ | 220 | $·9 \times 10^{-7}$ | $2·4 \times 10^9$ |
| Air | $3·5 \times 10^{11}$ | 225 | $·7 \times 10^{-7}$ | $3·2 \times 10^9$ |
| Hydrogen | $3 \times 10^{11}$ | 250 | $1·0 \times 10^{-7}$ | $2·5 \times 10^9$ |

connexion with the inner cylinder to ·15 microfarad, and to make the galvanometer exceedingly sensitive, as the rise in temperature of the thermo-electric junction was in these experiments only about ·5 degrees C. on the average. The results obtained in this tube are given in the Table under the heading, Tube 3.

The results of a series of measurements with these tubes are given in the table on the previous page.

It will be noticed that the value of m/e is considerably greater for Tube 3, where the opening is a small hole, than for Tubes 1 and 2, where the opening is a slit of much greater area. I am of opinion that the values of m/e got from Tubes 1 and 2 are too small, in consequence of the leakage from the inner cylinder to the outer by the gas being rendered a conductor by the passage of the cathode rays. It will be seen from these tables that the value of m/e is independent of the nature of the gas. Thus, for the first tube the mean for air is ·40 × $10^{-7}$, for hydrogen ·42 × $10^{-7}$, and for carbonic acid gas ·4 × $10^{-7}$, and for the second tube the mean for air is ·52 × $10^{-7}$, for hydrogen ·50 × $10^{-7}$, and for carbonic acid gas ·54 × $10^{-7}$.

Experiments were tried with electrodes made of iron instead of aluminium; this altered the appearance of the discharge and the value of v at the same pressure: the values of m/e were, however, the same in the two tubes; the effect produced by different metals on the appearance of the discharge will be described later on. In all the preceding experiments, the cathode rays were first deflected from the cylinder by a magnet, and it was then found that there was no deflection either of the electrometer or the galvanometer, so that the deflections observed were entirely due to the cathode rays; when the glow mentioned previously surrounded the cylinders there was a deflection of the electrometer even when the cathode rays were deflected from the cylinder. Before proceeding to discuss the results of these measurements I shall describe another method of measuring the quantities m/e and v, of an entirely different kind from the preceding; this method is based upon deflection of the cathode rays in an electrostatic field. If we measure the deflection experienced by the rays when traversing a given length under a uniform electric intensity, and the deflection of the rays when they traverse a given distance under a uniform magnetic field, we can find the values of m/e and v in the following way: Let the space passed over by the rays under a uniform electric intensity F be L, the time taken for the rays to traverse this space is L/v, the velocity in the direction of F is therefore:

$$\frac{Fe}{m} \frac{L}{v},$$

so that $\theta$, the angle through which the rays are deflected when they leave the electric field and enter a region free from electric force, is given by the equation

$$\theta = \frac{Fe}{m} \frac{L}{v^2},$$

If, instead of the electric intensity, the rays are acted on by a magnetic force H at right angles to the rays, and extending across the distance L, the velocity at right angles to the original path of the rays is

$$\frac{Hev}{m} \frac{L}{v}$$

so that $\phi$, the angle through which the rays are deflected when they leave the magnetic field, is given by the equation

$$\phi = \frac{He}{m} \frac{L}{v}.$$

From these equations we get

$$v = \frac{\phi}{\theta} \frac{F}{H}$$

and

$$\frac{m}{e} = \frac{H^2 \theta . L}{F \phi^2}.$$

In the actual experiments H was adjusted so that $\phi = \theta$; in this case the equations become

$$v = \frac{F}{H}$$

$$\frac{m}{e} = \frac{H^2 L}{F \theta}.$$

The apparatus used to measure v and m/e by this means is that represented in fig. 2. The electric field was produced by connecting the two aluminium plates to the terminals of a battery of storage cells. The phosphorescent patch at the end of the tube was deflected, and the deflection measured by a scale pasted to the end of the tube. As it was necessary to darken the room to see the phosphorescent patch, a needle coated with luminous paint was placed so that by a screw it could be moved up and down the scale; this needle could be seen when the room was darkened, and it was moved until it coincided with the phosphorescent patch. Thus, when light was admitted, the deflection of the phosphorescent patch could be measured.

The magnetic field was produced by placing outside the tube two coils whose diameter was equal to the length of the plates; the coils were placed so that they covered the space occupied by the plates, the distance between the coils was equal to the radius of either. . . . A series of experiments was made to see if the electrostatic deflection was proportional to the electric intensity between the plates; this was found to be the case. In the following experiments the current through the coils was adjusted so that the electrostatic deflection was the same as the magnetic:

| GAS | $\theta$ | H | F | L | m/e | v. |
|---|---|---|---|---|---|---|
| Air | 8/110 | 5·5 | $1·5 \times 10^{10}$ | 5 | $1·3 \times 10^{-7}$ | $2·8 \times 10$ |
| Air | 9·5/110 | 5·4 | $1·5 \times 10^{10}$ | 5 | $1·1 \times 10^{-7}$ | $2·8 \times 10$ |
| Air | 13/110 | 6·6 | $1·5 \times 10^{10}$ | 5 | $1·2 \times 10^{-7}$ | $2·3 \times 10$ |
| Hydro-gen | 9/110 | 6·3 | $1·5 \times 10^{10}$ | 5 | $1·5 \times 10^{-7}$ | $2·5 \times 10$ |
| Carbonic acid | 11/110 | 6·9 | $1·5 \times 10^{10}$ | 5 | $1·5 \times 10^{-7}$ | $2·2 \times 10$ |
| Air | 6/110 | 5 | $1·8 \times 10^{10}$ | 5 | $1·3 \times 10^{-7}$ | $3·6 \times 10$ |
| Air | 7/110 | 3·6 | $1 \times 10^{10}$ | 5 | $1·1 \times 10^{-7}$ | $2·8 \times 10$ |

The cathode in the first five experiments was aluminium in the last two experiments it was made of platinum; in the last experiments Sir William Crookes' method of getting rid of the mercury vapour by inserting tubes of pounded sulphur, sulphur iodide, and copper filings between the bulb and the pump was adopted. In the calculation of $m/e$ and $v$ no allowance has been made for the magnetic force due to the coil in the region outside the plates; in this region the magnetic force will be in the opposite direction to that between the plates, and will tend to bend the cathode rays in the opposite direction: thus the effective value of H will be smaller than the value used in the equations, so that the values of $m/e$ are larger and those of $v$ less than they would be if this correction were applied. This method of determining the values of $m/e$ and $v$ is much less laborious and probably more accurate than the former method; it cannot however be used over so wide a range of pressures.

From these determinations we see that the value of $m/e$ is independent of the nature of the gas, and that its value $10^{-7}$ is very small compared with the value of $10^{-4}$, which is the smallest value of this quantity previously known, and which is the value for the hydrogen ion in electrolysis.

Thus for the carriers of the electricity in the cathode rays $m/e$ is very small compared with its value in electrolysis. The smallness of $m/e$ may be due to the smallness of $m$ or the largeness of $e$, or to a combination of these two. That the carriers of the charges in the cathode rays are small compared with ordinary molecules is shown I think, by Lenard's results as to the rate at which the brightness of the phosphorescence produced by these rays diminishes with the length of path travelled by the ray. If we regard this phosphorescence as due to the impact of the charged particles, the distance through which the rays must travel before the phosphorescence fades to a given fraction (say $1/e$ where $e = 2 \cdot 71$) of its original intensity, will be some moderate multiple of the mean free path. Now Lenard found that this distance depends solely upon the density of the medium, and not upon its chemical nature or physical state. In air at atmospheric pressure the distance was about half a centimetre, and this must be comparable with the mean free path of the carriers through air at atmospheric pressure. But the mean free path of the molecules of air is a quantity of quite a different order. The carrier, then, must be small compared with ordinary molecules.

The two fundamental points about these carriers seems to me to be (1) that these carriers are the same whatever the gas through which the discharge passes, (2) that the mean free paths depend upon nothing but the density of the medium traversed by these rays. . . . The explanation which seems to me to account in the most simple and straightforward manner for the facts is founded on a view of the constitution of the chemical elements which has been favourably entertained by many chemists: this view is that the different atoms of the different chemical elements are aggregations of atoms of the same kind. In the form in which this hypothesis was enunciated by Prout, the atoms of the different elements were hydrogen atoms; in this precise form the hypothesis is not tenable; but if we substitute for hydrogen some unknown primordial substance X there is nothing known which is inconsistent with this hypothesis which is one that has been recently supported by Sir Norman Lockyer for reasons derived from the study of the stellar spectra. If, in the very intense electric field in the neighbourhood of the cathode, the molecules of the gas are dissociated and are split up, not into the ordinary chemical atoms, but into these primordial atoms which we shall for brevity call corpuscles; and if these corpuscles are charged with electricity and projected from the cathode by the electric field, they would behave exactly like the cathode rays. They would evidently give a value of $m/e$ which is independent of the nature of the gas and its pressure, for the carriers are the same whatever the gas may be; again, the mean free paths of these corpuscles would depend solely upon the density of the medium through which they pass. For the molecules of the medium are composed of a number of such corpuscles separated by considerable spaces; now the collision between a single corpuscle and the molecule will not be between the corpuscles and the molecule as a whole, but between this corpuscle and the individual corpuscles which form the molecule; thus the number of collisions the particle makes as it moves through a crowd of these molecules will be proportional, not to the number of the molecules in the crowd, but to the number of the individual corpuscles. The mean free path is inversely proportional to the number of collisions in unit time, and so is inversely proportional to the number of corpuscles in unit volume; now as these corpuscles are all of the same mass, the number of corpuscles in unit volume will be proportional to the mass of unit volume, that is the mean free path will be inversely proportional to the density of the gas. We see, too, that so long as the distance between neighbouring corpuscles is large compared with the linear dimensions of a corpuscle the mean free path will be independent of the way they are arranged, provided the number in unit volume remains constant, that is, the mean free path will depend only on the density of the medium traversed by the corpuscles, and will be independent of its chemical nature and physical state: this, from Lenard's very remarkable measurements of the absorption of the cathode rays by various media, must be a property possessed by the carriers of the charges in the cathode rays.

Thus on this view we have in the cathode rays matter in a new state, a state in which the subdivision of matter is carried very much further than in the ordinary gaseous state: a state in which all matter, that is, matter derived from different sources such as hydrogen, oxygen, &c. is of one and the same kind; this matter being the substance from which all the chemical elements are built up. With appliances of ordinary magnitude, the quantity of matter produced by means of the dissociation at the cathode is so small as to almost preclude the possibility of any direct chemical investigation of its properties. Thus the coil I used would, I calculate, if kept going uninterruptedly night and day for a year, produce only about one three-millionth part of a gramme of this substance.

The smallness of the value of m/e is I think due to the largeness of e as well as the smallness of m. There seems to me to be some evidence that the charges carried by the corpuscles in the atom are large compared with those carried by the ions of an electrolyte. In the molecule of HCl, for example, I picture the components of the hydrogen atoms as held together by a great number of tubes of electrostatic force, the components of the chlorine atom are similarly held together while only one stray tube binds the hydrogen atom to the chlorine atom. The reason for attributing this high charge to the constituents of the atom is derived from the values of the specific inductive capacity of gases: we may imagine that the specific inductive capacity of a gas is due to the setting in the electric field of the electric doublet formed by the two oppositely electrified atoms which form the molecule of the gas. The measurements of the specific inductive capacity show, however, that this is very approximately an additive quantity: that is, that we can assign a certain value to each element, and find the specific inductive capacity of HCl by adding the value for hydrogen to the value for the chlorine; the value of $H_2O$ by adding twice the value for hydrogen to the value for oxygen, and so on. Now the electrical moment of the doublet formed by a positive charge on one atom of the molecule and a negative charge on the other atom would not be an additive property; if, however, each atom had a definite electrical moment, and if this were large compared with the electrical moment of the two atoms in the molecule, then the electrical moment of any compound, and hence its specific inductive capacity, would be an additive property. For the electrical moment of the atom, however, to be large compared with that of the molecule, the charge on the corpuscles would have to be very large compared with those on the ion.

If we regard the chemical atom as an aggregation of a number of primordial atoms, the problem of finding the configurations of stable equilibrium for a number of equal particles acting on each other according to some law of force – whether that of Boscovich, where the force between them is a repulsion when they are separated by less than a certain critical distance, and an attraction when they are separated by a greater distance, or even the simpler case of a number of mutually repellent particles held together by a central force – is of great interest in connexion with the relation between the properties of an element and its atomic weight. Unfortunately the equations which determine the stability of such a collection of particles increase so rapidly in complexity with the number of particles that a general mathematical investigation is scarcely possible. We can, however, obtain a good deal of insight into the general laws which govern such configurations by the use of models, the simplest of which is the floating magnets of Professor Mayer. In this model the magnets arrange themselves in equilibrium under their mutual repulsions and a central attraction caused by the pole of a large magnet placed above the floating magnets. A study of the forms taken by these magnets seems to me to be suggestive in relation to the periodic law. Mayer showed that when the number of floating magnets did not exceed 5 they arranged themselves at the corners of a regular polygon; 5 at the corners of a pentagon, 4 at the corners of a square, and so on. When the number exceeds 5, however, this law no longer holds: thus 6 magnets do not arrange themselves at the corners of a hexagon, but divide into two systems consisting of 1 in the middle surrounded by 5 at the corners of a pentagon. For 8 we have two in the inside and 6 outside; this arrangement in two systems, an inner and an outer, lasts up to 18 magnets. After this we have three systems: an inner, a middle, and an outer; for a still larger number of magnets we have four systems, and so on. Mayer found the arrangement of magnets was as follows:

| 1 | 2 | 3 | 4 | 5 |
|---|---|---|---|---|
| $\begin{cases} 1.5 \\ 1.6 \\ 1.7 \end{cases}$ | $\begin{cases} 2.6 \\ 2.7 \end{cases}$ | $\begin{cases} 3.7 \\ 3.8 \end{cases}$ | $\begin{cases} 4.8 \\ 4.9 \end{cases}$ | 5.9 |

$$
\begin{cases} 1.5.9 \\ 1.6.9 \\ 1.6.10 \\ 1.6.11 \end{cases}
\begin{cases} 2.7.10 \\ 2.8.10 \\ 2.7.11 \end{cases}
\begin{cases} 3.7.10 \\ 3.7.11 \\ 3.8.10 \\ 3.8.11 \\ 3.8.12 \\ 3.8.13 \end{cases}
\begin{cases} 4.8.12 \\ 4.8.13 \\ 4.9.12 \\ 4.9.13 \end{cases}
\begin{cases} 5.9.12 \\ 5.9.13 \end{cases}
$$

$$
\begin{cases} 1.5.9.12 \\ 1.5.9.13 \\ 1.6.9.12 \\ 1.6.10.12 \\ 1.6.10.13 \\ 1.6.11.12 \\ 1.6.11.13 \\ 1.6.11.14 \\ 1.6.11.15 \\ 1.7.12.14 \end{cases}
\begin{cases} 2.7.10.15 \\ 2.7.12.14 \end{cases}
\begin{cases} 3.7.12.13 \\ 3.7.12.14 \\ 3.7.13.14 \\ 3.7.13.15 \end{cases}
\begin{cases} 4.9.13.14 \\ 4.9.13.15 \\ 4.9.14.15 \end{cases}
$$

where for example, 1.6.10.12 means an arrangement with one magnet in the middle, then a ring of six, then a ring of ten, and a ring of 12 outside. Now suppose that a certain property is associated with two magnets forming a group by themselves; we should have this property with two magnets, again with 8 and 9, again with 19 and 20, and again with 34, 35, and so on. If we regard the system of magnets as a model of an atom, the number of magnets being proportional to the atomic weight, we should have this property occurring in elements of atomic weight 2, (8, 9), 19, 20, (34, 35). Again, any property conferred by three magnets forming a system by themselves would occur with atomic weights 3, 10, and 11; 20, 21, 22, 23, and 24; 35, 36, 37 and 39; in fact we should have something quite analogous to the periodic law, the first series corresponding to the arrangement of the magnets in a single group, the second series to the arrangement in two groups, the third series in three groups, and so on.

# HENRI BECQUEREL
## 1852–1908

## THE DISCOVERY OF RADIOACTIVITY

ONE of the most remarkable 'accidental' discoveries in the history of science was that of radioactivity – the spontaneous radiations which are emitted by certain atoms. The man responsible for this discovery was Henri Becquerel, who, in 1896, investigated the nature of the fluorescence which occurred under the influence of Röntgen's X-rays. He himself tells us, 'For my part, from the first day I had knowledge of the X-ray discovery of Professor Röntgen, there came to me the idea of seeing whether the property of emitting rays was not intimately bound up with phosphorescence.'

Becquerel had thought of using photographic plates to investigate the penetrating rays. A box of such plates, wrapped in light-protective paper, happened to be in a drawer which also contained some uranium salts. When, later, the plates were developed, Becquerel discovered that they had apparently been affected by the uranium. Further experiments, described in the following selection (taken from Magie's *A Sourcebook in Physics*, Harvard University Press, 1935), convinced Becquerel that the uranium salt was itself capable of giving off radiation independent of the action of the X-rays or of sunlight to stimulate its fluorescence. Quite clearly, the fluorescent properties of uranium were not responsible for the exposure of his photographic plates. But Becquerel did not completely understand the meaning of his observations and it remained for Pierre and Marie Curie to isolate and discover radioactive elements.

Becquerel was a member of a family which contributed much to science. His grandfather, Antoine César Becquerel (1788–1878), was awarded the Royal Society's Copley medal in 1837 for his pioneer work in electrochemistry, and made special studies in magnetism and telegraphy. His father, Alexandre Edmond Becquerel (1820–91), continued in the same tradition, contributing especially to the study of light, phosphorescence, and photochemistry. Antoine Henri took over his father's professorship at the Musée d'Histoire Naturelle in 1892 and was professor at the École Polytechnique in Paris from 1895. At the same time he held the position of chief engineer of the ministry of bridges and roads, an organization associated with the names of many of France's most famous scientists.

Becquerel was awarded the Nobel Prize in physics in 1903 for his discovery of radioactivity, sharing the prize with the Curies.

---

## ¶ *The Radiation from Uranium*

AT a former meeting M. Ch. Henry announced that phosphorescent sulphide of zinc introduced in the path of the rays emanating from a Crookes tube increased the intensity of the radiations which passed through the aluminium.

Further M. Niewenglowski perceived that phosphorescent calcium sulphide emits radiations which pass through opaque bodies.

The same fact appears with several other phosphorescent bodies, and in particular with salts of uranium, of which the phosphorescence lasts only for a short time.

With the double sulphate of uranium and potassium, of which I possess crystals in the form of a thin transparent crust, I have made the following experiment:

I wrapped a Lumière photographic plate with bromized emulsion with two sheets of thick black paper, so thick that the plate did not become clouded by exposure to the sun for a whole day. I placed on the paper a plate of the phosphorescent substance, and exposed the whole thing to the sun for several hours. When I developed the photographic plate I saw the silhouette of the phosphorescent substance in black on the negative. If I placed between the phosphorescent substance and the paper a coin or a metallic screen pierced with an open-work design, the image of these objects appeared on the negative.

The same experiments can be tried with a thin sheet of glass placed between the phosphorescent substance and the paper, which excludes the possibility of a chemical action resulting from vapours which might emanate from the substance when heated by the sun's rays.

We may therefore conclude from these experiments that the phosphorescent substance in question emits radiations which penetrate paper that is opaque to light, and reduce silver salts.

\*

I particularly insist on the following fact, which appears to me exceeding important and not in accord with the phenomena which one might expect to observe: the same encrusted crystals placed with respect to the photographic plates in the same conditions and acting through the same screens, but protected from the excitation of incident rays and kept in the dark, still produce the same photographic effects. I may relate how I was led to make this observation: among the preceding experiments some had been made ready on Wednesday the 26th and Thursday the 27th of February and as on those days the sun only showed itself intermittently I kept my arrangements all prepared and put back the holders in the dark in the drawer of the case, and left in place the crusts of uranium salt. Since the sun did not show itself again for several days I developed the photographic plates on the 1st of March, expecting to find the images very feeble. The silhouettes appeared on the contrary with great intensity. I at once thought that the action might be able to go on in the dark, and I arranged the following experiment.

At the bottom of a box made of opaque cardboard, I placed a photographic plate, and then on the sensitive face I laid a crust of uranium salt which was convex, so that it only touched the emulsion at a few points; then alongside of it I placed on the same plate another crust of the same salt, separated from the emulsion by a thin plate of glass;

this operation was carried out in the dark room, the box was shut, and then enclosed in another cardboard box and put away in a drawer.

I did the same thing with a holder closed by an aluminium plate, in which I put a photographic plate and then laid on it a crust of uranium salt. The whole was enclosed in an opaque box and put in a drawer. After five hours I developed the plates, and the silhouettes of the encrusted crystals showed black, as in the former experiment, and as if they had been rendered phosphorescent by light. In the case of the crust which was placed directly on the emulsion, there was a slightly different action at the points of contact from that under the parts of the crust which were about a milli-metre away from the emulsion; the difference may be attributed to the different distances of the sources of the active radiation. The action of the crust placed on the glass plate was very slightly enfeebled, but the form of the crust was very well reproduced. Finally, in passing through the plate of aluminium, the action was considerably enfeebled but nevertheless was very clear.

It is important to notice that this phenomenon seems not to be attributable to luminous radiation emitted by phos-phorescence, since at the end of one hundredth of a second these radiations become so feeble that they are scarcely perceptible.

\*

## § *Emission of new Radiations by Metallic Radiation*

Some months ago I showed that uranium salts emit radia-tions whose existence has not hitherto been recognized, and that these radiations possess remarkable properties, some of which are similar to the properties studied by M. Röntgen. The radiations of uranium salts are emitted not only when the substances are exposed to light but when they are kept in the dark, and for more than two months the same pieces of different salts, kept protected from all known exciting radiations, continued to emit, almost without perceptible enfeeblement, the new radiations. From the 3rd of March to the 3rd of May these substances were enclosed in a box of opaque cardboard. Since the 3rd of May they have been in a double box of lead, which has never left the dark room. A very simple arrangement makes it possible to slip a photographic plate under a black paper stretched parallel to the bottom of the box, on which rests the substances which are being tested, without exposing them to any radiation which does not pass through the lead.

In these conditions the substances studied continued to emit active radiation.

*

All the salts of uranium that I have studied, whether they become phosphorescent or not in the light, whether crystallized, cast, or in solution, have given me similar results. I have thus been led to think that the effect is a consequence of the presence of the element uranium in these salts, and that the metal would give more intense effects than its compounds. An experiment made several weeks ago with the powdered uranium of commerce, which has been for a long time in my laboratory, confirmed this expectation; the photographic effect is notably greater than the impression produced by one of the uranium salts, and in particular by the sulphate of uranium and potassium.

Before publishing this result, I waited until our fellow member, M. Moissan, whose beautiful investigations on uranium have just been published, could put at my disposal some of the products which he had prepared. The results were still sharper and the impressions obtained on the photographic plate through the black paper were much more intense with crystallized uranium, with a casting of uranium, and with uranium carbide than with the double sulphate used as a check on the same plate.

The same difference appears again in the phenomenon of the discharge of electrified bodies. The metallic uranium provokes the loss of charge at a greater rate than its salts do.

# PIERRE CURIE
## 1859–1906

# MARIE CURIE
## 1867–1934

### POLONIUM AND RADIUM
### ARE DISCOVERED

In a memorial statement following the death of Marie Curie, Albert Einstein said: 'Her strength, her purity of will, her austerity towards herself, her objectivity, her incorruptible judgement – all these were of a kind seldom found joined in a single individual. . . . The greatest scientific deed of her life – proving the existence of radioactive elements and isolating them – owes its accomplishment not merely to bold intuition but to a devotion and tenacity in execution under the most extreme hardships imaginable, such as the history of experimental science has not often witnessed.' Marie Curie revealed all of this and more in her selfless dedication to one task, the search for truth in her scientific work, intensified in the last twenty-eight years of her life, if that were possible, following the tragic and untimely death of her husband in a street accident.

The intensity of her tragedy can be appreciated when the nature of her relationship with her husband is known. For Marie and Pierre Curie were more than wife and husband; they functioned as a team in their scientific endeavours in a unique collaboration which produced some monumental researches.

Pierre Curie did his early work in crystallography and magnetism and, with his brother Jacques, discovered the phenomenon of piezoelectricity, in which certain crystals, when subjected to pressure, produce a difference of electrical potential. From 1882 he was the director of laboratories at the Municipal School of Physics and Chemistry of Paris.

Marie was born Marie Sklodowska, daughter of a professor of physics in Warsaw. Her interest in science was kindled by her father and in 1891 she came to Paris to continue her studies at the Sorbonne.

Pierre and Marie were married in 1895. Marie originally undertook some independent research at her husband's laboratory. Becquerel had discovered radioactivity and this, because of the Curies' association with Becquerel, led them to the work that dominated their lives. Marie found that pitchblende, the ore from which uranium is extracted, was considerably more radioactive than the uranium it contained. This suggested the presence of a new element in the pitchblende, and at this point in the research Pierre joined his wife.

After two years of strenuous, incredibly difficult labour the Curies announced, in 1899, the discovery of two new elements, polonium and radium, each more radioactive than uranium, the radium more than one million times more radioactive. This discovery was destined to be revolutionary in upsetting the current concepts of atomic structure, of radiation, and of the nature of chemical reactions, and in leading to a broadening of the horizons of modern chemistry and physics.

The Curies shared the Nobel Prize in 1903 with Becquerel. Pierre was killed in 1906 and Marie found solace in the continuation of her researches, which brought her an unprecedented second Nobel award in 1911, this time in chemistry, for her further studies on radium and radioactivity. It is more than coincidence that one of the daughters of the Curies, Irène, who later became Irène Curie-Joliot (1897–1956), and her husband, Frédéric Joliot (1900–58), shared the Nobel Prize in chemistry for 1935 for the artificial production of radioactive substances, a pioneering work in a new and vast field of modern research.

The selection that follows is taken from Leicester and Klickstein's *A Source Book in Chemistry* (Harvard University Press, 1952).

¶ *Chapter II*

§ *Method of Research*

The results of the investigation of radioactive minerals, announced in the preceding chapter, led M. Curie and myself to endeavour to extract a new radioactive body from pitchblende. Our method of procedure could only be based on radioactivity, as we know of no other property of the hypothetical substance. The following is the method pursued for a research based on radioactivity: The radio-activity of a compound is determined, and a chemical decomposition of this compound is effected; the radio-activity of all the products obtained is determined, having regard to the proportion in which the radioactive substance is distributed among them. In this way, an indication is obtained, which may to a certain extent be compared to that which spectrum analysis furnishes. In order to obtain comparable figures, the activity of the substances must be determined in the solid form well dried.

§ *Polonium, Radium, Actinium*

The analysis of pitchblende with the help of the method just explained, led us to the discovery in this mineral of two strongly radioactive substances, chemically dissimilar: Polonium, discovered by ourselves, and radium, which we discovered in conjunction with M. Bémont.

*Polonium* from the analytical point of view, is analogous to bismuth, and separates out with the latter. By one of the following methods of fractionating, bismuth products are obtained increasingly rich in polonium:

1. Sublimation of the sulphides *in vacuo;* the active sulphide is much more volatile than bismuth sulphide.

2. Precipitation of solutions of the nitrate by water; the precipitate of the basic nitrate is much more active than the salt which remains in solution.

3. Precipitation by sulphuretted hydrogen of a hydro-chloric acid solution, strongly acid; the precipitated

sulphides are considerably more active than the salt which remains in solution.

*Radium* is a substance which accompanies the barium obtained from pitchblende; it resembles barium in its reactions, and is separated from it by difference of solubility of the chlorides in water, in dilute alcohol, or in water acidified with hydrochloric acid. We effect the separation of the chlorides of barium and radium by subjecting the mixture to fractional crystallization, radium chloride being less soluble than that of barium.

A third strongly radioactive body has been identified in pitchblende by M. Debierne, who gave it the name of *actinium*. Actinium accompanies certain members of the iron group contained in pitchblende; it appears in particular allied to thorium, from which it has not yet been found possible to separate it. The extraction of actinium from pitchblende is a very difficult operation, the separations being as a rule incomplete.

All three of the new radioactive bodies occur in quite infinitesimal amount in pitchblende. In order to obtain them in a more concentrated condition, we were obliged to treat several tons of residue of the ore of uranium. The rough treatment was carried out in the factory; and this was followed by processes of purification and concentration. We thus succeeded in extracting from thousands of kilogrammes of crude material a few decigrammes of products which were exceedingly active as compared with the ore from which they were obtained. It is obvious that this process is long, arduous, and costly. . . .

§ *Extraction of the new Radioactive Substance*

The first stage of the operation consists in extracting barium with radium from the ores of uranium, also bismuth with polonium and the rare earths containing actinium from the same. These three primary products having been obtained, the next step is in each case to endeavour to isolate the new radioactive body. This second part of the treatment consists of a process of fractionation. The difficulty of finding a very perfect means of separating closely allied elements is well known; methods of fractionation are therefore quite suitable. Besides this, when a mere trace of one element is mixed with another element, no method of complete separation could be applied to the mixture, even allowing that such a method was known; in fact, one would run the risk of losing the trace of the material to be separated.

The particular object of my work has been the isolation of radium and polonium. After working for several years, I have so far only succeeded in obtaining the former.

Pitchblende is an expensive ore, and we have given up the treatment of it in large quantities. In Europe the extraction of this ore is carried out in the mine of Joachimsthal, in Bohemia. The crushed ore is roasted with carbonate of soda, and the resulting material washed, first with warm water and then with dilute sulphuric acid. The solution contains the uranium, which gives pitchblende its value. The insoluble residue is rejected. This residue contains radioactive substances; its activity is four and a half times that of metallic uranium. The Austrian Government, to whom the mine belongs, presented us with a ton of this residue for our research, and authorized the mine to give us several tons more of the material.

It was not very easy to apply the methods of the laboratory to the preliminary treatment of the residue in the factory. M. Debierne investigated this question, and organized the treatment in the factory. The most important point of his method is the conversion of the sulphates into carbonate by boiling the material with a concentrated solution of sodium carbonate. This method avoids the necessity of fusing with sodium carbonate.

The residue chiefly contains the sulphates of lead and calcium, silica, alumina, and iron oxide. In addition nearly all the metals are found in greater or smaller amount (copper, bismuth, zinc, cobalt, manganese, nickel, vanadium, antimony, thallium, rare earths, niobium, tantalum, arsenic, barium, &c.). Radium is found in this mixture as sulphate, and is the least soluble sulphate in it. In order to dissolve it, it is necessary to remove the sulphuric acid as far as possible. To do this, the residue is first treated with a boiling concentrated soda solution. The sulphuric acid combined with the lead, aluminium, and calcium passes, for the most part, into solution as sulphate of sodium, which is removed by repeatedly washing with water. The alkaline solution removes at the same time lead, silicon, and aluminium. The insoluble portion is attacked by ordinary hydrochloric acid. This operation completely disintegrates the material, and dissolves most of it. Polonium and actinium may be obtained from this solution; the former is precipitated by sulphuretted hydrogen, the latter is found in the hydrates precipitated by ammonia in the solution separated from the sulphides and oxidized. Radium remains in the insoluble portion. This portion is washed with water, and then treated with a boiling concentrated solution of carbonate of soda. This operation completes the transformation of the sulphates of barium and radium into carbonates. The material is then thoroughly washed with water and then treated with dilute hydrochloric acid, quite free from sulphuric acid. The solution contains radium as well as polonium and actinium. It is filtered and precipitated with sulphuric acid. In this way the crude sulphates of barium containing radium and calcium, of lead and of iron, and of a trace of actinium are obtained. The solution still contains a little actinium and polonium, which may be separated out as in the case of the first hydrochloric acid solution.

From one ton of residue 10 to 20 kilogrammes of crude sulphates are obtained, the activity of which is from thirty to sixty times as great as that of metallic uranium. They must now be purified. For this purpose they are boiled with sodium carbonate and transformed into the chlorides. The solution is treated with sulphuretted hydrogen, which gives a small quantity of active sulphides containing polonium. The solution is filtered, oxidized by means of chlorine, and precipitated with pure ammonia. The precipitated hydrates and oxides are very active, and the activity is due to actinium. The filtered solution is precipitated with sodium carbonate.

The precipitated carbonates of the alkaline earths are washed and converted into chlorides. These chlorides are evaporated to dryness, and washed with pure concentrated hydrochloric acid. Calcium chloride dissolves almost entirely, whilst the chloride of barium and radium remains insoluble. Thus, from one ton of the original material about 8 kilogrammes of barium and radium chloride are obtained, of which the activity is about sixty times that of metallic uranium. The chloride is now ready for fractionation.

§ *Polonium*

As I said above, by passing sulphuretted hydrogen through the various hydrochloric acid solutions obtained during the course of the process, active sulphides are precipitated, of which the activity is due to polonium. These sulphides chiefly contain bismuth, a little copper, and lead; the latter metal occurs in relatively small amount, because it has been to a great extent removed by the soda solution, and because its chloride is only slightly soluble. Antimony and arsenic are found among the oxides only in the minutest quantity, their oxides having been dissolved by the soda. In order to obtain the very active sulphides, the following process was employed: The solutions made strongly acid with hydrochloric acid were precipitated with sulphuretted hydrogen; the sulphides thus precipitated are very active, and are employed for the preparation of polonium; there remain in the solution substances not completely precipitated in presence of excess of hydrochloric acid (bismuth, lead, antimony). To complete the precipitation, the solution is diluted with water, and treated again with sulphuretted hydrogen, which gives a second precipitate of sulphides, much less active than the first, and which have generally been rejected. For the further purification of the sulphides, they are washed with ammonium sulphide, which removes the last remaining traces of antimony and arsenic. They are then washed with water and ammonium nitrate, and treated with dilute nitric acid. Complete solution never occurs; there is always an insoluble residue, more or less considerable, which can be treated afresh if it is judged expedient. The solution is reduced to a small volume and precipitated either by ammonia or by excess of water. In both cases the lead and the copper remain in solution; in the second case, a little bismuth, scarcely active at all, remains also in solution.

The precipitate of oxides or basic nitrates is subjected to fractionation in the following manner: The precipitate is dissolved in nitric acid, and water is added to the solution until a sufficient quantity of precipitate is formed; it must be borne in mind that sometimes the precipitate does not at once appear. The precipitate is separated from the supernatant liquid, and redissolved in nitric acid, after which both the liquids thus obtained are reprecipitated with water, and treated as before. The different fractions are combined according to their activity, and concentration is carried out as far as possible. In this way is obtained a very small quantity of a substance of which the activity is very high, but which, nevertheless, has so far only shown bismuth lines in the spectroscope.

There is, unfortunately, little chance of obtaining the isolation of polonium by this means. The method of fractionation just described presents many difficulties, and the case is similar with other wet processes of fractionation. Whatever be the method employed, compounds are readily formed which are absolutely insoluble in dilute or concentrated acids. These compounds can only be redissolved by reducing them to the metallic state, *e.g.,* by fusion with potassium cyanide. Considering the number of operations necessary, this circumstance constitutes an enormous difficulty in the progress of the fractionation. This obstacle is the greater because polonium, once extracted from the pitchblende, diminishes in activity. This diminution of activity is slow, for a specimen of bismuth nitrate containing polonium only lost half its activity in eleven months.

No such difficulty occurs with radium. The radioactivity remains throughout an accurate gauge of the concentration; the concentration itself presents no difficulty, and the progress of the work from the start can be constantly checked by spectral analysis.

When the phenomena of induced radioactivity, which will be discussed later on, were made known, it seemed obvious that polonium, which only shows the bismuth lines and whose activity diminishes with time, was not a new element, but bismuth made active by the vicinity of radium in the pitchblende. I am not sure that this opinion is correct. In the course of my prolonged work on polonium, I have noted chemical effects, which I have never observed either with ordinary bismuth or with bismuth made active by radium. These chemical effects are, in the first place, the extremely ready formation of insoluble compounds, of which I have spoken above (especially basic nitrates), and, in the second place, the colour and appearance of the precipitates obtained by adding water to the nitric acid solution of bismuth containing polonium. These precipitates are sometimes white, but more generally of a more or less vivid yellow, verging on red.

The absence of lines other than those of bismuth does not necessarily prove that the substance only contains bismuth, because bodies exist whose spectrum reaction is scarcely visible.

It would be necessary to prepare a small quantity of bismuth containing polonium in as concentrated a condition as possible, and to examine it chemically, in the first place determining the atomic weight of the metal. It has not yet been possible to carry out this research on account of the difficulties of a chemical nature already mentioned.

If polonium were proved to be a new element, it would be no less true that it cannot exist indefinitely in a strongly radioactive condition, at least when extracted from the ore. There are therefore two aspects of the question: First, whether the activity of polonium is entirely induced by the proximity of substances themselves radioactive, in which case polonium would possess the faculty of acquiring atomic activity permanently, a faculty which does not appear to belong to any substance whatever; second, whether the activity of polonium is an inherent property, which is spontaneously destroyed under certain conditions, and persists under certain other conditions, such as those which exist in the ore. The phenomenon of atomic activity induced by contact is still so little understood, that we lack the ground on which to formulate any opinion on the matter. . . .

## § *Preparation of the Pure Chloride of Radium*

The method by which I extracted pure radium chloride from barium chloride containing radium consists in first subjecting the mixture of the chlorides to fractional crystallization in pure water, then in water to which hydrochloric acid has been added. The difference in solubility of the two chlorides is thus made use of, that of radium being less soluble than that of barium.

At the beginning of the fractionation, pure distilled water is used. The chloride is dissolved, and the solution raised to boiling-point, and allowed to crystallize by cooling in a covered capsule. Beautiful crystals form at the bottom, and the supernatant, saturated solution is easily decanted. If part of this solution be evaporated to dryness, the chloride obtained is found to be about five times less active than that which has crystallized out. The chloride is thus divided into two portions, A and B – portion A being more active than portion B. The operation is now repeated with each of the chlorides A and B, and in each case two new portions are obtained. When the crystallization is finished, the less active fraction of chloride A is added to the more active fraction of chloride B, these two having approximately the same activity. Thus there are now three portions to undergo afresh the same treatment.

The number of portions is not allowed to increase indefinitely. The activity of the most soluble portion diminishes as the number increases. When its activity becomes inconsiderable, it is withdrawn from the fractionation. When the desired number of fractions has been obtained, fractionation of the least soluble portion is stopped (the richest in radium), and it is withdrawn from the remainder.

A fixed number of fractions is used in the process. After each series of operations, the saturated solution arising from one fraction is added to the crystals arising from the following fraction; but if after one of the series the most soluble fraction has been withdrawn, then, after the following series, a new fraction is made from the most soluble portion, and the crystals of the most active portion are withdrawn. By the successive alternation of these two processes, an extremely regular system of fractionation is obtained, in which the number of fractions and the activity of each remains constant, each being about five times as active as the subsequent one, and in which, on the one hand, an almost inactive product is removed, whilst, in the other, is obtained a chloride rich in radium. The amount of material contained in these fractions gradually diminishes, becoming less as the activity increases.

At first six fractions were used, and the activity of the chloride obtained at the end was only 0·1 that of uranium.

When most of the inactive matter has been removed, and the fractions have become small, one fraction is removed from the one end, and another is added to the other end consisting of the active chloride previously removed. A chloride richer in radium than the preceding is thus obtained. This system is continued until the crystals obtained are pure radium chloride. If the fractionation has been thoroughly carried out, scarcely any trace of the intermediate products remain.

At an advanced stage of the fractionation, when the quantity of material in each fraction is small, the separation by crystallization is less efficacious, the cooling being too rapid and the volume of the solution to be decanted too small. It is then advisable to add water containing a known quantity of hydrochloric acid; this quantity may be increased as the fractionation proceeds.

The advantage gained thus consists in increasing the quantity of the solution, the solubility of the chlorides being less in water acidified with hydrochloric acid than in pure water. By using water containing much acid, excellent separations are effected, and it is only necessary to work with three or four fractions.

The crystals, which form in very acid solution, are elongated needles, those of barium chloride having exactly the same appearance as those of radium chloride. Both show double refraction. Crystals of barium chloride containing radium are colourless, but when the proportion of radium becomes greater, they have a yellow coloration after some hours, verging on orange, and sometimes a beautiful pink. This colour disappears in solution. Crystals of pure radium chloride are not coloured, so that the coloration appears to be due to the mixture of radium and barium. The maximum coloration is obtained for a certain degree of radium present, and this fact serves to check the progress of the fractionation.

I have sometimes noticed the formation of a deposit composed of crystals of which one part remained uncoloured, whilst the other was coloured, and it seems possible that the colourless crystals might be sorted out.

The fractional precipitation of an aqueous solution of barium chloride by alcohol also leads to the isolation of radium chloride, which is the first to precipitate. This method, which I first employed, was finally abandoned for the one just described, which proceeds with more regularity. I have, however, occasionally made use of precipitation by alcohol to purify radium chloride which contains traces of barium chloride. The latter remains in the slightly aqueous alcoholic solution, and can thus be removed.

M. Giesel, who, since the publication of our first researches, has been preparing radioactive bodies, recommends the separation of barium and radium by fractional crystallization in water from a mixture of the bromides. I can testify that this method is advantageous, especially in the first stages of the fractionation.

§ *Determination of the Atomic Weight of Radium*

In the course of my work I determined at intervals the atomic weight of the metal contained in specimens of barium chloride containing radium. With each newly obtained product I carried the concentration as far as possible, so as to have from 0·1 grm. to 0·5 grm. of material containing most of the activity of the mixture. From this small quantity I precipitated with alcohol or with hydrochloric acid some milligrammes of chloride for spectral analysis. Thanks to his excellent method, Demarcay only required this small quantity of material to obtain the photograph of the spark spectrum. I made an atomic weight determination with the product remaining.

I employed the classic method of weighing as silver chloride the chlorine contained in a known weight of the anhydrous chloride. As control experiment, I determined the atomic weight of barium by the same method, under the same conditions, and with the same quantity of material, first 0·5 grm. and then 0·1 grm. The figures obtained were always between 137 and 138. I thus saw that the method gives satisfactory results, even with a very small quantity of material.

The first two determinations were made with chlorides, of which one was 230 times and the other 600 times as active as uranium. These two experiments gave the same figure as the experiment with the pure barium chloride. There was therefore no hope of finding a difference except by using a much more active product. The following experiment was made with a chloride, the activity of which was about 3500 times as great as that of uranium; and this experiment enabled me, for the first time, to observe a small but distinct difference; I found, as the mean atomic weight of the metal contained in this chloride, the number 140, which showed that the atomic weight of radium must be higher than that of barium. By using more and more active products, and obtaining spectra of radium of increasing intensity, I found that the figures obtained rose in proportion. . . .

From its chemical properties, radium is an element of the group of alkaline earths, being the member next above barium.

From its atomic weight also, radium takes its place in Mendeleev's table after barium with the alkaline earth metals, in the row which already contains uranium and thorium.

## § *Characteristics of the Radium Salts*

The salts of radium, chloride, nitrate, carbonate, and sulphate, resemble those of barium, when freshly prepared, but they gradually become coloured.

All the radium salts are luminous in the dark.

In their chemical properties, the salts of radium are absolutely analogous to the corresponding salts of barium. However, radium chloride is less soluble than barium chloride; the solubility of the nitrates in water is approximately the same.

The salts of radium are the source of a spontaneous and continuous evolution of heat. . . .

## § *Conclusions*

I will define, in conclusion, the part I have personally taken in the researches upon radioactive bodies.

I have investigated the radioactivity of uranium compounds, I have examined other bodies for the existence of radioactivity, and found the property to be possessed by thorium compounds. I have made clear the atomic character of the radioactivity of the compounds of uranium and thorium.

I have conducted a research upon radioactive substances other than uranium and thorium. To this end I investigated a large number of substances by an accurate electrometric method, and I discovered that certain minerals possess activity which is not to be accounted for by their content of uranium and thorium.

From this I concluded that these minerals must contain a radioactive body different from uranium and thorium, and more strongly radioactive than the latter metals.

In conjunction with M. Curie, and subsequently MM. Curie and Bémont, I was able to extract from pitchblende two strongly radioactive bodies – polonium and radium.

I have been continuously engaged upon the chemical examination and preparation of these substances. I effected the fractionations necessary to the concentration of radium and I succeeded in isolating pure radium chloride. Concurrently with this work, I made several atomic weight determinations with a very small quantity of material, and was finally able to determine the atomic weight of radium with a very fair degree of accuracy. The work has proved *that radium is a new chemical element.* Thus the new method of investigating new chemical elements, established by M. Curie and myself, based upon radioactivity, is fully justified.

I have investigated the law of absorption of polonium rays, and of the absorbable rays of radium, and have demonstrated that this law of absorption is peculiar and different from the known laws of other radiations.

I have investigated the variation of activity of radium salts, the effect of solution and of heating, and the renewal of activity with time, after solution or after heating.

In conjunction with M. Curie, I have examined different effects produced by the new radioactive substances (electric, photographic, fluorescent, luminous colorations, etc.).

In conjunction with M. Curie, I have established the fact that radium gives rise to rays charged with negative electricity.

Our researches upon the new radioactive bodies have given rise to a scientific movement, and have been the starting-point of numerous researches in connexion with new radioactive substances, and with the investigation of the radiation of the known radioactive bodies.

# ERNEST RUTHERFORD
## 1871–1937

# FREDERICK SODDY
## 1877–1956

## THE NATURE AND CAUSES OF
## RADIOACTIVITY

BECQUEREL'S discovery of the radioactivity of uranium and the Curies' observation of the same phenomenon in polonium and radium challenged scientists to explain the nature of radioactivity. Within a few years, in 1899, Ernest Rutherford determined that the radiation from uranium was composed of two types of ray, which he called alpha and beta. The alpha rays could not penetrate more than about 0·0002 cm. of aluminium, but the beta rays were about one hundred times more penetrating. Three years later he and Frederick Soddy, then working at McGill University, in Montreal, ascribed radioactivity to the instability of the atoms which caused a continuous spontaneous disintegration. Their experiments (as reported in *The Philosophical Magazine* in 1902) are described in the selection that follows.

Rutherford was a New Zealander who, after a period of research at Cambridge and of teaching at McGill, went to Manchester University in 1907 and in 1919 succeeded J. J. Thomson as Cavendish Professor of Physics at Cambridge. His research proved to be the penultimate stage in the evolution of the modern concept of the atom. While still at Manchester, Rutherford had discovered, as the result of his study of radioactive disintegration, that the mass of the atom was, in fact, concentrated in a central *nucleus*, positively charged, around which electrons revolved at relatively great distances. The electrons being negatively charged to a degree which balanced the positive charge of the nucleus, the atom itself was neutral. When, in 1913, Niels Bohr, of

Copenhagen, reconciled Rutherford's theory of the nucleus with the quantum theory of energy, a 'model' of the atom became available which has remained the basis of the spectacular work in atomic physics and chemistry since that time. Rutherford's experiments showed, too, in 1919, that disintegration of an element could be effected artificially, and with J. Chadwick (b.1891) he transmuted many of the lighter elements. The release of energy observed during these experiments provided an occasion for demonstrating Einstein's theory of the equivalence of mass and energy.

Frederick Soddy's part in Rutherford's original work has been mentioned. After various appointments at London, Glasgow, and Aberdeen, Soddy became professor of inorganic and physical chemistry at Oxford. Like Rutherford in 1908, he received the Nobel Prize in chemistry, and it is not without significance that in the same year (1921) the winner of the prize in physics was Albert Einstein. Soddy was particularly interested in isotopes and, with Ramsay, in 1904, he noted the presence of helium in the radiation from radium, an observation which led to the association of helium with the alpha particle. As was subsequently discovered, the beta rays are streams of electrons and their penetrating power is in part the result of their high velocity, whereas the alpha particle, which is the nucleus of a helium atom, has great mass but lower velocity, which explains its small penetrating ability. A third type of emanation, the gamma ray, which could not be deflected in a magnetic field, was discovered in 1900. It has higher penetration than alpha and beta particles and, like X-rays and light rays, is a form of electromagnetic radiation.

---

¶ *The Cause and Nature of Radioactivity*

§ *I. Introduction*
The following papers give the results of a detailed investigation of the radioactivity of thorium compounds which has

thrown light on the questions connected with the source and maintenance of the energy dissipated by radioactive substances. Radioactivity is shown to be accompanied by chemical changes in which new types of matter are being continuously produced. These reaction products are at first radioactive, the activity diminishing regularly from the moment of formation. Their continuous production maintains the radioactivity of the matter producing them at a definite equilibrium value. The conclusion is drawn that these chemical changes must be subatomic in character.

The present researches had as their starting-point the facts that had come to light with regard to thorium radioactivity; besides being radioactive in the same sense as the uranium compounds, the compounds of thorium continuously emit into the surrounding atmosphere a gas which possesses the property of temporary radioactivity. This emanation, as it has been named, is the source of rays, which ionize gases and darken the photographic film.

The most striking property of the thorium emanation is its power of exciting radioactivity on all surfaces with which it comes into contact. A substance after being exposed for some time in the presence of the emanation behaves as if it were covered with an invisible layer of an intensely active material. If the thoria (thorium oxide) is exposed in a strong electric field, the excited radioactivity is entirely confined to the negatively charged surface. In this way it is possible to concentrate the excited radioactivity on a very small area. The excited radioactivity can be removed by rubbing or by the action of acids, as for example, sulphuric, hydrochloric, and hydrofluoric acids. If the acids be then evaporated, the radioactivity remains on the dish.

The emanating power of thorium compounds is independent of the surrounding atmosphere, and the excited activity it produces is independent of the nature of the substance on which it is manifested. These properties made it appear that both phenomena were caused by minute quantities of special kinds of matter in the radioactive state, produced by the thorium compound.

The next consideration in regard to these examples of radioactivity is that the activity in each case diminishes regularly with the lapse of time, the intensity of radiation at each instant being proportional to the amount of energy remaining to be radiated. For the emanation, a period of one minute, and for the excited activity, a period of eleven hours, causes the activity to fall to half its value.

These actions (1) the production of radioactive material, and (2) the dissipation of its available energy by radiation, which are exhibited by thorium compounds in the secondary effects of emanating power and excited radioactivity, are in reality taking place in all manifestations of radioactivity. The constant radioactivity of the radioactive elements is the result of an equilibrium between these two opposing processes.

*

§ III. *Separation of a Radioactive Constituent from Thorium Compounds*

During an investigation of the emanating power of thorium compounds, to be described later, evidence was obtained of the separation of an intensely radioactive constituent by chemical methods. It had been noticed that in certain cases thorium hydroxide, precipitated from dilute solutions of thorium nitrate by ammonia, possessed an abnormally low emanating power. This led naturally to an examination being made of the filtrates and washings obtained during the process. It was found that the filtrates invariably possessed emanating power, although from the nature of their production they are chemically free from thorium. If the filtrate is evaporated to dryness, and the ammonium salts removed by ignition, the small residues obtained exhibit radioactivity also, to an extent very much greater than that possessed by the same weight of thorium. As a rule, these residues were of the order of one thousandth part by weight of the thorium salt originally taken, and were many hundred, in some cases over a thousand, times more active than an equal weight of thoria. The separation of an active constituent from thorium by this method is not at all dependent on the purity of the salt used. By the kindness of Dr Knofler, of Berlin, who, in the friendliest manner, presented us with a large specimen of his purest thorium nitrate, we were enabled to test this point. This specimen, which had been purified by a great many processes, did not contain any of the impurities found in the commercial salt before used. But its radioactivity and emanating power were at least as great, and the residues from the filtrates after precipitation by ammonia were no less active than those before obtained. These residues are free from thorium, or at most contain only the merest traces, and when redissolved in nitric acid do not appear to give any characteristic reaction.

An examination of the penetrating power of the rays from the radioactive residue, showed that the radiations emitted were in every respect identical with the ordinary thorium radiation. In another experiment, the nature of the emanation from a similar intensely active thorium-free residue was submitted to examination. The rate of decay was quite indistinguishable from that of the ordinary thorium emanation; that is substances chemically free from thorium have been prepared possessing thorium radioactivity in an intense degree.

The thorium hydroxide which had been submitted to the above process was found to be less than half as radioactive as the same weight of thorium oxide. It thus appeared that a constituent responsible for the radioactivity of thorium had been obtained, which possessed distinct chemical properties and an activity of the order of at least a thousand times as great as the material from which it had been separated.

Sir William Crookes succeeded in separating a radioactive constituent of great activity and distinct chemical nature from uranium and gave the name UrX, to this substance. For the present, until more is known of its real nature, it will be convenient to name the active constituent of thorium, ThX, similarly.

*

*The influence of Time on the activity of Thorium and ThX*

The preparations employed in our previous experiments were allowed to stand over during the Christmas vacation. On examining them about three weeks later it was found that the thorium hydroxide, which had originally possessed only about thirty-six per cent of its normal activity had almost completely recovered the usual value. The active residues on the other hand, prepared by both methods, had almost completely lost their original activity. The chemical separation affected was thus not permanent in character. At this time M. Becquerel's paper came to hand; in which he shows that the same phenomena of recovery and decay are presented by uranium after it has been partially separated from its active constituent by chemical treatment.

A long series of observations was at once started to determine:

(1) The rate of recovery of the activity of thorium rendered less active by removal of ThX.

(2) The rate of decay of the activity of the separated ThX; in order to see how the two processes were connected. The results led to the view that may at once be stated. The radioactivity of thorium at any time is the resultant of two opposing processes:

(1) The production of fresh radioactive material at a constant rate by the thorium compound.

(2) The decay of the radiating power of the active material with time.

*The normal or constant radioactivity possessed by thorium is an equilibrium value, where the rate of increase of radioactivity due to the production of fresh active material is balanced by the rate of decay of radioactivity of that already formed.* It is the purpose of the present paper to substantiate and develop this hypothesis.

§ *IV. The Rates of Recovery and Decay of Thorium Radioactivity*

A quantity of the pure thorium nitrate was separated from ThX in the manner described by several precipitations with ammonia. The radioactivity of the hydroxide so obtained was tested at regular intervals to determine the rate of recovery of its activity. For this purpose the original specimen of ·5 gram was left undisturbed throughout the whole series of measurements on the plate over which it had been sifted, and was compared always with ·5 gram of ordinary de-emanated thorium oxide spread similarly on a second plate and also left undisturbed. The emanation from the hydroxide was prevented from interfering with the results by a special arrangement for drawing a current of air over it during the measurements.

Fig. 1 shows the curves obtained by plotting the radio-

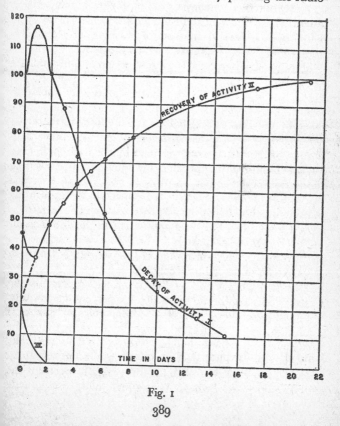

Fig. 1

activities as ordinates, and the time in days as abscissae. Curve II illustrates the rate of recovery of the activity of thorium, curve I, the rate of decay of activity of ThX. It will be seen that neither of the curves is regular for the first two days. The activity of the hydroxide at first actually diminished and was at the same value after two days as when first prepared.

The activity of the ThX, on the other hand, at first increases and does not begin to fall below the original value till after the lapse of two days. These results cannot be ascribed to errors of measurement, for they have been regularly observed whenever similar preparations have been tested. The activity of the residue obtained from thorium oxide by the second method of washing decayed very similarly to that of ThX, as shown by the above curve.

If, for present purposes, the initial periods of the curve are disregarded and the later portions only considered, it will be seen at once that the time taken for the hydroxide to recover one half of its lost activity is about equal to the time taken by the ThX to lose half its activity, viz., in each case about 4 days, and speaking generally the percentage proportion of the lost activity regained by the hydroxide over any given interval is approximately equal to the percentage proportion of the activity lost by the ThX during the same interval. If the recovery curve is produced backwards in the normal direction to cut the vertical axis, it will be seen to do so at a minimum of about 25 per cent and the above result holds even more accurately if the recovery is assumed to start from this constant minimum, as, indeed, it has been shown to do under suitable conditions.

This is brought out by Fig. 2, which represents the recovery curve of thorium in which the percentage amounts of activity recovered, reckoned from this 25 per cent minimum, are plotted as ordinates. In the same figure the decay curve after the second day is shown on the same scale. The activity of ThX decreases very approximately in a geometrical progression with the time, i.e. if $I_0$ represent the initial activity and $I_t$ the activity after time $t$,

$$\frac{I_t}{I_o} = e^{-\lambda t}, \quad\dots\dots\dots\dots\dots(1)$$

where $\lambda$ is a constant and $e$ the base of natural logarithms.

The experimental curve obtained with the hydroxide for the rate of rise of its activity from a minimum to a maximum value will therefore be approximately expressed by the equation

$$\frac{I_t}{I_o} = 1 - e^{-\lambda t}, \quad\dots\dots\dots\dots(2)$$

where $I_o$ represents the amount of activity recovered when the maximum is reached, and $I_t$ the activity recovered after time $t$, $\lambda$ *being the same constant as before.*

Now this last equation has been theoretically developed in other places to express the rise of activity to a constant maximum of a system consisting of radiating particles in which

(1) The rate of supply of fresh radiating particles is constant.

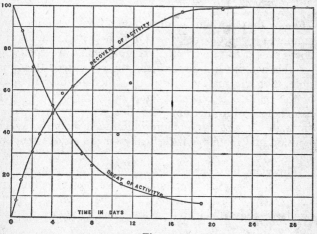

Fig. 2

(2) The activity of each particle dies down geometrically with the time according to equation (1).

It therefore follows that if the initial irregularities of the curves are disregarded and the residual activity of thorium is assumed to possess a constant value, the experimental curve obtained for the recovery of activity will be explained if two processes are supposed to be taking place:

(1) That the active constituent ThX is being produced at a constant rate;

(2) That the activity of the ThX decays geometrically with time.

Without at first going into the difficult questions connected with the initial irregularities and the residual activity, the main result that follows from the curves given can be put to experimental test very simply. The primary conception is that the major part of the radioactivity of thorium is not due to the thorium at all, but to the presence of a non-thorium substance in minute amount which is being continuously produced.

## § V. Chemical Properties of ThX

The fact that thorium on precipitation from its solutions by ammonia leaves the major part of its activity in the filtrate does not of itself prove that a material *constituent* responsible for this activity has been chemically separated. It is possible that the matter constituting the non-thorium part of the solution is rendered temporarily radioactive by its association with thorium, and this property is retained through the processes of precipitation, evaporation, and ignition and manifests itself finally on the residue remaining.

This view, however, can be shown to be quite untenable, for upon it, any precipitate capable of removing thorium completely from its solution should yield active residues similar to those obtained from ammonia. Quite the reverse, however, holds.

When thorium nitrate is precipitated by sodium or ammonium carbonate, the residue from the filtrate by evaporation and ignition is free from activity, and the thorium carbonate possesses the normal value for its activity.

The same holds true when oxalic acid is used as the precipitant. This reagent even in strongly acid solution precipitates almost all of the thorium. When the filtrate is rendered alkaline by ammonia, filtered, evaporated, and ignited, the residue obtained is inactive.

In the case where sodium phosphate is used as the precipitant in ordinary acid solution, the part that comes down is more or less free from ThX. On making the solution alkaline with ammonia, the remainder of the thorium is precipitated as phosphate, and carries with it the whole of the active constituent, so that the residue from the filtrate is again inactive.

In fact ammonia is the only reagent of those tried capable of separating ThX from thorium.

The result of Sir William Crookes with uranium, which we have confirmed, working with the electrical method, may be here mentioned. UrX is completely precipitated by ammonia together with uranium, and the residue obtained by the evaporation of the filtrate is quite inactive.

There can thus be no question that both ThX and UrX are distinct types of matter with definite chemical properties. Any hypothesis that attempts to account for the recovery of activity of thorium and uranium with time must of necessity start from this primary conception.

\*

§ *VII. Influence of conditions on the changes occurring in Thorium*

It has been shown that in thorium compounds the decay of radio-activity with time is balanced by a continuous production of fresh active material. The change which produces this material must be chemical in nature, for the products of the action are different in chemical properties from the thorium from which they are produced. The first step in the study of the nature of this change is to examine the effects of conditions upon its rate.

*Effects of Conditions on the Rate of Decay*

Since the activity of the products affords the means of measuring the amount of change, the influence of conditions on the rate of decay must be first found.

It was observed that, like all other types of temporary radioactivity, the rate of decay is unaltered by any known agency. It is unaffected by ignition and chemical treatment, and the material responsible for it can be dissolved in acids and re-obtained by the evaporation of the solution, without affecting the activity. The following experiment shows that the activity decays at the same rate in solutions as in the solid state. The remainder of the solution that had been used to determine the decay curve of ThX was allowed to stand, and at the end of 12 days a second quarter was evaporated to dryness and ignited, and its activity compared with that of the first which had been left since evaporation upon its original platinum dish. The activities of the two specimens so compared with each other were the same, showing that in spite of the very different conditions the two fractions had decayed at equal rates. After 19 days a third quarter was evaporated, and the activity, now very small, was indistinguishable from that of the fraction first evaporated. Resolution of the residues after the activity had decayed does not at all regenerate it. The activity of ThX thus decays at a rate independent of the chemical and physical condition of the molecule.

Thus the rate of recovery of activity under different conditions in thorium compounds affords a direct measure of the rate of production of ThX, under these conditions. The following experiments were performed:

One part of thorium hydroxide newly separated from ThX was sealed up in a vacuum obtained by a good Topler pump, and the other part exposed to air. On comparing the samples 12 days later no difference could be detected between them either in their radioactivity or emanating power.

In the next experiment a quantity of hydroxide freed from ThX was divided into two equal parts; one was exposed for

20 hours to the heat of a Bunsen burner in a platinum crucible, and then compared with the other. No difference in the activities was observed. In a second experiment one half was ignited for 20 minutes on the blast, and then compared with the other with the same result. The difference of temperature and the conversion of thorium hydroxide into oxide thus exercised no influence on the activity.

Some experiments that were designed to test in as drastic a manner as possible the effect of the chemical condition of the molecule on the rate of production of ThX brought to light small differences but these are almost certainly to be accounted for in another way. It will be shown later that about 21 per cent of the normal radioactivity of thorium oxide under ordinary conditions consists of a secondary activity excited on the mass of the material. This portion is of course a variable, and since it is divided among the total amount of matter present, the conditions of aggregation, &c., will affect the value of this part.

This effect of excited radioactivity in thorium makes a certain answer to the question difficult, and on this account the conclusion that the rate of production of ThX is independent of the molecular conditions is not final. The following experiment however makes it extremely probable.

A quantity of thorium-nitrate as obtained from the maker was converted into oxide in a platinum crucible by treatment with sulphuric acid and ignition to a white heat. The de-emanated oxide so obtained was spread on a plate, and any change in radioactivity with time, which under these circumstances could certainly be detected, was looked for during the first week from preparation. None whatever was observed, whereas if the rate of production of ThX in thorium nitrate is different from that in the oxide, the equilibrium point, at which the decay and increase of activity balance each other, will be altered in consequence. There should have occurred therefore, a logarithmic rise or fall from the old to the new value. As, however, the radioactivity remained a constant, it appears very probable that the changes involved are independent of the molecular condition.

It will be seen that the assumption is here made that the proportion of excited radioactivity in the two compounds is the same, and for this reason compounds were chosen which possess but low emanating power.

Uranium is a far simpler example of a radioactive element than thorium, as the phenomena of excited radioactivity and emanating power are here absent. The separation of UrX and the recovery of the activity of the uranium with time appear, however, analogous to these processes in thorium, and the rate of recovery and decay of uranium activity are at present under investigation. It is proposed to test the influence of conditions on the rate of change more thoroughly in the case of uranium, as here secondary changes do not interfere.

\*

## § IX. *The initial portions of the curves of decay and recovery*

The curves of the recovery and decay of the activities of thorium and ThX with time suggested the explanation that the radioactivity of thorium was being maintained by the production of ThX at a constant rate. Before this can be considered rigidly established, two outstanding points remain to be cleared up. 1. What is the meaning of the early portion of the curves? The recovery curve drops before it rises, and the decay curve rises before it drops. 2. Why does not the removal of ThX render thorium completely inactive? A large proportion of the original radioactivity is not affected by the removal of ThX.

A study of the curves (Fig. 1) shows that in each case a double action is probably at work. It may be supposed that the normal decay and recovery are taking place, but are being masked by a simultaneous rise and decay from other causes.

From what is known of thorium radioactivity, it was surmised that an action might be taking place similar to that effected by the emanation, of exciting radioactivity on surrounding inactive matter. It will be shown later that the

ThX, and not thorium, is the cause of the emanating power of thorium compounds. On this view, the residual activity of thorium might consist in whole or in part of a secondary or excited radioactivity produced on the whole mass of the thorium compound by its association with the ThX. The drop in the recovery curve on this view would be due to the decay of this excited radioactivity proceeding simultaneously with, and at first, reversing the effect of the regeneration of ThX. The rise of the decay curve would be the increase due to the ThX exciting activity on the matter with which it is associated, the increase from this cause being greater than the decrease due to the decay of the activity of the ThX. It is easy to put this hypothesis to experimental test. If the ThX is removed from the thorium as soon as it is formed, over a sufficient period, the former will be prevented from exciting activity on the latter, and that already excited will decay spontaneously. The experiment was therefore performed. A quantity of nitrate was precipitated as hydroxide in the usual way to remove ThX, the precipitate redissolved in nitric acid, and again precipitated after a certain interval. From time to time a portion of the hydroxide was removed and its radioactivity tested. In this way the thorium was precipitated in all 23 times in a period of 9 days, and the radioactivity reduced to a constant minimum. The following table shows the results:

|  | Activity of Hydroxide, per cent |
| --- | --- |
| After first precipitation | 46 |
| After precipitations at three intervals of twenty-four hours | 39 |
| At three more intervals each of twenty-four hours and three more each of eight hours | 22 |
| At three more each of eight hours | 24 |
| At six more each of four hours | 25 |

The constant minimum thus attained – about 25 per cent of the original activity – is thus about 21 per cent below that obtained by two successive precipitations without interval, which has been shown to remove all the ThX separable by the process. The rate of recovery of this 23 times precipitated hydroxide was then measured (Fig. 3). It will be seen that it is now quite normal, and the initial drop characteristic of the ordinary curve is quite absent. It is in fact almost identical with the ordinary curve (Fig. 1) that has been produced back to cut the vertical axis, and there is thus no doubt that there is a residual activity of thorium unconnected apparently with ThX, and constituting about one fourth of the whole.

The decay-curves of several of the fractions of ThX separated in this experiment after varying intervals of time were taken for the first few days. All of them showed the initial rise of about 15 per cent at the end of 18 hours and then a normal decay to zero. The position is thus proved that the initial irregularities are caused by the secondary radiation excited by ThX upon the surrounding matter. By suitably choosing the conditions the recovery-curve can be made to rise normally from a constant minimum, and the decay-curve be shown to consist of two curves, the first, the rate of production of excited radioactivity, and the second, the rate of decay of the activity as a whole.

So far nothing has been stated as to whether the excited radioactivity which contributes about 21 per cent of the total activity of thorium is the same or different from the known type produced by the thorium emanation. All that has been assumed is that it should follow the same general law; *i.e.*, the effect will increase with the time of action of the exciting cause, and decrease with time after the cause is removed. If the rate of rise of the excited activity be worked out from the curves given (Fig. 4) it will be found to agree with that of the ordinary excited activity, *i.e.*, it rises to half value in about 12 hours.

Curve 1 is the observed decay curve for ThX; curve 2 is the theoretical curve, assuming that it decreases geometrically with time and falls to half value in four days. Curve 3 is obtained by plotting the difference between these two, and therefore constitutes the curve of excited activity. Curve 4 is

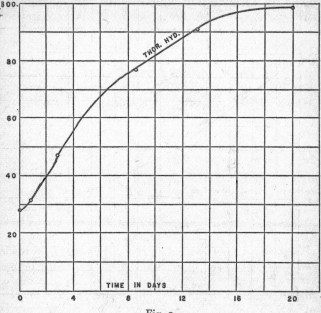

Fig. 3

the experimental curve obtained for the rise of the excited radioactivity from the thorium emanation when the exciting cause is constant. But the exciting cause (ThX) in the present case is not constant, but is itself falling to half value in 4 days, and hence the difference curve, at first almost on the other, drops away from it as time goes on, and finally decays to zero. There is thus no reason to doubt that the effect is the same as that produced by the thorium emanation, which is itself a secondary effect of ThX. Curve 3 (Fig. 1) represents a similar difference curve for *the decay* of excited activity, plotted from *the recovery curve* of thorium.

\*

§ *X. The non-separable radioactivity of thorium*

It has not yet been found possible by any means to free

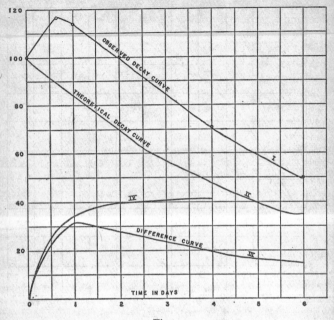

Fig. 4

thorium from its residual activity, and the place of this part in the scheme of radioactivity of thorium remains to be considered. Disregarding the view that it is a separate phenomenon, and not connected with the major part of the activity, two hypotheses can be brought forward capable of experimental test, and in accordance with the views advanced on the nature of radioactivity, to account for the existence of this part. First, if there was a second type of excited activity produced by ThX similar to that known, but with a very slow rate of decay, it would account for the existence of the non-separable activity. If this is true it will not be found possible to free thorium from this activity by chemical means, but the continuous removal of ThX over a very long period would, as in the above case, cause its spontaneous decay.

Secondly, if the change which gives rise to ThX produces a second type of matter at the same time, *i.e.*, if it is of the type of a decomposition rather than a depolymerization, the second type would also in all probability be radioactive, and would cause the residual activity. On this view the second type of matter should also be amenable to separation by chemical means, although it is certain from the failure of the methods already tried that it resembles thorium much more closely than ThX. But until it is separated from the thorium producing it, its activity will not decay spontaneously. Thus what has already been shown to hold for ThX will be true for the second constituent if methods are found to remove it from the thorium.

It has been shown that uranium also possesses a non-separable radioactivity extremely analogous to that possessed by thorium, and whatever view is taken of the one will in all probability hold also for the other. This consideration makes the second hypothesis, that the residual activity is caused by a second non-thorium type of matter produced in the original change, the more probable of the two.

# MAX PLANCK
## 1858–1947

### THE QUANTUM ENTERS PHYSICS

THE developments in physics which are illustrated in the extracts in this section may all be grouped about a central theme – the inner structure of the atom. The discovery of X-rays, of the electron, and of radioactivity, represent the beginnings of a new phase in the investigation of the material world. The new phenomena were to demand new ways of thinking, and the first indication of the great changes to come occurred, to the convenience of the historian, in the year 1900. At a meeting of the Berlin Physical Society on 14 December Planck introduced, in his discussion of a problem on radiation, the concept of the 'quantum', and with this step initiated a revolution in physics.

Max Planck was born in Kiel, when it was still part of Denmark, and became a professor of physics in that city, before moving to Berlin. From early in his career Planck worked in the field of thermodynamics. This important branch of physics was concerned with those general laws which govern all thermal processes, and through the work of such men as Carnot (1796–1832), Helmholtz (1821–94), and Clausius (1822–88), was coming to play an increasingly important part in physics. In his *Scientific Autobiography* (Philosophical Library, 1949), from which the following extract is taken, Planck tells of the difficulties he had in getting his ideas recognized by the leaders in the field, and, at one point, he states that it was 'one of the most painful experiences of my entire scientific life that I have but seldom, in fact, I might say, never, succeeded in gaining universal recognition for a new result, the "truth" of which I could demonstrate by a conclusive, albeit only theoretical, proof'. Yet recognition was to come in deeper form than simple tribute, for Planck was to transform the thinking of his fellow physicists.

In the reading which follows Planck describes the problem which stimulated these new ideas and comments on the break with the classical notions of physics which was involved. For Planck himself the implied rejection of the concepts of Newtonian physics was announced with something approaching regret, and much of his later work was devoted to the attempt to accomplish a reconciliation between the old ideas and the new. Many of his contemporaries accepted the revolution with greater enthusiasm, and from their endeavours were born the theories of the atomic world which we know today; yet in the attitude of Planck himself we may see, perhaps, not only a quirk of personal psychology, but also a tribute to the manner in which the concepts and ideas of classical physics had come to play so intrinsic a part in the thinking of scientific men, ideas which, when first formulated by such men as Galileo and Newton, were themselves the heralds of revolution.

———

My attention, therefore, was soon claimed by quite another problem, which was to dominate me and urge me on to a great many different investigations for a long time to come. The measurements made by O. Lummer and E. Pringsheim in the German Physico-Technical Institute, in connexion with the study of the thermal spectrum, directed my attention to Kirchhoff's Law, which says that in an evacuated cavity, bounded by totally reflecting walls, and containing any arbitrary number of emitting and absorbing bodies, in time a state will be reached where all bodies have the same temperature, and the radiation, in all its properties including its spectral energy distribution, depends not on the nature of the bodies, but solely and exclusively on the temperature. Thus, this so-called Normal Spectral Energy Distribution represents something absolute, and since I had always regarded the search for the absolute as the loftiest goal of all scientific activity, I eagerly set to work. I found a direct method for solving the problem in the application of Maxwell's Electromagnetic Theory of Light. Namely, I assumed the cavity to be filled with simple linear oscillators or resonators, subject to small damping forces and having different periods; and I expected the exchange of energy caused by the reciprocal radiation of the oscillators to result, in time, in a stationary state of the normal energy distribution corresponding to Kirchhoff's Law.

This extended series of investigations, certain ones of which could be verified by comparisons with known observational data, such as the measurements of damping by V. Bjerknes, resulted in establishing the general relationship between the energy of an oscillator having a definite period, and the energy radiation of the corresponding spectral region in the surrounding field when the exchange of energy is stationary. From this there followed the remarkable result that this relationship is absolutely independent of the damping constant of the oscillator – a circumstance which was very pleasing and welcome to me, because it permitted the entire problem to be simplified, by substituting the energy of the oscillator for the energy of the radiation, thus replacing a complicated structure possessing many degrees of freedom, by a simple system with just one degree of freedom.

To be sure, this result represented a mere preliminary to the tackling of the real problem, which now loomed all the more formidably before me. My first attempt to overcome it was unsuccessful, for my original silent hope that the radiation emitted by the oscillator would differ, in some characteristic way, from the absorbed radiation, turned out to have been mere wishful thinking. The oscillator reacts only to those rays which it is capable of emitting, and is completely insensitive to adjacent spectral regions.

Moreover, my suggestion that the oscillator was capable of exerting a unilateral, in other words irreversible, effect on the energy of the surrounding field, drew a vigorous protest from Boltzmann, who, with his wider experience in this domain, demonstrated that according to the laws of classical dynamics, each of the processes I considered could also take place in the opposite direction; and indeed in such a manner, that a spherical wave emitted by an oscillator could reverse its direction of motion, contract progressively until it reached the oscillator and be reabsorbed by the latter, so that the oscillator could then again emit the previously absorbed energy in the same direction from which the energy had been received. To be sure, I could exclude such odd phenomena as inwardly directed spherical waves, by the introduction of a specific stipulation – the hypothesis of a natural radiation, which plays the same part in the theory of radiation as the hypothesis of molecular disorder in the kinetic theory of gases, in that it guarantees the irreversibility of the radiation processes. But the calculations showed ever more clearly that an essential link was still missing, without which the attack on the core of the entire problem could not be undertaken successfully.

So I had no other alternative than to tackle the problem once again – this time from the opposite side, namely, from the side of thermodynamics, my own home territory where I felt myself to be on safer ground. In fact, my previous studies of the Second Law of Thermodynamics came to stand me in good stead now, for at the very outset I hit upon the idea of correlating not the temperature but the entropy of the oscillator with its energy. It was an odd jest of fate that a circumstance which on former occasions I had found unpleasant, namely, the lack of interest of my colleagues in the direction taken by my investigations, now turned out to be an outright boon. While a host of outstanding physicists worked on the problem of spectral energy distribution, both from the experimental and theoretical aspect, every one of them directed his efforts solely towards exhibiting the dependence of the intensity of radiation on the temperature. On the other hand, I suspected that the fundamental connexion lies in the dependence of entropy upon energy. As the significance of the concept of entropy had not yet come to be fully appreciated, nobody paid any attention to the method adopted by me, and I could work out my calculations completely at my leisure, with absolute thoroughness, without fear of interference or competition.

Since for the irreversibility of the exchange of energy between an oscillator and the radiation activating it, the second differential quotient of its entropy with respect to its energy is of characteristic significance, I calculated the value of this function on the assumption that Wien's Law of the Spectral Energy Distribution is valid – a law which was then in the focus of general interest; I got the remarkable result that on this assumption the reciprocal of that value, which I shall call here $R$, is proportional to the energy. This relationship is so surprisingly simple that for a while I considered it to possess universal validity, and I endeavoured to prove it theoretically. However, this view soon proved to be untenable in the face of later measurements. For although in the case of small energies and correspondingly short waves Wien's Law continued to be confirmed in a satisfactory manner, in the case of large values of the energy and correspondingly long waves, appreciable divergences were found, first by Lummer and Pringsheim; and finally the measurements of H. Rubens and F. Kurlbaum on infra-red rays of fluorspar and rock-salt revealed a behaviour which, though totally different, is again a simple one, in so far as the function $R$ is proportional not to the energy but to the square of the energy for large values of the energy and wave-lengths.

Thus, direct experiments established two simple limits for the function $R$: For small energies, $R$ is proportional to the energy; for larger energy values $R$ is proportional to the square of the energy. Obviously, just as every principle of spectral energy distribution yields a certain value for $R$, so also every formula for $R$ leads to a definite law of the distribution of energy. The problem was to find such a formula for $R$ which would result in the law of the distribution of energy, established by measurements. Therefore, the most obvious step for the general case was to make the value of $R$ equal to the sum of a term proportional to the first power of the energy and another term proportional to the second power of the energy, so that the first term becomes decisive for small values of the energy and the second term for large values. In this way a new radiation formula was obtained, and I submitted it for examination to the Berlin Physical Society, at the meeting on 19 October, 1900.

The very next morning, I received a visit from my colleague Rubens. He came to tell me that after the conclusion of the meeting he had that very night checked my formula against the results of his measurements, and found a satisfactory concordance at every point. Also Lummer and Pringsheim, who first thought to have discovered divergences, soon withdrew their objections; for, as Pringsheim related it to me, the observed divergences turned out to have been due to an error in calculation. Later measurements, too, confirmed my radiation formula again and again – the finer the methods of measurement used, the more accurate the formula was found to be.

But even if the absolutely precise validity of the radiation formula is taken for granted, so long as it had merely the standing of a law disclosed by a lucky intuition, it could not be expected to possess more than a formal significance. For this reason, on the very day when I formulated this law, I began to devote myself to the task of investing it with a true physical meaning. This quest automatically led me to study the interrelation of entropy and probability – in other words, to pursue the line of thought inaugurated by Boltzmann. Since the entropy $S$ is an additive magnitude but the probability $W$ is a multiplicative one, I simply postulated that $S = k \cdot \log W$, where $k$ is a universal constant; and I investigated whether the formula for $W$, which is obtained when $S$ is replaced by its value corresponding to the above radiation law, could be interpreted as a measure of probability.

As a result,[*] I found that this was actually possible, and that in this connexion $k$ represents the so-called absolute gas

[*] This finding, containing the introduction of the ultimate energy quanta for the oscillator, was reported by Max Planck again before the Physical Society of Berlin on 14 December, 1900. That was the birthday of the Quantum Theory.

constant, referred not to gram-molecules or mols, but to the real molecules. It is, understandably, often called *Boltzmann's constant*. However, this calls for the comment that Boltzmann never introduced this constant, nor, to the best of my knowledge, did he ever think of investigating its numerical value. For had he done so, he would have had to examine the matter of the number of the real atoms – a task, however, which he left to his colleague J. Loschmidt, while he, in his own calculations, always kept in sight the possibility that the kinetic theory of gases represents only a mechanical picture. He was therefore satisfied with stopping at the gram-atoms. The letter $k$ has won acceptance only gradually. Even several years after its introduction, it was still customary to calculate with the Loschmidt number $L$.

Now as for the magnitude $W$, I found that in order to interpret it as a probability, it was necessary to introduce a universal constant, which I called $h$. Since it had the dimension of action (energy $\times$ time), I gave it the name, *elementary quantum of action*. Thus the nature of entropy as a measure of probability, in the sense indicated by Boltzmann, was established in the domain of radiation, too. This was made especially clear in a proposition, the validity of which my closest pupil, Max von Laue, convinced me in a number of conversations – namely, that the entropy of two coherent pencils of light is smaller than the sum of the entropies of the individual pencils of rays, quite consistently with the proposition that the probability of the happening of two mutually interdependent reactions is different from the product of the individual reactions.

While the significance of the quantum of action for the interrelation between entropy and probability was thus conclusively established, the part played by this new constant in the uniformly regular occurrence of physical processes still remained an open question. I therefore, tried immediately to weld the elementary quantum of action $h$ somehow into the framework of the classical theory. But in the face of all such attempts, this constant showed itself to be obdurate. So long as it could be regarded as infinitesimally small, i.e.

when dealing with higher energies and longer periods of time, everything was in perfect order. But in the general case difficulties would arise at one point or another, difficulties which became more noticeable as higher frequencies were taken into consideration. The failure of every attempt to bridge this obstacle soon made it evident that the elementary quantum of action plays a fundamental part in atomic physics, and that its introduction opened up a new era in natural science. For it heralded the advent of something entirely unprecedented, and was destined to remodel basically the physical outlook and thinking of man which, ever since Leibniz and Newton laid the groundwork for infinitesimal calculus, had been founded on the assumption that all causal interactions are continuous.

# THE MODERN ERA

In the foregoing pages we have witnessed the rise of the classical physical sciences, but the extracts in the final section have shown that the coming of the twentieth century revealed limitations to the scope of these theories that were to result in the rise of radically new ideas. It would be wrong, however, to conclude that classical physics and chemistry are outdated or that their interest is mainly historical. Rather does it show us the need for a more widely based approach to the investigation of physical phenomena than was evident in earlier centuries.

The fundamental ideas of classical science provide us, as it were, with a language in terms of which we can discuss and analyse a chosen realm of experience. Within its own domain the language of classical science has proved magnificently successful. But this great success must not blind us to the fact that if we turn our attention to a new realm of experience, to the interior of the atom or to the farthest reaches of the universe, we have no right to expect that the classical language of physics will prove appropriate to these new realms.

When first the scientist encounters new phenomena he naturally talks of them in the physical language to which he is accustomed, using, that is, the ideas which have proved themselves in the past. It may, however, happen that as the new investigations proceed there emerge puzzling and curious features which are in sharp conflict with his expectations. When scientists first explored the structure of the atom they naturally used the language of classical physics in order to describe their results. Two fundamental concepts in this language were the 'particle' and the 'wave'. For the classical physicist the distinction between the two concepts was clear cut. Each concept was useful in its appropriate place, but they were used to describe quite different types of physical situation.

Investigation of the atomic world, however, revealed a very strange state of affairs. The electron, when discovered, was considered to be a 'particle', and indeed behaved as such in many experiments. But later experiments, instigated by new theories, showed clearly that the electron could display those phenomena which had always been thought of as characteristic of 'waves'. The electron appeared to have equally good claims to be titled both 'particle' and 'wave'.

This ambiguous behaviour was by no means confined to the electron, but was found to be characteristic of the atomic world in general. The dual nature of atomic matter was one of several curious features which emerged from the studies of atomic physics.

We might speak of this situation in the following manner. The world of the atom is far removed from the world of everyday experience, most notably in the size of the objects we study. Atoms cannot be handled as can the familiar objects of the world about us. We cannot measure an atom with a ruler, nor weigh it with a balance. In order to experiment with atoms we must conduct very subtle and delicate experiments. It is not, then, altogether surprising that the language appropriate to the phenomena of classical physics should not be applicable to the very different phenomena of the atomic world. If we insist on using the older and more familiar language we must be prepared for it to break down in the face of a task for which it was not designed. Such enigmas as the wave-particle duality of the electron are thus a symptom of this state of affairs.

In an earlier section mention has been made of the rise of relativity. This revolution in outlook came about in response to a very similar situation. The investigation of phenomena involving velocities very much greater than those normally encountered was another example of the penetration into regions remote from the familiar world. The very concepts of space and time that classical physics accepted as such an obvious feature of our conception of the world were found to require a drastic reappraisal.

The situations which gave rise to the theories of quantum mechanics and relativity were turning-points in the history of the physical sciences. It is not, perhaps, too fanciful to characterize this breakdown in the language of the classical scientist with the words of a modern poet, T. S. Eliot.

> Words strain,
> Crack and sometimes break, under the burden,
> Under the tension, slip, slide, perish,
> Decay with imprecision, will not stay in place,
> Will not stay still.

In response to this breakdown of traditional modes of thought the scientist is confronted with the construction of a new language, a new type of science, in order to discuss and analyse the new physical phenomena. This is a formidable task, the accomplishment of which is tantamount to the establishment of an entirely new viewpoint on the nature of the physical world. The enormity of the problem is well illustrated by the fact that, following Planck's discovery of the quantum nature of certain physical interactions in 1900, a quarter of a century of intense research was to take place before the language of the atomic world – the quantum theory – was formulated by Heisenberg and Schrödinger. This quantum language has a logical structure dictated by experimental observation of atomic events and, not surprisingly, has many features which, from the classical viewpoint, appear very bizarre.

The importance of the double revolution, the quantum theory and the theory of relativity, lies not only in the particular achievements of the new theories, great as they have been, but also in the deeper understanding of the nature of the physical inquiry which for so many centuries has been such an important part of man's investigations of his environment.

These changes have made an increasingly important impact on chemical thought, for the atom and the molecule have remained fundamental to the chemist's interpretation of his subject. As the physical picture (or today one might almost say the mathematical picture) of the atom has changed, so has the chemist sought to relate the new ideas to his chemical experience. He has, for example, thought of chemical bonds not merely as the formal lines drawn on paper to connect the symbols for various atoms, but in terms of a theory of how atoms are physically held together; he uses the idea that pairs of electrons are shared between atoms, whether attention is focused on the 'particle' or the 'wave' nature of the electron.

More definite ideas about the nature of chemical bonds have led to more definite ideas about how these bonds are rearranged when molecules react. This may be more complex than might be expected from simple chemical equations. Unstable intermediate entities are often formed, which are not represented in the equation because they have only fleeting existence. Sometimes a self-perpetuating sequence of such intermediates is found, so that the reaction proceeds by a cycle of two or three simple stages repeated indefinitely. Each stage is dependent on its predecessor, so the process is known as a 'chain-reaction', a term very familiar in chemistry before it came to be applied to analogous processes in nuclear physics.

The investigation of molecular shape has continued, and alongside it has developed an accurate sense of molecular size. In spite of the equivocal nature of subatomic particles, it is still useful to most chemists to think of molecules in fairly concrete terms, and to make models of them. An indication of molecular size is given by the scale of such models which can conveniently be $10^8$:1 (i.e. 1 cm. to 1Å). The interpretation of the physical properties of substances in terms of the nature of their molecules has extended beyond the characteristics of solidity or volatility to the hardness of diamond, the lubricating properties of graphite, the elasticity of rubber, the fibre-forming properties of wool, cellulose, nylon, and Terylene.

The field of organic chemistry which produced a new range of synthetic materials when coal-tar became available as a raw material, has more recently produced a new wave of products (of which synthetic detergents and fibres are the most familiar) from petroleum products. At the same time, interest in naturally occurring substances has remained strong, and the development of more subtle analytical and synthetic methods has enabled the chemistry of 'natural products' to be increasingly understood. Spectacular achievements have been made in the investigation of the colouring matter in the petals of flowers, the gums exuded from soft fruits, the vitamins and hormones which can influence animal health in quite minute quantities, the drugs for which certain plants have long been famous. A very recent success was the synthesis of chlorophyll, the pigment in green leaves on which the 'breathing' of plants depends.

In such ways and many others, chemistry has made an impact on the biological sciences, most specifically on physiology. Biochemistry grew up as a new branch of science exploiting more fully the application of chemical ideas to biological processes. The term 'bio-physical chemistry' has even been used to describe such activities as the endeavour to understand the fundamental structure of the materials of which living cells are composed.

Such increasing diversification of scientific inquiry has led to a degree of specialization which has frequently been deplored. The necessarily narrow range of the individual scientist's research has given rise to a situation in which the worker in one field may well have little more than a vague idea of the activities of his scientific colleagues. The disadvantages of such a state of affairs need hardly be emphasized, and the remorseless intensification of research would seem to lead to greater and greater divergencies. Yet such a picture does less than justice to the trends of contemporary scientific research.

It has become almost a commonplace remark that much of the most interesting work of the last two or three decades has taken place in the 'borderline' sciences. Most often such comments have primarily referred to such new subjects as biochemistry and biophysics, which have succeeded to the extent that they have usefully brought together ideas from the physical and the biological sciences. Such studies are still in their infancy, but it now seems that the more each side advances, the more useful it will be to the other. Alongside the diversification, and in some ways as a consequence of specialization, is coming a greater unification in science than we have known for some centuries.

The future path of science cannot be charted with exactitude. Past history clearly shows the sudden twists and turns that reveal new vistas and perspectives previously unsuspected. The extracts in this book represent but a few of the milestones on this journey. But they are more than a historical record. They present a picture of human endeavour and achievement which continues to the present day and inspires with hope the journeyings of tomorrow.

# INDEX

# INDEX

# MORE ABOUT PENGUINS
## AND PELICANS

*Penguinews*, which appears every month, contains details of all the new books issued by Penguins as they are published. From time to time it is supplemented by *Penguins in Print*, which is a complete list of all books published by Penguins which are in print. (There are well over three thousand of these.)

A specimen copy of *Penguinews* will be sent to you free on request, and you can become a subscriber for the price of the postage. For a year's issues (including the complete lists) please send 4s. if you live in the United Kingdom, or 8s. if you live elsewhere. Just write to Dept EP, Penguin Books Ltd, Harmondsworth, Middlesex, enclosing a cheque or postal order, and your name will be added to the mailing list.

More Pelican books on Science are described on the following pages.

Note: *Penguinews* and *Penguins in Print* are not available in the U.S.A. or Canada

# THE ORIGINS AND GROWTH
# OF PHYSICAL SCIENCE

## VOLUME I

The beginnings of the scientific approach are described in this first volume, from the ideas and discoveries of Aristotle, Archimedes, and the ancient Greeks down to the more specialized work which followed the Renaissance – the theories of Copernicus, Brahe, Kepler, Galileo, and Newton in astronomy, and of Pascal, Boyle, Priestley, Cavendish, and Lavoisier in chemistry. In Volume 2 the story is continued, by way of modern chemistry and electricity, to the atomic physics of today.

*The Origins and Growth of Biology*, a companion volume, is also published in Pelicans.

# VIBRATIONS AND WAVES

Norman Feather

In *Mass, Length and Time* Norman Feather, who is Professor of Natural Philosophy at Edinburgh, provided – without formal recourse to the calculus – a systematic introduction to first principles and to the methods of measurement in physics. His later study, *Vibrations and Waves*, treats in greater detail of one particular fundamental principle in its many ramifications. The two volumes, taken together, afford a reasonably complete introduction to physics at the undergraduate level – if electricity and magnetism be excluded.

In this second-year course, throughout which the calculus is necessarily employed, the author formulates and elaborates the classical concept of waves, which in a dualism with the classical concept of particles (developed in the earlier volume) forms the basis of the quantum physics of today. Although he does not neglect to discuss certain fundamental ideas in electricity and magnetism, his main concern is with mechanical vibrations, with waves on water, with sound and light. As before, Professor Feather has touched in the history of his subject with biographical notes on the many physicists mentioned in his text.